GEORGE WASHINGTON'S
Secret Navy

HOW THE
AMERICAN REVOLUTION
WENT TO SEA

JAMES L. NELSON

New York Chicago San Francisco Lisbon London Madrid Mexico City
Milan New Delhi San Juan Seoul Singapore Sydney Toronto

Library of Congress Cataloging-in-Publication Data

Nelson, James L.
     George Washington's secret navy / James L. Nelson.
        p.   cm.
     Includes bibliographical references and index.
     ISBN 0-07-149389-1 (acid-free paper)
       1. United States—History—Revolution, 1775–1783—Naval operations.
     2. United States. Navy—History—Revolution, 1775–1783.   3. Washington,
George, 1732–1799.   I. Title.

     E271.N45   2008
     973.3′5—dc22   2008005355

1 2 3 4 5 6 7 8 9 10 11 12 13 14 15 16 17 18 19 20   DOC/DOC 0 9 8

ISBN 978-0-07-149389-5
MHID   0-07-149389-1

McGraw-Hill books are available at special quantity discounts to use as premiums and sales promotions or for use in corporate training programs. To contact a representative, please visit the Contact Us pages at www.mhprofessional.com.

This book is printed on acid-free paper.

"Finding we were not likely to do much in the Land Way, I fitted out several Privateers, or rather armed Vessels, in behalf of the Continent, with which we have taken several Prizes."

GENERAL GEORGE WASHINGTON,
Commander-in-Chief of the Continental Army,
to Colonel Benedict Arnold,
December 5, 1775

For Abigail Marie-Thérèse Nelson,
my darling little one

Contents

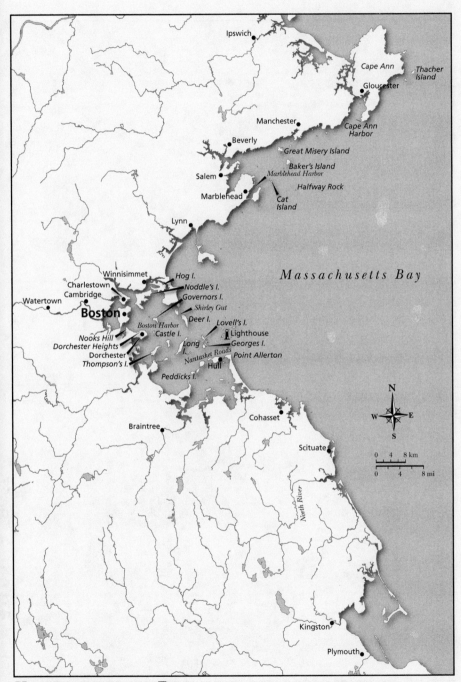

Ipswich

Cape Ann

Thacher
Island

Gloucester

Manchester

Cape Ann
Harbor

Beverly

Great Misery Island

Baker's Island
Salem   Marblehead Harbor

Halfway Rock
Marblehead

Cat
Island

Lynn

Massachusetts Bay

Winnisimmet   Hog I.
Charlestown   Noddle's I.
Cambridge   Governors I.
Watertown   Shirley Gut
Boston   Deer I.   Lovell's I.
                    Boston Harbor   Lighthouse
                    Castle I.
Nooks Hill   Long   Georges I.
Dorchester Heights   I.   Point Allerton
    Dorchester   Nantasket Roads
Thompson's I.   Hull
            Peddicks I.

N
W   E
S

Cohasset

Braintree

Scituate

0   4   8 km
0   4   8 mi

North River

Kingston

Plymouth

MASSACHUSETTS BAY

NORTH ATLANTIC COAST

NEWFOUNDLAND

St. John's

Cape Race

GRAND BANKS

Gulf of St. Lawrence

Cabot Strait

CAPE BRETON

Louisbourg

Strait of Canso

Cape Canso

I. of St. Johns

Charlottetown

NOVA SCOTIA

Halifax

Cape Sambro

Lunenburg

Cape Sable

ATLANTIC OCEAN

NEW BRUNSWICK

St. John

Bay of Fundy

Machias

Penobscot River

Penobscot Bay

Kennebec River

Falmouth

Merrimack R.

Portsmouth

Isles of Shoals

Newburyport

Gloucester

Cape Ann

Massachusetts Bay

Boston

Plymouth

Cape Cod

Cape Cod Bay

Providence

Martha's Vineyard

Nantucket

Newport

Block Is.

Narragansett Bay

New London

CANADA

Québec

Montréal

St. Lawrence River

Lake Champlain

Ticonderoga

Lake George

Saratoga

St. Johns

Albany

Hudson River

NEW ENGLAND

Connecticut River

Hartford

Middletown

New Haven

Long Island Sound

Long I.

New York

Sandy Hook

NEW YORK

NEW JERSEY

PENNSYLVANIA

Trenton

Philadelphia

Delaware River

Delaware Bay

N E S W

0 50 100 km
0 50 100 mi

PROLOGUE: *A Very Delightful Country*

THE COUNTRYSIDE is foreign to him but charming, lovely in its summer greens. He rides down the muddy road from his headquarters in Cambridge to the most prominent of the American defenses on Prospect Hill, about a mile away. He is considered one of the great horsemen of the age, and the horse between his legs is the one thing that is familiar to him. Everything else is completely new.

George Washington has the mark of a leader, tall and erect in the saddle, a manner that others call noble and even majestic. A small sword hangs at his side; a black cockade adorns his hat. He is wearing a uniform, one of the few so dressed, even though he is in the midst of more than fourteen thousand soldiers.

He is general and commander-in-chief of the Continental Army and has been for eighteen days. It has been more than a decade and a half since he last commanded troops in the field, and then, during the French and Indian War, he was colonel of a regiment of Virginia Provincials.

A mist rises from the fields as the sun burns off the wet from yesterday's heavy rains. The road is soft and muddy, and the horse steps through pools of standing water. The air is fine with the soft, clean smell that comes on the heels of a storm. It carries a scent of cooking fires and the tang of salt air.

Major General Charles Lee is riding at Washington's side. Gangly, slovenly dressed, and profane, he is in many ways Washington's polar opposite, but he is considered the greatest military mind on the American side. He has accompanied Washington from Philadelphia and has been pleased to share in the adulation that has surrounded the new commander-in-chief on his nine-day trip by horseback from the seat of government to the seat of war.

Behind Lee rides Joseph Reed, a young lawyer from Philadelphia who will be Washington's personal secretary. Lee's dogs race madly around the little parade of mounted officers.

The men, newly arrived from Philadelphia, have spent their first night in the pretty little village of Cambridge and have just ridden from Washington's Brattle Street headquarters past the wide common, the smattering of houses, and the buildings of Harvard College. Many of Cambridge's eight hundred inhabitants are Tories, and they are now gone. There are almost no civilians still living there—the houses and the college buildings are nearly all occupied by troops.

The generals ride through open country now. Green hills roll along like ocean swells, and here and there stands of oak and elm trees rise in bursts of leaves. In any direction the odd church spire can be seen, brilliantly white in the morning sun, like fingers pointing to heaven.

Washington, the farmer and eager land speculator, cannot help but assess the countryside. He likes what he sees. "The Village I am in, is situated in the midst of a very delightful Country, and is a very beautiful place itself," he will shortly write his brother Samuel. But he is on other business now.

Ahead of him rises Prospect Hill, standing proud above the smaller hills surrounding it. Its top is scarred and turned in two places where redoubts have been constructed to keep the British, now entrenched on Bunker Hill, from pushing onto the mainland. The dirt and the wooden ramparts are only a few weeks old. The brown earth looks freshly dug, and it all looks bright and clean in the sun.

The day is getting warmer, warm enough for Washington to feel uncomfortable in his wool regimental coat and waistcoat, but he gives no indication of this. He rides on, approaching the camps at the base of Prospect Hill and the soldiers stationed there. They are drawn up in ranks to welcome him. There has been no real parade, no assembly of the army to greet the new commander-in-chief. It is expected that the British will lead an assault on the American lines at any time, and the men cannot leave their positions for such a ceremony.

Washington rides slowly down the line of men standing at attention, muskets on their shoulders. He will later tell John Hancock, president of the Continental Congress, that these men are the stuff from which a good army might be made, but privately he is not so sure. None of them have uniforms, which is only to be expected from an army that assembled spontaneously, but what clothes they do have are little more than rags, filthy from the near constant work of improving the defensive lines. There are boys and black men in the ranks. Washington cannot distinguish officers from common soldiers. There is nothing about the troops to indicate that they enjoy any sort of discipline or order.

Upon his arrival in Watertown, seat of the Massachusetts Provincial Congress, Washington received a welcoming letter from that body that was in part a warning of what he was going to find. "We wish you may have found such Regularity, and Discipline already establish'd in the Army, as may be agreeable to your Expectations," the Provincial Congress wrote, and then went on to explain why he would not find such things. The army had been assembled in a great hurry, at a time when there was no real government at work in Massachusetts. The soldiers were naturally brave and intelligent but had little or no military experience. "The Youth in the Army are not possess'd of the absolute Necessity of Cleanliness in their Dress, and Lodging, continual Exercise, and strict Temperance." Washington can see that the Provincial Congress was not exaggerating.

As commander of his Virginia Provincials, he saw to it that his men were better outfitted, better equipped, and better drilled than the British regulars they fought beside. It was a point of pride for him. His new command could not be further from that ideal. But Washington gives no indication of his concern.

He rides on through the camp. The living quarters that the men have set up for themselves are perhaps the oddest, most unmilitary arrangement he has ever seen. There are massive tents made out of discarded sails, the work of troops from seaport towns. There are huts built of boards, or stone and turf, or brick and brush. Some have been thrown together, while others are carefully constructed with doors and windows. A few regiments, he is relieved to see, have proper tents and marquees. But only a few.

Washington will soon request that Congress send tents and ten thousand simple hunting shirts by way of uniform, but he will get neither.

As he and Lee and their entourage pass through the camp, past the lines of soldiers drawn up to welcome them, the Yankee privates and the aristocratic Virginian regard one another warily, withholding final judgment. Washington continues up the road, the mud turning quickly to dust under the rising sun, up to the crest of Prospect Hill where men in sweat-stained, dirt-smeared shirts, sleeves rolled up to their elbows, struggle to make the entrenchments more formidable yet. They have no engineers with experience in such things. They don't even have enough shovels.

From the crest of Prospect Hill Washington looks to the north and south. The visibility is good, unlike yesterday, and he is able to get his first real look at the enemy's lines.

Less than a mile away is Breed's Hill, where the Massachusetts troops were driven from their works as he was riding to Boston, and Bunker Hill, where the British are now entrenched. The green slopes are covered with white tents in neat rows, laid out the way a proper encampment should be laid out—no old sails or huts built of sod. The works that the Americans built in a single night are much improved now. The British will not easily be dislodged from there.

The town of Charlestown, huddled at the base of Bunker Hill, is still mostly a blackened ruin from the fires that started there on the day of the battle.

Beyond Bunker Hill Washington can see three floating batteries moored in the Mystic River, their guns trained on the thin neck leading to the high ground, the only land approach. On the flat water between Charlestown and Boston a twenty-gun ship swings at anchor. From that distance it looks like a delicate model, its masts and yards impossibly thin, though it is, in fact, more powerful than anything Washington could put to sea.

His eyes move toward the south, toward the near-island city of Boston. Most of the town is hidden on the far side of Beacon Hill, with its tall spire reaching high above the town. The steeples of Boston's fourteen churches rise above the tight clusters of wood frame houses at the north end of town. South of that, partially visible past Beacon Hill and Mount Whoredom, the Boston Common makes a wide swath of green. Through a glass Washington can see the lines of tents there, the British entrenchments, the long guns aimed at the Americans across the Charles River.

He looks at the river below, noting the vulnerable places where the British could easily land troops, and begins to form a mental picture of what defenses he will strengthen to stop that from happening. He looks up at the city again and then beyond it to the low islands that lead like stepping stones out to the sea.

The sea. It glitters and winks and stretches far away to the bright line of the horizon. Washington understands that he is looking at an unbroken highway to England, a highway carrying supplies and reinforcements to General Thomas Gage in the city he is trying to surround. It is a strategic advantage that the British enjoy, one he will have to contend with. He has no notion how he will do it.

CHAPTER *I* *The British Command*

BY THE TIME George Washington arrived at Cambridge, the lines were all but drawn, the two sides settled into what would become nearly a year's stalemate. It would take Washington some time to understand exactly what sort of war he was fighting. That was not the case for the British commanders in Boston, who had been under siege for a month and a half before Washington's arrival. They understood already that the fight in the near term would not be for territory but for supplies and *matériel.*

George Washington's opposite number, the commander of the British forces in Boston, was General Thomas Gage. Gage and Washington had fought side by side during the French and Indian War, most notably in the disastrous battle under General Edward Braddock at the Monongahela River, in which Gage had been wounded. As happened often during the Revolution, the former companions in arms were now enemies.

Thomas Gage was fifty-four years old, a seasoned veteran with military experience that far exceeded Washington's. He had participated in some of the bloodiest fighting of the mid-eighteenth century, including the 1745 Battle of Fontenoy in Belgium, where the British suffered a bloody defeat at the hands of the French, and the Battle of Culloden in Scotland during the Jacobite Rebellion, when the highland clans under Bonnie Prince Charlie were smashed by British troops.

Like many of his fellow senior officers, Gage had spent a good portion of his career in America, nearly twenty years in all. He was a solid general but not a great one. He lacked the genius and drive of a James Wolfe, who had stormed Quebec in 1759, or the flash and political savvy of a John Burgoyne, who would ingratiate his way into a major command during the Revolution. Gage's reputation, borne out by his years of service, was for dependable, brave, reliable but uninspired soldiering.

After the French and Indian War Gage had remained in America as commander-in-chief of British forces there, a position he held through years marked by taxation issues and a growing revolutionary spirit. He returned briefly to England in 1773, his first visit home since leaving for America with Braddock, but the next year he sailed again for British America, arriving in Boston in May 1774. As punishment for the Boston Tea Party, Parliament had passed the Massachusetts Regulatory Act, which altered the royal charter of that colony and stripped the colonial government of much of its authority. Gage would now serve as both military commander-in-chief of the British army in America and as governor of Massachusetts. That act, along with the Boston Port Act, which closed Boston Harbor, and other coercive measures aimed at the rebellious citizenry of Massachusetts, had been prompted largely by suggestions from Gage.

Gage was a strong believer in the rule of law and the rights of Englishmen as understood to flow from King and Parliament, but he had no enthusiasm for New England–style democracy, which he felt was "too prevalent in America, and claims the greatest attention to prevent its increase." He probably knew more about America than any other general officer in the British army. Despite that, he made the mistake, common in England, of believing that the colonies would never band together in common cause but would remain thirteen independent states, jealous of one another.

One common mistake he did not make was to think that the colonists, once having risen in rebellion, would easily be put down. Concord and Lexington and Bunker Hill only confirmed his belief to the contrary. To Secretary of State Lord Barrington he wrote, "These People shew a Spirit and Conduct against us, they never shewed against the French."

It was the general consensus in England that the fighting that Americans had done during the French and Indian War had been halfhearted at best. Many assumed the same would be true in the brewing rebellion, and Gage felt that that miscalculation had already led to serious missteps. "They are now spirited up by a Rage and Enthousiasm, as great as ever People were possessd of." This was the difference between people fighting for their own liberty and those fighting for someone else's empire.

Gage was an early advocate of overwhelming force. In a letter to Barrington he advised, "If you think ten thousand Men sufficient, send twenty, if one million [in money] is thought enough, give two, you will save both Blood and Treasure in the end." Unfortunately for Gage, by the time there were men in office in England who agreed with him, he was gone.

Gage found himself in a political and military bind prior to the outbreak of fighting at Lexington and Concord. He understood that any decisive military action on his part would touch off open revolt, leaving his small force to face a great cohort of local militia who had been arming and training for a year or more. Even if the colonials could not match British regulars for martial ability, they could overwhelm them with numbers.

King George III and his ministers, far removed from the growing tensions in Massachusetts, did not understand this. By the early part of 1775 many in the king's cabinet were tired of what they perceived as Gage's inactivity and were determined to recall him to England. But despite his own irritation with Gage, the king still liked and respected the man and would not humiliate him with a summary dismissal. Instead he sent three major generals to assist Gage: William Howe, Henry Clinton, and John Burgoyne.

"A corrupt Admiral without any shadow of capacity"

While Gage was head of the land forces, the Royal Navy on the North American station came under the command of Vice Admiral Samuel Graves. Graves was sixty-three years old, having first attained flag rank thirteen years earlier. He claimed to have "rose to his present rank and obtained his late command without political interest." Certainly there was little of the refined gentleman about him. He was a lifelong sailor, described as "a tough, boisterous man."

As if to demonstrate those qualities, in August of 1775 Graves would go so far as to engage in the ungentlemanly act of brawling on the streets of Boston, an incident that caused quite a stir. "A curious Event has taken place here yesterday," wrote Hugh, Lord Percy, an officer stationed in Boston, to a friend. "Our Admiral has been boxing in the Street with one of the Commissioners of the Custom."

For some time, Graves and Commissioner Benjamin Hallowell had been involved in a running dispute concerning permission to harvest hay on one of the islands in Boston Harbor. When Hallowell encountered Graves on the street and asked why he had had no response to four letters he had written the admiral, Graves informed him that he simply chose not to respond. Tempers flared and Graves threw "both his fists in Mr. Hallowell's face."

As the altercation escalated, Graves twice drew his sword and twice sheathed it after being called "a rascal and a scoundrel" for drawing on an unarmed man. Punches were exchanged. Finally, "lest the Admiral Should again draw his sword Mr. Hallowell wrested it from him and broke it, and then they were parted." That at least was Hallowell's version, writing in the third person to General Gage, but the rumor that reached Lord Percy suggested that "the Admiral has had the worst of it in every respect," and other accounts seemed to verify as much. One person in Boston, writing to a friend in England, claimed that "In his own department, the Admiral is more hated and despised, if possible, than he is by the army and the rebels."

In the spring and summer of 1775, when not fighting with customs officials, Graves spent a good deal of time disagreeing with Gage. The two men disliked each other, each deeming the other incompetent. Of the two, Gage was more likely right. Undersecretary of State William Eden referred to the two men as "A worthy General, with parts inferior to his situation, and a corrupt Admiral without any shadow of capacity."

During the course of his career, Graves had managed to participate in a few major naval engagements, most notably the Battle of Quiberon Bay in 1759—the pivotal naval engagement of the Seven Years War with France and a resounding victory for Britain—but he was never one of those bold, visionary leaders who made the Royal Navy the most potent force on the sea. Rather, he was a mediocrity, a cautious and unimaginative man, frightened of taking action. He was happy to quarrel with his fellow officers and civilians, but he seemed to have no interest in fighting the rebellious Americans, relying on the absence of a formal declaration of war to justify inaction.

Not all of the problems with the navy were the admiral's fault. Graves faced any number of difficulties. One was the inadequate size of his fleet, which was sufficient for peacetime operations but not for waging war. In the summer of 1775 the squadron consisted of four ships of the line: the flagship *Preston*, of sixty guns; the *Boyne*, of seventy guns; and the *Somerset* and the *Asia*, both sixty-fours. They were not in the best condition. Soon after the *Somerset*'s arrival, Graves wrote, "she was so leaky in her passage from England, that two hand pumps were kept continually working, and . . . ever since, though lying still in the Harbor, it has required one hand pump constantly going to Keep her free." Even after substantial work was done in Boston, the *Somerset* still leaked prodigiously. The other capital ships were not much better.

The admiral also had under his command seven frigates and eighteen sloops and schooners. These smaller vessels were far more useful for the sorts of action the British navy was likely to see in the American theater. The larger ships of the line were cumbersome and unwieldy, a major handicap given the tricky navigation along the northeast coast from New York to the Canadian border, where tides, currents, numerous islands, and underwater hazards made simply getting underway a dangerous proposition. (*Somerset* was one of many ships of the Royal Navy that would end her career wrecked on the coast of New England.) Nor were the Americans likely to send to sea anything that would require the power of a sixty-four-gun man-of-war. Smaller ships that could chase lightly armed smugglers and privateers into shallow bays and rivers were what was needed on the North American station.

In April 1775, a week before the fighting at Lexington and Concord, Graves hired an additional sloop and a schooner from a shipowner in Massachusetts. A month later, after the shooting started, he managed to purchase two more schooners for the naval service. And that was the end of that. There would be no more buying ships or much of anything else from the Americans.

For more than a year the people of Massachusetts had taken every opportunity to make things as hard as possible for Graves. The previous fall, Graves had sent to New York for "a few Shipwrights, Sailmakers, caulkers and Ropemakers, for not withstanding Boston at that time abounded with artificers of all sorts necessary for Shipping, yet very few cared to work for Government."

Such passive resistance increased as time passed, and with the onset of fighting, the people of Massachusetts withdrew all remaining support. Shipowners put their vessels out of commission, removing and hiding the sails and rudders, rather than risk their being of service to the British military. "The Fears of a few well disposed people to risk their Vessels," Graves informed Philip Stevens, Secretary to the Admiralty, "and the determination of the rest to prevent the Army and Navy having Supplies of provisions and Fuel, have caused most of the Vessels in this province to be dismantled and laid up."

Realizing that he could acquire no more vessels in the colonies, Graves requested a few of the navy's old fifty-gun ships, which he thought "handy Ships, and from their easy Draught of Water can go in and out of Harbors without the great Risque and Delay which constantly attends the piloting of those now with me." He also requested that more boats be sent, because "the principal part of the Duty here is done in Boats," and there was no place left save Halifax, Nova Scotia, where boats could be built or repaired.

A shortage of vessels was less of a problem than a shortage of sailors to man them. The *Preston* had carried only three hundred men, her peacetime complement, when she arrived on station in July 1774, and the other ships were similarly undermanned for wartime duty. The following year Graves reported that through death and desertion the squadron was "upwards of 160 short," and that number would only increase.

By early 1775 Graves was sending his vessels to seaport towns to press sailors into the Royal Navy. "Necessity obliges me, contrary to my inclination, to use this method to man the Kings Ships," Graves informed the Admiralty, assuring them that impressment would be carried out "with all possible moderation." In pressing sailors from American towns, however, the navy introduced unreliable, bitter men into the service and further inflamed colonial anger and resentment. Morale was already a problem aboard many of the ships. In late May, a boat crew of six sailors, rowing guard duty in Newburyport, Massachusetts, mutinied against the two officers in the boat. "[T]he tars, not liking the employ," the *Essex Journal* reported, "tied their commanders, then run the boat ashore, and were so impolite as to wish the prisoners good night, and came off."

Like the army, the navy would eventually get the reinforcements it needed for war on a continental scale. Like Gates, however, Graves would be gone before those reinforcements could do him any good.

"Very great Pains have been taken to starve the Troops"

Despite the years of unrest in the colonies, despite the steady militarization of the people, and despite the training of militias and the organization of alarms and minutemen, the siege of Boston took the British completely by surprise. While King George, his ministers, and Parliament had anticipated some sort of fighting—violence having already flared up on more than one occasion—they had not envisioned a massive army rising up and trapping their troops in Boston. Even those with more insight, such as General Gage, were caught off guard by the speed with which events unfolded. "The whole country was assembled in arms with surprising expedition," was Gage's understated description to the Earl of Dartmouth.

To Gage and Graves, bottled up in Boston, it soon became clear what sort of war they would be fighting. Graves had good reason to be less concerned with the possibility of frontal attack than with the rebels' determination "to prevent the Army and Navy having Supplies of provisions and Fuel." The day after the shooting war started at Lexington and Concord, the war for *matériel* began.

During the French and Indian War, the British Department of Treasury had developed a system by which London firms were contracted to supply the troops in America, and those firms in turn subcontracted to colonial firms. When that war ended, the system had continued as a means to supply the peacetime garrisons that remained on the American continent.

As tensions began to mount through 1775, some in London understood that this supply system could be threatened. Even before Lexington and Concord, the chief contractor for supplies to the British army, the firm of Nesbitt, Drummond and Franks, warned the Treasury that the American colonies might prevent *matériel* from reaching Boston. Once the shooting started, the flow of supplies from colonial firms stopped. With the colonial army encircling the city, nothing could get through. As one British officer wrote, "In the course of two days, from a plentiful town, we are reduced to the disagreeable necessity of living on salt provisions, and were fairly blocked up in Boston."

That left only the sea lanes, but a majority of seaborne supplies arrived from other ports in America. There were still firms in the colonies that were willing to sell to the British, either out of loyalty to the Crown or simply for the profit to be had, but patriots in the port towns kept a careful eye on the cargo and destination of every ship preparing to get under way. Gage would soon write to Dartmouth:

> Very great Pains have been taken to starve the Troops and the Friends of Government in Boston, for no Article Necessary for the Support of Life is Suffered to be Sent from any of the Provinces from New Hampshire to South Carolina, and in most of the Sea-Ports Persons are appointed to examine everything that is embarked and where it is going.

The amount of supplies required just to keep the army fed was staggering. The garrison in Boston, including the women and children attached to it, amounted to around forty-six hundred people, who consumed around eight tons of food per day at full rations.

The civilian population prior to the siege was around seventeen thousand. Gage at first agreed to let those sympathetic to the Revolution leave Boston and let Tories enter, but those in the city feared that once only loyalists and soldiers were left there would be nothing to stop the rebels from burning the place. After several tortured negotiations and agreements, during which some of the population left the city, all passage over Roxbury Neck was stopped. By mid-July there were around sixty-five hundred civilians left, and they, too, had to be fed.

It did not take long for the suffering to begin. In the brutal summer heat, soldiers and civilians began to die of scurvy, dysentery, and other conditions brought on by a lack of adequate food. The elderly and those already sick were the first to go. "Very sickly," wrote one citizen of Boston, "from ten to thirty die in a day." Gage ordered that no bells should toll for the dead, presumably because their constant ringing would discourage the people in the city and alert the enemy to the troubles.

"How the times are changed!" wrote Massachusetts Attorney General Jonathan Sewall, a Tory who had once been a close friend of John Adams:

> If a quarter of a poor, half-starved dead sheep is carry'd thro' the street, people fly to their doors and windows to view the wonderful sight, in the same manner as they formerly did to see the funeral of a person of distinction, while in return a funeral passes along . . . unheeded . . . and this

is natural eno', for when there is not a supply of victuals for all[,] the sur-
vivors will feel less regret at seeing the crowd thin off.

Sewall would sail for London with his wife and children after the battle
of Bunker Hill in June, leaving behind his capacious home in Cambridge, one of a cluster of Tory-owned mansions on Brattle Street that
had come to be known collectively as Tory Row. The Georgian home of
his former neighbor John Vassall, a merchant and British sympathizer
who had fled to England in 1774, would soon become George Washington's headquarters.

On the high seas, the battle for supplies and *matériel* began prior to
Washington's arrival, and it continued for months, growing increasingly
more violent, before Washington even became aware of it.

CHAPTER 2 *The Greatest Events . . . in the Present Age*

GENERAL THOMAS GAGE and Vice Admiral Samuel Graves were not the only men trying to keep up with the headlong pace and unpredictable direction of events in America. The leaders of the American colonies were taken equally by surprise. The Second Continental Congress convened for the first time on May 10, 1775, just as the political and military situation in the thirteen colonies was spinning out of control.

When the First Continental Congress had adjourned the previous October, it had sent a petition to King George in England blaming Parliament for the difficulties in America and explaining to the monarch that they wished to "fly to the foot of his throne and implore his clemency for protection against them [Parliament]." The petition said in part:

> We ask but for Peace, Liberty, and Safety. . . . Your Royal authority over us, and our connection with Great Britain, we shall always carefully and zealously endeavor to support and maintain.

This was a very different sentiment than would be expressed in 1776, but when it was written, no significant blood had been shed between American and British forces. By the time the Second Continental Congress met, that was no longer the case.

In the wake of the fighting at Lexington and Concord, an army had formed out of the companies of mostly Massachusetts militia that had responded to the alarm and then failed to go home. It was a spontaneous thing, the army coming together with no formal plan or forethought. Timothy Pickering, thirty years after the event, penned the only remaining reminiscence of the decision made on April 20 to create an army:

I rec^d notice that a number of militia officers assembled at Cambridge, desired to see me. I went thither. Genl Warren was among them. They were consulting of the formation of an army. To me the idea was new & unexpected. I expressed the opinion which at the moment occurred to me . . . *the immediate formation of an army did not appear to me to be necessary.*

Despite Pickering's misgivings, the army was formed. Exactly how big it was is a matter of conjecture, though it was certainly between fifteen thousand and twenty thousand men strong. This ad hoc force, ragged though it was, was large enough to bottle up the British troops of around four thousand effectives under Gage's command within the confines of Boston.

As if the bloodshed at Lexington and Concord and the siege of Boston had not created issues enough, on the very morning the Second Continental Congress convened, about eighty Green Mountain Boys under the joint command of Ethan Allen and Benedict Arnold captured Fort Ticonderoga with its small garrison of British regulars in the colony of New York. Events, it seemed, were galloping like a runaway horse, and Congress was just trying to hang on. At the end of April, even before the taking of Ticonderoga, William Emerson, a reverend from the town of Concord and the grandfather of Ralph Waldo Emerson, would write, "This Month remarkable for the greatest Events taking Place in the present Age."

If things were confused and uncertain for the delegates in Philadelphia, they were far more so for the members of the Massachusetts Provincial Congress, in whose colony the war had broken out. That body, which had formed in defiance of Gage and the Crown and whose only authority was what it granted itself, now found itself responsible not only for the governance of a colony but for the organization and maintenance of a sizable army. On April 23, Joseph Warren, president pro tem, wrote to the Provincial Congress of New Hampshire to tell them that Massachusetts had made official what the meeting on April 20 attended by Pickering had informally resolved: "[T]his Congress, after solemn deliberation and an application to Heaven for direction in the case, have this day *unanimously resolved,* That it is our duty to immediately establish an Army." Massachusetts would provide 13,600 troops and looked to the other New England colonies to provide the rest. Warren added that he would have included letters and depositions attesting to British "depre-dations, ruin, and butcheries," but he could not, because of the "great confusions in this Colony."

On May 3 Warren wrote to the Continental Congress "to be conven'd at Philadelphia, on the tenth of May, Instant," informing the Congress of the creation of the 13,600-man army and the proposals to New Hamp-shire, Rhode Island, and Connecticut that those colonies furnish troops "in the same proportion." He included various depositions from men who had fought at Lexington and Concord.

If the letter was meant to suggest that the Continental Congress assume the management of the army, it was too subtle for the delegates. After considering the letter and the depositions, as well as an address to the inhabitants of Great Britain that Warren had also included, they resolved to have the documents published in newspapers and then went on to other business.

On May 16 the Massachusetts Provincial Congress dispatched Dr. Ben-jamin Church with a less subtle message to the Continental Congress. It was read by that body on June 2. This letter, also penned by Joseph War-ren, informed the Congress that the people of Massachusetts "tremble at having an army (although consisting of our countrymen) established here without a civil power to provide for and control them."

In closing, Dr. Warren suggested a remedy to prevent further trem-bling. "As the Army now collecting from different colonies is for the gen-eral defense of the right of America," he wrote, "we w^d beg leave to suggest to y^r consideration the propriety of y^r taking the regulation and general direction of it."

Warren and the Massachusetts Provincial Congress were correct, of course, that the army should be under the control of a pan-colonial body, given the increasingly national character of the uprising. But like the Provincial Congress, the Continental Congress was struggling to clar-ify the breadth of its own authority and the nature of the war that seemed to be breaking out around it. Silas Deane, a delegate from Con-necticut, wrote to his wife, saying, "our business has run away with us."

Unsure what to do with Fort Ticonderoga, which had been dumped in their laps, the Continental Congress suggested that the colony of New York remove the cannon and stores to the south end of Lake George and take an exact inventory "in order that they be safely returned, when the restoration of the former harmony between Great Britain and these Colonies, so ardently wished for by the latter, shall render it prudent."

A Congress unwilling to take responsibility for a few dozen cannon seemed unlikely to take responsibility for an army of more than fifteen thousand men. And yet, they did.

There is, oddly, no record of a formal decision by the Continental Congress to assume the management of the army. John Adams, in his diary, recorded that he "made a motion, in form, that Congress would adopt the army at Cambridge, and appoint a General." Adams did not indicate what day that was and said that the motion was postponed.

It appears that the Congress took on the responsibility bit by bit, like a bather easing himself into scalding water. The day after Warren's letter was read, the Congress resolved to form a committee of five to "take into consideration the letter from the Convention of Massachusetts bay." That same day the delegates also resolved to borrow six thousand pounds for "the purchase of gunpowder for the use of the Continental Army." (Without authority beyond what each colony chose to grant it, Congress could pass resolutions but not laws.) Thus, even before the committee began reviewing the request of the Massachusetts Provincial Congress, the troops assembled around Boston had become the Continental Army.

On June 9 the committee charged to consider the letter from the Massachusetts Provincial Congress met and reported. But the answer Congress sent to Massachusetts, though based on the committee's work, did not address the governance of the army. Rather, it touched on another issue raised in the letter, the fact that Massachusetts had no official government—or at least the rebellious part of its population did not.

The Continental Congress suggested that since Parliament had altered the charter of the colony, no obedience was due Parliament, and the people should choose their own representatives to "exercise the powers of Government, until a Governor, of his Majesty's appointment, will consent to govern the colony according to its charter." It was one extra-legal government body suggesting the creation of another, but the reference to the king appointing a governor reflected the unwillingness of

Congress as a whole to entertain the notion of a break with England. Yet that same day they ordered up "five thousand barrels of flour for the use of the Continental Army."

By June 15 Congress had ordered that companies of riflemen be raised from Pennsylvania, Maryland, and Virginia; had set the pay of the officers and privates; and had formed a committee to draft rules and regulations for the army. There was no question at this point that the army surrounding Boston was the Army of the United Colonies. But one of the largest issues had yet to be resolved: Who would be the commander-in-chief?

The Choice for Command

When the army first formed around Boston, it came under the leadership of General Artemas Ward, who had been made commander-in-chief by the Massachusetts Provincial Congress on May 19 as they waited for a decision from the Continental Congress. Ward was forty-eight years old, a veteran of the French and Indian War, during which he had risen to the rank of lieutenant colonel. Despite his experience, he was not considered competent to continue in command of the army, and that feeling was reinforced after the battle of Bunker Hill. Elbridge Gerry of Marblehead wrote that Ward was "an honest Man, but I think Wants the Genius of a General in every Instance." James Warren claimed that he was "destitute of all Military Ability and Spirit of Command."

Only three men were under serious consideration for the position of commander-in-chief: Horatio Gates, Charles Lee, and George Washington. All three, like Thomas Gage in Boston, had fought with Braddock during the French and Indian War and had taken part in the fight at the Monongahela. Of the three, Washington had the least military experience.

Horatio Gates was the son of a butler whose employer, the Duke of Leeds, had helped secure a place in the British army for the boy. Gates fought in America in the French and Indian War, rising as high as major before a lack of family influence or money prevented further promotion. After quitting the army he settled in Virginia until the outbreak of the Revolution. Service in the regular British army, as opposed to service in an American militia or provincial force, was considered by Americans the highest of credentials. Despite his *curriculum vitae* and the general esteem in which he was held, however, Gates was not one of the front-runners for the position of commander-in-chief.

Charles Lee had a better military pedigree than Gates, certainly better than Washington. His father had been a general in the regular British army, and Lee had followed in his footsteps, if not as far. Lee had served with distinction in several engagements, had risen to lieutenant colonel, and had fought with the Polish army after the conclusion of the French and Indian War.

Retired from the British army and sensing opportunity in the brewing trouble in the colonies, Lee had arrived in America in 1773 and soon made himself conspicuous with anyone who might do him any good. He positioned himself as the greatest military mind on the continent, convincing more than a few that such was the case.

Charles Lee was eccentric to say the least, with a poor sense of personal hygiene and a vocabulary more resembling a mule skinner than an officer and a gentleman. As one person who dined with Lee recalled:

> General Lee is a perfect original, a good scholar and soldier, and an odd Genius; full of fire and passion, and but little good manners; a great sloven, wretchedly profane, and a great admirer of dogs,—of which he had two at dinner with him, one of them a native of Pomerania, which I should have taken for a bear had I seen him in the woods.

No doubt Lee's strange qualities only enhanced his reputation for genius. John Adams would express a high opinion of "General Lees Learning, general Information and especially of his Science and experience in War," though most of what Adams knew about Lee must have come from Lee himself, whom Adams had come to know while Lee was hanging around the First Continental Congress.

From the time the Second Continental Congress convened, the New England delegates in particular were under great pressure from their constituency to adopt the army. "Every Post brought me Letters, from my Friends," John Adams recalled, urging that Congress take over the army and appoint a commander-in-chief.

The choice was Lee or Washington. James Warren wrote to John Adams from Watertown, Massachusetts, describing the chaos in the army and saying, "they seem to me to want a more Experienced direction. I could for myself wish to see your Friends Washington and L at the Head of it." Warren did not write out Lee's name, perhaps not wanting unauthorized readers to know of that recommendation.

There was one overriding objection to both Gates and Lee, despite their being, in Adams's words, "officers of such great experience and confessed abilities." They were not Americans.

Elbridge Gerry, a Marblehead native who would represent Massachusetts in the Continental Congress beginning in 1776, wrote that "General Lee . . . is a stranger and cannot have the Confidence of a Jealous people when struggling for their Liberty. I revere him as an Officer and wish he had been born an American." Gerry was an early proponent of Washington.

One of the core themes of the Revolution was the widening gulf between the Americans and the British, and the United Colonies simply could not accept an Englishman at the head of the American army. And deep down, Lee and Gates, who had internalized the prejudices of regular British army officers, had no confidence in the ability of colonials to fight. Washington from the beginning envisioned an aggressive war against the British, but both Lee and Gates argued for avoiding any major set-piece battles, which they did not think American troops could win. Both Lee and Gates would serve as general officers but end the war in disgrace.

CHAPTER *3* *Noddles Island*

ON MAY 25, while the Second Continental Congress wrestled with what seemed more and more like the outbreak of a war, the British frigate *Cerberus* arrived in Boston Harbor from England. On board were the generals William Howe, John Burgoyne, and Henry Clinton, dispatched by King George to help Thomas Gage put down the American insurrection. With them under Royal seal was Graves's promotion to Vice Admiral of the White. On the morning of May 27 Graves hoisted the white ensign for the first time aboard his flagship *Preston*, and each vessel of the squadron saluted with thirteen guns. That same afternoon, however, the admiral would suffer the first in a series of naval embarrassments at the hands of the rebellious colonists, the first defeat in the burgeoning war for supplies.

At the time of the Revolution, Boston Harbor was a tricky maze of islands, shallows, and narrow channels. Less than half a mile northeast of the town were Noddles and Hog islands, both large and mostly uninhabited. In modern-day Boston, Logan Airport sits on fill extending from the old Noddles Island, which is now called East Boston. The two islands, along with most of the distinctive features of the harbor around Boston, have melded into one large urban center.

In the summer of 1775, Noddles and Hog islands were used mostly for growing hay and grazing cattle, both of which the British needed desperately. The islands were susceptible to attack, particularly as the water that separated them from the mainland was only about knee-deep at low tide, and the rebels planned to exploit that vulnerability.

A week earlier Graves had successfully removed several tons of hay from another island farther south in the harbor before Americans had driven off the British and burned the rest. The Massachusetts Provincial

Congress did not care to allow Graves to secure any more and made plans to strip Noddles and Hog islands of anything useful to the enemy.

Learning through an informer of the Americans' designs, Gage wrote to Graves on May 25 that he had "Information that the Rebels intend this Night to destroy, and carry off all the Stock & on Noddles Island." Graves accordingly ordered two guardboats to row "as high up as possible between Noddles Island and the Main, to Alarm in Case any attempt is made by the Rebels to go over." The admiral suggested to Gage that the most effective means of stopping the rebels was to station troops on the island, a step Gage apparently did not take.

In the early-morning darkness of May 27, unseen by either of the patrolling guardboats, around six hundred American soldiers splashed through the shallows from the small town of Chelsea to Hog Island. While some of the men began driving the stock from that island, others waded across the narrow channel to Noddles, where hundreds of sheep and several cows and horses were grazing.

Around two o'clock in the afternoon the rebels set fire to the hay on Noddles Island. Great billows of black smoke rising through the still air gave the British their first indication that things were not well. The flagship signaled for the marine companies on all vessels in the harbor to land on the island. Longboats and pinnaces were hauled around to the ship's sides, and blue-jacketed sailors held their oars erect in two lines as the marines with their red coats and white crossbelts clambered down the boarding ladders and took their places on the thwarts. The *Preston, Somerset, Glasgow, Cerberus,* and *Mercury* soon had "all boats mann'd & arm'd to land the Marines on Noddles Island."

Of greater concern to Graves than the hay and livestock was a storehouse on Noddles Island that he had hired to warehouse naval stores from the *Glasgow* and "tar, pitch, junk, lumber and many other articles" that would not fit on board the store schooner. Graves considered the preservation of those supplies his first priority, given "the almost impossibility of replacing them at this Juncture." Along with the marines, Graves ordered the schooner *Diana*, commanded by his nephew, Thomas Graves, to make her way up Chelsea Creek, the stretch of water between the north shore of the islands and the mainland, and use her four 4-pounders and her swivel guns to cut off the rebels' escape. "[T]here was no time to be lost," Graves wrote in his report, adding caustically, "and assistance from the Army was not immediately to be had."

It was around five o'clock in the afternoon when the marines landed on Noddles Island and began advancing on the rebel forces. By then the island was blazing, with barns full of hay and several houses engulfed in flame, though not, apparently, Graves's storehouse. The American troops fell back quickly in the face of the marines' disciplined fire and steady advance. The *Cerberus* landed two 3-pounder fieldpieces and a party of seamen to fire them, and those guns added their more lethal discharge to the fight.

As they were pushed back across the island, a handful of Americans took refuge in a ditch and stood their ground, returning fire even as they endured the marines' volleys, the fire from the fieldpieces, and the broadsides of the *Diana*, which had made her way up Chelsea Creek and now lay just off their position. But despite all the flying iron, no Americans were killed during the action. Amos Farnsworth, an American soldier, recorded in his diary, "thanks be unto God that so little hurt was Done us when the Bauls Sung like Bees Round our heds."

The entrenched Americans could not long endure the combined fire of the marines and sailors and the *Diana*'s guns. They fell back from Noddles and Hog islands across the shallow water to Chelsea. The schooner had worked as far up shallow Chelsea Creek as she could, and Thomas Graves was under orders from his uncle not to remain in that narrow waterway once the tide began to fall. Accordingly, with the tide still flooding, he came about and began to work his way back toward the harbor. He nearly made it. It was early evening as the schooner passed the middle of Noddles Island, just off the town of Winnesimit on the mainland. Then the wind died away.

Hours of gunfire and the sight of smoke and flames lifting off the islands had alarmed the entire countryside. Private Phineas Ingalls wrote in his diary, "About sunset we heard they were upon Hog Island. . . . Heard firing all night. At night about 200 went down to Lichmore Point." American troops flocked to Winnesimit and from the shore poured small-arms fire into the *Diana*, which drifted at extreme musket range about two hundred feet away. The *Diana* responded with her broadsides and swivels, and soon a steady barrage of gunfire was raging between the schooner and the waterfront.

Seeing the *Diana* becalmed, Graves ordered the fleet's boats and the sloop *Britannia*, tender to the flagship, to her assistance. The boats pulled through the storm of musket balls and took the schooner in tow, the oarsmen straining to pull her back toward the safety of the fleet moored off Boston's waterfront.

As the evening grew dark, General Israel Putnam arrived on the shore of Winnesimit with more troops and two fieldpieces, which he turned on the schooner and the boats towing her off. The report to the Massachusetts Committee of Safety stated that "two 3 Pounders coming to Hand that Instant, began to play upon them, & soon obliged the Barges to quit her."

Left alone under the Americans' guns, Lieutenant Graves and his men continued to fight back with everything they had. Then, with the tide ebbing, the *Diana* touched bottom. The schooner's company struggled desperately to get her free, all the while enduring a desultory fire from the Americans, who were by now shooting in the dark. It was no use. The tide was falling fast, and the *Diana* settled deeper and deeper into the mud. Finally, at low water, around 3 A.M., the schooner rolled onto her beam ends. Unable to man the guns or even stand on the nearly vertical deck, Graves and his men abandoned the *Diana*, taking to the ship's boat and rowing over to the *Britannia*, which was anchored nearby.

For a while the *Britannia* took up the fight, but the small-arms and cannon fire from the shore were too much for the small vessel. Unable to sail in a contrary wind with damaged rigging, *Britannia* slipped her anchor cable and was towed to safety by the fleet's boats. "The sloop was disabled," wrote one American observer, "and obliged to be towed off by the Men of War's Boats; the Remains of them are returned to their den."

Around 7 A.M. the fighting died off. Later that day the Americans made their way to the stranded and deserted *Diana*, which was apparently too damaged to be worth refloating, and "got out of the wreck, 12 four pounders, 6 swivels, and every thing else that was valuable, without molestation." It was a nice windfall for the artillery-starved army.

With the *Diana* stripped of her valuable guns, the rebels stuffed hay through the great cabin windows and set the vessel on fire. Soon she was fully engulfed, the flames racing up her masts, consuming her tarred shrouds and stays, and turning her gray canvas sails into floating bits of flaming debris. The column of smoke would have been clearly visible from the waterfront in Boston.

The British forces had suffered two men killed in the fighting, the Americans none. While Graves managed to save a "great part of the King's stores," a great deal was lost, along with the schooner. Worse, though Graves seemed not to understand or at least not to acknowledge it, the Americans had managed to drive off more than a thousand sheep and lambs from the two islands, livestock crucial to maintaining the British presence in Boston.

Samuel Graves's nephew, Lieutenant Thomas Graves, was acquitted by a court-martial of any wrongdoing in the loss of his vessel, not surprising given the stubborn fight he kept up until the last possible moment. He would go on to command the seventy-four-gun *Bedford* in the Battle of the Virginia Capes in September 1781, in which his cousin, the unfortunate Admiral Thomas Graves, conceded victory to the French and doomed Lord Cornwallis to surrender at Yorktown. In 1801, as Rear Admiral of the White, Lieutenant Graves would be Admiral Horatio Nelson's second-in-command at the Battle of Copenhagen.

Samuel Graves himself did not fare so well, at least not in the eyes of his fellow officers. Lord Percy wrote, "They [the rebels] have lately amused themselves with burning the houses upon an island just under the Admiral's nose. . . . This is not the most agreeable thing that could have happened."

It was certainly not an agreeable result to anyone on the side of King and Parliament. But even as the barns, hay, and schooner were going up in flames, events were under way that would embarrass the British navy even more.

Firewood

Food and forage were not the only necessities lacked by the troops and civilians in Boston. Of the many shortages in that besieged city, one of the most severe and urgent was a lack of firewood.

It might seem odd that, in the middle of a particularly hot summer, one described as a drought by several diarists, firewood should be so crucial a commodity. But firewood was the primary means of cooking and of heating water to wash clothing. The only other option was coal, which could only be had from England and which, because of difficulties in transport, never proved a viable alternative.

A soldier's diet centered on meat and bread, and with the siege in place that became the diet of the civilians in Boston as well. Wood was needed to heat the baking ovens that produced the bread. With fresh meat virtually nonexistent, the residents of Boston were forced to rely on salted beef and pork that might have been a year or more in the cask. Salt meat had to be thoroughly boiled just to render it edible, which was about the best one could hope for. Tons of salt provisions were consumed every day, and an extraordinary amount of wood was required to boil it all.

Ideally the British army would have had on hand at all times a six-month supply of provisions, but even a month before Lexington and Concord the army in Boston had been running short in every category. The shortage of firewood, which was bulky and hard to transport, could only get worse when the summer ended and wood was needed for heat as well as cooking. "Great Difficulties now arose in procuring Fuel," Graves wrote, "not only for present consumption but for the next Winter."

All firewood was put under the army's control. Near the end of June, General William Howe, who had command of the troops stationed in Charlestown, issued orders saying, "The Barrack Mas^r is to Collect all the Timber and fire Wood in Charleston, and to lodge it for the use of Government, No other person is allow'd to take any Timber and fire Wood from Charleston." As with the meager fresh provisions, care was taken that the sick in the hospitals were supplied first. Orders were given to deliver from each regiment two companies' allotment of firewood to the hospital, "As Wood cannot be got, but at an Extravagant Price."

"The wilderness is impervious and vessels we have none"

As it happened, the city of Boston was not the only place on the seaboard starving for supplies. In far-off Machias, Maine (then a district of Massachusetts), about 240 miles by water northeast from Boston and only about 25 miles from the border with Canada, the population was also suffering from deprivations brought on by the growing conflict.

Machias was a small outpost huddled around the wide Machias River, a town of around eighty families, a number of which were quite large,

and one hundred single men. The town made its living from the seemingly endless forest at its back, cutting and exporting lumber and firewood, a lucrative industry in the best of times. What little farming the
inhabitants did was for subsistence, and a severe drought in the fall of
1774 had prevented the people from laying in sufficient stores to get
them through the winter and following spring. Only the arrival of a few
ships over the winter, carrying provisions, had kept the town alive

In late May 1775, a number of Machias inhabitants sent a petition to
the Massachusetts Provincial Congress seeking relief from their increasingly desperate situation. "We dare not say we are the foremost in supporting the glorious cause of American liberty," they wrote by way of
establishing their credentials, "but this we can truly affirm, that we have
done our utmost to encourage and strengthen the hand of all the advocates for America with whom we have been connected."

Part of that encouragement, they explained, involved not purchasing
any goods from anyone suspect of being a Tory, "except when con-
strained by necessity." That policy, combined with the drought and their
location far from any source of supply, a small settlement carved out of
the woods, had put them in real danger of starving. "We . . . have no
country behind us to lean upon, nor can we make escape by flight; the
wilderness is impervious and vessels we have none."

The petitioners were not asking for a handout, but rather that supplies be sent and the town be allowed to "pay the whole amount in lumber, the only staple of our country." Before the Massachusetts legislature
could respond, however, help came from another, less likely source.

Icabod Jones was a wealthy merchant and landowner in Machias who
had done a good business, as Thomas Gage wrote to Graves, "Supplying
this Garrison with Wood Lumber &c for his Majesty's use." His unswerv-
ing loyalty to the Crown and his efforts to supply the troops in Boston,
"having exerted himself for the Service of Government," made him a
friend to General Gage and Admiral Graves.

The rebellious Americans were less enthusiastic about Jones. The
Providence Gazette referred to him as "Capt. Icabod Jones, an infamous
Tory." James Warren called him simply "a dog." Jones, who was living in
Boston at the time of the siege, had begun to realize that supplying the
British garrison had a downside. His market was assured, but his source

of supply was not. "Mr. Jones . . . ," Gage wrote to Graves, "is threatened by the Inhabitants of the Eastern parts of this Province, to intercept and destroy his Vessels."

The people of Machias were thought to be well armed courtesy of the British navy. A few months earlier His Majesty's schooner *Halifax*, while trying to enter the river at Machias, had run up on the rocks making seven and a half knots before a fresh gale and quickly broke apart. As Graves understood it, the locals had salvaged the guns and were ready to use them against their former owners.

Icabod Jones approached Thomas Gage with his proposal. Jones wanted to sell the British firewood and lumber to build barracks to house the troops over the winter, both of which they desperately needed. Jones either knew or suspected that the people of Machias were dangerously short of supplies and believed that their predicament would make them more flexible in their choice of trading partners. The resulting transaction could be beneficial to all, particularly to Icabod Jones.

After meeting with Jones, Gage wrote to Graves explaining that the merchant "has my permission to carry Twenty Barrels Pork, and Twenty Barrels Flour, from this for the use of the New Settlers at Mechias—as he promises to continue as usual every Supply in his power."

Jones understood that, hungry or not, the people of Machias might make trouble, particularly if they were armed with the *Halifax*'s guns. He concluded that "an Armed Vessel's being sent there, to bring them [the guns] away, may have good effect, and prevent their fitting out Vessels from those parts to annoy his Majesty's Subjects, and to encourage the Inhabitants to the Eastward to bring fuel, Lumber, &c. to the Port of Boston." Lexington and Concord had apparently taught him nothing about the advisability of trying to strong-arm Americans and confiscate their munitions.

Some years later, Admiral Graves would sum up the entire experience:

> Mr Ichabod Jones, who, having some property about Machias, imagined from his acquaintances with the People there that he could furnish the Army with a considerable quantity of Firewood. . . . But the event proved how totally mistaken Mr Jones was in the temper of his Countrymen, and also shewed what we had generally to expect.

The armed vessel Graves chose to accompany Jones's sloops was the schooner *Margaretta*. She was one of the smaller vessels Graves had hired to augment his fleet about two months before. Though manned with as good a crew as one could wish, twenty sailors chosen from the flagship *Preston*, she was as lightly armed as a naval vessel could be and still be considered a fighting ship. She carried only swivel guns mounted on the rails and muskets, pistols, and cutlasses for the crew. She had on board four 3-pounder carriage guns, but for some reason they were stored down in the hold, not mounted. *Margaretta* was not much by Royal Navy standards, but Graves figured she was enough to overawe backwoods colonials.

On May 26 Graves ordered Midshipman James Moore, who commanded *Margaretta*, to sail in convoy with Jones's vessels to Machias and "remain for their Protection while they are lading." He was then to return to Boston. En route he was to use his "utmost Endeavours to take or destroy all armed Vessels that are acting illegally or that are annoying any of his Majesty's loyal and peaceable subjects," though it was hard to imagine Moore would encounter any armed vessel with less firepower than *Margaretta*. He was also to endeavor to secure the guns salvaged from *Halifax* and to assure whoever had salvaged them that they would be paid for their effort.

Moore's orders were simple enough and would most likely have gone off without much difficulty if Icabod Jones had not managed to miscalculate and blunder at every step.

CHAPTER *4* *Machias Sons of Liberty*

ON JUNE 2, as the Continental Congress was considering whether to take control of the army in Massachusetts, the little convoy consisting of Icabod Jones's sloops *Unity* and *Polly*, accompanied by the *Margaretta*, arrived in Machias Bay. The vessels worked their way up the wide, muddy river, past humps of islands bristling with pine and a series of headlands jutting out from the shore.

The morning was cold, the season lagging two or three weeks behind Boston. The scattered oaks and maples were still in flower and just showing their bright and wispy new foliage. A forest of massive, old-growth pine, fir, and spruce lined the shore and marched away into the backcountry, lining the crests of the low hills that ringed the town. Here and there a granite outcrop pushed the meager soil aside. In this place men wrestled a living from the woods and sea, not the soil.

Machias was a small settlement cut into an inhospitable forest, but thanks to its burgeoning lumber business, merchant ships routinely called there during the months of good weather. The cluster of houses and wharves was situated mainly at the confluence of the Machias and Middle rivers, and there the *Margaretta, Unity*, and *Polly* came to anchor. Burnham Tavern was the center of village life, and that was where Jones headed the next day when he went ashore to negotiate with the townspeople.

Word of the fighting at Lexington and Concord had recently reached the far-off town, and like most Americans, the people of Machias were in no mood to trade with any friend of the British army. But they were also desperate for provisions, and in their desperation they would have put their feelings aside and made a deal, as they had before, if Jones had handled the situation with any sensitivity.

But he did not. No doubt emboldened by the armed schooner riding at anchor within easy gunshot of the town, Jones began to make demands. He circulated an agreement that "required the signers to indulge Capt Jones in carrying Lumber to Boston, & to protect him and his property, in all events." Only those who signed would be allowed to trade for the salt pork and flour he was carrying.

The people of Machias bridled at these coercive tactics, and Jones got nowhere with his efforts. A few days later, on June 6, a meeting was assembled to seek some compromise. Having had a few days to stew on the issue, the people of Machias were angrier still, so much so that Jones felt compelled to have Moore move the *Margaretta* farther upriver so that "her Guns would reach the Houses." Moore rigged spring lines onto the anchor cable that would allow him to swing the ship side to side and bring her guns to bear on any target on shore.

With that protection in place, Jones met with the assembled inhabitants of Machias. The people considered themselves "nearly as prisoners of war," trapped between their loathing of Jones and the British government he worked for on the one hand and the very real possibility of starving on the other. Grudgingly they "passed a Vote, that Capt Jones might proceed in his Business as usual without molestation, that they would purchase provisions he brought into the place and pay him according to the Contract."

Thus assured of having his way, Jones ordered his two sloops to warp up to the town wharf and begin to discharge the provisions in their holds. The distribution of the food, like the negotiations that preceded it, might have passed without incident if Jones could just have left things as they were. Instead, when the provisions were landed, he announced that he would distribute them only to those people who had voted at the town meeting in favor of his being allowed to carry lumber to Boston.

Those people whom Jones would thereby have slighted were those who had voted against supplying the British even in the face of possible starvation. It is reasonable to imagine that they represented the most radical element of Machias society. Unsurprisingly, "they determined to take Capt Jones, if possible, & put a final stop to his supplying the Kings troops with any thing."

Foremost among the rebel leaders in Machias were Benjamin Foster, a lieutenant of militia and business partner of Icabod Jones, who lived in East Machias, four miles from Machias proper, and thirty-one-year-old Jeremiah O'Brien. O'Brien was the eldest of Morris and Mary

O'Brien's nine children, one of the many large families in the area. Morris had moved to Machias with his sons Jeremiah and Gideon in 1764. After establishing a lumber business, they had brought the rest of the family to town the following year.

Through hard work and the bountiful resources of the virgin territory, the O'Briens had prospered and become leaders in the community, with Jeremiah most prominent among them. O'Brien family legend had it that Morris had fled his native Ireland after participating in an unsuccessful revolt against British tyranny. True or not, the revolutionary spirit was strong in him and his sons. When outrage at Jones's demands moved the locals to action, Jeremiah O'Brien was at their head.

Word was sent to the nearby settlements of Mispecka and Pleasant River, and soon men from all around had gathered in the woods near the O'Brien homestead to plot their move. It was agreed that if they could grab Jones and the officers on shore, the vessels could be taken with little effort. With that in mind, the ad hoc militia set off for town.

June 11 was a Sunday, and the men of Machias correctly guessed that Moore and Jones would be at Sunday services in the meeting house. In the early afternoon, "thirty Men in Arms and many more went to the Meeting House there to take up Ichabod Jones and Captain Moore," according to Jabez Cobb, master of a brigantine that happened to be in Machias at the time.

Seated in the pew with Jones and Moore were the *Margaretta*'s first officer, a young midshipman named Stillinsfleet, and Jones's nephew, Stephen Jones. The latter, then in his late thirties, was in fact a captain in a militia company in Machias and did not share his uncle's Tory leanings. He would later become one of Machias's leading citizens, but for the moment he would find himself tarred with Icabod's brush.

The four men were apparently unaware of the hostility they had engendered—or at least were convinced that the colonists would not molest them for fear of the *Margaretta*'s guns or of losing the provisions Jones had brought. And indeed, during the nine days they had been at Machias, "the officers of the schooner was daily on shore, and behaved with civility."

Suddenly, over the preacher's voice, there rose the sound of an approaching mob, and the men realized at last how wrong they were.

Jones "looked out of the Window & saw a Number of People Armed making toward the House." The doors to the meeting house burst open and O'Brien, Foster, and the angry men of Machias came charging down the aisle. Moore, Stillinsfleet, and the Joneses leapt to their feet in surprise and, "alarmed that they were pursued by Armed Men, jumped out of the Window and escaped."

The officers, resplendent in the long blue coats and white waistcoats and breeches of their dress uniforms, raced to the waterfront, the shouting mob close behind them. An officer on the deck of the *Margaretta*, seeing the commotion in the streets and his superiors racing for the wharf, dispatched a boat to collect them "before their pursuers (who were very numerous) came up with them." Tumbling into the boat, the officers managed to get out to the *Margaretta* before being seized by the colonists. Icabod Jones ran the other direction and disappeared into the thick woods that crowded against the settlement. Of the four, only Stephen Jones was apprehended.

Once back on board the *Margaretta*, Moore hoisted the ensign and no doubt cleared the schooner for action. He then sent a message ashore telling the people that he had orders to protect Jones and his vessels, and "he was determined to do his duty whilst he had life; & that, if the people presumed to stop Capt Jones's vessels, he would burn the town."

It was a bold threat from a midshipman with only twenty men and a schooner armed with swivel guns, and the men of Machias were not impressed. They shouted out across the water, ordering Moore to "strike to the sons of Liberty and come on shore," but Moore declined.

One of Jones's sloops, likely the *Polly*, was still tied to the wharf. Some of the armed patriots, who numbered around one hundred, descended on this sloop and stripped her of sails and rigging, presumably to stop anyone from sailing her away. The other sloop, the *Unity*, was at anchor farther downstream. A second band of men rowed out to that vessel, boarded her, and moved her upriver. They anchored her close to the wharf where the *Polly* was tied up, downstream of the *Margaretta*. Moore did not try to stop them.

For a few hours a tense and uneasy truce fell on the town and the armed schooner riding at her anchor, as each waited for the other to make a move. Midshipman Moore was the first to act. Around 8:30 in the evening, as dusk was settling over the town and the water, Moore quietly weighed anchor and let the *Margaretta* drop downriver toward the *Unity*, anchored below. The men who had shifted the *Unity* closer to the wharf had gone ashore, but once they saw what Moore was up to they scrambled into their boats and pulled for the sloop in an effort to board their prize before the British could retake her.

Reaching the sloop first, the Americans swarmed over her low sides and, with no time to haul up the anchor, let go the cable. The sloop was swept up in the current and ran aground in the soft mud near the shore. *Margaretta* came to anchor no more than fifteen yards from the grounded sloop.

Most of the local men may have considered themselves no more than concerned Americans before, but now they thought of themselves as Sons of Liberty, and they were ready to fight. Armed men swarmed to the shoreline, while others climbed into boats and canoes and pulled for a spot along the riverbank near where the schooner now swung at her anchor.

Moore was ready to fight back. All along the *Margaretta*'s deck, blue-jacketed sailors loaded their sea-service muskets and crouched behind the low bulwark. Shot and charge were rammed down the muzzles of the swivel guns, the heaviest ordnance in the fight.

Someone among the crowd of armed rebels hailed Moore, "desiring him to strike to the Sons of Liberty, threatening him with death if he resisted." Accounts of Moore's reply vary. Nathaniel Godfrey, pilot on board the *Margaretta*, testified that Moore called out "he was not ready yet." James Lyons of the Machias Committee recalled him saying, "Fire and be damn'd." The one thing everyone did agree on was that once Moore refused to surrender, the shooting began.

The Americans fired first, a blast of musket shot. Lead balls whipped over the heads of the sailors on board the *Margaretta* and thudded into the schooner's sides. Midshipman Moore immediately ordered his men to return fire. All along the gunwale British muskets fired back, and the swivels blasted away at point-blank range.

The two sides continued this "smart engagement" for some time, the flash from their muzzles bright in the growing darkness. There is little agreement on how long the fight lasted, reports ranging from fifteen minutes to two and a half hours. Nathaniel Godfrey, the *Margaretta*'s pilot, whose writing reflects the careful precision of a ship's master, noted, "The firing continued about an hour and a half." All agreed that the shooting was swift and intense. Incredibly, no one was hurt, perhaps owing to the darkness.

Finally Moore had had enough. Eager to break off the fight, he ordered the schooner's cable cut. The *Margaretta* dropped downriver about half a mile and came to anchor again near a sloop commanded by a man named Samuel Tobey. Tobey had come to Machias to pick up a cargo of lumber. His vessel was loaded with boards, and Tobey was waiting for first light to get under way.

Even after that prolonged and intense exchange, the Americans still had some fight left in them. Once again armed men loaded into boats and canoes and, with night full on, pulled downriver to where the *Margaretta* lay. They closed with the schooner, intent on boarding her, but "were beat off from a brisk fire from the Swivels & obliged to quit their Boats, four of which in the Morning were left upon the Flats full of holes." One man was injured on board the British schooner.

Moore knew the Americans were not done with him, and he likewise realized how inadequate a man-of-war his converted merchant schooner made. He passed lines to Tobey's sloop and hauled her alongside the *Margaretta*. The navy bluejackets gathered boards from the sloop's cargo, passed them across to the *Margaretta*, and "made a Barricadoe fore & Aft to defend ourselves from Small Arms." *Margaretta* spent the rest of the night tied alongside Tobey's sloop, her men no doubt keeping eyes and ears trained intently into the dark.

The First Sea Fight of the War

At some point in the night, Midshipman James Moore realized that his mission was over and that he could do nothing further for Icabod Jones, who was still cowering somewhere in the forest. At first light Moore ordered the *Margaretta* cast off from Tobey's sloop. Sails were set, and with the schooner's boats towing astern the *Margaretta* stood downriver toward the sea. Samuel Tobey, "being well acquainted with the River," was taken against his will to serve as pilot. The breeze filled in and the

Margaretta slipped past the thickly wooded shores of the Machias River. Local patriots peppered the schooner with musket fire as she passed.

The Machias Sons of Liberty, meanwhile, were preparing for battle. Forty men under the command of Jeremiah O'Brien manned Jones's sloop, the *Unity*. While the *Margaretta*'s men were armed with matching sea-service muskets, pistols, and cutlasses, O'Brien's crew was armed with "guns, swords, axes & pick forks." At first light they got under way, dropping downriver in pursuit of the *Margaretta*.

O'Brien's men may not have had decent weapons, but Benjamin Foster lacked even a ship. The *Polly* had been stripped of sails and rigging, and there was no time to put her back together. There was, however, a small schooner called the *Falmouth Packet* at Machias at the time. Her master, Thomas Flinn, had had the misfortune to arrive "the 10th of said June where he found every thing Quiet," not realizing that everything would explode the next day.

Foster and the twenty men under his command boarded the *Falmouth Packet* and demanded its use. Flinn refused, but Foster assured him "it was in vain to Refuse as they would take her by Force." Foster also insisted that Flinn and his crew join the men from Machias, and again Flinn refused. This time Foster relented and put the *Falmouth Packet*'s crew ashore, and then he and the twenty men with him followed in O'Brien's wake. Like the men on board *Margaretta*, Foster and O'Brien's men built "breast works of pine boards, and any thing they could find in the Vessels, that would screen them from the enemy's fire."

With Samuel Tobey as pilot, the *Margaretta* negotiated the Machias River and stood for the sea beyond. The breeze was building as Machias Bay opened in front of them. With a considerable distance between the *Margaretta* and the pursuing Americans, Moore was all but in the clear when he committed a fatal error in seamanship. While jibbing the schooner—turning her stern through the wind—he allowed the breeze to catch the sails on the wrong side and swing them across the deck. The mainsail's boom and gaff, the spars that supported the bottom and top edges of the sail, swept in a great, violent arc from one side to the other and then slammed into the shrouds supporting the mast and shattered. Just a few miles short of escape, the *Margaretta* was crippled.

Moore once again came to anchor as his men cleared away the wreckage. About three miles away was a sloop, also at anchor. Moore sent a party of armed sailors off in the *Margaretta*'s boat. They boarded the sloop, which turned out to be from Norwich, Connecticut, and was commanded by a man named Robert Avery. Moore's men took possession of her, weighed the sloop's anchor, and "brought her alongside, took her Boom and Gaff & fixed them in the Schooner."

The crew of the *Margaretta* was just finishing their work when they spotted the *Unity* and the *Falmouth Packet* charging downriver toward them. Moore "immediately weighed Anchor & stood out for the Sea." Like Samuel Tobey, Robert Avery was made to go with the schooner to serve as pilot.

Even undamaged *Margaretta* was "a very dull sailor." Moore ordered the boats that were towing astern to be set adrift so they would not slow the schooner, and his men set all sail the ship could carry. It was not enough, and soon the Americans were overhauling them. "[T]hey coming up with us very fast," wrote Nathaniel Godfrey, "we began to fire our Stern Swivels, & small Arms as soon as within reach."

For nearly an hour the Americans plunged on through the rain of musket balls. By one report Moore ordered Tobey to "take up his Gun in Defense of the Vessel" or he would "send a Brace of Balls through him," but Tobey refused. The same offer was made to Robert Avery, and Avery, who was either a Tory or more easily intimidated, agreed to aid in the *Margaretta*'s defense.

Soon the Americans were within hailing distance, and once again they called for Moore to "strike to the Sons of Liberty," promising the English good treatment if they did and death if they did not.

Moore could not escape, and he was not about to strike his colors, so he turned to fight. He luffed the *Margaretta* into the stiff breeze, her sails flogging and her broadsides bearing on the approaching Americans. The British poured swivel shot and small-arms fire into the *Unity* and the *Falmouth Packet*, but the Americans stood on, knowing their advantage lay in numbers and could only be realized in hand-to-hand combat.

As the two attackers closed, "Captain Moore imployed himself at a box of hand granades and put two on board our vessel," wrote Joseph Wheaton, a crewman aboard *Unity*, "which through our crew into great disorder." But even those small exploding shells did not stop O'Brien and Foster. The *Unity* rammed the *Margaretta*'s starboard quarter, her bow-sprit running right through the main shrouds and ripping through the mainsail. The *Falmouth Packet* piled against the *Margaretta*'s larboard bow.

The attacking ships were perfectly positioned, one forward, one aft, and on either side of the *Margaretta*, with the British sailors caught between them as the Americans swarmed over the bulwarks and onto the *Margaretta*'s deck. Men from the *Unity* climbed onto the schooner's quarterdeck, swinging discharged muskets like clubs and driving the British sailors forward. Muskets and pistols banged out on all sides, and shouting Americans plunged into the crowd of British sailors with axes and pitchforks.

Midshipman Moore was shot down in the initial rush, a musket ball in his chest and another in his belly. He collapsed bleeding to the deck. Young midshipman Stillinsfleet was wounded in the side—not danger-ously, but enough to make him flee in terror to his cabin, where he was found later. The unfortunate Robert Avery, who just a few hours before had been peacefully at anchor on board his own ship, was shot and killed.

The fighting surged along the deck as more and more Americans clambered over the rails. The British superiority in small arms was moot once the weapons were fired with no time to reload, and, crude as they were, the Americans' axes and pitchforks proved effective for hand-to-hand fighting. The Americans had a three-to-one advantage in numbers. The battle on the *Margaretta*'s deck was over quickly.

The British lost one man killed and five wounded. One American was killed and six wounded, though one of those later died. The mortally wounded Midshipman Moore was carried down to his cabin and laid on his bunk. According to Nathaniel Godfrey, when asked why he did not strike his colors, Moore "look'd up and told them 'he preferred Death before yielding to such a sett of Villains.'" Moore was later carried to the empty home of Icabod Jones, where he died the following day.

The jubilant Americans squared away the three vessels, secured the *Margaretta*'s crew, and "carried her up to Mechais, in great triumph, with their Colours flying." The colors might well have been some variation of a red flag with a white canton and a pine tree.

A few weeks later, the Massachusetts Provincial Congress resolved to express their thanks to:

> Captain Jeremiah Obrian and Captain Benjamin Foster, and the other brave men under their command, for their courage and good conduct in taking one of the Tenders belonging to our enemies, and two Sloops belonging to Ichabod Jones, and for preventing the Ministerial Troops being supplied with Lumber.

The Provincial Congress decreed that the three vessels—*Unity*, *Polly*, and *Margaretta* (the *Falmouth Packet* having been returned to Thomas Flinn)—should remain in the possession of the people of Machias under the command of O'Brien and Foster. The *Margaretta* being such a poor sailer, it was decided that the *Polly* would be fitted out as an armed vessel for the protection of Machias, which the people rightly thought might now be the object of unwanted attention from the British navy. The *Polly* was fitted out with the *Margaretta*'s guns, including the 3-pounders that had been lying uselessly in her hold. Renamed *Machias Liberty*, she was given to Jeremiah O'Brien to command.

Though intensely displeased, Admiral Graves felt certain he would have his revenge. To the governor of Nova Scotia he wrote, "the Pirate [Jeremiah O'Brien] will soon reap the Reward for his Perfidy. Two armed Schooner have gone in quest of him." The next vessels to call at Machias, however, were the armed schooner *Diligent* and the shallop *Tatamagouche*. Both vessels were captured by O'Brien and his followers without a shot fired after their officers, "unacquainted with the disposition of the people at Mechias," recklessly went ashore. The *Diligent* became part of O'Brien's growing fleet.

Thus the first ship-to-ship naval action of the American Revolution, which would come to be known as the "Lexington and Concord of the Sea," ended as an American victory. For Samuel Graves, the loss of twenty prime seamen was a much greater calamity than the loss of an insignificant schooner. For the people in Boston, the worst of the loss was two shiploads of firewood. In writing about the event to John Adams, James Warren noted, "this is doing great Service. they are reduced to great straits for wood as well as fresh provisions in Boston. it is said it would fetch three Gueneas a Cord. they have already Burnt all the fences &c."

Despite the dramatic loss of the *Margaretta* and Jones's sloops, the British navy did enjoy some success in plundering American shipping. As James Moore and Icabod Jones were sailing to Machias, a few of Graves's cruisers captured American ships laden with flour and sent them into Boston. Gage wrote to Graves that the captures "have been of very great use to the Service, but we still are in great want of Pork, or Beef." On the day that Graves learned of the *Margaretta* disaster, the blow was softened by the news that His Majesty's schooner *Hope* had arrived in Boston with two prizes, each loaded with wood.

While the two armies looked at one another across the water surrounding Boston, the seaborne fight for supplies was well under way.

CHAPTER 5 *"The amiable, generous and Brave George Washington, Esquire"*

WHILE GENERAL GAGE, Admiral Graves, and the patriots around Boston and Machias engaged in combat, the Continental Congress continued to debate the role it would play in the growing war and who would lead it.

In hindsight, given the near-mythological status George Washington has assumed in the collective American memory—a status not altogether undeserved—it seems amazing that the question of whether Horatio Gates or Charles Lee should be made commander-in-chief over Washington persisted through much of the Revolution. Even among his fellow Virginians, and despite the fact that he was America's best-known native-born soldier, Washington's nomination to the post was hardly a given.

By the time of the Second Continental Congress, George Washington had been famous for more than twenty years. As a major in the Virginia militia, the twenty-one-year-old Washington had led a small party through the wilderness to present-day Erie, Pennsylvania. His charge was to deliver a letter from Virginia Governor Robert Dinwiddie to the commander of the French outpost there. On Dinwiddie's urging, Washington published the journals of that harrowing winter trek, full of heart-pounding escapes from Indian attacks and near-drownings. The popularity of those accounts spread Washington's fame throughout the colonies as well as England.

At the outbreak of the French and Indian War, Washington tried and failed to secure a commission in the regular British army. Unwilling to sit on the sidelines, he volunteered his services in General Braddock's campaign against the French in present-day Pittsburgh, Pennsylvania. Washington's bravery and leadership were conspicuous during the ambush of Braddock's forces on the Monongahela River, during which Braddock was shot down and Washington assumed command.

Although Braddock's campaign was a debacle, Washington received only praise for his actions on the Monongahela. Soon afterward he was made commander of the newly formed Virginia Regiment, which came to be known as the "Virginia blues" after the distinctive uniform that Washington himself designed.

For more than three years Washington headed up the regiment, fighting continually along the frontier of Virginia and the Ohio Country. Washington's goal was to make the Virginia Regiment more than a provincial unit and far more than a militia company. His aims were to have his men outfitted and drilled to match any regular army unit and to make them the foremost experts in the practice of wilderness fighting. In these he succeeded admirably, but a commission in the regular British army, which Washington coveted, still eluded him.

Frustrated by the lack of recognition his regiment received from his superiors in the British army, and understanding at last that he, an American with no influence, would never receive a commission, Washington resigned from command of the Virginia Regiment in 1758. He would not wear a uniform again for another seventeen years.

Washington was elected to represent Virginia at the First Continental Congress, during which he remained largely silent. He was more active during the Second Continental Congress, which, unlike the first, had an army to consider. He served on several committees dealing with military preparations, including "a committee to bring in a dra't of Rules and regulations for the government of the army."

John Adams, at least according to his autobiography, was largely responsible for the nomination and subsequent election of George Washington as commander-in-chief. He would later joke that Washington was always selected for a leadership role because he was always the tallest man in the room, which was generally true. But if Adams would later, on cool reflection, take an ironic view of Washington's nomination, at the time he was much impressed with the soldier from Virginia. He wrote to his wife, Abigail, that Washington's "great experience and abilities in military matters, is of much service to us." A few weeks later he referred to Washington as "the modest and virtuous, the amiable, generous and Brave George Washington, Esquire."

Swept up in the military fervor that Washington's presence inspired, Adams went on to write, "Oh that I were a soldier! I will be. I am reading military books. Everyone must, and will, and shall be a soldier." Adams certainly would never have expressed such a romantic sentiment to anyone but his beloved "Portia," as he called his wife, and one can well imagine Abigail smiling and shaking her head to read such a thing from her short, stout, middle-aged, decidedly unmilitary husband.

Washington was in almost every way Adams's opposite. Adams was one of the most vocal and prolix of the delegates to Congress, while Washington was generally silent. Adams was a fearless leader in the political theater but no military man; Washington, so effective at leading men in the field, took no leadership role in Congress. Adams was a hardworking lawyer who earned a tolerable income through his labor. Washington was a wealthy Virginia aristocrat who worked tirelessly overseeing his plantation but had no profession per se.

Physically, Washington was certainly Adams's opposite. While Adams was short, balding, and round, Washington was around six foot two, a tall man for the age or indeed for any age. He was also well proportioned, with a strength that was legendary and had not waned by the fifth decade of his life. Washington looked like everyone's idea of a military leader. After meeting him, Abigail Adams, whose head was not easily turned, wrote to John saying:

> I was struck with General Washington. You had prepared me to entertain a favorable opinion of him, but I thought the half was not told me. Dignity with ease and complacency, the gentleman and soldier, look agreeably blended in him.

Abigail went on to quote the lines by the poet John Dryden of which Washington put her in mind: "Mark his majestic fabric; he's a temple/Sacred by birth, and built by hands divine." Such enthusiasm no doubt fanned John Adams's growing jealousy of Washington.

Of Charles Lee, Abigail said tersely, "The elegance of his pen far exceeds that of his person."

George Washington wished to make clear to everyone at the Continental Congress that, unlike Adams and the rest, he was a soldier. To reinforce the favorable impression made by his physical presence, he apparently attended Congress in his uniform. Though this has become a standard part of the Washington story, it, like much of Washington's ascendancy to commander-in-chief, comes to us only through Adams, who wrote about it to Abigail.

It is not even clear what uniform he may have worn. The uniform of the Virginia Regiment, the Virginia blues, was a blue broadcloth coat with scarlet facings, a scarlet waistcoat, and blue breeches. It would have been impressive indeed if the forty-three-year-old Washington could still fit into a uniform he had not worn in almost two decades, though this is the uniform he is shown wearing in a 1772 portrait by Charles Willson Peale.

A little more than a month later, army surgeon James Thatcher would see Washington in his familiar "blue coat with buff-colored facings," so it is possible that he had that uniform before the Second Continental Congress. But whatever the colors of the uniform, the message would have been unmistakable.

Adams could see that Congress was dividing along various lines, and one of those divisions was North versus South. Southern delegates were displeased by the prospect of a "New England Army under the Command of a New England General." The Southerners were looking mainly to Washington, though several, including a few from the Virginia delegation, were opposed to his nomination.

Despairing of finding any unanimity among the delegates, Adams decided at last to force them to some decision. Some time before June 14 he made a motion "that Congress would Adopt the Army at Cambridge and appoint a General." He went on to say that he "had but one Gentleman in mind for that important command."

John Hancock, the wealthy, ostentatious Boston merchant who was then serving as President of the Continental Congress, had himself in mind for command of the army. It was certainly true, as Adams wrote, that Hancock's "Exertions, Sacrifices and general Merit in the Cause of his Country, had been incomparably greater than those of Colonel Washington," but that was not enough to overcome "his entire Want of Experience in actual Service."

Nonetheless, as Adams began, Hancock listened with "visible pleasure," sure that the nomination was his. When Adams reached the part about "a Gentleman from Virginia who was among us," Hancock's expression changed. "I never remarked a more sudden and sinking

Change of Countenance," Adams observed. Washington, who had been sitting by the door, discreetly "darted into the Library Room."

The ensuing debate ended in nothing close to a consensus, so the motion was tabled. Only after additional days of lobbying by Adams and other Washington supporters did so great a majority of Congress clearly favor Washington that "the dissentient Members were persuaded to withdraw their Opposition." On June 15 Washington was again nominated, this time by Thomas Johnson of Maryland, and this time was unanimously elected.

Washington went to great lengths to assure everyone that he had not sought the post of commander-in-chief. Three days after his nomination and acceptance, he wrote to his wife, Martha, saying in part, "I assure you, in the most solemn manner, that, so far from seeking this appointment I have used every endeavor in my power to avoid it." It was a refrain that would play through every letter he wrote concerning his post.

It is unlikely that Washington lied about his ambitions—such a thing would not have been in keeping with his character. But neither is it credible that a man who apparently wore his uniform to Congress (the only member to do so, though others held commissions in militia units) and who served on every committee having to do with military affairs was not hoping on some level to be chosen to lead the armed forces.

Surely there was some subtle, perhaps even subconscious campaigning on Washington's part, and indeed, any campaign would have to have been subtle. The standards of the eighteenth century made it unseemly to seek any office actively. One needed to serve reluctantly, at the behest of the people; raw ambition was an ungentlemanly trait even among the ambitious men of the Continental Congress. More than a decade later, candidates for president of the United States would not actively campaign for themselves. When Washington accepted that office, and when he accepted the chairmanship of the Constitutional Convention, he similarly protested that he had not sought or desired those positions.

Washington does seem to have had genuine misgivings about accepting command of the army, as well he might, given how unrealistic it was to think that a mob of ill-trained and ill-equipped colonials—a "rabble in arms," as General John Burgoyne described the troops around Boston—could beat back one of the greatest armies on earth. To his fellow Virginian Patrick Henry, Washington privately confided, "From the day I enter upon the command of the American armies, I date my fall, and the ruin of my reputation." It was a valid insight into the potential hazards of the command he had accepted, a command that would most likely have been the ruin of a lesser man.

To Martha, Washington wrote that "it was utterly out of my power to refuse this appointment without exposing my Character to such censures as would have reflected dishonor upon myself." Having brought about his own nomination, consciously or otherwise, he would have appeared ridiculous if he had then declined the position, opening himself to accusations of moral if not physical cowardice. The eighteenth-century gentleman served not out of his own desire but because others clamored for him to lead, and when he was clamored for, it was his duty to accept. And Washington surely coveted the command. The only thing worse for him than being appointed commander-in-chief would have been for someone else to be named in his stead.

A little more than two weeks after he accepted the nomination, Washington would come to fully understand the grim circumstance into which he had plunged himself.

Cambridge

George Washington left Philadelphia for Boston on June 23, traveling on horseback in the company of Charles Lee (who had been commissioned as a major general, second to Artemas Ward) and Philip Schuyler, also a major general. There was no skimping on pomp and circumstance.

All of the Massachusetts delegates, complete with carriages and servants, were there to see the men off, as were delegates from other colonies. John Adams wrote to Abigail that the parade included "a large troop of light horse in their uniforms; many officers of militia besides, in theirs, music playing, etc., etc. Such is the pride and pomp of war." And then, having apparently abandoned his earlier enthusiasm for soldiering, he added, "I, poor creature, worn out from scribbling for my bread . . . must leave others to wear the laurels which I have sown."

Much of the nine-day, nearly four-hundred-mile journey from Philadelphia to Boston was like that, with citizens in every one of the more than fifty towns along the route turning out to welcome and celebrate the famous soldiers. Washington would complain to John Hancock that his trip was "retarded by necessary Attentions to the successive Civilities which accompanied me in my whole Route."

Schuyler left the company in New York, from where he would proceed to Ticonderoga and take command there, while Washington and Lee continued on to Cambridge. They were welcomed in Watertown on the first of July with yet more ceremony, courtesy of the Massachusetts Provincial Congress, who had more reason than anyone in the United Colonies to be happy to see them. The next day the two men, accompanied again by a large parade of citizens and a troop of light horse, rode through the rain to their final destination, Cambridge and the headquarters of the American army. Arriving in camp at last, Washington found something he had yet to encounter—a body of men who were not impressed.

The soldiers living in their disorganized camps, toiling at the entrenchments, turning out for various alarms, and exchanging cannon fire with the British in Boston took only passing notice of the great man's arrival. George Washington, of course, did not then enjoy the status he would attain after eight years of war and victory over England. He was simply the Southerner whom Congress had selected to take the place of Artemas Ward, who was popular with many of the troops.

To further add to the men's distraction, the day before Washington's arrival the British had begun a furious cannonading of the American lines, which many thought a prelude to an attack. The men braced for an assault that only the driving rain of July 2, it was thought, had prevented. Washington's arrival was not foremost on people's minds. Phineas Ingalls, a private from Andover, wrote in his journal, "July 2. Rained - a new general from Philadelphia." James Stevens, who was stationed in Cambridge, noted only, "nothing heppeng extrorderly we preaded [paraded] three times." Because of the rain, the few troops who had been turned out to greet the arriving generals were dismissed before their arrival.

That is not to say that the presence of a new commander-in-chief went entirely without notice. William Emerson in his diary noted simply, "This Day arrived at Cambridge his Excellency General Washington." The next day Joseph Hodgkins, a junior officer in Cambridge, wrote to his wife, "geaneral Washington & Leas got into Cambridge yesterday and to Day thay are to take a vew of ye Army & that will be atended with a grate deal of grandor there is at this time one and twenty Drummers & as many feffors a Beting and Playing Round the Prayde." Despite Hodgkins's prediction of grandeur, there is little evidence to suggest much was done. Washington and Lee were too eager to tour the lines to spend time on any elaborate ceremony.

Cambridge was nearly five hundred miles from Mount Vernon as the crow flies, but it might as well have been on another continent for all the differences between Massachusetts and Virginia. Washington found the countryside pleasing. The inhabitants, however, took more getting used to.

Washington had been in Boston once before, nineteen years earlier, to plead his case to the commander of the British army in North America for higher pay and a regular army commission, neither of which he received. He had stayed only two days, not enough time to plumb the New England character. Now he was in for a shock.

The master of Mount Vernon was horrified by the relationship he discovered between the officers and men of the Massachusetts regiments. A former member of the Virginia House of Burgesses, a part of the Tidewater's ruling elite, Washington found the leveling spirit of the Yankees utterly foreign. He complained that in New England, "the principles of democracy so universally prevail." Such a sentiment, coming from a man leading his country's fight for freedom from aristocracy, seems odd to the modern ear, but it underlines the differences between Southern republicanism and New England town meeting–style democracy.

To Washington, an army officer was a gentleman first and an officer second, and one did not become a gentleman through any democratic process. It galled the commander-in-chief that the Massachusetts officers were of much the same social class as their men, though such was hardly surprising given that New England had nothing like Virginia's clear social strata. Writing to fellow Virginian Richard Henry Lee, Washington complained of "an unaccountable kind of stupidity in the lower class of these people, which believe me prevails too generally among the Officers . . . who are nearly of the same Kidney with the Privates."

Worse yet, the officers were, in democratic New England fashion, elected by the troops, and so rather than assiduously seeing that orders were carried out, they were more apt to "curry favour with the men (by whom they are chosen, & on whose Smiles possibly they may think they may again rely)" in order that they might retain their rank. The army around Boston was still thinking and acting like a local militia, not the Army of the United Colonies. Changing that, and turning the army into a truly continental force, was one of Washington's primary goals.

CHAPTER *6* *New Lords, New Laws*

THE MORE Washington learned of his new command, the more horrified he became. His General Orders of July 7 included, in one document, the phrases, "It is with inexpressible concern," "The General . . . is highly displeased," "may prove . . . the fatal Instrument of our ruin," "A complaint of the most extraordinary kind," "the General . . . will punish them with the utmost severity," and other like warnings and admonitions.

The American lines were impossibly long, stretching five miles from the thin neck at Roxbury, where the Americans had "thrown up a strong Work on the Hill," around the shores of Back Bay to "Intrenchments on Winter & Prospect Hills, the Enemies Camp in full View at a Distance of little more than a Mile," so close that American and British pickets ahead of the lines could almost talk to one another. Despite the entrenchments already in place and the great amount of work done prior to Washington's arrival, the commander-in-chief found the defenses inadequate, the situation precarious. "Between you and me," he wrote privately to Richard Henry Lee, "I think we are in an exceeding dangerous situation."

Washington knew that transports filled with British troops had been arriving in Boston over the past month, and he believed, incorrectly, that the British had nearly as many men as he did. In fact the arriving troops, part of a reinforcement sent from Ireland, raised the British strength to only about six thousand effectives.

The British army was short of numbers, but they had experience, discipline, training, and equipment. They were working on inside lines, and with their naval strength they could easily focus an attack at any point of the sprawling American defenses, while it would take the Americans precious time to shift troops to counter such a move.

Washington believed that an attack was imminent. He wrote to Richard Henry Lee that once "their new Landed Troops have got a little refreshd, we shall look for a visit, if they mean, as we are told they do, to come out of their lines—their great Command of Artillery, & adequate Stores of Powder &ca gives them advantages which we have only to lament the want of."

To guard against disaster Washington began immediately to strengthen the entrenchments and lines of defense. Just five days after the commander-in-chief's arrival, William Emerson noted:

> Thousands are at work every Day from 4 to 11 o'clock in ye Morning 'tis surprising ye Work that has been done. . . . The Lines are almost extended from Cambridge to Mistick River, so that very soon it will be morally impossible for ye Enemy to get to ye Works, excepting in one Place, which is supposed to be purposely left unfortified to toll ye Enemy out of their Fortress.

Washington meant to improve both the physical works and the discipline and regulation of the camp. Emerson further observed, "There is great overturnings in ye Camp as to Order & Regularity. New Lords, new Laws." He went on to describe how Washington had set about eradicating from the army not only disorder but also the New England spirit of egalitarianism:

> The Generals Washington and Lee, are upon ye Lines every Day, new Orders from his Excellency are read to ye respective Regiments every Morning after Prayers, ye strictest Government is taking Place: great distinction made between Officers and Soldiers, everyone is made to know his place and keep in it, or be immediately triced up and receive (not 1000) but 30 or 40 Lashes, according to the Nature of his Crime.

Washington issued a steady stream of general orders; orders for proper returns (i.e., troop counts), orders for troop movements in case of alarm, orders for soldiers to stop enlisting in multiple regiments for the bonus money, orders for officers to wear colored ribbons across their chests to distinguish them from privates, and orders for numerous courts-martial for a variety of offenses. Washington would later tell Richard Henry Lee, "I have made a pretty good Slam among such kind of officers as the Massachusetts Government abound in. . . . I spare none

& yet fear it will not all do, as these Peeple seem to be too inattentive to every thing but their Interest."

After just a few weeks of furious activity, Washington began to feel that his defenses were strong enough to dissuade the British from challenging them. He wrote to his brother Samuel that he had initially expected the enemy to attack, but "as we have been incessantly (Sundays not excepted) employed in throwing up Works of defense I rather begin to believe now, that they think it rather a dangerous experiment; and that we shall remain sometim watching the Motions of each other."

Though Washington was growing more comfortable with the strategic picture, it would take him quite a bit longer to warm up to the Yankees. To Boston native John Hancock, Washington would write, "I have the sincere Pleasure in observing that there are Materials for a good Army, a great Number of able-bodied Men, active zealous in the Cause & of unquestionable Courage." But to his cousin Lund Washington, the overseer at Mount Vernon, he would write almost two months after arriving in Cambridge that "their Officers generally speaking are the most indifferent kind of People I ever saw. . . . they are by no means such Troops in any respect, as you are lead to believe of them from the Accts which are published. . . . they are an exceedingly dirty and nasty people."

New Terrain

In George Washington's acceptance speech upon being unanimously elected to the post of commander-in-chief, he had said in part, "I feel great distress, from a consciousness that my abilities and military experience may not be equal to the extensive and important Trust." The sentiment may have been sincere, or he may have been expressing the modesty expected of a gentleman, or he may have been trying to lower expectations in the event things did not work out. Perhaps all three motivations were at work. While history would ultimately prove his abilities equal to the trust, he was correct about one thing. He did not have the military experience for the job.

During his brief army career prior to 1775, Washington had never commanded anything larger than a regiment. Even more important, he was a stranger to the kind of fighting that would dominate the main theaters of combat during the Revolution, the European style of warfare that employed closed ranks of men maneuvering in open country.

All of Washington's experience had involved fighting in the unsettled backcountry of the American frontier. He had watched Braddock's British regulars slaughtered at the Monongahela precisely because they stood in closed ranks and fired volleys at an enemy hidden in the forest. Only the Provincials, who had plunged into the woods at the first contact with the enemy and fought the way the Indians did, had managed to put up any effective defense.

As commanding officer of the Virginia blues, Washington had drilled his men in the mobile tactics necessary to counter the French and the Indians, who would be employing the same tactics against him. For years Washington led his men in that type of irregular combat, so different from the orderly marching and volley fire of more conventional eighteenth-century warfare. He and his Virginia Provincials became battle-tested and skilled, but that experience had nothing to do with the sort of fighting he faced as commander-in-chief of the Continental Army.

Beyond the sheer size of his command, Washington now had to reckon with military issues he had never before had to deal with in a meaningful way. He had no real experience with the use of field artillery. He had little practical experience in siege warfare involving extensive entrenchments and fortifications. He would be some time learning how to choose the best ground for a fight, and he would never learn to make battle plans that were not overly complicated.

And with his new command, Washington encountered another element that had played no part in the Virginia backcountry—the sea.

For the first time in his career, Washington had to consider the sea in his strategic thinking. It was no idle concern—every major city in the American colonies was directly accessible from the sea. Even Philadelphia, the largest city in British America with nearly thirty thousand inhabitants, was a busy port despite sitting more than one hundred miles up the Delaware River. The British enjoyed a naval superiority that the Americans could never dream of approaching. Already Washington understood that his position around Boston was placed in jeopardy by the Royal Navy and that their "complete command of the water" could enable the British to direct an attack at any point along the American lines—or along the American continent.

Washington knew nothing of ships and the sea. He had made only one ocean voyage in his life, accompanying his half-brother Lawrence to Barbados in 1751. Lawrence had made the trip hoping the climate would provide a cure for his tuberculosis. Instead George had contracted smallpox, which left him with barely discernible pockmarks on his face as well as an immunity to the disease that would kill thousands of his fellow soldiers during the Revolution.

At one time Washington had almost made a career of going to sea. When he was fourteen years old and casting about for a profession, Lawrence suggested that George consider a berth as a midshipman in the Royal Navy, something Lawrence thought he could arrange. George apparently was ready for the adventure, but his mother, Mary Washington, was hesitant. A friend found that she "offers several trifling objections such as fond and unthinking mothers naturally suggest."

Had Washington grown up in a New England seaport town such as Marblehead or Beverly, a career at sea would have seemed perfectly normal, even expected, regardless of his family's social standing. For a member of the Virginia aristocracy, it was unheard of. All thoughts of sending George to sea ended when Mary received a letter from her brother in London, Joseph Ball, to whom she had appealed for advice. Ball was of the same mind as Samuel Johnson, who famously said that "no man will be a sailor who has contrivance enough to get himself into a jail." Ball told Mary that George would be better off "apprentice to a tinker," because if he shipped out as a common sailor in the merchant service, he would soon be pressed into the navy where they would "cut him and staple him and use him like a Negro, or rather, like a dog."

Nor did Ball think much of George's prospects of entering the navy as a midshipman with the hope of advancement and eventual command. "And as for any considerable preferment in the Navy," he wrote, "it is not to be expected, there are always too many grasping for it here [London], who have interest and he has none." Even if Washington became the master of a Virginia ship, "which will be very difficult to do," he would never earn more than a man who owned a moderate plantation. Setting himself up as a planter, beginning modestly and building wealth slowly, Ball felt, "will carry a man more comfortably and surely through the world, than going to sea, unless it is by great chance indeed."

Joseph Ball had a valid point, several in fact. While Washington, with his physical strength, ambition, native intelligence, and dedication to hard work, might have flourished shipboard, there were few opportunities for advancement at sea and even fewer for gaining wealth. The navy would have been a better route than the merchant service. The command structure of a man-of-war would have appealed to Washington's propensity for order and discipline, and the navy offered a much greater chance of advancement based on merit than the army. Army commissions, for one thing, were bought and sold for great sums of money, but that did not happen in the navy. The army could afford a few officers who were incompetent, absent, or both, but a ship could not sail without men on board who knew what they were doing.

That said, advancement in the navy was no less a scramble than in the army, one that depended on powerful friends and family influence. Officers with the right connections advanced, while those without connections often spent their lives as midshipmen or lieutenants, never making the leap to post captain. Washington, a colonial with no influence at all, might well have moldered his life away in the wardroom of some British man-of-war.

Instead Washington found his father's old surveying equipment, and his life spun off on an entirely different trajectory. And when it came to building wealth, Washington chose a method even more expedient than that suggested by his uncle; he married it.

Now, twenty-nine years later, Washington was looking at the sea in a radically different light. This great, open expanse of water was the gaping back door into Boston, and his siege was only half a siege, with no chance of being anything more, as long as the British controlled the sea lanes.

His appreciation of the naval side of the equation is evident in his General Orders of July 9. In these, Washington instructed the commanding officer at Roxbury, the point in the American lines closest to Boston, to send a written, sealed report to headquarters every day noting any important happening in the city and "mentioning particularly, all Arrivals of Ships and Vessels in the bay; and what changes and alterations are made, in the Stations of the Men of war, Transport's, and floating batteries &c."

As he stared across Boston's Back Bay at row after precise row of British regular army tents spread out on the Boston Common and Bunker Hill, and as he furiously prepared for the attack he still thought might be imminent, George Washington could not predict the sort of war he would be facing over the coming year. He could not guess at that point that the British would show no interest in an assault on the American lines or that the conflict would be a stalemate for the land forces.

Only slowly would Washington come to understand that the real war in the New England theater during that first year was a fight not for territory but for *matériel* and that it would be fought at sea. In fact, that war had already begun at Noddles Island, Machias, and other places along the seaboard where Americans were putting to sea in armed vessels of every type. It would take Washington two months to understand this— and longer still before he joined the fight.

CHAPTER 7 *"We Have the Utmost Reason to Expect Any Attack"*

WASHINGTON WANTED for a great many things. His letters to Congress included requests for a paymaster, a commissary general, a muster master general, and a quartermaster general. He asked for a war chest, for engineers and entrenching tools, for tents, and for hunting shirts in lieu of uniforms. The lack of uniforms was so pronounced that no one could "distinguish the Commissioned Officers from the non Commissioned, and the Non Commissioned from the private."

But Washington did not lack food or fuel. With all the bounty of summertime America at its back, the Continental Army was well supplied in those areas. Joseph Reed wrote to his wife, "Provisions of all kinds cheap and plenty," while less than a mile away the British and loyalists were literally dying for lack of food.

Washington was well aware of the shortages in Boston and the strategic value they represented. Keeping the British army destitute became an important element of his strategy. "The great Scarcity of fresh Provisions in their Army has led me to take every Precaution to prevent a Supply," he wrote to Congress in mid-July. "[F]or this Purpose I have ordered all the Cattle & Sheep to be drove from the low Grounds & Farms within their Reach."

Increasingly as time went by in his new command, Washington came to recognize the naval component of the struggle. For some time, patriots around Boston Harbor and beyond had been tormenting the British with lightning attacks carried out in whaleboats—small, handy craft that could move fast under oar or sail. Armed men in a fleet of upward of a hundred boats burned hay and lighthouses on the islands and destroyed navigational aides in Boston Harbor. Washington could see the usefulness of this sort of seaborne cavalry, and he ordered the commanding officers of each regiment to "report the Names of such Men in their respective Corps as are the most expert in the management of whale boats."

A week after that order he reported to Congress, "I have ordered all the Whale Boats along the Coast to be collected, & some of them are employed every Night to watch the Motions of the Enemy by Water, so as to guard as much as possible against any Surprize."

Though Washington was starting to recognize a maritime component in his strategy (one can imagine that he had only just learned what a whaleboat was), he was still thinking small and defensively. As of yet he had no interest in sending to sea anything more substantial than a large rowboat.

It was only natural, of course, that Washington's energies be directed toward defense. His troops were untrained and undisciplined, and he was facing what was arguably the best army in the world. In late July he wrote to Congress saying, "As the season is now advanced, and the enemy considerably re-enforced, we have the utmost reason to expect any attack that may be made will not be much longer delayed."

Despite the easy flow of intelligence between the British and American camps, which meant that each side had a pretty good idea what the other was up to, Washington did not know that General Gage had no intention of fighting his way out of Boston. Just days after Washington wrote to Congress about the possibility of imminent attack, Gage wrote to the Earl of Dartmouth, the American Secretary in London, explaining why, even with the newly arrived reinforcements, he would not be going on the offensive. "[T]here is but one way out of the Town by Land, and that a Narrow pass commanded on all sides," he wrote. But the difficulty of crossing Roxbury Neck, and the memory of Bunker Hill, did not concern Gage as much as the thought of what he would do once he was out of Boston.

Gage did not have enough men to both secure Boston and "move out with the Remainder in Force Sufficient to Subdue the Country." The Americans could sweep the countryside of food ahead of the British forces, and a lack of water transport and a shortage of wagons left Gage with no means of establishing a supply line. "There is no Rivers for the Transportation of Supplys, and Land Carriages are not to be procured,"

Gage wrote. A lack of fresh provisions was turning the British stay in Boston into a hellish experience, but a shortage of men and wagons kept them from doing anything about it.

Gage's officers generally agreed with that assessment, including General Burgoyne and Lord Percy, who wrote to a friend and fellow officer, "Here we are still cooped up, and are now so surrounded with lines & works as not to be able to advance into the country without hazarding too much. For our army is so small that we cannot even afford a victory, if it is attended with any loss of men."

Lord Dartmouth likewise agreed with Gage's reasoning and informed the general that London did not expect any further operations that year. Instead, Dartmouth, the king, and the war ministers turned their thoughts to the campaigning season of 1776.

The Article of Powder

In his very first letter to Congress, written on July 10, Washington mentioned the army's dire lack of gunpowder. "We are so exceedingly destitute," he wrote, "that our artillery will be of little use, without a supply both large and seasonable. What we have must be reserved for the small-arms, and that managed with the utmost frugality."

Gunpowder was not an item readily available in the colonies. As trouble mounted, King George III had had the good sense, as early as October 1774, to prohibit the export of gunpowder, arms, and ammunition to any part of his kingdom. That order was renewed in April 1775, two weeks before Lexington and Concord.

Nearly all of the gunpowder used by the American military had to be imported from some place other than England. Manufacture of powder was all but nonexistent in the colonies, and those few places that did have powder mills were hampered by a lack of saltpeter. Congress offered inducements for ship captains to import powder, but few took them up on the offer.

Despite his warning to Congress, Washington was not then aware of the full extent of the crisis. The commander-in-chief's mention of powder came only after his letter had bemoaned a shortage of tents, uniforms, and sundry other items, and gunpowder was not mentioned

again in the subsequent letters Washington wrote to Congress during
the month of July. The lack of gunpowder was an issue but not the central issue. Not yet.

Soon after his arrival at Cambridge, Washington had been given a
return showing an available store of 303½ barrels of gunpowder, enough
to mostly fill the cartridge boxes of every man and sustain the Americans' heavy artillery for a day's fighting but no more. He made the
improvement of that supply a priority, but it was just one of many pri-
orities that occupied him in his first month.

Then, on August 3, Washington received shocking news. "[O]n
ordering a new supply of cartridges," he wrote Congress, "I was
informed, to my very great astonishment, that there were no more than
thirty-six barrels." That total was a mere 9,937 pounds, enough for only
nine shots per man with none for heavy artillery. There was not enough
gunpowder to sustain the army through even an hour of major combat.

Washington was certain that the army had not, since his arrival, gone
through nearly thirty-seven tons of powder, and he made a thorough
inquiry to discover the reason for the startling discrepancy. It turned out
that the Committee of Supplies, which had put together the return of
early July, had through some misunderstanding given Washington a total
of all powder "which had been collected by the Province, so that the
report included not only what was on hand, but what had been spent"—
including what had been burned in the battle of Bunker Hill and subsequent skirmishes. Brigadier General John Sullivan wrote, "The
General was so struck he did not utter a word for half an hour."

"Our situation in the article of powder," Washington wrote the next
day to Congress, "is much more alarming than I had the most distant
idea of." He met secretly with the speaker of the Massachusetts House
of Representatives to devise some way of acquiring gunpowder "in such
a manner as might prevent our poverty from being know; as it is a secret
of too great consequence to be divulged."

Washington was in a delicate position. He wanted to make his desperate situation clear to his friends while keeping it from his enemies.
"[T]he existence of the Army, and the salvation of the Country," he
informed Congress, "depend upon something being done for our relief,
both speedy and effectual, and that our situation be kept a profound
secret."

The next day Washington began to fire off letters. To Jonathan Trumbull of Connecticut he wrote "in strict confidence, to acquaint you, that our necessities in the article of powder and lead are so great, as to require an immediate supply." He added that "No quantity, however small, is beneath notice." In nearly identical language he wrote to the New Hampshire Committee of Safety and to Rhode Island's deputy governor Nicholas Cooke, who would become governor three months later following the departure of Tory sympathizer Joseph Wanton.

Results were mixed. While Trumbull regretted that he had no powder to send, Richard Henry Lee assured Washington that Congress had already sent six tons, which were en route, and five tons more would be coming. Meanwhile, Washington turned to conserving all the powder he could. Soldiers in camp had long practiced the undisciplined habit of firing their guns whenever they felt like it, sometimes going out beyond the pickets to take potshots at the British. Washington renewed his efforts to put a stop to that. The day after learning of the powder crisis, he issued a general order stating, "It is with indignation and shame the General observes, that notwithstanding the repeated orders which have been given to prevent the firing of guns in and about camp, it is daily and hourly practiced."

He pointed out that the constant firing might prevent the troops from recognizing a real alarm when it came, and that "there is not the least probability of hurting the enemy." Washington ordered that each man's cartridge box be examined every evening to make certain no rounds had been fired, and that any man who passed beyond the guards should be regarded as the enemy and shot. He did not mention the dire lack of gunpowder as the reason for such Draconian measures. If the rank and file were to discover the truth, it was guaranteed that the British soon would as well.

Gunpowder was one of the few things the British in Boston were not lacking, and they kept up a constant barrage on the American lines to which the Americans could make no reply. Joseph Reed wrote to a friend, "The enemy having more ammunition to sport with than we have, divert themselves every day with cannonading our lines." The British shot had little effect except when the American troops did something stupid. Two men were killed, Reed wrote, while "running after cannon-shot."

Through conservation and pleading with Congress and the New England governments, Washington hoped to preserve and replenish his powder supply. But then another alternative presented itself, one that intrigued Washington, but one that would require a ship.

Bermuda Powder

After pleading for powder, Washington's August 5 letter to Nicholas Cooke informed Rhode Island's deputy governor that "One Harris is lately come from Bermuda, where there is a very considerable Magazine of Powder in a remote Part of the Island." Harris had informed Washington that the people of Bermuda were supporters of the American cause and would be happy to help liberate the powder for the use of the Continental Army. The Americans needed only a vessel, preferably an armed vessel, to go and get it.

Washington informed Cooke of this because Rhode Island had established a naval force. That colony had long been on the forefront of naval activity and had begun fighting the war at sea with Great Britain nearly a decade before anyone else in the colonies knew there was a war to fight.

Since the autumn of 1774, the Colony of Rhode Island had suffered a string of depredations by the Royal Navy, and in particular by the frigate *Rose*, commanded by the efficient James Wallace. Admiral Graves had sent *Rose* to

> winter in Newport in Rhode Island, where the few Friends to Government will be rejoiced to behold some Countenance and protection, and the refractory Spirits deterred from very violent proceedings against them. The *Rose* being at Rhode Island will I also hope be a severe Checque to the prodigious smuggling carrying on there with Impunity.

For a year *Rose* had dominated Narragansett Bay. Fed up at last, the Rhode Island General Assembly had voted on June 12, 1775, to order the Committee of Safety to "charter two suitable vessels, for the use of the colony, and fit out the same in the best manner to protect the trade of this colony."

The first vessel chosen was a sloop named *Katy*, owned by Providence merchant and patriot John Brown, who was already in hot water with

James Wallace for his active resistance to British authority. Command of *Katy* was given to portly forty-two-year-old Captain Abraham Whipple, a former privateersman of the French and Indian War and, as subsequent action would prove, one of the most able naval officers in the American service.

The instructions given to Whipple by Nicholas Cooke informed the captain that he was "employed by the Government for the Protection of the Trade of this Colony . . . to kill, Slay and Destroy, by all fitting Ways enterprizes and Means, whosoever, all and such Person and Persons, as Shall attempt or enterprize the Destruction, Invasion Detriment or Annoyance of the Inhabitants of this Colony." That meant, in particular, James Wallace and the *Rose*, and yet, in keeping with the general uncertainty of the summer of 1775, Whipple was enjoined to carry out his mission against the Royal Navy "in His Majesty's Name George the Third."

Katy was around sixty feet long, armed with six 4-pounders and a number of swivels. For most of the summer of 1775 she and her smaller consort, *Washington*, played a game of cat and mouse with Wallace and the *Rose* all over Narragansett Bay, brazenly removing cattle from islands within sight of the frigate and even recapturing a prize taken by *Rose*.

Though Washington was far from ready to arm a vessel of his own, he saw the usefulness of borrowing one from someone else. "We understand there are two armed Vessels in your Province commanded by Men of known Activity & Spirit," he wrote to Cooke. He proposed that one be sent on the mission to Bermuda, with Harris acting as agent, for a price. Washington acknowledged the risks and the real possibility of failure but pointed out that "No Danger is to be considered when put in Competition with the Magnitude of the Cause."

Cooke appreciated Washington's position but told the commander-in-chief that Rhode Island's ships were needed for Rhode Island business and were not available for the use of the United Colonies. Nor did the Bermuda mission require such a well-armed vessel. Cooke proposed arming a packet ship currently at Providence, manning her with volunteers from Washington's army, and sending her instead.

Negotiations dragged on through August. Cooke became more interested after hearing a report that a delegation from Bermuda had met with the Continental Congress and promised tacit support for the American cause in exchange for continued trade. That support included information on the powder stores near the government house in the island town of St. George.

Cooke, however, could not dispatch the ship without permission from the Rhode Island General Assembly, but he did not want to bring the secret plan before that group. "[T]he Nature of the Business," he wrote to Washington, "was such that I did not think it proper to lay it before so large a Body." Cooke knew that secrecy would go out the door if so many were let in on it. Instead he contrived to have a small committee appointed to meet during the upcoming recess of the assembly with the authority to send *Katy* to Bermuda.

On September 2 Cooke informed Washington that the committee "have come to a Resolution to make the Attempt" to retrieve the powder from Bermuda. Abraham Whipple, who had earlier been too sick to go, was now recovered.

By this time Washington was becoming more open to the possibilities of naval warfare. He had always been quick to dedicate resources to intelligence-gathering efforts, and now he knew that a mail packet from England was due to arrive in New York soon. "I need not mention to you the vast Importance of gaining Intelligence of the Enemy's motions & Designs," Washington wrote to Cooke. He proposed that *Katy* "cruize for a few Days off Sandy Hook," where he felt certain she would be able to capture the packet, which, he told Cooke, was armed with "none but Swivels & only mann'd with 18 Men."

Washington, who previously had shown no interest and even an active dislike for the idea of American naval power, not only suggested using the *Katy* to intercept the mail packet but gave detailed instructions on how she should do it. He suggested that if *Katy* could not patrol off Sandy Hook, another vessel should be found that could. Even more radical for the cash-starved commander-in-chief, he suggested that the other vessel could be sent "at the Continental Expense."

On September 14 Cooke informed Washington that "Capt. Whipple sailed on Tuesday with Sixty-one Men on board; his Vessel being clean and every Way in good Order." Whipple had instructions to cruise off Sandy Hook for two weeks and then proceed to Bermuda if he had not managed to capture the mail packet in that time. Later that day, however, Cooke read in the Cambridge newspaper an extract of a letter from

Bermuda claiming that the gunpowder had already been removed from the island. He wrote again to Washington suggesting that Whipple return to Rhode Island after cruising for the mail packet. "His Station in the River is very necessary as Capt. Wallace hath equipped a Sloop with Six and a Schooner with Four Carriage Guns who may be very troublesome here," he wrote.

Washington agreed, and Cooke dispatched a vessel to inform Whipple, but Whipple was not to be found. Whipple, it turned out, had discovered that the mail packet had eluded him, and so he abandoned his patrol and sailed for Bermuda.

By late October Whipple was back in Rhode Island. His passage to Bermuda had been a long one, meeting first with "light flattering winds" and then "with a violent Gale." On his finally making the island, "the Inhabitants, taking him to be an armed Vessel belonging to the King, were thrown into the utmost Confusion, and the Women and Children fled into the Country."

Bermuda, like continental America, was a British colony. Since agriculture had never worked well on the island, which had no natural source of water, Bermuda's four to six thousand residents relied on trade, mainly with the American colonies, for income as well as food. As in most British colonies, a significant anti-British strain ran through the population, though ultimately Bermuda would remain loyal to the Crown.

Whipple landed and showed the members of the King's Council his papers. Happily the Council was not of a loyalist bent. When the people realized *Katy* was an American vessel they greeted Whipple warmly but informed him that he was too late. The powder was gone. Both missions to which he had dedicated a month and a half had ended in failure.

George Washington was sanguine. "[I]t is not in our power to Command Success," he wrote to Cooke, "tho' it is always our duty to deserve it." The commander-in-chief was not discouraged by the failure of his first stab at naval warfare. In fact, by the time Whipple returned from Bermuda, Washington had become a genuine advocate of naval power and had created and sent to sea a secret navy of his own.

CHAPTER *8* *The Congressional Navy Cabal*

THE CONTINENTAL CONGRESS showed little inclination during the summer of 1775 to create a navy of the United Colonies. The army had essentially been created for them, and they had only to adopt it. Not so a navy. A navy would have to be created from the bottom up; ships would have to be purchased or built, guns and gunpowder acquired, officers commissioned, and hundreds of seamen found to man the vessels. The task would consume money and time, neither of which Congress could spare, and it would further provoke England when many still believed a rapprochement possible. It was not an idea whose time had come.

At least it was not for most of the delegates. There was in Congress a small cabal of men who were intensely interested in maritime affairs. Foremost among them was John Adams, delegate from Massachusetts.

Short and stout, slightly jowled, his head capped with a small white wig ringed with tight curls, Adams's appearance belied his fiery, radical nature. Of all the delegates to Congress, Adams was perhaps the most forward thinking and eager to act, forever chafing at those who failed to see things his way.

In the first few months of the Second Continental Congress, while most delegates were still feeling their way along, unsure of the scope and nature of the conflict, Adams complained to his friend James Warren, a leader in Massachusetts politics, "[t]he Congress is not yet so much alarmed as it ought to be." Adams felt that Congress had deceived itself into thinking Parliament would back off once news of Lexington and Concord reached London. He himself felt that Americans would experience only "Deceit and Hostility, Fire, Famine, Pestilence and Sword." In that, Adams was closer to being right.

Adams wrote those words on July 6, less than three months after the fighting at Lexington had turned the cold war hot. Two weeks later he complained to Warren, "We ought to have had in our hands a month ago the whole Legislative, executive and judicial of the whole Continent, and have completely modeled a Constitution; to have raised a naval Power, and opened all our Ports wide; to have arrested every Friend of Government [Parliament] and held them Hostages for the poor Victims in Boston."

Adams, as ever, was way out in front. It would take more than a decade to accomplish all that he had hoped to do in two and a half months. But much of what he envisioned he was already discussing with others, and that most certainly included the establishment of a navy.

John Adams considered himself something of an authority on maritime affairs, "[a]s a considerable part of my time, in the Course of my profession, had been spent upon the Sea coast of Massachusetts in Attending the Courts." Adams had spoken at length with codfishermen, whalers, and merchant seamen. He had "heard much of the Activity, Enterprize, Patience, Perseverance and daring Intrepidity of our Seamen" and had come to the conclusion that if those men were let loose against British shipping, "they would contribute greatly to the relief of our Wants as well as to the distress of the Ennemy."

Washington would ultimately reach the same conclusion regarding the potential utility of New England mariners, but he would never come to agree with Adams's rosy assessment of their character. To be sure, Adams's words were written many years after the success of American arms was a *fait accompli*.

Also at the center of Congress's naval cabal was fifty-one-year-old Christopher Gadsden, a delegate from South Carolina and one of the few Southerners with an interest in maritime affairs. Gadsden had served as an officer in the British navy during his younger years and so had a more realistic view of British naval power than those who were overawed by the Royal Navy's reputation.

Not long after Congress had taken over management of the army, Gadsden and Adams began to talk about naval matters. Adams, writing of Gadsden to his friend Elbridge Gerry in Marblehead, said, "He has several Times taken Pains to convince me that this Fleet is not so formidable to America as we fear." Gadsden felt it would not be too difficult for American forces to capture small vessels of the British navy—sloops, schooners, and cutters—as had already been proved in Machias. Less realistic was his opinion that the crews of large men-of-war would not fight "british Americans" but rather in battle would rise up against their oppressive officers.

Elbridge Gerry showed the letter containing Gadsden's thoughts to James Warren, who heartily approved, writing to Adams, "I thought it very happy to have so great an authority [as Gadsden] confirming my own sentiments." Warren, in fact, proposed to the Massachusetts legislature that the colony undertake such a maritime venture, and he used Adams's letter to support his arguments. But the majority of leaders in Massachusetts, like those in Congress, shied away from such a step.

For all the high talk that swirled around the creation of a navy, nothing of that sort was formally advanced in the Continental Congress. In part this was because Congress had its hands full debating other issues, the foremost being whether to open American ports to trade with other countries. Cost, too, was a factor. Ships were expensive, and while an army could be put in the field and then supplied as needed, a ship had to be fully stocked with food and ammunition before it went to sea.

And there were the political implications of naval warfare to weigh. The many delegates in Congress who still hoped for reconciliation with England clung to the fiction that the army was purely for defensive purposes. It had come together as a reaction to British aggression and was maintained for the defense of the country against "ministerial butchers"—meaning Parliament's troops, not those of the beloved king.

Organized local militia had been a colonial tradition for more than a hundred years. The concept of citizen-soldiers taking up arms in defense of their homes was ingrained in the American character, and the battles of Lexington and Concord and Bunker Hill and the siege of Boston were looked on as defensive necessities. Indeed, Washington's commission made clear that the army was "for the defense of American liberty, and for repelling every hostile invasion thereof."

A navy would be different. Sending ships onto the high seas to hunt down and capture British vessels could not be construed as defensive. Such blatant American aggression would signal an unwelcome change in colonial ambitions. The establishment of a navy could reasonably be construed as a tacit declaration of sovereignty.

Last, the southern colonies looked on the idea of a navy with suspicion. With the exception of Gadsden and later Richard Henry Lee, most viewed a navy as a New England affair that would result in big costs and few benefits to the South. Though Washington had left Congress long before any discussion of a navy was heard on the floor, he would likely have agreed with the majority Southern view on the subject.

Given all the arguments against the idea, no delegate was likely to propose the creation of a navy unless instructed to do so by his colonial legislature. In early August, that happened.

It was not Massachusetts leading the way this time but Rhode Island. The shooting war on land might have broken out in Massachusetts in April 1775, but the naval war had started years before in Rhode Island. The most violent and audacious of the Rhode Islanders' many acts of resistance in the years before to the Revolution had taken place in June 1772, and it led, ultimately, to the creation of the navy of the United States.

The Gaspee Affair

Even more than its neighbors, Rhode Island and Providence Plantations had always been a maritime colony, arrayed as it was on its long axis around the waters of Narragansett Bay. Though the colony with its fifty-five thousand inhabitants was only about one-fifth as populous as Massachusetts in 1775, virtually every one of its free men was involved in shipping and maritime commerce in some capacity and degree. From the beginning of the eighteenth century ships had sailed regularly between Rhode Island and the islands of the Caribbean. Traders carried beef, pork, butter, cheese, horses, lumber, and barrels south and then filled their holds for the return trip with bar iron, ironmongery, textiles, and other manufactured goods from Europe that were scarce in the nonindustrialized American colonies.

As this trade increased, two products from the "Sugar Islands" began to dominate: rum made from molasses, which was a by-product of the islands' sugarcane processing, and raw molasses itself with which to feed the growing number of distilleries in New England. This would eventually become one leg of the infamous triangle trade in which rum from New England was exchanged for slaves in Africa who were then traded for sugar and molasses in the West Indies.

Seeing a fresh revenue opportunity in this trade, the Crown began to place duties on imports. In particular, the Sugar Act of 1764 levied a tax on molasses and sugar entering America from any non-English port. This led Rhode Island captains to invent ever more elaborate ways of evading the duties—the colony's 380 miles of convoluted coastline being rife with hidden places to land smuggled goods—which led in turn to more heavy-handed enforcement. The escalating tension played out against a mounting colonial revulsion at such examples of "taxation without representation" (a phrase that had been in use in Ireland for a generation or more) such as the Stamp Act of 1765 and the Townshend duties of 1767, and violence erupted on several occasions, reaching its ultimate expression in the second week of June 1772.

At around noon on June 9 the small coasting packet *Hannah* stood out of the harbor of Newport, Rhode Island. With Goat Island off her larboard side, she shaped a northerly course for the town of Providence, twenty-five miles up Narragansett Bay. The wind was blowing from the north, and the *Hannah*'s captain, Benjamin Lindsey, braced the ship's yards hard around and hauled taut the sheets on the fore-and-aft canvas as the packet plunged close-hauled across the bay.

Hannah had arrived at Newport the previous day after a short voyage from New York. Lindsey, according to the local press, had dutifully reported his cargo at the customs house in Newport. If he did, he was showing more respect for His Majesty's revenue laws than was generally granted by Rhode Island's merchant captains.

As *Hannah* made her way up the bay, Lindsey saw a familiar vessel to the south, also beating north against the wind. She was His Majesty's armed schooner *Gaspee*, of eight guns, under the command of Lieutenant William Dudingston. The schooner, sent by the British admiral in Boston to enforce the Crown's customs laws, was entirely familiar to and universally loathed by the men who sailed on Narragansett Bay.

There could be no doubt that *Gaspee* was giving chase. Lindsey understood perfectly well that Lieutenant Dudingston expected *Hannah* to heave to so that *Gaspee*'s boarding party might inspect the vessel's cargo, but he had no intention of complying with that wish.

Tack on tack *Hannah* and *Gaspee* raced north. The *Gaspee* was likely the faster of the two, and she was certainly better manned. Mile by mile the armed schooner began to overtake the fleeing merchantman.

North of Warwick Point, Narragansett Bay begins to narrow into the Providence River. With banging sails, a stamp of feet, and the squeal of yards bracing around, the two ships made short tacks across increasingly confined waters. By two o'clock in the afternoon the tide began to ebb, slowing their progress.

The water was still high but falling fast an hour later when Lindsey swung the *Hannah* around on a larboard tack and stood to the east. To the south of him Dudingston did the same, covering *Hannah*'s every maneuver.

Just to the north of *Hannah*'s track, and still covered by water, a sand spit called Namquit Point made out from the western shore. If Dudingston ever knew of the bar's existence he had forgotten it, not having been to Providence since his return to Narragansett Bay that spring. But Lindsey, a Yankee captain with local knowledge, knew full well that the hazard was there.

Hannah held her easterly course as Lindsey, standing on her quarterdeck, carefully gauged his position relative to the hidden bar. Satisfied at last that he had cleared the end of the point, he ordered the vessel about. Once again *Hannah* spun into the wind, her sails flogging as she came around to starboard tack, making to the westward. South of him, as Lindsey had known he would, Dudingston also tacked.

The two vessels settled on their new courses, crossing the river east to west. *Hannah* had tacked around the end of Namquit Point and stood into clear water to the north, but *Gaspee*, to the south, had not. Lindsey no doubt savored the sight as the hated *Gaspee*, under full sail and driving hard, came to a sudden and jarring stop, her bow slamming into the sands of Namquit Point on a falling tide.

As he continued upriver to Providence, Lindsey could be fairly certain of one thing: *Gaspee* was not going anywhere for at least nine or ten hours.

"[T]o go and destroy that troublesome vessel"

Hannah came to anchor off Providence's busy waterfront around sunset. No sooner was the hook down than Lindsey went ashore to search out Providence's leading citizen and foremost revolutionary, John Brown.

The Browns had arrived in Rhode Island with Roger Williams at the founding of the colony and had been among its most prominent families ever since. John Brown would go on to become one of Rhode Island's leaders in the Revolution and would later establish Brown University, but on the night of June 9, 1772, his primary concern was the schooner *Gaspee*, which Lindsey reported hard and fast on Namquit Point.

It is quite possible that the men of Providence—of whom 726, according to a 1776 survey, were capable of bearing arms—had already decided on the action they would take and were waiting only for the opportunity. Certainly when the chance presented itself, they wasted little time in discussion.

Brown went right to work. He passed an order to the master of one of his ships to

> collect eight of the largest long boats in the harbor, with five oars each; to have the oars and row-locks well muffled, to prevent noise, and to place them at Fenner's Wharf, directly opposite of the dwelling of Mr. James Sabin, who kept a house of board and entertainment for gentlemen.

Sabin's Tavern was a meeting place for men in Providence with a revolutionary bent. Just after sunset, as the shops along the waterfront were shuttering their windows and closing their doors, a drummer marched down the street beating a tattoo to muster attention. He informed the locals of the *Gaspee*'s situation and invited anyone inclined "to go and destroy that troublesome vessel" to gather at Sabin's. Among those who heeded that call was a young man named Ephraim Bowen, who hurried home to borrow his father's gun and collect his powder horn and bullets before arriving at Sabin's around nine o'clock.

He found the tavern crowded with men, mainly mariners from Providence who saw the chance to rid themselves of a great impediment to their lucrative smuggling. Some were arranging to get under way while others were hurriedly melting lead for bullets over the tavern's kitchen fire. Bowen loaded his gun and prepared to go.

Also among the Americans was Dr. John Mawney, who had hurried to the tavern on hearing the drummer in the streets. He agreed to accompany the expedition as surgeon.

Around ten o'clock the order came for the men to move out. Filing out of Sabin's they crossed the street to Fenner's Wharf and took their places in the longboats collected there. Mawney later wrote, "we stopped at Capt. Cooke's Wharf, where we took in staves and paving stones." With guns in short supply, the attackers would be armed mainly with sticks and rocks.

A ship's captain took the tiller of each boat. Leading the expedition was a familiar figure along the Providence waterfront, first among equals, Captain Abraham Whipple, who would later command the Rhode Island navy's sloop *Katy* and then a ship in the Continental Navy.

Whipple was thirty-nine years old on that June night in 1772 when he settled into the sternsheets of the boat that would pull him downriver to the stranded *Gaspee*. He had attained a portly figure, and his broad face and wide mouth made him look more like a kindly uncle than the fighting captain he was. In the attack on the *Gaspee* and over the course of the Revolution, he would get the chance to prove how deceptive his avuncular looks could be. Like many who would take to the sea during the American Revolution, Whipple had learned his trade as a privateer captain during the French and Indian War. Back then he had commanded the ship *Game Cock*, which became something of a legend under his leadership. In one cruise alone *Game Cock* scooped up twenty-three prizes, and Whipple gained firsthand experience in fighting at sea.

At Fenner's Wharf, Ephraim Bowen climbed into a boat commanded by John B. Hopkins, who, like Whipple, would go on to command a vessel in the Continental Navy. One by one the boats pushed off. Muffled oars were lowered into their thole pins as the flotilla pulled out into the stream. Manned by expert seamen, the boats formed a line abreast, with Whipple's boat on the right wing and Hopkins's on the left. In near silence they pulled down the river through the still-moonless night, toward the unsuspecting schooner.

Lieutenant Dudingston was in an awkward position, with his vessel stranded on a sandbar on a coast whose inhabitants had already demonstrated their willingness to attack the king's ships. Under those circumstances one might have expected him to set a vigilant watch, but he did not. Had he kept his men at quarters and under arms, the outcome of the night's events might have been different. But at midnight, when the night watch was called on deck, it consisted of only one man, an illiterate seaman named Bartholomew Cheever.

Cheever no doubt paced the deck and stared out into the dark night, the moon still more than an hour from rising. After about forty-five minutes he detected some movement on the water. Peering over the *Gaspee's* bow he could see a line of boats, "six or seven in number," according to his affidavit, "full of men, drawing near to the schooner." Cheever raced below to inform the sleeping Lieutenant Dudingston.

Dudingston rushed to the deck dressed only in his nightshirt, a pistol in one hand and a sword in the other. Standing by the starboard foreshrouds he stared out in the direction Cheever pointed until he, too, saw the ghostly line of boats.

The lieutenant climbed up onto the starboard rail, shouting, "Who comes there?" When he heard no answer he shouted again.

Abraham Whipple, in the foremost boat, was about sixty yards off. "I am the sheriff of the County of Kent, Goddamn you!" he shouted in reply. ("Sheriff" or "head sheriff" was Whipple's nom de guerre, just as "captain" was John Brown's.) "I have got a warrant to apprehend you, Goddamn you, so surrender!"

Whipple knew his business when it came to attacking a man-of-war. Once the *Gaspee* had come in sight he ordered the boats to move from a line abreast to a line ahead, a move carried out easily by the experienced boat crews. In that formation they could attack the stranded vessel right at her bows and out of the arc of fire of her broadside guns.

Dudingston replied that "the sheriff could not be admitted on board at that time of night," but he realized his danger. He shouted for all hands on deck. As surprised men tumbled out of their hammocks and up to the weather deck, Dudingston ordered the foremost cannons hauled up to the bow where they would bear on the attacking boats. But it was too late for that.

Abraham Whipple called for his men to spring to their oars. With a shout the men pulled hard and the longboats shot ahead, closing fast with the *Gaspee.* Seeing that he had no chance of getting his great guns to bear, Dudingston ordered his men forward with small arms, ready to repel boarders.

Dr. Mawney was in the lead boat. Closing with the schooner, Mawney saw a rope hanging down from her bow, and he seized it to haul himself on board. The rope slipped through his hands and he fell waist-deep into the water, but "being active and nimble, I recovered, and was the first of our crew on deck."

Dudingston was standing on the rail, slashing at the Americans with his sword. Farther back in the line of boats, Ephraim Bowen, gun in hand, was watching the action. Joseph Bucklin, standing beside him, said, "Ephe, reach me your gun, and I can kill that fellow."

Bowen handed the gun to Bucklin, and Bucklin took aim at the lieutenant. The report of the musket cut through the shouts of struggling men on the *Gaspee*'s bow, and Lieutenant Dudingston crumpled. "I have killed the rascal," Bucklin exclaimed.

But Bucklin's diagnosis was premature. The bullet clipped Dudingston's left arm and penetrated his groin. Dudingston cried out, "Good God, I'm done for!" and staggered down from the rail.

The men of the *Gaspee* fired back, and their small-arms fire was met with a volley from those Americans who had firearms. Others, wielding barrel staves like cutlasses, swarmed over the schooner's side and fell on the *Gaspee*'s crew, knocking them to the deck.

The *Gaspee*'s boatswain, John Johnson, "received several blows with a stick." Dudingston tried to get his men to fall back and make a stand at close quarters, "but soon saw that most of them were knocked down, and myself twice, (after telling them I was mortally wounded)."

As Dr. Mawney gained the deck, a fellow American named Simeon Olney handed him a stave. Mawney made to strike down a man by the windlass whom he took for a British seaman when a voice he recognized as Captain Samuel Dunn called out, "John, don't strike!"

As Americans and the men of the *Gaspee* struggled in the bow, three of Whipple's boats pulled around the schooner's quarter. Suddenly more Americans were pouring over the side, and the British sailors found themselves caught between two lines of attack.

The fight did not last long. Some of the *Gaspee*'s men fled into the hold ahead of the shouting, stave-wielding Americans. The schooner's midshipman, William Dickinson, later reported, "In the three boats which boarded us upon the quarter, there were thirty or forty men, at least; and in the whole I suppose about one hundred and fifty in number, on which we thought proper (the lieutenant being wounded,) to surrender."

The order rang out along the deck for the *Gaspee*'s crew to call for quarter, and the fight was over as abruptly as it had begun. Those British sailors who remained on deck were hustled below, and once order was restored, the *Gaspee*'s men were ushered back up one at a time. On deck their arms were pinioned and their hands tied with tarred cord, after which they were shoved into the boats alongside. The Americans assured the British they would not be hurt, but their treatment was none too gentle.

John Mawney was in the hold helping to organize prisoners when John Brown called down to say he was wanted on deck. When Mawney replied using Brown's name, Brown said, "Don't call names, but go immediately to the cabin, there is one wounded and will bleed to death."

Dudingston had staggered aft to the companionway that led to his cabin before slumping to the deck, weak from loss of blood. When Brown and Whipple found him there, according to Midshipman Dickinson, Brown threatened to smash the lieutenant's head with a heavy wooden bar called a handspike.

The lieutenant showed the Americans that he was wounded. Perhaps unwilling to acknowledge the shooting and possible killing of a king's officer, one of the Americans replied, "Damn your blood, you are shot by your own people." Dudingston's servant was untied, and he and Dickinson were ordered to carry their commanding officer down into his cabin. Dudingston was laid on the after lockers, "bleeding profusely," according to Mawney.

Applying pressure to Dudingston's wound, Mawney directed Joseph Bucklin to break open Dudingston's trunk and search for cloth. Bucklin did so and then held Dudingston's wound while the doctor tore the cloth into bandages and gave Dudingston "drops," most likely laudanum, for the pain. It is unclear whether Mawney knew that it was Bucklin who had shot the British lieutenant.

While his wound was being dressed, Dudingston had a chance to observe the dozen or so men crowded into his little cabin. To his surprise they did not appear to be an unwashed mob but "merchants and masters of vessels." Likewise, Dickinson observed that "many of them appeared like men of credit and tradesmen; and but few like common men."

Men of credit or not, the men rifled Dudingston's trunks and drawers and took away the ship's papers and the orders under which he had been operating. Soon his wounds were bound, and still in his nightshirt, his coat draped over his shoulders, Dudingston was lowered into a boat for the trip ashore.

Abraham Whipple ordered the boat's crew to land Dudingston and return immediately, but Dudingston responded that they may as well throw him overboard, as he did not have the strength to walk from the shore to anyplace where he might find help. Relenting, Whipple decided to land five of Dudingston's crew with him on Pawtuxet Point, and the British sailors were given a blanket on which to carry their officer.

The sky to the east was turning a pale blue as the men climbed back into their boats for the pull upriver to Providence. The leaders of the expedition gathered in a single boat, and as the others pulled away they set the hated *Gaspee* on fire.

Dudingston was landed at the Still-House Wharf at Pawtuxet, and as his men carried him ashore he heard, far off, the *Gaspee*'s guns going off as if in a final act of defiance. The fire had spread to the still-loaded cannons, and as the schooner burned to the waterline she seemed to be flailing out at an enemy already long gone.

Though no longer well known in American history, the burning of the schooner *Gaspee*, with the near-fatal wounding of her lieutenant, was regarded in England as the most outrageous and unforgivable act ever committed by a colony, and it would retain that distinction until the fighting at Concord. The Boston Tea Party of December 1773, with its nonviolent destruction of private property, was a minor thing compared with the Rhode Islanders' audacious act. Their transgression would not go unnoticed or unpunished.

The Royal Navy Reacts

For nearly two years after the destruction of the *Gaspee*, the people of Rhode Island suffered no consequences. It was not that the Crown was not outraged, but simply that the volatile situation in Boston required the British military's complete attention.

That respite came to an end in November 1774 when the twenty-gun frigate *Rose*, under the ruthless and unyielding command of Captain James Wallace, arrived in Newport Harbor. While the people of Rhode Island had mounted armed resistance against the various schooners and sloops sent by the Royal Navy, they were helpless to oppose a powerful man-of-war.

Wallace set about harassing Narragansett Bay shipping with an efficiency Dudingston could only have dreamed of. Commerce and, more important, smuggling ground nearly to a halt, and the economy of the once prosperous colony staggered under the pressure. Soon after the battle of Lexington and Concord, Wallace arrested James Brown for smuggling. Wallace knew but could not prove that Brown was guilty of leading the *Gaspee* affair. Only desperate negotiations with General Gage in Boston prevented Brown from being sent off to England for trial.

For ten months Wallace and the *Rose* dominated Rhode Island, and there was little Rhode Island could do to fight back. They commissioned the tiny sloop *Katy*, with Abraham Whipple in command, and the even smaller *Washington*, but the two vessels were no more significant to the *Rose* than yipping dogs to a bull.

Not until the convening of the Second Continental Congress did the Rhode Island General Assembly see a chance to end the *Rose*'s depredations. While a small colony acting alone did not have the resources for such a thing, the United Colonies, which now had a standing army, must surely be able to afford a navy as well.

On August 26, 1775, the Rhode Island legislature drafted instructions concerning a navy to its delegates to Congress, Stephen Hopkins and Samuel Ward. The instructions were couched in the ostentatiously conciliatory language in which every radical idea was presented in those early months of the Revolution. After explaining how the Americans had taken "wise and pacifick measures" to bring about a reconciliation with Great Britain, and how the Ministry had nonetheless sent "Troops and Ships-of-War into America, which destroy our Trade, plunder and burn our Towns, and murder the good people of these Colonies," the General Assembly voted and resolved that "this Colony most ardently wish to see the former friendship, harmony and intercourse between Britain and these Colonies restored," and so on in that vein for another one hundred and ten words before getting to the heart of the matter.

"[T]his Assembly is persuaded," they wrote at last,

> that the building and equipping an American Fleet, as soon as possible, would greatly and essentially conduce the preservation of the lives, liberty

and property of the good people of these Colonies; and therefore instruct their Delegates to use their whole influence, at the ensuing Congress, for building, at the Continental expense, a Fleet of sufficient force for the protection of these Colonies.

It would be another month and a half before the Rhode Island delegates were able to test their influence by introducing the measure, but with those words the Rhode Island Assembly set in motion the events that would lead to the United States Navy.

CHAPTER *9* "Our Weakness & the Enemy's Strength at Sea"

BY MID-AUGUST 1775, most of the military action in the American Revolution, apart from minor skirmishes and the digging of fortifications, was taking place on the water. Despite American efforts to starve the British out of Boston, supplies and *matériel* continued to slip in through Boston's wide-open back door, past the many low islands scattered around Boston Harbor. Ships from Britain and sloops and schooners sent by loyalists in other colonies were warped creaking up to Long Wharf, and dockworkers, sweating in the midsummer heat, hoisted casks from dark holds and livestock from the 'tween decks.

In the second week of August, General Washington wrote a note of polite but clear reprimand to the New York Provincial Congress. A ship that had been allowed to leave New York, supposedly bound for St. Croix in the Virgin Islands "with fresh Provisions and other Articles," he told the legislature, "Has just gone into Boston." He reminded them that "the Disstresses of the Ministerial Troops, for fresh Provisions and any other Necessaries, at Boston, were very great; It is a Policy, Justifiable by all the Laws of War, to endeavour to increase them."

A few weeks previously he had sent word to Connecticut, New York, and Rhode Island that three men-of-war and a number of transports had sailed from Boston steering east southeast. Washington guessed that "the great distress they are in at Boston for fresh provisions makes it extreamly probable they make some depredations along the Coasts."

He was right. On August 19 the ships returned after raiding the eastern end of Long Island. British army captain Francis Hutcheson, the assistant deputy quartermaster general in Boston, reported with delight that the fleet had liberated "1900 Sheep 103 Black Cattle 110 Cord of Wood a few Piggs and some Poultry which has put us all in good Spirits." Two ships sent to Quebec had just returned with beef, pork, flour, oats, and entrenching tools in their holds, and General Gage had opened the port of Boston, previously closed to all traffic, to any ship that would bring in fresh provisions or fuel. Admiral Graves's cruisers had scooped up several American ships loaded with flour and diverted them to the city, leading Hutcheson to predict, "we shall therefore be in no want of that necessary Article." That may have been wishful thinking, however. Just a few days before, a private in the 35th Regiment of Foot had been sentenced to five hundred lashes for stealing flour, and a few shiploads would not long alleviate such a severe shortage.

Yet despite the increasing dearth of supplies in Boston, the successful capture of three British armed vessels in Machias, and various other minor naval actions in New England waters, Washington remained dead set against any American naval initiative.

On August 10 a committee of the newly formed General Court of Massachusetts approached Washington with the idea of establishing a naval force. The General Court, its members elected by the towns, had replaced the Provincial Congress on July 19 in a nominal return to the colony's 1691 charter. The General Court had immediately chosen from its delegates an upper body, or executive council, which was to be headed by the colonial governor if and when King George appointed someone acceptable. General Gage, of course, was not acceptable. The reestablishment of the General Court was exactly what the Continental Congress had advised the Massachusetts Provincial Congress to do in May—a gesture of conciliation with the Crown. By August, however, a peaceful resolution of the conflict with England seemed increasingly remote, and in that light the establishment of a navy seemed more and more desirable.

General Washington gently but thoroughly rejected the suggestion. "As to the furnishing of Vessells of Force," he wrote, "You Gentlemen will Anticipate me in pointing out our Weakness & the Enemy's Strength at Sea." Washington believed that any armed vessels in the Continental service would "fall an easy Prey" to the British navy before they could do any good.

Washington had too little experience in naval matters to imagine what a few small ships could do. A man such as Nicholas Cooke, a native of maritime Rhode Island, could see the benefit of a ship like *Katy*, a David against *Rose*'s Goliath. Jeremiah O'Brien, born and bred by the sea, could imagine the utility of small armed vessels patrolling the waters off Machias. To General Gage and Admiral Graves, whose experiences had been in the grand theater of European conflict, the juxtaposition of land and naval forces was such a natural part of warfare that it hardly warranted comment. But Washington, the frontier soldier, could not yet embrace what was to him the alien concept of naval action.

The vulnerability of armed Continental ships was not Washington's only objection. "I could offer many other Reasons against it," he went on, "some of which I doubt not will suggest themselves to the Hon: Board." But one overriding consideration trumped all others—he had no gunpowder to spare. Thus, Washington concluded, "[I]t is unnecessary to enumerate [other reasons] when our Situation as to Ammunition absolutely forbids our Sending a Single Ounce out of the Camp at present."

Like the rebel leaders of Rhode Island, however, those of maritime Massachusetts could see the benefit of armed vessels. Two months earlier the Massachusetts Provincial Congress had rejected James Warren's proposal for a limited naval campaign, but now the committee of the General Court elected a subcommittee to consider Washington's letter and soon after resolved to fit out vessels anyway. Ten days after Washington dismissed the idea, another committee was formed to "consider in what manner the Armed Vessels established by the Resolve of this Court, shall be supplied with Provisions and Ammunition."

One after another the individual colonies were concluding that a naval force was necessary to their defense, but still Washington resisted.

And then he changed his mind.

The Fishermen Soldiers of Marblehead

It is not clear why, in the space of a few weeks, George Washington did a complete about-face on the matter of armed vessels.

One factor, no doubt, was an increase in his supply of powder. Bit by bit during the month of August, his constant pleading and cajoling began to pay dividends, as supplies trickled in from various sources. On August 29 Washington wrote to Richard Henry Lee that "we have only one hundred and eighty-four barrels of powder in all, including the late supply from Philadelphia." While his phrasing indicated that he was far from satisfied with that amount, still it was five times more that he had had just three weeks before.

Joseph Reed wrote to a friend on August 21 saying, "I can hardly look back without shuddering at our situation before this increase to our stock." Clearly the anxiety as to the article of powder was easing, and the need to horde every ounce was not quite so great.

Restlessness might have been another contributing factor. Washington was too active a man to be satisfied with the stalemate in which he found himself. There was a note of frustration in the words he penned to Lund Washington on August 20, around the time of his decision regarding a fleet: "Our Lines of Defense are now completed, as near so at least as can be—we now wish them to come out, as soon as they please, but they (that is the Enemy) discover no Inclination to quit their own Works of Defense."

Not long after, Washington would dispatch Benedict Arnold with a thousand-man column to Canada to try to get things moving on that front. In a letter describing the Arnold expedition to his brother, John Augustine Washington, George added, "The inactive state we lie in is extremely disagreeable, especially as we can see no end to it." He would put forth various plans for launching an attack against Boston, all of which his senior officers would wisely reject.

Some months later Washington would write to William Ramsay, "Finding we had no great prospect of coming to close Quarters with the Ministerial Troops in Boston, I fitted out at the Continental Expence, several Privateers." Thus his apparently sudden change of heart regarding a fleet might well have been related to his desire to break a status quo that was unbearable to a man of action. He might also have been influenced, however, by an officer who had arrived at camp the month before at the head of a newly augmented regiment. That man was Colonel John Glover of Marblehead.

Though they were opposites in appearance—Glover being short and stocky—John Glover and George Washington had much in common. They were the same age, both natural leaders and fighting men. They were both men of means. Each man represented his colony's ideal image of a civic leader, though that image as it manifested in Virginia was very different from that of Massachusetts. Washington was a Tidewater aristocrat, the lord of the manor, born a member of society in a colony where a rise from humble beginnings did not necessarily create an enviable personal narrative. Glover was a self-made New Englander, a wealthy merchant who had worked his way up from a poor, fatherless childhood to a position of leadership in Marblehead society.

John Glover had been four when his father died. When he was old enough to work he turned his hand to various trades, including shoemaking and cordwaining. At twenty-four he was granted "Liberty to retail strong Liquors" in Marblehead and likely opened a tavern to cater to the many fishermen and sailors in that harbor town.

By the 1760s Glover had become a shipowner. His vessels traded between Marblehead, Spain, and the West Indies, carrying salted cod to Catholic Europe and returning from the Caribbean with sugar, molasses, and rum. It is likely that Glover, like many shipowners, commanded his own vessels at least part of the time.

Typical of the Marblehead fleet, Glover's vessels served a double purpose, carrying cargo around the Atlantic and fishing the Grand Banks for cod. This wildly lucrative fishery quickly elevated him to a place in the "codfish aristocracy" of Marblehead along with the likes of Elbridge Gerry, Jeremiah Lee, and Azor Orne. In the years leading up to the war, as Parliament passed various acts taxing and restricting colonial trade, that legislation hit mercantile Marblehead hard, exacerbating the town's already radical New England tendencies. Glover and his fellow civic leaders became active in the growing unrest. Glover himself was made second in command of the Marblehead Militia under Jeremiah Lee.

The militia trained diligently and even turned out for a few alarms, but they did not participate in the battles of Lexington and Concord. Ashley Bowen, a Marblehead ship rigger and faithful diarist, recorded the March 1775 sailing of the fishing fleet from Marblehead to the Grand Banks. His entry of March 11, one of several in a similar vein, read, "This day wind at WSW. Sailed nearly fifty of our fishermen for the Isle of Sable." The men of Marblehead missed the start of the American Revolution because they had gone fishing.

In the first week of May, Bowen noted the return of many of the fishing schooners from the banks. The British navy's enforcement of the Boston Port Bill and the colonies' nonimportation agreements had made work scarce for mariners, so many of the returning fishermen found themselves unemployed, and unemployed sailors have always been a formula for trouble. Happily the army offered them an outlet. Dr. Edward Holyoke of Salem, Massachusetts, noted, "Our men are enlisting very fast here, between three and four hundred gone from this town: the sailors and fishermen, as they have no other employment or support, go to ye army, and we are told there is a whole regiment of fishermen gone from Marblehead—good riddance!"

The people of Marblehead did indeed waste little time plunging into the fight. Bowen noted on May 22, "The fishermen are enlisting quite quick. . . . Drums and fife goes about town to enlist men." The town meeting selected representatives to the Massachusetts Provincial Congress, and these included Azor Orne, Elbridge Gerry, and Jonathan Glover, John's older brother.

John Glover, militia leader, had no time for politics. On the night before the battles of Lexington and Concord, Elbridge Gerry, Jeremiah Lee, and Azor Orne had been meeting with Sam Adams and John Hancock at the Black Horse Tavern at Menotomy. After the meeting Hancock and Adams had departed for Lexington, but the three Marbleheaders decided to spend the night where they were. Sometime past midnight they were awaked by a detachment of redcoats crashing into the inn in search of rebel leaders. Gerry, Lee, and Orne, wearing only their nightshirts, raced out the back door as the British stormed in the front.

The men huddled in a nearby cornfield and were never found, but Jeremiah Lee caught a chill, and three weeks later he was dead. Command of the Marblehead Militia, officially known as the 21st Massachusetts Regiment, devolved to John Glover.

On June 22 Ashley Bowen noted in his diary, "This morning at 3 o'clock our new Regiment marched off for Cambridge. All well." But Bowen's mind was not on the coming fight with England, and he added that "about the time our troops set off I dreamed of being in close hug with a poor rich widow of this town."

The 21st Massachusetts was initially housed in the elegant Cambridge mansion of loyalist John Vassall, only to be evicted a few weeks later when the newly arrived George Washington chose the Vassall home for his headquarters. A number of the Marbleheaders were kept on as a guard detail, however, and it is likely then that John Glover and George Washington first met.

John Glover and his Marbleheaders would be there for Washington at some of the most crucial moments of the war. A year after the men met, Glover's seagoing regiment would ferry Washington's army to Manhattan when the British had them trapped against the East River following the disastrous Battle of Long Island. Four months later Glover's troops would man the Durham boats that carried Washington over the Delaware for the pivotal attack on Trenton. His regiment, renamed the 14th Continental, would participate in the heaviest fighting that day.

Glover may or may not have given Washington the idea of fitting out schooners and sending them to sea. The genesis of that decision is now lost. But there is no question that once Washington embraced the notion, it was John Glover to whom he turned for expertise, manpower, and a ship.

Hannah

John Glover was the right man to ask for a ship. It just so happened that he had one to rent.

Glover was the owner of a small schooner he called *Hannah* after his wife or daughter. The schooner has proved an elusive vessel for historians to track, a task rendered harder by the ubiquity of the name Hannah in colonial America. Shipping records from the Marblehead area show eighteen schooners named *Hannah* within eight years of the Revolution, including one owned by Jonathan Glover, John's brother, who named the vessel after his own daughter.

John Glover's *Hannah* was a Marblehead schooner, one of the tough little boats used for fishing and trade, generally to the West Indies. Admiral Graves in Boston appreciated the qualities of those vessels and saw how useful they could be as armed cruisers. In August 1774, one year before Washington began fitting out his fleet, Graves had written to Secretary of the Admiralty Philip Stevens that "three or four good Marblehead schooners would do considerable Service in the present weak State of the Squadron." *Margaretta* may have been such a vessel.

Hannah was about ten years old when Glover hired her out to Washington, and she and Glover had already had a run-in with the British navy more than two months before. On June 6 Ashley Bowen had seen a schooner standing in to Marblehead, a white flag with a blue diamond snapping at her masthead. It was John Glover's private ensign, announcing *Hannah*'s return to her home port under the command of Captain John Gale.

Ashley Bowen was not the only one watching the vessel's arrival. From shore John Glover could see *Hannah* making for the harbor, while from the quarterdeck of His Majesty's sloop-of-war *Merlin*, Captain William Burnaby was also watching *Hannah*'s approach. Burnaby had been sent to Marblehead the week before to "prevent all kinds of illicit and contraband Trade," and he meant to do so now. He sent the *Merlin*'s barge to intercept the schooner and stop her for inspection. Glover, seeing this, leapt into his own boat and pulled hard for the *Hannah*'s side.

Bowen watched the whole thing.

John Glover went off and met her, and the *Merlin*'s barge met her at the same time. The officer of the barge ordered her to bring to. Glover ordered her not, and the schooner run under the ship's stern, paid no regard to her and run alongside the wharf. All is well that ends well.

It was not the last time *Hannah* would find herself running from His Majesty's forces.

By the middle of August, rumors of schooners being turned into men-of-war were circulating around the area. "No cruisers to fit out in Beverley as was talked of," Bowen noted on August 18, but this time the diarist was wrong. By August 21 at the latest, *Hannah* was indeed being fitted out as a cruiser in the Continental service.

The schooner's conversion took place in Beverly, across the water from Marblehead. Though Glover was from Marblehead, in 1774 he had purchased from Benjamin Beckford "a certain parcle of upland & flats ground being situate in said Beverly with a warehouse, cooper shop and wharf." It was from there that Glover ran his little fleet. The land was located near what today is the end of Front Street.

In his ledger book Glover recorded for the date August 24, "To Schoo^n Hannah Portledge Bill: 44-5-4." The term "portledge" referred to wages paid to a vessel's sailing crew, indicating that *Hannah* was manned as of that date and that the men were to be paid 44 pounds, 5 shillings, and 4 pence. And indeed, on that same day Ashley Bowen noted, "This day fair weather. Came from town a company of volunteers for privateering. They came from Camp at Cambridge and are to go on board Colonel Glover schooner."

Glover's ledger entry went on to say, "To the hier of ditto Sch°° 78 tons @ one dollar per ton per month for two months & 21 days is 208 dollars: 32..8..0." For the perfectly reasonable rate of 78 dollars per month, Glover was leasing his schooner to the army of the United Colonies and allowing her to be sent into harm's way. After nearly two months of hesitancy, during which he had gone from rejecting naval forces outright to embracing them at last, Washington, at the cost of a dollar per ton per month, finally had a navy.

Washington may have had yet another reason to hesitate as long as he did. As a former delegate to Congress he was familiar with the political landscape. He certainly understood that this was not a minor tactical decision but one with much broader implications for Continental policy.

And it was a decision he did not actually have the authority to make.

CHAPTER *10* *George Washington's Secret Navy*

WHEN WASHINGTON was appointed commander-in-chief on June 17, his commission gave him "full power and authority to act as you shall think for the good and welfare of the service." Though frequently prone to micromanagement, the Continental Congress clearly meant to grant the general considerable latitude. After all, who could predict in June 1775 where events were headed? After a few specifics concerning returns, not disbanding troops, field promotions, and victuals, the instructions issued to Washington on June 20 went on to say:

> And whereas all particulars cannot be foreseen, nor positive instructions for such emergencies so beforehand given, but that many things must be left to your prudent and discreet management, as occurrences may arise upon the place, or from time to time fall out, you are, therefore, upon such accidents, or any occasions that may happen, to use your best circumspection; and (advising with your Council of War) to order and dispose of the said Army under your command as may be the most advantageous for obtaining the end for which these forces have been raised.

Between his commission and his instructions, it might have seemed at first blush that Washington had leeway to do just about anything he wished. But the commission, written in a flush of patriotic enthusiasm for the tall commander-in-chief, was more a ceremonial document than a formal job description. What's more, it went on to say that Washington was "punctually to observe and follow such orders and directions, from time to time, as you shall receive from this or a future Congress."

Likewise, the instructions of June 20 were not so open-ended as they at first appeared. Rather than giving Washington carte blanche in every circumstance, Congress was simply acknowledging that he might have to deal with unforeseen emergencies. A battlefield initiative to meet a sudden and short-lived crisis—"occurrences" or "accidents" in the Congressional phrasing—was quite different from a major policy initiative like the creation of a navy.

As the summer wore on, most delegates in Congress supported some level of coastal defense. A month before Washington made the decision to arm *Hannah*, Congress resolved that "each colony, at their own expense, make such provision by armed vessels or otherwise . . . for the protection of their harbours and navigation of their sea coasts, against all unlawful invasions, attacks and depredations, from cutters and ships of war." As with the troops in the field, however, armed vessels were to be for defense only. A majority of delegates—John Adams and his naval cabal notwithstanding—were not yet ready to authorize something as blatantly offensive as the pursuit and capture of British ships on the high seas. This opposition was particularly pointed among Washington's fellow Southerners, a fact of which he was undoubtedly aware.

While there is no indication in Washington's correspondence that he knew he was exceeding his authority, there are hints in what he did not write. On August 23, after work on *Hannah* had begun and one day before she was officially hired as an armed vessel, Washington wrote a long letter to Congress that was typical of the updates he regularly sent to his civilian leadership. He elaborated many details of his current military situation but somehow failed to mention the ship.

Similarly, in letters of that time to all the men in whom he confided his military plans—Richard Henry Lee, Philip Schuyler, John Augustine Washington, Joseph Trumbull, and Nicholas Cooke—he said nothing about his nascent navy. Secrecy was not the issue. Washington freely discussed in his correspondence many top-secret issues, including the critical shortage of gunpowder, Benedict Arnold's march to Quebec, Abraham Whipple's mission to Bermuda, and his thoughts and concerns regarding the ongoing siege of Boston. Indeed, there was hardly any aspect of the military situation he did not discuss with his close correspondents or with Congress. But with regard to the arming of *Hannah* and other plans for a fleet, he was silent.

Washington understood that he was pushing the limits of his authority, and he was likely waiting for some success on *Hannah*'s part before announcing her existence and mission. As it happened, *Hannah*'s first capture would not be a success but rather an embarrassment that would anger and compromise the commander-in-chief.

"The First Armed Vessell Fitted out in the Service of the United States"

The harbor at Marblehead, Massachusetts, is bordered to the northwest by the high rocky edge of Marblehead itself and to the southeast by lower-lying Marblehead Neck. The harbor is nearly rectangular, a long, narrow slot between the unforgiving rocky shorelines that border it on three sides. It is a well-sheltered place but easy to blockade and hard to get out of if the wind is not right.

For years Marblehead had been a thorn in the side of Admiral Graves. In February 1775, the Committee of Inspection, a local body charged with enforcing the Continental Congress's rules regarding trade, impounded two boxes of wax candles that Graves had imported by way of Marblehead for his own use. In retaliation Graves ordered the twenty-gun frigate *Lively* to blockade the harbor and press seamen off incoming ships. From that point on, Marblehead was never without a man-of-war outside the harbor entrance waiting for a chance to "harrass and impress the seafaring inhabitants of that town."

About three and a half nautical miles to the northwest, arrived at by way of a tortured channel through mudflats, sat the harbor of Beverly. Where Marblehead was a deep, narrow cut, Beverly was an all but open roadstead, just a gentle curve in the coastline with its harbor formed by the protecting arm of Salem Neck. Though neither harbor is visible from the other, the two communities have been figuratively staring at one another for three hundred years.

Beverly was a busy seaport town of some three thousand people at the outbreak of the Revolution. It was home to a large fleet of fishing vessels and small merchantmen, including *Hannah* and the rest of John Glover's ships. With Salem Neck standing like a rampart between the waterfront and the sea, and mudflats making any approach to the town a slow and tricky affair, Beverly was better protected from the Royal Navy than was Marblehead.

Tied to Glover's Wharf at the western end of Beverly Harbor, *Hannah* was transformed during the last weeks of August from a merchantman to a man-of-war. Gunports were cut into her sides, and four 4-pounder carriage guns and swivels were hoisted aboard. Platforms to house men were constructed below where before her open hold had housed only cargo or cod. Blacksmiths, shipwrights, cordwainers, masons, and joiners from Beverly contributed to her fitting out. It is likely that she was rigged with a square topsail on her foremast, speed being more crucial in her new career.

On August 24 soldiers from Glover's 21st Regiment marched from Cambridge to Beverly to form the ship's crew. Uniformed in short blue jackets and tarred trousers, they were returning to their natural element, the sea. Recruits were no doubt easy to find. Siege duty was as dull for the privates as it was for the commander-in-chief. What's more, the generally accepted practice in naval warfare was to award the crew a certain percentage of the value of any ship and cargo taken. Though Washington had not yet written the formal orders and terms of service, the men no doubt expected prize money.

For help in finding a captain for *Hannah*, Washington again turned to Glover, who recommended his old friend and business partner Nicholson Broughton. Broughton was a Marbleheader, fifty-five years old, and had been a ship master for twenty years. Like most in Marblehead he had often endured the harassment of the Royal Navy. Ashley Bowen noted on June 20, "This afternoon as Captain Nick Broughton was coming from Salem by water the *Merlin*'s boat brought him too and carried him alongside, but he was soon aquitted."

Broughton was serving as a captain in Glover's 21st Regiment when he was "appointed to the Command of the first Armed Vessell fitted out in the Service of the United States." A third of Broughton's company were selected for *Hannah*'s crew.

Washington's instructions to Nicholson Broughton, issued on September 2, directed him to "take Command of a detachment of said Army and proceed on Board the Schooner *Hannah*, at Beverly, lately fitted out & equipp'd with Arms, Ammunition and Provisions at the Continental Expence." Broughton was to "Cruize against such Vessels. . . in the Service of the ministerial Army," to carefully search any prizes for important documents, to treat prisoners "with Kindness and Humanity, as far as is consistent with your own Safety," and to send prizes into whatever safe port lay nearest to Cambridge. Broughton was to avoid "any Engagement with any armed Vessel of the Enemy," since the object of the cruise was to "intercept the Supplies of the Enemy" and not to run the risk of battle. That was one order the captain would strictly follow.

Despite the supplies of powder that had recently arrived at camp, Washington warned Broughton to be "extremely careful and frugal of your Ammunition" and not to waste any in salutes or anything else that was not absolutely necessary.

If the men recruited from the 21st were hoping for prize money, Washington's orders did not disappoint. Though not as generous as the prizes Congress would later award or those that could be taken by a privateer, Washington's orders granted "one third Part of the Cargo of every vessel by you taken, and sent into Port, (military and naval Stores excepted)." Washington specified the number of shares to go to the captain, lieutenants, ship's master, gunner, boatswain, and others. But in an interesting acknowledgment that this was an army affair and not a formal navy, he did not refer to the lowest rankings as seamen or landsmen. Rather, his orders read, "Privates 1 Share each."

No prize money was to be allotted if the prize was retaken from an enemy ship—that is, an American ship that had been captured by a British cruiser and then recaptured by *Hannah*. In that case Washington would recommend to the owner that "a suitable Compensation" be made to *Hannah*'s crew.

One of the most revealing of the ten specific points in Washington's orders was number eight: "As there may be other Vessels imployed in the same Service with yourself, you are to fix upon proper signals." Even before *Hannah* had proved the worth of armed vessels, even before she had sailed, Washington was thinking of expanding his fleet.

"[T]he dayly Piratical Acts of Graves's Squadron"

Washington was not the only one looking to escalate the war at sea. On the other side of the Atlantic, decisions were being made that would turn the naval action in Massachusetts into a fight enveloping all the American colonies.

The Foreign Ministry in London was well aware of the suffering of its army and navy in Boston and had arranged by early September to send reinforcements and supplies. The reinforcements consisted of two companies of artillery aboard the transports *Charming Nancy* and *Baltick Merchant*, which were to be accompanied by the ordnance storeships *Nancy*, *Juno*, and *Williamson*, their holds crammed with military supplies. Six victuallers carried much-needed food.

The small convoy assembled in the choppy waters of Spithead and anchored off St. Helens on the Isle of Wight near Portsmouth, England. Escorting the unarmed merchant ships was the powerful forty-four-gun *Phoenix* under the command of Captain Hyde Parker. Parker instructed the masters of the convoy's ships to "Obey all orders & Signals you shall from time to time receive and you are to strictly follow the form of sailing"—that is, to maintain the designated formation. Even as he was writing those instructions, however, Parker might well have considered the pointlessness of issuing them. Convoys were easily scattered by storms or fog, and masters of merchant vessels were notorious for ignoring their escort's directions and wandering off.

While protecting convoys, British men-of-war also served as mail packets for the constant stream of orders and correspondence flowing between England and its American colonies. *Phoenix* carried a new directive to Admiral Samuel Graves from the Lords Commissioners of the British Admiralty. It was time to inflict more pain on the rebellious colonies.

Since July, Parliament's New England Restraining Act had sought to cool the insurrection by prohibiting New Hampshire, Massachusetts, Rhode Island, and Connecticut from importing or exporting goods from or to any port outside Great Britain or one of her West Indian colonies. Ships violating the act were fair game for the Royal Navy. In a typical report, Graves wrote to Secretary of the Admiralty Philip Stephens on September 26 that "the *Savage* put back with three Vessels seized under the restraining Act for the Northern Colonies."

By the time the *Phoenix* was ready to sail, the rebellion had spread. Graves's new orders informed him (as if he did not already know) that nearly all the colonies had "arrayed themselves in Arms and committed Acts of Open and Actual Rebellion." The only colony not mentioned was Georgia, which had been slow to join with the others in resisting the Intolerable Acts.

Graves was now to instruct his captains "to seize all Ships and Vessels belonging to any of the said Colonies or owned by the Inhabitants thereof," save for those that carried papers proving they were bound to or returning from a British port. Any ship carrying arms or ammunition was to be seized no matter where it came from or where it was headed, unless it was sailing under license from the British government.

What was more, any ship captured on the high seas was to be taken to a British port outside the twelve rebellious colonies, which could mean that American crews would be detained far from their homes. In practice this part of the order would prove less workable, as a man-of-war capturing an American ship off Marblehead could hardly be expected to take her to Halifax rather than Boston. But it did represent an escalation and toughening of the British navy's control of American shipping.

John Adams, Christopher Gadsden, and their ilk were not the only Americans who considered it ridiculous to simply endure the depredations of the British navy while taking no offensive action in return. William Tudor, a Harvard classmate of Adams and a judge-advocate on Washington's staff, expressed his frustration in a letter to Adams. Commenting on the capture of a British merchantman by locals at Cape Ann, he wrote:

> This is but a small Retaliation for the dayly Piratical Acts of Graves's Squadron. There is scarce a Vessel that escapes the Clutches of the Cutters and Men of War that infest the Coast. The Week before last they carried eleven Sail of Vessels into Boston, where after the Formality of a Trial in an admiralty Court, they are confiscated, to the Use of Graves and his Harpies. Notwithstanding these continual Depredations, our Assembly will not be prevail'd on to fit out Privateers. The Delicacy is absurd surely.

Tudor's frustration was shared by others, including, by that time, Washington himself. It is interesting to note that Tudor, though attached to the headquarters at Cambridge, was apparently unaware of Washington's naval efforts—another indication of the general's desire for secrecy.

Happily for advocates of a navy, attitudes were changing. And no one would help change them more than Graves and the Lords Commissioners, who grew more heavy-handed in reaction to the growing spirit of revolution.

On September 8 the convoy of artillery and supplies set sail from St. Helen's and soon encountered hard luck and bad weather. A few days after they put to sea, a gale roared up on them in the night. The convoy reduced sail and spread out for fear of running into one another in the dark. When dawn came, three of the victuallers were gone, blown beyond the horizon by the storm. With *Phoenix* hovering nearby, the rest plunged on toward Boston.

On September 29 the Lords Commissioners of the Admiralty took yet another step toward increasing the pressure on the rebellious colonies. They addressed a letter to Molyneux Shuldham, the fifty-eight-year-old rear Admiral of the White who had first hoisted his broad pennant the previous spring. "Whereas it is expedient His Majesty's Service that Vice Adml. Graves should return to England," they wrote, "And Whereas we have thought fit that you should succeed him. . . . You are hereby required and directed to repair, without loss of time, to Portsmouth, and hoist your Flag on board His Majts. Ship the *Chatham*."

Both Admiral Samuel Graves and General Thomas Gage were on their way out, recalled to England, to be replaced by men the administration hoped would be more successful in stamping out rebellion. Neither man knew it yet. Gage would find out in a matter of weeks, but Graves would continue his blundering indecisiveness months longer with no idea he was being recalled. Not until the end of 1775 and the arrival of Shuldham in Boston would he become aware of the displeasure of the Lords Commissioners.

CHAPTER *II* Hannah *Puts to Sea*

AT TEN O'CLOCK in the morning on September 7, 1775, the "privates" who manned the *Hannah* stretched along her halyards and hauled away, heaving on the throat halyards until the luffs of the foresail and mainsail were bar taut, then swaying away the peaks, heave and belay. With all hands on duty, thirty-nine men jammed the schooner's deck.

It had been blowing a strong gale earlier, but the wind had moderated and blew fair for the schooner to work her way through the tricky channel from Beverly to the open sea. *Hannah* was on the prowl.

Her sailing did not go unnoticed in the neighborhood. Ashley Bowen noted, "sailed on an unknown expedition a schooner of Captain John Glover's, Nick Broughton, Captain of Marines, and John Gale, master of the schooner." John Gale, Glover's brother-in-law and the former captain of the *Hannah*, the man who had been commanding her when she slipped past *Merlin*, was shipping out as her sailing master. Broughton's second in command was Lieutenant John Glover, Colonel Glover's son. One of Washington's officers would later write, "Colonel Glover has given the strongest proofs of his good opinion of the Schooner commanded by Captain Broughton, he has ventured his brother & his favorite son on board her."

All that morning and afternoon *Hannah* sailed slowly northeast with the wind astern, following the coastline, perhaps veering off in various directions in search of prey. By five o'clock that evening she was only fifteen or twenty miles from Beverly, somewhere northeast of Cape Ann, when two sails were sighted to the southwest, astern and upwind. *Hannah*'s patrol had taken her right into the arms of the Royal Navy.

"[A]bout 5 oClock saw two ships of War, they gave me Chace," Broughton later reported to Washington. The ships were likely the *Lively* of twenty guns and the eight-gun sloop *Savage*. On August 28 Graves had ordered them to patrol an area from the Isles of Shoals, off Portsmouth, New Hampshire, to Cape Cod, but strong contrary winds had kept them bottled up in Boston Harbor. Unfortunately for Broughton, the British men-of-war were finally able to get under way the same day he did.

Lively's journal of September 5 recorded, "hove short at 1 A.M. weigh'd and came to Sail." She stood northeast from the outer reaches of Boston Harbor, making for her cruising grounds between the Isles of Shoals and Cape Ann with the wind off her starboard quarter, sailing roughly the same course as *Hannah*. Hours later, with the sun approaching the horizon, her lookouts spied the American schooner. *Lively* hauled her wind and bore off to the northeast, setting courses and topgallants in an effort to overhaul the strange sail.

Broughton turned on his heel and raced toward Cape Ann Harbor, now known as Gloucester Harbor. Captain Thomas Bishop, in command of *Lively*, realized he would not be able to intercept the schooner and broke off the chase. That night Broughton lurked around the mouth of the harbor, the safe haven under his lee. The next morning he ventured offshore again and again was greeted by "a ship under my lee quarter." Once more Broughton put up his helm and headed for safety, this time running clean into Cape Ann Harbor.

Through the daylight hours *Hannah* remained safely at anchor. Meanwhile *Lively*, lurking around Cape Ann, was enjoying good hunting. *Lively*'s journal for September 6 read, "at ½ past 5 P.M. Fired a Shot and bro^t to a Brig Sent the Boat on board found her to be from Pescatuway [Piscataqua, the river on which Portsmouth, New Hampshire, is situated] with Lumber bound to St Vincent Sent a Petty Officer & 3 men on board her & took her hands out."

Around sunset the Marbleheaders on board *Hannah* weighed anchor and stood out to sea once again. With "Light airs and fair Weather" Broughton steered south through the dark, no doubt hoping to avoid the men-of-war lurking to the northeast around Thatcher's Island. The schooner plunged on close-hauled through the night. Then, with the sun coming up on the morning watch, they spied a ship to leeward.

"I perceived her to be a large ship," Broughton wrote. Once again he ordered *Hannah* to come about. With headsails flogging and hands tending sheets and braces, the *Hannah* tacked and headed for shore. But this time the large ship did not pursue her.

Seeing that, Broughton "put about & stood towards her again and found her a ship of no force." She was, in fact, the merchant ship *Unity*, which *Lively* had taken the day before, now bound for Boston under the command of her small prize crew. Broughton closed with her and drew abreast, hailing to ask where she came from and where bound. The answer came back that she hailed from Piscataqua and was bound for Boston.

That last was enough for Broughton. Any ship bound for Boston was fair game by his orders. He ordered a boat cleared away and sent an officer, most likely Lieutenant Glover, to examine the ship. Glover concluded, correctly, that *Unity* was a legitimate capture. Broughton told the officer in command of *Unity* that "he must bear away and go into Cape Ann, but being very loth I told him if he did not I should fire on him, on that he bore away." Whether Broughton and *Hannah*'s crew understood then that *Unity* was in fact a recapture and would yield no prize money is unclear. Given the degree of disappointment to follow, it is likely they did not and believed rather that they had just achieved a major score.

While *Hannah* was retaking *Lively*'s prize, *Lively* continued to hover around Thatcher's Island, scooping up American merchantmen. A few hours after *Unity* was recaptured, Captain Thomas Bishop took "a sloop from St. Lucia bound for Cape Ann with Cocoa." The next day he captured a sloop "Loaded with Horses from Casco Bay for the West Indies." Perhaps thinking that horses were more bother than they were worth in Boston, given the city's chronic shortage of fodder, Bishop placed his burgeoning community of prisoners from American merchant ships on board the sloop and let her go.

Hannah escorted *Unity* to Gloucester, where the British prize crew were turned over to the Gloucester Committee of Safety to be escorted to Washington's headquarters at Cambridge. Word spread quickly. That same day Ashley Bowen wrote, "The Essex Cruiser retook a ship bound for Boston, taken by His Majesty's Ship the *Lively*, and carried her into Cape Ann. Grand doing!"

George Washington's navy had just made its first capture, and the headaches were about to begin.

Mutiny

On Saturday, September 9, the prize crew captured with *Unity* arrived at Washington's headquarters, presumably along with the ship's papers. Washington could not have been pleased with what he found.

Unity was indeed an American vessel, taken by the British while making a legitimate voyage from New Hampshire to the West Indies. While it was a stroke of luck that the ship had been retaken, it also created an awkward situation. Washington still hoped to keep his armed vessels a secret from Congress, but as it happened, *Unity* belonged to John Langdon, one of the New Hampshire delegates to that body. Capturing a congressman's ship would not help the goal of secrecy.

But before he could address that issue, Washington found he had more immediate problems. Nicholson Broughton and the crew of *Hannah* felt that *Unity* was in fact a legitimate prize, originally bound for Boston, and not a recapture for which no prize money would follow.

By way of evidence, Broughton wrote to Washington that the treatment his boarding officer received from the man commanding *Unity* "was such as I would rather have expected from a polite Enemy than a Friend to our Cause." It is unclear exactly who this officer was, and it is possible that Broughton and Lieutenant Glover did not know themselves. Presumably it was *Lively*'s petty officer, who had been assigned to command the prize for the short run into Boston. The *Unity*'s original crew had been removed, and even if her American captain, a man named Flagg, was still on board, it seems unlikely that the British petty officer would have let him do the talking. A "polite Enemy" is very likely whom Broughton and Glover met, but that did not prove their case.

As further proof, Broughton claimed that the *Unity* carried "a much greater Quantity of Naval Stores than is customary to export to our Ports." What's more, Langdon's ship had on board, in his opinion, more provisions than were quite necessary for her crew, as well as "a Considerable Quantity of raw Fish," which was contrary to the resolves of the Massachusetts General Assembly.

For these and other reasons Broughton felt *Unity* should be condemned as a prize and he and his men given the one-third share of the sale of cargo that a prize would yield. Broughton went on to recommend that *Unity* be moved from Gloucester to Beverly, "a Place of much greater Security." He added in a postscript that *Hannah* remained in Gloucester and had not yet returned to sea because Lieutenant John Glover had been accidentally injured, how he did not say.

Whatever reply Washington made to Broughton is lost, but it is clear that he was unimpressed with Broughton's arguments and no doubt eager to put the entire embarrassing affair behind him. He most certainly was not going to condemn and sell a ship owned by a member of the Continental Congress. It was the commander-in-chief's intention to return the *Unity* to Langdon's agent and to recommend to Langdon that *Hannah*'s crew be given some compensation per his original orders regarding recaptures. But when word of this reached *Hannah* in Gloucester, the men took their protest one step further than Broughton might have wished; they mutinied.

Details of the mutiny are few, but a major factor—if not the single factor—leading to the uprising was certainly the crew's disappointment over losing their shares of prize money. George Washington had already been horrified by the egalitarian spirit of New Englanders and their inability to suffer any perceived injustice. Now he was getting his first introduction to the attitudes of New England's deepwater sailors, whose jealous protection of their perceived rights and privileges made most land-bound New Englanders look like compliant servants.

Sailors worked more nearly as a collective unit than any other laborers in the eighteenth century. Soldiers certainly functioned cooperatively, but soldiers were not limited to the confines of a ship, and only in combat were they obliged to place their lives in their comrades' hands. Sailors by contrast had to rely regularly on cooperative efforts to survive grave danger on the open sea, a circumstance that led to a rare degree of group solidarity.

Compounding that collectivism was the fact that sailors were among the first wage laborers long before the Industrial Revolution made such a contract common. Then too, sailors worked in the immediate proximity of their captains and mates, who often mistreated them both physically and financially (hence Washington's uncle's warning that the boy not be sent to sea).

Sailors pushed back against abuses with collective resistance. The very term "strike" comes from London seamen in the 1760s who removed, or "struck," the yards and sails from their ships to protest labor conditions. New England sailors, thrown out of work by Britain's Intolerable

Acts, took to the streets and helped foment the early violent resistance that led to the American Revolution. In 1765, Gage wrote of the Americans engaging in the Stamp Act riots, "The sailors . . . are the only people who may be properly stiled Mob." Crispus Attucks, the first man shot during the Boston Massacre, was a seaman.

And so, when Washington denied to the men of the *Hannah* what they thought was rightfully theirs, they reacted collectively. Their protest took the form of mutiny, which, next to turning pirate, was the most drastic form of resistance open to a mariner. The collectivism of the *Hannah*'s crew was no doubt made more virulent by the fact that they were all from the same town, a bond not often shared by a ship's company.

Washington, a stranger to the ways of the sea and sailors, did not understand this, and even if he had it would not have made the least difference to him. In the coming months, as his naval efforts expanded, he would gain a greater understanding of New England seafarers, and that understanding would lead to the Virginia aristocrat's utter loathing of the species.

The *Hannah* mutiny did not last long, nor was it particularly violent. Ashley Bowen noted on September 11 that a company of Marblehead minutemen had been dispatched to Cape Ann, likely ordered there to arrest the mutineers. *Hannah*'s men apparently did not resist. One well-connected observer in Cambridge wrote simply, "The rascals are brought down here under guard, and I hope will meet with their deserts."

By September 22 the crew had been tried and found guilty of "Mutiny, Riot and Disobedience of orders." A sailor named Joseph Searle, presumably the ringleader, was sentenced to "thirty-nine Lashes upon the bare back and be drum'd out of the Army." Harsh as that was, one might compare Searle's sentence for one of the gravest of military crimes to the five hundred lashes a British private in Boston received that same summer for stealing flour.

Thirteen others were sentenced to twenty lashes and dismissal from the army, and twenty-two more were fined twenty shillings each. Three of those fined were recommended as "proper objects of mercy," and their fines were remitted. Possibly as a salve to the rest of Glover's regiment, the countersign for the guards' password on the day the sentences were announced was "Marblehead."

The next day Phineas Ingalls wrote in his journal, "About 9 [A.M.] twelve Marblehead men are to be whipped—20 lashes each. One only was whipped." Washington, apparently, showed mercy to the mutineers at the last minute, likely reserving punishment for Searle alone.

Around the time of the court-martial, and two weeks after *Unity* was taken, Washington finally wrote a letter to John Langdon. "E're this you must have heard of the taking, and retaking of your Ship," he wrote, "and my ordering it to be delivered up to your Agent." He told Langdon that he had promised the officers he would "recommd them to your notice & compensation" and would have done the same for the men "but for their exceeding ill behaviour upon that occasion." Rather than fiscal reward, he wrote, "I hope to bestow a reward of a different kind upon them for their Mutinous behaviour."

In explaining how Langdon's ship had been captured by a Continental armed vessel, a thing Congress did not know existed, Washington was evasive and coy. He wrote parenthetically, "(for you must know the Vessell which retook yours was fitted out at the Publick expence and manned with Soldiers for a particular Expedition)."

In claiming that *Hannah* was for a "particular Expedition" the commander-in-chief gave the impression that she had been armed for a single discrete mission, like the ships he hired to transport Benedict Arnold's troops to Maine or like the sloop *Katy* he'd sent off to Bermuda. Such a mission could be construed as one of the "occurrences" or "accidents" that "may arise upon the place, or from time to time fall out," for which his orders gave him discretion to act.

That was how Washington wished it to sound. His letter obfuscated the fact that he had unilaterally decided on a broad, ongoing policy of naval warfare and was at that moment making plans to expand his fleet. With Broughton's poor performance the only thing he had to show for his bold initiative, Washington was not yet ready to reveal his navy's existence to Congress.

Washington's obfuscation must have had its desired effect, because the revelation of a Continental armed vessel did not trouble Langdon. About four weeks after Washington dispatched the letter, his secretary

Joseph Reed sent sixty dollars to Broughton, forty dollars to Lieutenant John Glover, and thirty dollars to Lieutenant John Devereaux, *Hannah*'s second lieutenant, "as a Compliment from Capt Langdon for retaking his Vessel."

If Broughton's dubious and insistent arguments that *Unity* was a legitimate prize troubled Washington, the commander-in-chief was not concerned enough to sack his first sea captain. It would, in fact, take many months for Washington to realize how incompetent the man was. Meanwhile Broughton remained in command, with *Hannah* languishing in Beverly through most of September. Finally, on September 28, Broughton got under way again. Bowen noted, "Captain Broughton schooner out on her cruise, but soon returned."

On October 7 Broughton sailed again and "pursued a ship toward Boston but could not catch her." She was a British transport, and Broughton showed what was for him unusual aggressiveness, even firing four shots at her as he chased her into Boston Harbor. It was that very aggression that would bring about the near destruction of his first naval command.

CHAPTER *12* Dolphin *and* Industry

A FRESH GALE blew out of the south southeast on September 26, kicking up a steep chop along the North Shore of Massachusetts. White water cascaded from the tops of gray seas, and bursts of cold, early-autumn rain swept through, soaking anyone unfortunate enough to be standing a deck.

Hannah rode at her anchor, snug in Beverly Harbor, not having ventured out since bringing the *Unity* in. Just a few miles away, corkscrewing through the chop, the schooner *Industry* found herself running north before the gales under shortened canvas. Though bound for Boston with supplies for the British army, for some reason she had been unable to make her way into Boston Harbor. Instead she put into Marblehead, standing into the harbor around 10 A.M. Her master, Francis Butler, expected to find a British man-of-war on station, and when he did not he spun around and headed back out to sea. Later that day, however, deciding perhaps that his chances were better among the rebels than on the lee shore of Cape Ann, he once again put into Marblehead, this time coming to anchor.

The Marbleheaders guessed that *Industry* was in the service of the "ministerial army" and did not wait to act. Ashley Bowen wrote that "a number of our Marblehead men took a small schooner from our wharf and went and boarded her and turned her to our wharves."

Industry had sailed from Boston to the island of New Providence in the Bahamas. The clearance papers for her return trip claimed that she was bound for Salem, but her logbook revealed that in fact she intended to return to Boston. Butler did not help his cause by simultaneously claiming that he was bound for Salem and assuring the Marbleheaders that he would sooner have run the schooner up on the rocks than let it fall into their hands.

Though *Industry* had not in truth been bound for Salem, that is where she ended up when the Marblehead men took her around to that place. Her hold was stuffed with an exotic cargo, including, among other things, one hundred and fifty turtles, nineteen barrels of limes, and thousands of lemons and oranges.

The cargo was more amusing than helpful to the Americans. William Tudor wrote to John Adams, "The Lovers of Turtle in the Camp are like to be indulg'd with a feast of it. . . . This is no very great Acquisition for Us, but will be a severe Disappointment to our ministerial beseig'd Enemy." Certainly the fruit would have been more than a mere luxury to the people in Boston, who were dying for lack of fresh provisions.

It was still blowing hard the next day, and twenty miles northeast of where *Industry* now rode at anchor, the brigantine *Dolphin* pounded hard into the seas, laboring south close-hauled under a reefed topsail. The ship's cargo was unhappy and let the men on deck know it, the bleating and bellowing of sixty-eight sheep and forty-five oxen rising muted through the battened hatches.

Unable to make any southing against the wind, the *Dolphin*'s master, William Wallace, tucked in behind Thatcher's Island and came to anchor. The ship's presence did not go unnoticed in nearby Gloucester. Two local men, "Captains Somes & Smith," rowed out to the anchored brigantine and hailed her master, inquiring where she was from and where bound.

Wallace replied that he was from Quebec and bound for St. Eustatia and that he had come to anchor there because he was in need of water. That answer was only partly true—the part about hailing from Quebec—and Somes and Smith suspected as much. They pulled back to Gloucester and "invited men to go off in boats and Seize her." The invitation was eagerly taken up, and men from Gloucester armed themselves and pulled back for the brigantine. Boarding her apparently without resistance, they claimed her as a prize, though a prize for whom was not entirely clear.

Dolphin proved more valuable than *Industry*. Her cargo of sheep, cattle, and forage had been "a present from the Tory merchants, etc. to the sick and wounded in Boston." In two days of spontaneous action, the people of Marblehead and Gloucester had done what Broughton and *Hannah* had failed to do in nearly a month, capturing British supply vessels that would enrich the Americans and further deprive the British army in Boston. Six days later a group of citizens in Portsmouth, New Hampshire, captured a ship called the *Prince George*, loaded with more than 1,880 barrels of flour, when her master, bound for Boston, mistakenly put in there.

These captures by local civilians were typical of the sort of impromptu action that had marked most naval activity until that time, including the taking of the *Margaretta* in Machias. But just as the men of Marblehead, Gloucester, and Portsmouth had no real authority to do what they did beyond an understanding that America was engaged in an undeclared war with the British army, so they had no legal mechanism by which to dispose of their prizes. Unsure what to do next, they did what everyone did in similar circumstances—they asked George Washington.

Expanding the Fleet

Washington did not consider the question of what to do with the *Dolphin* and *Industry* any of his business. The ships had been taken by Massachusetts men, not Continental soldiers, so he redirected the question to the General Court of Massachusetts. The commander-in-chief was not, however, a disinterested party. He had his eye on the ships.

On September 21, while still embroiled in the fallout from the *Hannah* mutiny, Washington had written to John Hancock, president of the Continental Congress, which was the formality he used when writing Congress as a whole. Once again he delved into the minutia of army affairs, including the pay for artificers (i.e., engineers), returns for the rifle companies, the need for a regular payroll, and the lack of tow-cloth hunting shirts. He revealed that he had set in motion a plan he had been considering for some time—an attack on Quebec by a column of men sent north through the wilderness of Maine. "I am now to inform the Honbl. Congress . . . ," he wrote, "that encouraged by the repeated Declarations of the Canadians & Indians, & urged by their Requests, I have detached Col. [Benedict] Arnold with 1000 Men to penetrate into Canada."

Washington, ever restless, could indulge in vicarious warfare through the Arnold expedition, but he was itching for the real thing. "The State of Inactivity, in which this Army has lain for some Time, by no Means corresponds with my Wishes," he wrote in the same letter, "by some deci-sive Stroke to relieve my Country from the heavy Expense, its Subsis-tence must create." Ten days earlier Washington had called a council of war to suggest an attack on the troops in Boston by means of boats and a column sent across Roxbury Neck. After some discussion it was unan-imously agreed that such an attack "was not expedient."

The only local battle punctuating the abhorrent stalemate for Wash-ington was the seagoing fight for supplies, and the only genuinely proac-tive military step he could take was arming vessels and sending them to sea. A few months later he stated this explicitly in a letter to Benedict Arnold, writing, "Finding we were not likely to do much in the Land Way, I fitted out several . . . armed Vessels, in behalf of the Continent."

But once again in his otherwise detailed letter to Congress he failed to mention his naval activities. Whether or not Washington believed he had the authority to create a naval force, he clearly was not confident enough yet to make his efforts known to his civilian leadership.

Questions of authority notwithstanding, once Washington had decided on a course of action, he committed himself to it. His initial orders to Broughton, in which he mentioned the possibility of "other Vessels imployed in the same Service," showed that he intended to expand his fleet, and even Broughton's stunning lack of success did not temper his enthusiasm. Now, with *Industry* and *Dolphin* all but dropping from the sky, he saw an opportunity.

Washington left many of the details concerning the fleet to his able assistant, Joseph Reed. On September 30 Reed met with members of the Massachusetts House of Representatives (the legislative chamber of the General Court, carrying forward the Court's business in the absence of a recognized governor to head the executive council) and informed them that "his Excellency . . . has directed 3 vessels to be immediately equipped." Reed wrote to James Warren, Speaker of the House, a few days later, explaining that since Washington had left it up to the Gen-eral Court to dispose of *Industry* and *Dolphin* as they wished, it would be up to the Court to "Signify in some proper way that these Vessels are to be at the Direction of the General."

Even before a decision was made regarding the vessels, word had been flying around Marblehead that they would be the next armed ves-sels in Washington's fleet. Ashley Bowen, who seemed to miss nothing, wrote on October 2, "News from Headquarters of three cruisers to be fitted out with all speed . . . [a] small schooner which Captain Hugh Hill took at Marblehead and a brig which the Cape Ann men took . . . Captain Nicholas Broughton, Commodore." (Broughton, had he read Bowen's journal, might have been pleased with the promotion Bowen had given him, or he might have preferred that Bowen get his first name, Nicholson, correct.)

On October 3 the Massachusetts House of Representatives decided the fate of the two unhappy merchant ships. Their cargoes were to be sold and the money deposited in the public treasury. Qualified men were to be appointed to make an appraisal of the vessels, and then each was to be "delivered to the Order of his Excellency General Washington, for him to improve as an Armed Vessel, he giving his Receipt for the same."

The following day, and before learning of the decision of the House of Representatives, Washington sent John Glover to determine whether *Dolphin* and *Industry* were suitable for his purposes. When he heard of the House's resolution later that day, however, it was not to his liking.

It is unclear what his objections were, though most likely he took the House's insistence that he sign a receipt as an indication that the ships were his only on loan and still ultimately under the control of the Colony of Massachusetts, conditions he could not accept. Reed sent a note to Glover informing him, "The Vote of the General Court is at length received but upon such Terms & in such a Manner; that his Excellency the General does not chuse to meddle with either of the Vessels." But Washington's naval ambitions were not over, and Glover was further instructed to "take up two other Vessels the most suitable for our Purpose."

Reed's letter seemed to suggest that Washington was not only fully convinced of the usefulness of armed vessels but now regretted not having acquired them earlier. Certainly as September lapsed into October and the weather became increasingly harsh in the North Atlantic, fewer and fewer fat British merchantmen would come lumbering down the New England coast. If Washington did not already understand that, John Glover would have made him aware of the realities of navigating autumn and winter seas. There is a sense of urgency in Reed's instructions to Glover: "let them [the ships] be prime Sailors, put them in the best

Order & loose no Time—A great Number of Transports are hourly expected at Boston from England and elsewhere." The tone of urgency and frustration would grow even more strident in the coming weeks.

"I have directed 3 Vessels to be equipped"

John Glover was on a mission, and he carried with him a list of explicit instructions in which Washington was finally codifying and formalizing the rather ad hoc policy he had formed in sending *Hannah* out on the high seas. Glover was to find two vessels that appeared to be good sailers and in good condition. He was to have the potential vessels inspected by "indifferent People" and then arrange to hire them at a reasonable rate. Washington promised to ratify and confirm any contracts Glover entered into. Once the vessels were nearly ready for sea, Glover was to send notice to headquarters, and the ships' officers and crew, picked from the regiments of seafaring towns, would be ordered to march for Beverly. In each seaport where prizes might be sent, he was to nominate "Persons of approved good Character & known Substance" to act as prize agents.

It was a tall order, and Glover would need help. "As you may have more men upon your Hands than you will be able to manage," Reed wrote to the Marbleheader, "Mr Moyland the Muster Master General is associated with you in this Business."

Stephen Moylan was thirty-eight years old, born in Ireland, and in 1775 a resident of Philadelphia. He was a man with more foreign experience than most Americans, having been educated in Paris before spending several years in the shipping business in Lisbon. For all that, however, Moylan was very much a part of the tough American merchant class, having ultimately made a career in Philadelphia's maritime trade.

Moylan had been appointed mustermaster general of the army less than two months earlier, on August 11, in which position he was responsible for maintaining the muster rolls and for inspecting the men and their equipment. But the waterfront was Moylan's preferred territory, and his familiarity with the ways of shipping and those who serviced the maritime industry, from shipwrights and chandlers to sailors and ship's officers, made him an ideal candidate for overseeing Washington's fleet.

Just as important, and perhaps one of the reasons Washington chose him, was that Moylan was a stranger to Marblehead and Beverly, with no friends or relatives there whom he might favor. While Glover could be expected to tread carefully around neighbors and business associates, Moylan would have no reason to show anything more than common diplomacy and patience when dealing with local businessmen.

George Washington found the complexity of his naval affairs mounting in the first week of October. He had one vessel fitted out for cruising and men searching for two more. Armed men in seaport towns had been snatching up British ships for months when the opportunity presented itself, but now they were turning to him for adjudication of the prizes. Most significantly, Washington had authorized the establishment of prize agents to determine if vessels taken by his ships were legitimate military captures and what would become of them if they were. Especially in this last, Washington was seriously overstepping the understood boundaries of a commander-in-chief under strict civilian control.

It was time to tell Congress.

On October 5 Washington again wrote to John Hancock. The bulk of the letter comprised a report on one of the most distressing events to occur thus far—indeed, what would be for Washington one of the most personally unsettling events to occur during the entire siege of Boston. About a week before, evidence had come to light that Dr. Benjamin Church, a prominent leader of the revolutionary faction in Massachusetts and the director general of the hospital in Cambridge, had been conducting an illicit correspondence with the British in Boston. Despite Church's protestations that the letter was meant as disinformation regarding American strength, a council of war found him guilty of treason.

Church was later tried again by the Massachusetts House of Representatives and again found guilty. Sentenced to solitary confinement, he was released some months later on sentence of exile from America. The ship on which he was sailing to the West Indies disappeared at sea.

Dr. Church's conviction was based largely on suspicion and the discovery of a single coded letter. There was no other hard evidence against him. Years later, however, those suspicions would prove correct when the papers of General Gage revealed that Church had carried on a lengthy correspondence with the general and had in fact been on the British payroll.

Toward the end of his October 5 letter to Congress, Washington wrote, "I have an express from Col. Arnold. . . . I am happy in finding he meets with no Discouragement." Arnold was then just entering the wilderness in Maine and beginning a harrowing journey to Quebec, having traveled by ship to present-day Augusta. Five years almost to the day after discovering Church's treason, Washington's trust would receive the most grievous wound of all when his much admired General Benedict Arnold was revealed as a traitor as well.

After explaining the matter of Benjamin Church, Washington proceeded to naval affairs. He chose as his segue the captures made by civilians in seaport towns, making particular mention of the *Prince George*, recently captured in Portsmouth with a load of flour for the British army. "I shall now beg Leave," he began, "to request the Determination of Congress as to the Property & Disposal of such Vessels & Cargoes as are designed for the Supply of the Enemy & may fall into our Hands. There has been an Event of this Kind at Portsmouth."

Washington clearly understood that authorizing the distribution of captured goods was beyond his authority. He continued, "I have directed the Cargo to be brought hither for the Use of the Army, reserving the Settlement of any Claims of Capture to the Decision of Congress."

It was only reasonable, of course, that Washington not mention captures made by his own naval force (which consisted of *Hannah*), since the only one thus far had been the unfortunate capture of *Unity*, which had been returned to its owner. But Washington had a new enthusiasm for naval operations and was optimistic that his growing fleet would soon be taking prizes. When his letter finally came around to mentioning his naval efforts, it did so with the same tone of optimism and urgency that Reed had conveyed to Glover:

> I am the more induced to request this Determination may be speedy, as I have directed 3 Vessels to be equipped in order to cut off the Supplies, & from the Number of Vessels hourly arriving it may be an Object of some Importance. In the Disposal of these Captures; for the Encouragement of the Officers & Men, I have allowed them one third of the Cargoes except

military Stores, which with the Vessels are to be reserved for the publick Use. I hope my Plan as well as the Execution will be favoured with the Approbation of Congress.

A month and a half after Washington had sent *Hannah* to sea, his letter to Congress implied that he was only now arming and fitting out men-of-war at Continental expense. He was clearly playing down the whole affair, but if he feared a brouhaha in Congress over his actions, luck was with him. When John Hancock responded to the October 5 letter, he made no mention of the commander-in-chief's initiatives regarding a navy. By that time, once again, everything had changed.

CHAPTER *13* *Building and Equipping an American Fleet*

ON AUGUST 1, 1775, after being in session for two and a half months, the Second Continental Congress went into recess. They had adopted an army, issued directions for its organization and management, and established an officer corps. They had provided the army with hundreds of thousands of dollars and had made great efforts to supply it with *matériel.* But they had shown no interest in a navy, and even the few naval-minded delegates, such as John Adams and Christopher Gadsden, the South Carolina delegate and former British naval officer, had made no official effort to change that.

During the August recess, however, the Rhode Island General Assembly instructed that colony's delegates to call for "building and equipping an American Fleet." Rhode Islanders were eager to see a force that could challenge James Wallace in the frigate *Rose,* free Narragansett Bay from the dominance of the British navy, and restore the colony's lucrative smuggling trade.

When the Continental Congress reconvened on September 5, Stephen Hopkins, Rhode Island's eloquent, well-read, sixty-eight-year-old delegate, once again returned to Philadelphia, as did Samuel Ward, the second half of the Rhode Island delegation. Not until September 13, however, did enough delegates drift back from the more distant colonies to constitute a quorum. Debate then quickly centered on whether or not to open American ports to foreign trade, a move which, like establishing a navy, smacked of sovereignty and carried political implications well beyond any practical considerations. These debates and others dragged on for weeks.

On October 3, a Tuesday, the Congress as usual turned to the hundred pressing issues with which it had to contend, including "accounts

of the committee of Trenton for waggonage and sundry expenses,"
whether Fredrick Blankenburg and Leonard Stein should be allowed to
keep the hussar uniforms that had been made for them (they were), and
whether Washington should be granted the discretion to pay a month's
wages to the families of anyone killed in an attack on Boston, should
one come to pass.

Finally, at the end of the day, one of the Rhode Island delegates—
most likely the venerable Hopkins—laid his colony's request before the
Congress. It was a watershed moment, signaling a major shift in legislative affairs. Hopkins's motion to establish a navy of the United Colonies
forced the delegates to confront the very issues they had so long avoided.

The immediate reaction, however, was underwhelming. The Congress postponed any discussion of the motion until the following Friday.

Quite likely those on both sides of the debate wanted a few days to
lobby their fellow delegates before the matter was brought up for discussion. Once again, however, the rapid unfolding of events overtook
Congress's deliberations and spun the issue in an entirely unforeseen
direction.

Two North Country Brigs

On October 5, two days after Rhode Island's motion had been tabled
and the very day Washington was writing to inform Congress that he was
fitting out three armed vessels, Congress once again resolved to "take
into farther consideration the state of trade of the 13 confederated
Colonies," and once again the delegates failed to reach any consensus.
They resolved to take up the issue again the next day.

Following the trade discussion, "Sundry letters rec^d. from London
were laid before Congress," one of which contained intelligence of
potentially great consequence. Two "north country built Brigs, of no
force" were reported to have sailed from England for Quebec on August
11 "loaded with arms, powder and other stores . . . without a convoy."

Suddenly the notion of sending armed ships to sea was no longer a
theoretical question but one of immediate and practical concern. Capturing those unarmed brigs would in one stroke achieve two critical
goals. It would deprive the defenders of Quebec, toward which Bene-

dict Arnold was then marching, of arms and supplies for the city's defense while infusing Washington's army with just the sort of military stores it so desperately needed.

A committee of three was immediately nominated "to prepare a plan for intercepting [the] two vessels." The three men nominated, as John Adams would recall many years later, were Silas Deane, John Langdon, and himself.

With that motion, which would lead to American ships hunting British vessels on the high seas, an action that could in no way be construed as defensive, a "most animated opposition and debate arose." Rhode Island's motion of two days before had served to factionalize those for and against an American navy, and their brewing passions now poured forth on the floor of the Pennsylvania State House, where Congress was meeting.

Edward Rutledge of South Carolina stood in opposition to the resolution. Adams had earlier described Rutledge as "a very uncouth, and ungracefull Speaker. He shruggs his Shoulders, distorts his Body, nods and wriggles his Head . . . and Speaks thro his Nose," but on this day Rutledge showed uncharacteristic rhetorical skills. A surprised Adams later suggested that Rutledge had been the target of much lobbying since the Rhode Island proposal had been laid before Congress. "He never appeared to me to discover so much Information and Sagacity," Adams recalled, "which convinced me he had been instructed out of Doors, by some of the most knowing Merchants and Statesmen in Philadelphia."

The discussion went on, "loud and vehement." Some called the idea of naval action "the most wild, visionary mad project that ever had been imagined. It was an Infant, taking a mad Bull by the horns"—which was, in fact, a tolerably accurate description of the American Revolution as a whole. Others argued that it would "corrupt the morals of our Seamen. It would make them selfish, piratical, mercenary, bent wholly upon plunder, &c. &c. &c." Whoever presented that argument clearly had not spent much time in the company of mariners. As George Washington was learning, Yankee seamen were pretty much there already.

"These formidable Arguments and the terrible Rhetoric," Adams wrote, "were answered by Us by the best reasons We could alledge, and the great Advantages of distressing the Ennemy, supplying ourselves, and beginning a System of maritime and naval Opperations, were represented in colours as glowing and animating."

In the end, the resolution passed and the committee to draft the plan—Adams, Deane, and Langdon—was elected. Congress could hardly have picked a committee more sympathetic to the idea of establishing a navy than those three men.

Adams, of course, had been talking and writing for some time about the need for a naval force. Deane was from Connecticut, and his family was deeply involved in maritime interests. He would ultimately help relatives secure posts as shipbuilders and officers in the Continental Navy. John Langdon was the merchant and shipowner from New Hampshire who just a few weeks before had received a cryptic note from George Washington explaining how a Continental armed schooner had happened to recapture one of his ships.

Adams, Deane, and Langdon left the ornately appointed chambers of the Continental Congress and met in private to hammer out the wording of the resolution. It did not take long. The three men, who, as Adams put it, "expressed much Zeal, in favor of the Motion" of intercepting the brigs, apparently had very similar ideas of how to proceed. Within a few hours they were back, resolution in hand.

The resolution called for a letter to Washington informing him of the brigs' sailing and the opportunity they presented. Congress, of course, did not yet know about the ships Washington was fitting out, as the commander-in-chief was only that day writing to explain his actions. As far as the committee knew, the most accessible armed vessels were the *Machias Liberty* and the *Diligent*.

Washington was instructed to "apply to the council of Massachusetts bay, for the two armed vessels in their service," and he was to "despatch the same, with a sufficient number of people, stores, &c. particularly a number of oars, in order, if possible, to intercept s^d two Brigs and their cargoes." The remonstrance to ship "a number of oars" was a characteristic bit of John Adams micromanagement.

The resolution further instructed Washington that his armed vessels should capture "any other transports laden with ammunition, cloathing or other stores, for the use of the ministerial army or navy in America." It would have been silly, after all, to ignore supply vessels simply because they were not the two brigs specified in the letter. This was also, how-

ever, a subtle way for the pro-navy men to expand the mission of the
armed vessels and ease the way toward the creation of a genuinely offensive fleet.

The committee of three did not stop there, further instructing that
Washington "be directed to employ s^d vessels, and others, if he judge
necessary, to effect the purposes afores^d." They also proposed that letters be sent to Governors Cooke in Rhode Island and Trumbull in Connecticut requesting the use of their armed vessels. All ships so employed
were "to be on the continental risque and pay."

John Hancock drafted the letter to Washington that same day, and
an express rider clattered off toward Cambridge with the sealed paper.
At the same time an express rider from Cambridge was spurring his
horse toward Philadelphia with Washington's letter admitting to having
ordered the fitting out of armed vessels on his own authority. Finally
God seemed to be smiling on American arms.

Hannah's *Last Stand*

By the first week in October the British command was growing tired of
the increasing depredations made by the rebels on their shipping,
including the capture of the *Industry, Dolphin*, and *Prince George*. General
Thomas Gage, who had just received word of his recall to England, wrote
to Lord Dartmouth of his hope to put a stop to the "Boats and Ships that
are in the several Harbours, and have brought Supplies to the Rebels;
and have also enabled them to stop Refreshments coming into Boston."
Gage, like Washington, had come to understand that the real struggle
between the armies in Massachusetts was a war of supplies.

On October 8 a lieutenant commanding a British transport reported
to Admiral Samuel Graves that "he had been chased in the bay by a
Rebel Schooner," which had fired four shots at the fleeing vessel. Graves
suspected the schooner was *Diligent*, which had been captured in
Machias in the spring, but he was wrong. The schooner was *Hannah*, and
it was Nicholson Broughton who had chased the transport to Boston.

While Washington had been laying the foundation of an expanded
fleet, Broughton had been sticking close to home. Since the end of September he had remained at anchor in Beverly Harbor, darting in and
out in the unfulfilled hope of snatching a passing ship before returning

to the safety of the harbor for the evening. Though he had not actually taken a prize, the act of chasing the transport into Boston and firing on it was too bold for Graves to ignore. The frigate *Lively* was in Maine, escorting a convoy gone for firewood, but the sixteen-gun sloop-of-war *Nautilus* had recently arrived in Boston from Rhode Island. Graves considered her "the best going Vessel of any then in Boston," as well as being "in all respects so proper for this sudden Service, to put to Sea immediately in quest of the Rebels."

At 10 P.M. on October 8, *Nautilus* "W^d. [weighed] and Came to Sail," standing northeast toward Cape Ann in her hunt for the audacious rebel ship. It was blowing a fresh gale, and *Nautilus*'s captain, John Collins, ordered topgallant yards struck down to the deck as he maintained his station off the dangerous coast of Massachusetts.

By October 10 *Nautilus* was five miles southeast of Halfway Rock, from where she had a view of the approaches to Marblehead, Beverly, Manchester, and Cape Ann. The day before Broughton had made two forays out of the harbor to chase passing ships but had somehow managed to miss tangling with *Nautilus* both times. On her new station, however, the man-of-war could not be missed, though it is possible that observers from the shore did not recognize her for what she was. Ashley Bowen wrote in his journal simply, "I saw a ship off with her sails hauled up, laying too."

Or perhaps they did recognize *Nautilus*. According to Bowen, Broughton weighed anchor and stood out of Beverly Harbor around 11 A.M. Bowen wrote, "At 11:00 o'clock sailed schooner Decoy, Broughton, off and sailed as far as Halfway Rock, about and stood in again." Bowen seemed to suggest that Broughton was using *Hannah* to lure *Nautilus* into Beverly. Certainly Broughton had shown little enthusiasm in the past for going to sea in the presence of large, strange ships. Unfortunately, Bowen's allusion is the only hint we have of what might have been a cunning plan.

Aware of the danger or not, Broughton stood out to sea. The weather was good and the wind was on his starboard beam as he made his way toward Halfway Rock. Then, at 1 P.M., his luck ran out.

Broughton apparently spotted the *Nautilus* before the *Nautilus* spotted him, as *Hannah* was already running for safety when she caught the attention of the man-of-war's captain, John Collins. Collins later reported to Graves that he "saw standing into Salem a Schooner, the one I supposed I was in quest after."

Nautilus was five miles southeast of Halfway Rock. With a shout of "hands to stations for stays!" the men rushed to bring the sloop about, raising tacks and sheets and hauling on braces. With headsails flogging and topsails coming aback, *Nautilus* tacked and stood in after the fleeing schooner.

Hannah raced north, passing the exposed harbor of Marblehead, rounding Salem Neck, and making for Beverly Harbor, her refuge, where she came to anchor. Thus far Beverly had proven a safe haven that British vessels dared not enter, but this time it was different. With specific orders to run the rebel schooner to ground, Collins pressed on, boldly sailing toward Beverly's tricky approach channel bounded by bars and mudflats.

When it became clear to Broughton that *Nautilus* was still after him, he slipped *Hannah*'s anchor cable and tried to get farther into the harbor, but the schooner ran aground "very near the beach." The tide was ebbing, and it was clear that *Nautilus* would be up with her before *Hannah* could move again. The schooner's crew and "the People speedily assembled, stripped her, and carried her Guns, &c. ashore."

It is no mean task moving cannon off a grounded vessel and over mudflats to more solid ground. Even the little 4-pounders *Hannah* mounted were six feet long and weighed 1,200 pounds apiece. Luckily, the long lead *Hannah* had on her pursuer gave the men the time they needed to get the job mostly done before they fell under the sloop-of-war's guns.

It was 3:30 P.M. when *Nautilus* "Came too of Beverly near the said Schoonr." Collins let go a single anchor within a half mile of Beverly Church. *Nautilus* was within grapeshot range of the stranded schooner when Collins opened up with his great guns. The sloop's barrage was too hot for the rebels, who left the *Hannah* on the mud, retreating back to Beverly and returning *Nautilus*'s cannon fire with small arms and swivels.

At that point Collins "thought it best to endeavour setting her [*Hannah*] on fire." The *Nautilus*'s crew loaded the ship's boats with combustibles and swayed them over the side, but by then the tide was well out, and *Hannah*, high and dry, was no longer accessible by boat. Abandoning his attempt to burn the schooner, Collins continued to pour round shot into her.

By four o'clock, with the tide still falling, Collins's troubles were mounting. The people of Beverly lined the shore and peppered the *Nautilus* with musket and swivel gun fire. Across the narrow channel the people of Salem heard the gunfire, and two hundred or more raced out to Salem Neck, which overlooked the place where *Nautilus* had come to anchor. They dragged with them three 4-pounder cannons, which they positioned in well-sheltered places and began to fire on *Nautilus*, while others continued the assault with muskets.

Nautilus was caught in a cross fire and anchored on a lee shore. Collins wrote that the gun emplacements on Salem Neck were "so well chosen that I could not see them with my Glass." Realizing he could not destroy *Hannah* and that no purpose was served in staying where he was, Collins decided to get under way. With the wind setting the *Nautilus* on shore, the only way he could come to sail was to "cast" the ship—that is, to run a spring line from the after end of the ship to the anchor cable and haul that tight, swinging the *Nautilus* broadside to the wind before setting sail.

In a storm of small-arms, swivel, and cannon fire, the sloop-of-war's crew rigged the spring line. The capstan was manned and the cable hauled taut. The spring line lifted dripping from the water, quivering under the tension, and then broke.

The men of the *Nautilus* set to with the sort of professionalism for which the Royal Navy was famous. The journal of the *Nautilus* reads, "got a nother Spring. broke it in heaving. found ye Ship grounded." With the tide ebbing fast, *Nautilus* had settled on the mud, and heaving on spring lines was not going to get her off.

Collins had the smaller stream anchor carried out ahead of the ship to haul *Nautilus* off the bottom, but that was not going to happen until the tide had begun to flood. For nearly four hours the sloop-of-war found herself stuck in the mud under rebel fire, the same unhappy situation that had been the death of the schooner *Diana* off Noddles Island.

Finally, around 7:30 P.M., the tide lifted *Nautilus* off the bottom. Hands were sent to the capstan and the ship was hauled up to the stream anchor. Given the constant fire from Salem Neck and Beverly and the ship's precarious situation on a lee shore, there was no chance of recovering the anchors and cables. "Cut the B.B. [best bower] Cable & Spring . . . Left Behind the Bt Br Anchor & Cable & Stream Anchor & Cable with the Bueys & Rope—att which time ye Rebels Kept firing upon us with ye Above Cannon & Small Arms," the ship's journal recorded.

By 8 P.M. *Nautilus* was under sail at last, working her way out to sea and free from the harassing fire of the Americans. She was pretty badly cut up aloft, with a spritsail topsail yard and a topgallant studdingsail yard and sail shot away and several shrouds cut in two. Though Collins would write, "'tis very lucky they fired so high," the *Nautilus*'s hull came in for a beating as well. She was hit about twenty times through the hull and hammock netting. One of the great guns was dismounted and a swivel shot in two. One of the ship's company had his leg shot off, and another was wounded in the side. One of the two, likely the one who lost his leg, later died.

The Americans likewise suffered two casualties, neither inflicted by the *Nautilus*. One of the Salem gunners, David Newall, had his "hand blowed off in loading one of our Cannon." Broughton was the other American casualty. He apparently caught "a bad Cold, which he took at the time of Runing his Vesell on Shoar," no doubt while wading to dry land.

Hannah does not seem to have been too badly damaged, but her days as a man-of-war were over. With the new generation of Washington's navy fitting out, there were no resources to put toward the diminutive vessel. Though her period of hire, two months and twenty-one days per John Glover's ledger, would suggest that she remained a part of Washington's fleet at least into the early days of November, there is no further mention of her service.

Still, in her last act she helped inflict damage on and teach a lesson to a British man-of-war. Things might have gone worse still for *Nautilus* had American gunnery been more proficient, but it was not. As Salem resident William Wetmore wrote, "We fired very badly many times."

CHAPTER *14* *Marblehead Boats at Beverly*

WITHIN TWO DAYS of being sent to Salem and Marblehead to search for schooners to convert to armed vessels, John Glover and Philadelphia shipowner and mustermaster general of the army Stephen Moylan had their ships picked out. The ubiquitous Ashley Bowen wrote, "I hear Mr. Thomas Grant's schooner and Mr. Arch Selman's ditto are to fit out as cruisers."

Bowen's information was correct. Grant's schooner was the *Speedwell*, a Marblehead boat of seventy-two tons. After having "Cearfully Examined the hull, her Age, the Sails Riggen Cables & Anchrs together—with the Boat Stores & C., as She Now Lays at Beverly wharfe," Glover and Moylan's inspectors determined her value to the oddly precise amount of "Three Hundred Thirty one pounds Six Shillings & Eight pence."

The other vessel was the *Eliza*, a schooner of sixty tons owned by Archibald Selman and valued at three hundred pounds, three shillings, and, once again, eight pence. Like most Marblehead vessels, the two schooners were tied up at the safer port of Beverly. The "indifferent People" whom Glover and Moylan appointed to inspect the schooners were Jonathan Glover, John's brother, and Edward Fettyplace.

On Saturday, October 7, Glover and Moylan met with Joseph Reed and assured him that the newly armed schooners would be ready for sea in less than a week. By Monday, however, they were forced to confront reality. "We were to sanguine in our expectation," the men wrote to Reed from Salem, explaining, "[I]t is difficult to procure Carpenters to put them in the necessary order." The schooners, they announced, would not be ready before October 14.

Glover and Moylan were encountering other problems as well. *Eliza* and *Speedwell* carried the standard sail plan for a Marblehead schooner:

a single jib, a trapezoidal foresail with a boom at the foot and a gaff at the head attached to the foremast, and a similar though larger sail on the mainmast. Those three sails were, as Moylan put it, "sufficient for the Voyages they usually Make," but they did not offer the speed and flexibility required of an armed cruiser.

Washington's men wanted more canvas for their ships, certainly one or more square topsails on the foremast, perhaps a square topsail on the mainmast, and additional jibs and other light-air sails. The owners, however, objected that "were they to purchase the other sails Necessary for the present purpose, the hire of the vessells would be inadequate to the expence."

In the end, these and other niggling complaints were settled with an agreement that the owners would put their ships in the same "good order & Condition" as they would if the vessels were being hired for a trading voyage to the West Indies or elsewhere, and Glover and Moylan would cover the additional expenses.

On October 9, the day before her run-in with the *Nautilus*, Glover assured Washington that he had every confidence in *Hannah*'s fitness. But that opinion was apparently not universal, and Glover agreed that Broughton and his crew might shift to "a vessell of better fame for Sailing." Once *Hannah* had been shot up by the sloop-of-war, Moylan and Glover both knew they would need a new third vessel to join the two they had just acquired.

To that end Glover and Moylan hired the seventy-four-ton schooner *Two Brothers* from Thomas Stevens of Marblehead. The men assured Washington that the ship would be ready to cruise in twelve to fourteen days. Like the newly hired schooners, *Hannah* had apparently been fitted out with additional sails, which were to be shifted to the *Two Brothers*.

With that Moylan set off for Portsmouth, New Hampshire. Reed had written him that "the management of the Flour at Portsmouth may be attended with some Difficulty." Moylan was to straighten out the problems surrounding the *Prince George*'s cargo and send the flour on to Cambridge. The increase in naval activity was creating headaches for George Washington, and now the headaches were starting to run downhill.

Glover remained in Beverly to deal with the fitting out of the three new ships and the decommissioning of his own vessel, *Hannah*.

A Second Front

Even as Glover and Moylan were struggling to get their vessels fitted out and sent off to sea, General Washington was expanding his naval efforts into another base of operations. That base was to be Plymouth, Massachusetts, south of Boston Harbor. Staging a ship there would mean having armed vessels working both sides of the approaches to Boston. It would also mean not having to deal with Marblehead sailors, for whom Washington was developing a distaste. In the end, however, the Plymouth fleet would teach him that sailors were sailors no matter from where they hailed.

Before Washington had a ship to sail from Plymouth or anyone to oversee its fitting out, he had a captain. That man was Sion Martindale, a Rhode Island merchant captain of long experience with whom Washington was evidently impressed. On October 8 Washington issued instructions to Martindale appointing him "a Captain in the Army of the United Colonies" and advising him to take command of a vessel "lately fitted and equipp'd with Arms, Ammunition & Provisions at the Continental Expence." The instructions were all but identical to those issued to Broughton, with the exception that a surgeon was added to the ship's complement and awarded four shares of any prize money.

The vessel under discussion was the schooner *Triton*, owned by a merchant captain named Daniel Adams. Adams had apparently already spoken with Washington or Joseph Reed about his vessel and obtained a tentative agreement that she should be leased by the army and converted into a man-of-war.

During the second week in October, before *Triton* was officially hired and Washington sent his own man to oversee the work, Daniel Adams left Cambridge to begin the schooner's conversion. By October 12 she was being referred to by her new name, *Harrison*, in honor of Continental Congressman Benjamin Harrison, whom Washington had just learned would soon be visiting the army's headquarters at Cambridge. An account from that day for "The Schooner *Harrison* to Stephen Sampson for Sundry Iron Work" showed fifty-nine different items provided for the schooner. They ranged from the mundane, such as "strap for the mast" and "2 Copper Ladels" and "1 Candel Stick," to things that were found only on a man-of-war, such as "10 Primen [priming] wires" and "2 Double Wormers" and "Swifel for Gun."

On October 10 Washington found a crew for the ship he did not yet officially control. Hoping perhaps to avoid Marbleheaders and to give Martindale a ship's company from his native Rhode Island, Washington sent orders to Nathanael Greene that "The officers of the Rhoade Island Forces are Requested to Furnish Capt Martingale with a Party for a Sea Expedition." The men would be on standby for some time to come.

On Friday, October 13, Joseph Reed issued instructions to the man Washington had appointed to oversee the outfitting of the vessel at Plymouth, a young Rhode Island captain named Ephraim Bowen. This was the same Ephraim Bowen who in 1772 had participated in the burning of the Royal Navy schooner *Gaspee* near Providence. It was Bowen's borrowed gun that had been used to shoot the British commander, Lieutenant William Dudingston. Now he was once again taking part in the war at sea.

Bowen's instructions differed from those issued to Glover and Moylan nine days earlier. In part that was because Bowen did not have to find a vessel as Glover and Moylan had done. The *Triton* had already been chosen, and the instructions clearly indicated that Washington intended to fit out only one ship from Plymouth. Bowen was simply to make sure *Triton* would answer. To do so he was to "inquire at Plymouth what Character she has as a Sailor." The agreement with Daniel Adams was not ironclad, and if *Triton* had a poor reputation, Bowen was to "take up one instead of her which can be well recommended."

Other nuances of Bowen's instructions may reflect Reed's learning from prior mistakes. Bowen was to have the owner "fit her up with Sails suitable for the Service particularly Topsails," thus avoiding the dispute Glover and Moylan had encountered concerning their schooners' rigs. Glover and Moylan had been told to send directions for making proper gunpowder cartridges for the ships' guns, but Bowen was to send actual "formers," wooden dowels of the proper diameter around which the cartridges would be formed. Bowen was also told to keep a journal of his proceeding, which he did faithfully.

Bowen got under way the day he received his orders, stopping first in Watertown per his instructions to ask James Warren which "Person of approved good Character & known Substance" might be appointed as agent in Plymouth to provision the vessel and oversee the management of prizes. Warren recommended a Plymouth merchant named William Watson.

The next day Bowen rented a sulky—a small, two-wheeled cart—and headed south out of Watertown. The skies were clear but the wind was blowing a gale, no doubt making Bowen's little conveyance shudder as he bounced along the rough road hugging the coast south of Boston.

Bowen arrived at Plymouth that evening after a wearying journey of some forty miles, but he did not find Adams or his schooner there. The next day he drove his sulky to Kingston, about three miles north of Plymouth. There he found both Adams and the schooner and received assurances from Adams that the vessel would be in Plymouth the following day, which it was. When the *Harrison* arrived, Bowen was meeting with Watson and with the Plymouth Committee of Safety, to whom he presented a letter from Reed asking that the committee assist Bowen, particularly in finding guns, "As he is somewhat of a Stranger."

A few days later Bowen wrote to Washington informing him that the people of Plymouth considered *Triton* to be a fine sailing vessel. He had accordingly set carpenters to work converting her to a man-of-war. Daniel Adams felt the ship would be ready "in four or five days, if he is not oblig'd to wait for guns."

As to guns, Bowen wrote that the smattering of odd sizes available in Plymouth included four 3-pounders, seven swivel guns of various bores, "one Excellent Wall piece (& two Cohorns if wanted)." If those would not do, Bowen was certain he could find some in Bristol or Providence, Rhode Island. Last, he told the commander-in-chief that William Watson had agreed to serve as agent to the vessel, and he asked for further instructions.

Washington had originally intended to fit out just one ship at Plymouth but soon after Bowen left Cambridge had decided to fit out at least two. Joseph Reed sent his reply to Bowen with Sion Martindale, who was on his way to Plymouth to see about fitting out the second ship. Along with the letter, Martindale carried Washington's instructions to William Watson calling for him to oversee the business of not one but "the several armed Vessels fitting out at Plymouth."

Though at first intended for the command of the *Harrison*, Martindale—who would prove demanding indeed—set his sights instead on the second ship. He had in mind the schooner *Endeavour*, owned by local merchants George Ewing and Benjamin Wormwell, which came "highly recommended," though by whom is unclear. Nonetheless, Bowen was not to take the recommendation at face value but was to make "proper Inquiry about her."

Even before Sion Martindale had begun his service in Washington's fleet, the insightful Joseph Reed had the measure of the man. He reminded Bowen that the still critical lack of gunpowder "does not admit these Vessels being fitted out at all Points, nor will the Time admit. Captain Martindale having been used to a Vessel where nothing was wanted I fear will not make suitable Allowances." How right he was.

Bowen's suggestion that he go to Providence or Bristol to find guns was also a red flag to Reed, who was entertaining second thoughts about having sent John Glover to transact Continental business in his hometown of Marblehead. Bowen could go to Rhode Island if it was absolutely necessary, Reed wrote him, "but we have always found that when Gentlemen sent upon their Business go among their Friends, they are apt to stay too long & are induced to favor their Friends in such Articles as may be wanted to delay the Business." Though expressing his reservations in hypothetical terms, Reed told Bowen that he felt it "Necessary to give you this Caution." Bowen wrote back to assure Reed that "I have no Friends in Providence or Bristol who can Reap any advantage from this Business."

That day he and Martindale examined the *Endeavour* and concluded that she was a good candidate for conversion to a man-of-war. Martindale then began to display the very tendency Reed feared. "Capt Martindale Says he is to have Twelve Carriage Guns & 16 or 20 Swivels" for capturing unarmed merchant ships, Bowen reported. That was three times the number of guns any of Washington's other ships carried, but Martindale had full confidence in his own ability and was no doubt envisioning the capture of British men-of-war with glorious, thundering broadsides. "Capt Martindale Says he Should not desire So large a Number of Cannon," Bowen added, "but finds the Vessel to be able to Carry them, & Doubts not of Giving a Good account of them."

Bowen also informed Reed that he was not sending formers for making cartridges. "The Schooner will be Compleat for Sea by Saturday

Night," which was in two days, and there was not enough time to have ammunition made in camp. He urged Reed to send the *Harrison*'s crew to Plymouth and to supply them with paper to make up the cartridges there, before the ship sailed.

Like Moylan and Glover, Bowen was apparently in nearly complete denial about how long it would take to convert a trading schooner to a fighting ship.

CHAPTER *15* *"Not a Moment of Time be lost"*

EVEN BEFORE informing Congress of his maritime aspirations, George Washington had been anxious to get his ships fitted out and off to sea. Upon receiving word of the North Country brigs sailing for Quebec— exactly the sort of prize he dreamed of—and with it Congress's serendipitous sanction of naval efforts they knew nothing about, the commander-in-chief became more eager still. "It is Some Disappointment to us that the Vessels cannot be got ready sooner," Reed wrote to Glover and Moylan in response to their letter warning that the fitting out would take longer than first estimated. "The General therefore directs that you will immediately set every Hand to Work that can be procured & not a Moment of Time be lost in getting them ready."

The first two vessels under conversion in Beverly were slated to intercept the ordnance brigs in the St. Lawrence, but that would leave only one Beverly cruiser to patrol the approaches to Boston. Having heard Glover and Moylan's complaints about the difficulty of finding carpenters in Beverly, Washington and Reed thought it best to look elsewhere as well. The orders originally given to Glover and Moylan had directed them to seek vessels in Newburyport, Massachusetts, if none could be found in Salem or Marblehead. The fleet that had transported Benedict Arnold's column to Maine was from Newburyport and was by now presumably home and swinging idly at anchor. Reed wrote to Glover and Moylan ordering one of them to go there to acquire a fourth vessel. "[T]here are Carpenters, Guns, &c, to be had there in plenty," Reed assured the men and added, "let the Same Expedition be also used with the Vessel." The agent in Newburyport was to hire a ship "on the best Terms & let us know what he will want to equip the Vessel for Sea."

At the same time, Reed ordered that the ships fitting out at Beverly be provisioned for a cruise of six weeks and crews of seventy men. He added at the end of his instructions, "The General approves of the Steps taken respecting those [vessels] already engaged."

Meanwhile, as far as Congress knew, Washington had no men-of-war with which to intercept the British brigs, and only after they had sent word to Cambridge regarding the ordnance vessels would the delegates learn otherwise. Long before giving any serious thought to ships of war "on the Continental risque & pay," however, Congress had suggested to the various colonies that they establish their own naval forces. Now Congress turned to those colonies in the hope that their armed ships would be available for Continental use.

John Hancock understood that Massachusetts had two armed vessels in its employ, the *Machias Liberty* and *Diligent*, taken by Jeremiah O'Brien and Benjamin Foster in downeast Maine. Accordingly the President of the Continental Congress wrote the Massachusetts General Court that Washington would be asking for the use of their ships. Hancock wrote express orders in a similar vein to Jonathan Trumbull of Connecticut and Nicholas Cooke in Rhode Island, informing Cooke of the "two north Country built Brigs of no force" and asking him "with all possible expedition to dispatch the armed vessels of the Colony of Rhode island on this Service." Like Washington, Hancock and at least some of his fellow delegates may have regretted not thinking of this earlier.

Nicholas Cooke received Hancock's express orders on October 10, five days after Hancock had written them. That same day he wrote to Washington explaining why he could not help. "I think it my Duty to inform your Excellency that the large Sloop hath not yet returned from her Bermuda Expedition; and that the Small One is unfit for Service."

Jonathan Trumbull tried to be of help. The Colony of Connecticut had fitted out an armed brigantine named *Minerva*, which Trumbull ordered "to sail with all possible dispatch on a cruize to the River St Lawrence." Unfortunately, all but a dozen or so of the *Minerva*'s men refused to go, perhaps because they were unwilling to leave Connecticut waters, and so the vessel remained at home.

Nor did Massachusetts have any vessels to send to the St. Lawrence. *Machias Liberty* and *Diligent* had become a de facto Machias navy, cruising eastern Maine and only nominally under the control of the Massachusetts government. That left only the ships of George Washington's fleet. Had Washington not struck out on his own and authorized vessels without Congressional approval, there would have been no men-of-war at all to send on that important mission.

The commander-in-chief must have permitted himself a certain sense of satisfaction when he wrote to Hancock on October 12, "Before I was honoured with your favor of the 5th Instt I had given Orders, for the Equipment of some armed Vessels to intercept the Enemys Supplies of Provisions, & Ammunition." He had mentioned these ships before, of course, in his letter of October 5, but now he offered more detail. "One of them [*Hannah*] was on a Cruize between Cape Ann & Cape Cod when the Express arrived," he added, though in his previous letter he had implied that all three were just then fitting out. To give Congress a better idea of what he had been up to, he enclosed a copy of Broughton's instructions of September 2.

Washington informed Congress that Massachusetts and Rhode Island had no vessels to send north, leaving only those he had commissioned available for the job. Two of his vessels would be "immediately dispatch'd on the Duty, & every particular mentioned in your Favor of the 5th literally complied with."

There were two snags, only one of which he mentioned to Congress. In the matter of prize money, Congress had been much more generous than he, allowing the officers and men half rather than a third of the value of the prize and not exempting military stores as Washington had done. This would mean that the two vessels bound for the St. Lawrence would be operating under much more favorable terms than the rest of Washington's fleet. "I fear that the proposed Increase will create some Difficulty by making a Difference, between men engaged on similar Service," he wrote. Washington decided that he would simply not mention Congress's largesse to the ships' crews.

The other snag—which Washington chose not to mention—was that the schooners were not actually fitted out yet and so could not be "immediately dispatch'd." By the time Washington heard about the ordnance brigs from Congress, *Hannah* had been battered by *Nautilus* and was out of commission. The three new Beverly ships and the two in Plymouth were only just beginning their conversion to armed vessels.

Washington designated the two earliest-hired of the Beverly schooners for the St. Lawrence mission as they were further along than the Plymouth ships, which had only just been selected. But even the Beverly schooners needed considerable work before they could sail. Desperately eager to get the vessels off, Washington could only lean on Colonel John Glover and Mustermaster General Stephen Moylan to get the conversions done.

In his letter to Congress, Washington revealed how he had come to embrace the possibilities that armed ships represented and how he hoped sending the fleet to sea might reinvigorate an army grown moribund after nearly half a year of inactivity. "Nothing shall be ommitted to secure Success," he wrote, "a fortunate Capture of an Ordnance Ship would give new Life to the Camp, & an immediate Turn to the Issue of this Campaign."

The Maddest Idea

In passing the motion to arm two vessels and send them to intercept the North Country brigs, those in Congress who opposed a navy had given an inch to those who favored one. Now those in favor were ready to take a mile.

This faction started their maneuvering on October 6, the day after Hancock had sent Congress's orders concerning the brigs to Washington. The committee that had drawn up those orders—John Adams, John Langdon, and Silas Deane—presented a report calling for Congress to authorize the fitting out of two swift-sailing armed vessels to cruise for enemy transports. The report was ordered to "lie on the table, for the perusal of the members." Congress did not yet know about Washington's fleet, his letter explaining his actions being then en route.

Rhode Island's motion was also due to be discussed that day, but it was put off until the day following. It was then that the Continental Congress finally had its first genuine deliberation concerning the creation of an American navy, and a heated deliberation it was.

According to John Adams's notes on the debate, Samuel Chase of Maryland began the discussion. Adams described Chase as "violent and boisterous . . . tedious upon frivolous Points." Chase was not a big supporter of a navy.

"It is the maddest Idea in the World, to think of building an American fleet," Chase pronounced. "Its Latitude is wonderfull. We should mortgage the whole Continent." He favored the idea of two smaller vessels but only for gaining intelligence.

Stephen Hopkins saw immediately that things were not going Rhode Island's way. Preferring to table the motion rather than see it defeated, he stood and offered "No Objection to putting off the Instructions from Rhode Island, provided it is to a future date."

Robert Treat Paine of Massachusetts chose to needle Chase. "Seconds Chase's Motion," he said, "that it be put off to a future day Sine die [without a day]."

"The Gentleman from Maryland never made such a motion," Chase retorted. "The Gentleman is very sarcastic, and thinks himself very sensible."

John Zubly, a Swiss immigrant and delegate from Georgia, whom Adams called "a Man of warm and zealous Spirit," pointed out that "If the Plans of some Gentlemen are to take Place, an American Fleet must be a Part of it—extravagant as it is."

The problem, in part, was the lack of specificity in Rhode Island's motion. It called simply for "the building and equipping an American Fleet," without suggesting what was meant by that. Was it a half a dozen schooners? Was it a fleet of ships of the line? Christopher Gadsden took the motion to mean something closer to the latter, and though he was one of the firmest supporters of a navy in Congress, he balked. "I am against the Extensiveness of the Rhode Island Plan," he argued, "but it is absolutely necessary that some Plan of Defense by sea should be adopted."

With no shared understanding of what constituted an American fleet, the delegates argued in circles. John Rutledge, brother of Edward, said, "I shall not form a conclusive opinion till I hear the Arguments. I want to know how many Ships are to be built and what the cost."

Sam Adams was always one to take the most radical stand, but on this occasion he agreed with Rutledge. "The Committee cant make an Estimate untill they know how many Ships are to be built."

Silas Deane, one of the three who, along with Adams and Langdon, had drafted the plans to arm vessels and send them against the ordnance brigs, said, "It is like the Man that is appointed to tell the Dream and the Interpretation of it. The Expense is to be estimated, without knowing what Fleet there shall be, or whether any att all."

John Adams recorded, "Zulby, Rutledge, Paine, Gadsden lightly skir-mishing." In the end, the entire discussion was tabled once again.

On Friday, October 13, the naval question was again raised on the floor of Congress. This time the discussion was not of the Rhode Island resolution but of a more moderate and specific proposal by the com-mittee of Adams, Deane, and Langdon. This day would prove to be qui-etly momentous.

Before the committee reported, Washington's letter of October 5 was read to the Congress. Buried in that letter was his admission—six weeks after the fact—that he had "directed 3 Vessels to be equipped in order to cut off the Supplies," but by this time Congress was so enmeshed in naval considerations that the belated notification did not even warrant a comment.

After hearing Washington's letter, Congress took into consideration the plan of the three-man committee:

> *Resolved*, that a swift sailing vessel, to carry ten carriage guns, and a pro-portional number of swivels, with eighty men, be fitted out with all despatch, for a cruise of three months, and that the commander be instructed to cruise eastward, for intercepting such transports as may be laden with warlike stores and other supplies for our enemies, and for such other purposes as the Congress shall direct.

It was further resolved that "another vessel be fitted out for the same purposes." The specific description of the first vessel, as opposed to the vagueness of the second, suggests that Congress already had a certain ship in mind. That ship was likely Rhode Island's sloop *Katy*. *Katy*, unfor-tunately, was then on her way back from Bermuda, having gone looking for gunpowder for Washington's army, and missed her chance to be the first commissioned vessel of the United Colonies. Renamed *Providence*, however, she would end up as part of the Continental Navy and would sail as John Paul Jones's first command.

The resolve further called for "a Committee of the three be appointed to prepare an estimate of the expense, and lay the same before Congress, and to contract with proper persons to fit out the ves-sel." A vote was taken and a new committee was chosen, consisting again of Silas Deane and John Langdon. This time, however, Christopher Gadsden was appointed in John Adams's place, likely to prevent the appearance of a New England cabal. Gadsden certainly was as avid and knowledgeable a supporter of the navy as was Adams.

John Adams did not seem to mind being left off the committee. There was a muted jubilance in the letter he penned to James Warren that evening. "We begin to feel a little of a Seafaring Inclination here," he wrote. "I believe We shall take some of the twenty Gun Ships before long."

Adams had reason for his optimism. Modest as the Congressional resolution was, it authorized for the first time ships to be fitted out by the United Colonies and sent to sea to cruise for enemy shipping—not as an emergency expedient, as with the ordnance brigs, but as national policy. That date, October 13, 1775, is considered today to be the official birthday of the United States Navy.

"What is the Admiral doing?"

George Washington and the Continental Congress were not the only ones with naval actions on their minds in early October 1775. After months of inactivity, Samuel Graves in Boston was also thinking of engaging in maritime warfare. He was, after all, commander-in-chief of His Majesty's North American Squadron.

The Royal Navy had by then suffered numerous humiliations. The *Diana* had been destroyed, the *Margaretta* and *Diligent* captured, the *Nautilus* badly mauled in Beverly, and a number of transports snatched from under their guns. And Graves had done little in the way of fighting back.

A frustrated General John Burgoyne wrote of Graves's inactivity to a friend, "It may be asked in England, 'What is the Admiral doing?' I wish I were able to answer that question satisfactorily, but I can only say what he is not doing."

Burgoyne went on to enumerate that Graves was not supplying the army with fresh meat, not defending the flocks of sheep they had or the islands in Boston Harbor, and not using his ships for communications and intelligence gathering. "He is intent upon greater objects, you will think," Burgoyne continued, "supporting in the great points the dignity of the British flag,—and where a number of boats have been built for the enemy; privateers fitted out; prizes carried in; the King's armed vessels sunk; the crews made prisoners; the officers killed,—he is doubtless enforcing instant restitution and reparation by the voice of his cannon and laying the towns to ashes that refuse his terms? Alas! he is not."

The admiral's inaction was due in part to reticence and in part to a lack of direction from London as to how aggressive he should be toward the rebels. It would be several months before the king's proclamation declaring the colonies in revolt reached America, and until then no one on either side was quite certain of the official view of the insurrection.

As early as summer 1775, however, people in the ministry were beginning to grumble about Graves. Graves's friend the Earl of Sandwich, who was also First Lord of the British Admiralty, wrote privately to the admiral in August urging him to do "the utmost towards crushing the rebellion." Sandwich hinted that Graves might meet with disapproval for doing too little but not for doing too much.

Graves claimed to hope (ironically, like many in the Continental Congress) that a reconciliation between England and the colonies might still be possible. By late August, however, it was clear that the rebels were "seriously preparing for War" while Graves, in his own words, "was still without the least Instruction for his Guidance respecting the Rebellion." But even the admiral could see that it was time to act.

The plan that Graves hit upon was quite extraordinary, particularly considering the lack of aggression he had shown until that point. In order to "punish the people of the four New England Governments, for their many rebellious and pyratical Acts," Graves decided to "burn and lay waste the Towns and destroy the Shipping" of nearly all the major seaports in Connecticut, Rhode Island, Massachusetts, and New Hampshire. Graves's proposal constituted the most punitive and violent reaction yet to the growing rebellion, a wild swing from relative forbearance to scorched earth.

For help with his planned offensive he turned to General Thomas Gage, who was still in command in Boston. Graves requested transport vessels that could be fitted out with mortars and howitzers for naval bombardment and "a small detachment of the Royal Regiment of Artillery." Gage agreed to lend the admiral the army transport ship *Symmetry* and the sloop *Spitfire* to "fit up as you please." Sailors were in short supply, and Gage could spare none from his army transports, but he said he would see about carpenters and caulkers. Adding a dig to the offer of help, Gage wrote, "It is to be wished that something of this kind had

been proposed at an earlier Period." Gage apparently saw no downside
to the wholesale destruction of seaport towns.

The entire month of September was consumed in preparing the *Symmetry* and *Spitfire*. Considerable carpentry work was required before the
ships could receive mortars and ammunition. Much of the delay, Graves
felt, was due to a lack of cooperation on Gage's part. It would have been
done much quicker, he wrote, "if the Business had received that ready
assistance from all concerned which such an Undertaking might
expect." Preparations were also slowed by Graves's insistence on loading
the ordnance ships under cover of darkness to preserve the secrecy of
the mission.

On October 4, a few days before the squadron was ready to sail and
the day before Washington informed Congress of his schooner fleet, His
Majesty's sloop *Raven* arrived at Boston with orders for Admiral Graves
from the Lords Commissioners of the Admiralty. The new orders called
for Graves to do whatever he felt necessary along the New England sea-
coasts "for suppressing . . . the Rebellion which is now openly avowed &
supported in those Colonies." The orders, written on July 6, implicitly
endorsed what Graves had already decided to do.

To command the squadron Graves chose forty-one-year-old Lieutenant Henry Mowat, commander of the six-gun armed vessel *Canceaux*.
Mowat was pragmatic and tough and knew the coast of New England
intimately, having been engaged in survey work there since 1764.

Graves issued his orders to Mowat on October 6. He was to proceed
with *Canceaux* in company with *Symmetry, Spitfire*, and the schooner *Halifax* to Cape Ann Harbor and there "burn destroy and lay waste the said
Town together with all Vessels and Craft in the Harbour." That done,
the squadron was to continue north, destroying rebellious towns along
the coast.

"My Design," Graves wrote,

is to chastize Marblehead, Salem, Newbury Port, Cape Anne Harbour,
Portsmouth, Ipswich, Saco, Falmouth in Casco Bay, and particularly
Mechias, where the *Margueritta* was taken, the Officer commanding her
killed, and the People made Prisoners, and where the *Diligent* Schooner
was seized.

Graves was sending Mowat to sea with orders to turn every significant seaport north of Boston into a charred ruin. The resultant swath of devastation would have been incredible, yet no one in the British command seems to have found any fault with the plan.

Mowat's squadron got under way on October 9. Ashley Bowen watched them pass "without Halfway Rock" as they made their way northeast. It was night when the fleet reached the entrance to Cape Ann Harbor, and Mowat knew better than to try and work his way in through the tricky channels in the dark. The ships hove to for the night, but soon a gale sprang up from the northward, forcing the vessels to struggle along under close-reefed topsails. Finally, with the unwieldy *Symmetry* and *Spitfire* making heavy weather of it, Mowat decided to run for shelter at Cape Cod.

The next morning the wind shifted to the southwest and Mowat's squadron ran north back to Cape Ann Harbor. As they closed with the town, however, the artillery officer lent to the squadron by General Gage "gave it as his opinion, that the houses stood too scattered to expect success." To effectively bombard a town from the water, the squadron needed a sufficient density of buildings to support a massive fire. Fearing "the ill consequences of a disappointment," Mowat stood out to sea again, and the squadron headed north.

The next day the ships were off Cape Elizabeth, Maine, with Falmouth in sight, but another northwest gale drove them farther east and forced them to anchor near Squirrel Island in Boothbay Harbor. There they remained for several days until the storm blew itself out.

Finally, on October 16, the squadron got under way again. They did not continue east to Machias, as one might have expected. Instead, they retraced their steps for Falmouth, now known as Portland.

At first blush Falmouth might have seemed an unlikely choice of towns to make an example of. Though known for its rebel sympathies, Falmouth had caused less offense than nearly any other town Graves had slated for razing. It could hardly compare with Machias, Beverly, Marblehead, or even Portsmouth for its contributions to the armed insurrection. Mowat, however, had a good reason for choosing Falmouth, and it was personal.

CHAPTER *16* *The Empire Strikes Back*

THE TOWN OF Falmouth consisted of some two thousand people clustered mostly on a three-mile-long peninsula at the south end of Casco Bay. Two- and three-story wooden buildings were packed along narrow streets that climbed uphill from the busy waterfront. Though on the northern fringe of New England's commercial centers, Falmouth was a thriving town, its economy based mostly on the export of lumber. By 1768 Falmouth had been exporting four million feet of pine boards annually, almost ten times more than the combined exports of Kittery, Portsmouth, and Boston.

Maine was then a district of Massachusetts, and Falmouth, like most Massachusetts towns, was fervently revolutionary, complete with local militia and a Committee of Inspection to make sure the Continental Association, which banned trade with England, was properly observed.

In March 1775, a sloop from England had dropped anchor in Falmouth Harbor. In her hold were sails and rigging for a ship under construction in Falmouth, one that had been commissioned by a local businessman and loyalist named Thomas Coulson for a merchant in Bristol, England. Warned that his cargo might be in violation of the Continental Association, Coulson had applied to the local Committee of Inspection for permission to off-load it. After "a long and serious debate," the committee decided that, since the rigging and sails were from England and Coulson's ship was bound for England after launch, the cargo was indeed prohibited. They agreed, however, that "the case was hard, and would gladly have construed the Association in his favor."

Given the expense of building the ship and importing the sails and rigging, Coulson was unwilling to let the issue end there. He informed the Committee of Inspection that he was going to apply to the Massachusetts Provincial Congress for a ruling, but instead he went to a higher authority, General Thomas Gage in Boston, for whom the Continental Association was just another illegal act of rebellion. Coulson took with him a letter from the loyalist sheriff at Falmouth requesting that a man-of-war be sent to settle the affair.

Gage applied to Admiral Graves for a ship. The only one Graves had available was the *Canceaux*, which was slated to leave for Halifax for repairs. Graves ordered Henry Mowat to take *Canceaux* to Falmouth instead and see that Coulson was allowed to off-load his cargo. The sloop-of-war arrived there in early April, and under her protection Coulson would have been able to proceed except that now he could find no men to unload the ship.

For the next month the *Canceaux* remained while the sloop was slowly off-loaded, presumably by her own small crew. Tensions on both sides ran high. Falmouth patriots braced for an attack by *Canceaux*, while loyalists grew certain the patriots would imprison them. To make matters worse, a group of radicals from Brunswick and Topsham, at the other end of Casco Bay, threatened to march to Falmouth under the leadership of Colonel Samuel Thompson and launch an attack on *Canceaux*.

Still calm prevailed, and British sailors went ashore unmolested. Hoping to maintain that calm, and fearing that they would get the worst of any violent confrontation, the Falmouth Committee of Correspondence wrote to their counterparts in Brunswick asking that no attempt be made on *Canceaux*. Thompson assured them that he had dropped his plan to attack the man-of-war, but while this may have been true, he still intended to make trouble. On May 9, Thompson and around fifty of his armed men landed on the back of Falmouth Neck. Thrifty and resourceful Yankees that they were, each man's uniform consisted of "a small bough of spruce in his hat," and for a standard they carried "a spruce pole, with a green top on it."

Rather than launch an attack on *Canceaux*, the band laid low in a thick stand of trees, seizing and detaining anyone who passed by. Around 1 P.M. they hit the jackpot when Lieutenant Mowat, ashore for a walk with the *Canceaux*'s surgeon and a local Anglican minister named John Wiswell, wandered into their trap.

When word of Mowat's capture got back to *Canceaux*, the ship's master sent word that if Mowat was not released in a few hours "he would lay the Town in ashes." The *Canceaux*'s men "hove taught the Spring," swinging the ship "Broadside to the Town." With that, the smoldering anxiety of the past month exploded into a full-blown panic. As one observer wrote,

> You can hardly conceive of the consternation, confusion and uproar that immediately ensued. Our women were, I believe, every one of them in tears, or praying, or screaming; precipitately leaving their houses . . . and widows hurrying their goods into countrymen's carts, never asking their names, though strangers, and carrying their children either out of Town, or up to the south end, according to the greater or less irritability of their nerves.

The men, apparently, did not react much better. A delegation met with Thompson and urged him to release the prisoners, but Thompson "appeared inflexible, and even furious." Negotiations dragged on during the day, but Thompson refused to release the men and continued to insist that "Divine Providence had thrown them into his hands."

By that evening, however, it was clear to Thompson that all of Falmouth stood in opposition to his plans and that the reinforcements he had been counting on were not coming. God's will notwithstanding, he agreed to grant parole to Mowat on the condition that the lieutenant return the next day. Mowat was escorted to the waterfront and ferried out to *Canceaux*, and at the same time the *Canceaux*'s master released a number of prisoners he had rounded up that day to use as leverage for the return of his captain.

The next morning Mowat elected to violate his parole and remain on board the man-of-war, which was hardly a surprise. He sent a note explaining that his servant, who had gone ashore to take the lieutenant's dirty laundry to his washerwomen, had overheard several threats to Mowat's life.

When word of Mowat's breach of parole reached the various militia units that had converged on Falmouth, they were furious. They turned their anger on local Tories, who were tried in makeshift courts, pronounced guilty, and fined for their crimes. Plans were laid to destroy *Canceaux*, but the militias could not agree on how it might be done. A few days later a band of drunken militiamen fired on the man-of-war with their muskets, which was as close as they would come to attacking the ship, before finally drifting back to the towns from which they had come. "Thompson's War," as it came to be known, was neither a stellar success for American arms nor a shining example of the noble defense of a righteous cause.

"My Design is to chastize . . . Falmouth"

On October 16, six months and one week from the day he had been taken by Samuel Thompson, Mowat was back at Falmouth, anchored outside the harbor with a powerful squadron. The people of Falmouth had seen the ships pass a few days before and had concluded that the British navy was on a foraging expedition for the garrison in Boston. Falmouth militia had been dispatched to nearby islands to protect livestock and hay, but beyond that no precautions had been taken.

When the ships returned and anchored outside the harbor, however, fear began to spread. When no messages were sent ashore, uncertainty as to the squadron's intentions helped to fan the panic. Then, on the morning of October 17, the people of Falmouth learned that the ships were commanded by Henry Mowat, and they breathed a sigh of relief.

When Mowat had been released on parole the previous spring, he had "expressed his gratitude to the Town in strong terms" before going back aboard *Canceaux*. Falmouth residents felt that they had saved Mowat from the evil designs of a radical outsider, and they assumed that the lieutenant felt the same way and that he had "great reason to be bound in gratitude to several gentlemen" there. But Mowat did not draw such distinctions between the radicals of Falmouth and those of Brunswick. They were all, in his eyes, an unruly mob. Nor was Falmouth innocent of fomenting revolution. The town had earned its place on Samuel Graves's hit list.

That morning the squadron faced contrary winds, but Mowat was eager to get up to the town. The fleet began the laborious process of kedging, or warping—that is, moving a ship by dropping its anchor ahead, then hauling the vessel up to the anchor. "Employed carring out warps to warpe the ship ahead," the *Canceaux*'s log recorded.

By early afternoon a breeze came up and the squadron was able to make sail and cover the last distance to the Falmouth waterfront. According to *Canceaux*'s log, "at 3 . . . came too aline ahead abreast of the Town of Falmouth." With the ships arrayed to fire on the town, word spread at last that Mowat had come to do just that. The "inhabitants generally were in a state of alarm, and many began to move out for safety."

Once the ships were anchored, Mowat penned a letter to the town's inhabitants and sent his acting lieutenant, a man named Fraser, ashore to deliver it. By then Falmouth was in a fury of activity, with some residents rushing to leave town while others were gathering at the waterfront.

Fraser landed "amid a prodigious assembly of people," many of them carrying muskets. He was escorted by the mob "with uncommon parade and ceremony along the street to the Town House," where he and a number of leading citizens took seats in the courtroom. The rest packed in as best they could. One can only imagine what was running through Fraser's mind.

The crowd was called to silence, and Fraser handed Mowat's letter to a lawyer named John Bradbury, who read it aloud. Addressed to "the People of Falmouth," the letter began in just the sort of patronizing language rebellious Americans found so intolerable: "After so many premeditated Attacks on the legal Prerogatives of the best of Sovereigns After the repeated Instances you have experienced in Britain's long forbearance of the Rod of Correction; and the Merciful and Paternal extension of her Hands to embrace you, again and again, have been regarded as vain and nugatory."

Mowat went on to explain that the people of Falmouth were "guilty of the most unpardonable Rebellion" and that he had "orders to execute a just Punishment on the Town." What the punishment was he did not say, but the broadsides of the ships aimed at the town gave a sufficient hint. Mowat allowed the people two hours "to remove without delay the Human Species out of the said town." To those who had sought protection aboard *Canceaux* during Thompson's War, "the same door is now open." The letter concluded, no doubt to Lieutenant Fraser's relief, "The officer who will deliver the letter I expect to return unmolested."

Mowat's words were greeted with stunned silence. Bradbury was asked to read the letter again, which he did. "It is impossible to describe the amazement which prevailed upon reading this alarming declaration," one witness recalled, "a frightful consternation ran through the assembly, every heart was seized with terror, every countenance changed color, and a profound silence ensued for several minutes."

Rather than kill the messenger, the people pointed out to Fraser that the punishment was excessively severe and the time too short to remove the civilian population, especially with night coming on. Fraser told them that if they had a proposal for Mowat he would take it out to him, but he could not guarantee that the commodore would receive it.

The town leaders immediately appointed a committee of three, Jedediah Preble (who back in May had offered himself to Thompson as a prisoner in Mowat's stead and had indeed been imprisoned when Mowat broke his parole), Dr. Nathaniel Coffin, and Robert Pagan. They were to meet with Mowat and negotiate some sort of truce. The three men took a boat out to *Canceaux*, where they asked Mowat what "the nature of the chastisement" would be and reiterated that, with night coming on, there was insufficient time to get the women and children out of town.

Mowat told the committee that his orders "did not authorize him to give any warning to the inhabitants" but simply to come alongside the town and "burn, sink and destroy." He declared that they had no right to expect leniency thanks to the nature of their crimes, but, encouraged by "the known humanity of the British Nation," he was ready to deal. Mowat told the committee that if they were to deliver up all the arms and ammunition in town, along with a few prisoners of his choosing, he would put off destroying Falmouth until he had consulted with his superiors in Boston. Preble, Coffin, and Pagan argued that it would take time to comply with that demand.

At last the two parties came to an agreement, the details of which are unclear. In his report to Graves, Mowat claimed to have demanded that a number of arms as well as the five cannon he was certain were in town be delivered to him by eight o'clock that evening. The committee of three, however, in a report written three months later, claimed that Mowat demanded the arms and cannon be delivered by eight o'clock the following morning.

Likewise, according to the committee's report, Mowat asked for eight muskets to be delivered by eight that evening as a token of compliance. In his report to Graves, Mowat wrote that "they returned with Ten stand

only," suggesting that the committee delivered more than they thought
necessary but less than Mowat expected. The differences between the
two accounts might reflect faulty memories or genuine failures in communication, but in either case Lieutenant Mowat was not pleased.

When the paltry offering of ten muskets failed to satisfy him, Preble,
Coffin, and Pagan begged him to give them until nine o'clock the following morning to comply more fully or, if the people chose not to meet
all Mowat's demands, to get the women and children out of town. Mowat
agreed and told the committee to be aboard *Canceaux* with the arms and
cannon by 8:30.

The men returned to shore to find all of Falmouth in a disordered
panic, "where nothing occurred but scenes of tumult, confusion, and
bustle." People were driving ox- and horse-drawn wagons piled high with
household goods through the narrow streets, desperately making their
way off the peninsula and away from the leering guns of the enemy's
ships. To add to the confusion, militia from the surrounding countryside were pouring into town, mobilized by the militant patriots of Falmouth, and were threatening to burn the town if the citizens cooperated
with Mowat. To keep the militia from engaging in any aggressive acts
against the men-of-war and thus provoking a violent response, "a number of moderate gentlemen" took it upon themselves to form a citizens'
patrol.

The committee of three called together the leading men of Falmouth
and related Mowat's demands, but to their astonishment the people
were opposed to giving up their cannon or small arms, even in the face
of the men-of-war's guns. They agreed to make a final decision in the
morning, but the next morning that decision was "by no means to
deliver up the cannon or their arms." Despite the fourteen hours that
had passed since Mowat's initial letter had been read, many civilians still
remained in Falmouth. Preble, Coffin, and Pagan were asked to return
to *Canceaux* and "prolong the time on board as long as possible, that
more effects might be removed."

The three men did as asked, arriving on board *Canceaux* at 8 A.M. on
October 18. They informed Mowat that no more weapons would be
forthcoming. They did not even bother to ask if Mowat might spare the
town but only that he give them half an hour to get ashore and get clear

of the line of fire. That Mowat agreed to, and Preble, Coffin, and Pagan, after "expressions of thankfulness for the lenity that had been shown," left *Canceaux* at 8:30 and pulled for the Falmouth waterfront.

Mowat had set 9 A.M. as the time he would open up on the town, but from *Canceaux*'s quarterdeck he could see women and children still struggling through the streets. "I made it forty minutes after nine before the Signal was hoisted," he wrote, "which was done with a gun, at the same time the cannonade began."

"An horrible shower of balls"

Daniel Tucker, a Falmouth resident, was just making his way out of town when the firing began. "Mowat hoisted a red flag," he wrote, "and fired the first gun and the shot whistled along between me and the old meeting house." The Reverend Jacob Bailey observed, "the flag was hoisted to the top of the mast, and the cannon began to roar with incessant and tremendous fury."

The streets were still crowded, and it appeared to some observers that Mowat was purposely firing high to avoid civilian casualties, though there is nothing in Mowat's reports to suggest that he did so. But the destruction was immediately felt. The gunfire and smoke terrified the draft animals pulling wagons out of town and caused them to bolt, "dashing everything to pieces, and scattering large quantities of goods about the street."

Unlike Gloucester, Falmouth was perfectly situated for destruction by naval bombardment. The harbor was deep and broad and allowed the ships to anchor within point-blank range. The town's wooden buildings crowded close to one another so that flames could easily move from one to another, and the town was built on a hill sloping up from the harbor, so buildings farther inland stood exposed above those closer to the water. It did not take long before the real destruction began. "The first house that was fired . . . burned down without communicating with any other," Tucker wrote, "but it was only a short time before all the north part of the town was in a blaze."

The master's log of the *Canceaux* recorded the devastation in cold, official language: "at 10 several Houses was on fire the fire broke out with great violens in two or 3 houses of the Somost [southernmost] Part of the Town at Noon the fire begun to be general both in the town and vessles but being calm the fire did Not Sprede as wished for." Though most of the people had fled, a body of armed men remained in the town and desperately fought the fires as one building after another became fully involved.

The constant barrage of cannons and mortars continued on through the afternoon, "an horrible shower of balls, from three to nine pounds weight, bombs, carcasses [specialized shells used to set buildings on fire], live shells, grape-shot, and musket balls."

Around 1 P.M. a small breeze sprang up from the south and helped push the flames from building to building, but still the squadron did not let up its pounding of the town. Toward the south end of Falmouth were several detached buildings, too far removed to be caught up in the general conflagration. Those, and the Americans who had stayed behind to fight the fires, made it, in Mowat's opinion, "absolutely necessary for some men to be landed, in order to set fire to the vessels, wharfs, storehouses, as well as the many parts of town that escaped from the shells and carcases."

At 3 P.M. Lieutenant Fraser and thirty sailors and marines, along with Gage's artillery officer, went ashore to put the last of the structures to the torch. They were met by the armed men of Falmouth, who had been struggling to save the buildings. Musket fire flashed between the British and Americans as the marines held the militia at bay and the sailors "threw torches into the doors and windows of the houses and stores." With the last of the buildings blazing and the marines forming a rear guard, the British moved back to their boats and pulled for *Canceaux*. The only casualties were a midshipman and a marine, slightly wounded. Mowat did not bother to tell Graves that one man from the landing party deserted, surrendering himself to the militia and claiming "he chooses to fight for America."

By 6 P.M., with the sun near setting, "the body of the town was in one flame." With the *Canceaux* warmed and illuminated by the brilliant inferno just across the water, Mowat at last called for a cease-fire. Even the roar of the flames must have seemed muted and quiet after nearly nine hours of constant gunfire from the four men-of-war. From the waterfront, the armed Americans continued to pepper the British ships with musket shot, which did no damage. Still, *Canceaux* "made the Sigl to get under sail" and the squadron weighed and stood out of the harbor, coming to anchor again out of range of the muskets or any cannon the Americans might have.

Mowat's ammunition was all but expended and the *Spitfire* was "much shattered," presumably from the constant concussion of the guns, punishment which the converted merchant vessel was not designed to take. The troops were "in great distress, for want of necessaries," and many were falling sick. Mowat decided he had to return to Nantasket Roads and see to these issues "before I can attempt any other place."

Falmouth had received exactly the sort of scorched-earth treatment Graves had envisioned. Nearly every building that faced the water was a smoldering ruin. "In a word," Reverend Jacob Bailey wrote,

> about three quarters of the town was consumed and between two and three hundred families who twenty four hours before enjoyed in tranquility their commodious habitations, were now in many instances destitute of a hut for themselves and families; and as a tedious winter was approaching they had before them a most gloomy and distressing prospect.

Fallout

Atrocity as a military tactic is rarely successful. Rather than break the morale of those who are made to suffer, it tends rather to strengthen their resolve. And so it was with Falmouth.

Americans were shocked and outraged that such an act could be committed by people who had not so long ago been looked upon as countrymen. "This is savage and barbarous in the highest stage," James Warren wrote to John Adams. William Gordon also wrote to Adams wondering how many more towns would be burned before "every manly exertion of power & wisdom is to be exercised in opposing our Enemies!"

George Washington, on hearing of the event, wrote to Philip Schuyler to say the British navy attacked Falmouth "with every Circumstance of

Cruelty and Barbarity, which Revenge and Malice could suggest. We expect every Moment to hear other Places have been attempted and have been better prepared for their Reception."

Washington touched on one of the problems facing Graves. Prior to the destruction of Falmouth, most seaport towns were lightly if at all defended. After the Falmouth attack, every town that could be accessed from the sea began to frantically throw up defenses. By January a Canadian traveling through the area reported that "From Portsmouth to Casco every harbour and Creek has some insignificant Redoubt, Logwall, or other defense, and upon the least alarm the Country People come in."

But in fact Graves never tried such an attack again, despite his grandiose plans. By the time Mowat returned to Nantasket Roads the weather was deteriorating, Washington's schooners were beginning to make problems for the admiral, and myriad other things demanded his attention. And perhaps it had dawned on the old admiral that his idea was not a good one in the first place.

The destruction of Falmouth seems not to have caused much of a stir in England. At first the reports were dismissed as rebel propaganda, and when they were found to be true, it was assumed there must be some good reason for the attack. The American Secretary, George Germain, who had succeeded Dartmouth, demanded an explanation from Howe, who had succeeded Gage. When Howe reported the simple facts of the case, Germain was apparently satisfied.

The French, however, who were keeping close watch on the goings-on in America, recognized the destruction of Falmouth for the blunder it was. "I can hardly believe this absurd as well as barbaric procedure on the part of an enlightened and civilized nation," wrote France's foreign secretary, the Count de Vergennes, "more especially as the perpetrators of this terrible crime allegedly declared that the order had been to given to burn all maritime towns from Boston to Halifax."

Vergennes had excellent sources of information and a clear understanding of the issue. The radicals in America were fired up by the British atrocity, and their calls for independence became louder and more vociferous. But more important, many Americans who had previously been unsure of the wisdom of breaking from England were now persuaded of its necessity and came down firmly in the patriots' camp.

A month after Falmouth was razed and eight months before the Declaration of Independence, the *New England Chronicle* cried that the "savage and brutal barbarity of our enemies . . . is a full demonstration that there is not the least remains of virtue, wisdom, or humanity in the British court. . . . Therefore we expect soon to break off all kinds of connections with Britain, and form into a Grand Republic of the American Colonies."

In the same vein, William Whipple, a prominent citizen of Portsmouth, New Hampshire, wrote to John Langdon that "at present it seems to me to be the determination of every one to risque his all in support of his liberties & privileges, the unheard of cruelties of the enemy have so effectually united us that I believe there are not four persons now in portsmouth who do not justify the measures pursuing in opposition to the Tyranny of Great Britain."

In the end, Samuel Graves launched only one major offensive operation against the enemy, and it did nothing but strengthen the American cause.

CHAPTER *17* Hancock *and* Franklin

BY THE END of the second week of October, Washington was putting a great deal of thought and energy into his schooners. Orders flew from Joseph Reed's desk. "Lose no Time," he wrote to John Glover. "Every Thing depends upon Expedition." He sent word to Nicholson Broughton to "recruit your present Crew to 70 Men including Officers" and assured him further orders would be forthcoming.

Despite Broughton's complete lack of success and the mess over *Unity*'s capture, *Hannah*'s commander was to continue as senior captain of the fleet, in charge of the expedition to the St. Lawrence. He would be master of the *Speedwell* fitting out in Beverly, and under him, in command of the second vessel, *Eliza*, would be John Selman, a thirty-one-year-old Marblehead ship master and a captain in Glover's regiment.

Though Reed had ordered Glover or Stephen Moylan to proceed to Newburyport to find a fourth vessel for the fleet, Glover had instead hired another Marblehead boat, the *Hawk* of sixty-four tons, possibly doing so before Reed's orders arrived. Previously, with just two schooners fitting out in Beverly, Glover had complained about a lack of carpenters slowing up the refits. Now he had four schooners—the *Speedwell*, *Eliza*, *Two Brothers*, and *Hawk*—all needing attention.

Anxiety mounted at the headquarters in Cambridge, and Washington and Reed grew increasingly exasperated at delays they did not understand. On October 14 Reed wrote to Moylan, who was in Portsmouth arranging transport of the *Prince George*'s flour to Cambridge, "We are very anxious to hear of the armed Vessels being ready for Sea. Every Day, nay every Hour is precious. It is now fourteen days since they were set on Foot, Sure they cannot be much longer in preparing."

The next day Glover threw Reed a bone. "This will acquaint you," he wrote, "the two Vesells that the Captains Broughton, & Selman, are to Command, are ready to tack [take] the troops on board." Glover had been ordered to send for the crews when the ships were within a few days of being ready to sail. He may have believed the refits were nearly complete, or he may have been placating Reed, but in any event the ships were not as far along as he implied.

Reed had already ordered Broughton and Selman to recruit seventy men for each of their ships, but their efforts had not gone well. Broughton in fact had not recruited anyone, since he was still incapacitated with the cold he had caught when *Hannah* had gone aground.

The soldiers who would be sailors carried long infantry muskets, impractical weapons for shipboard use. Muskets used in naval combat were generally shorter "sea service" weapons, more handy in confined spaces. Glover wrote to Reed, "Would it not be best, that every man, be furnisht with a Spear, or Cutlash, & a pare of Pistles, if to be had, as Guns is Very unhandy in boarding." Such small arms were standard issue to Royal Navy boarding parties, but the munitions-starved Continental Army was able to supply its sailors with only a few such luxuries.

Glover reported that the two ships were provisioned save for "4000 weight of bread," which could not be purchased in Marblehead for less than the "Extravegent price" of thirty-two shillings per pound. Reed agreed that "The Price you mention for Bread is monstrous; but there must be no delay." He told Glover that Broughton and Selman had their orders and "must be immediately dispatched." The orders had been drafted that same day under the heading of "Add[l] Instruct[ns]," as they were supplements to the original instructions issued on September 2.

The orders came directly from Washington and began with the intelligence of the "two North Country Brigantines of no Force." (Sailors today make a careful distinction between a brig and a brigantine based on how the ship's mainmast is constructed, but the two terms were colloquial and used interchangeably in the eighteenth century. The rig would have included square sails on the foremast and a large, gaff-rigged fore-and-aft sail—with or without one or more additional square sails—on the mainmast.)

The commander-in-chief continued, "You are hereby directed to make all possible Dispatch for the River St. Lawrence and there to take such a Station as will best enable you to intercept the above Vessels." Broughton was to capture any vessel that might be in service to the ministerial army. He was to try to determine if the ordnance brigs had already passed, and if they had he was to maintain station "as long as the Season will admit." Washington was confident that Benedict Arnold, still fighting his way through the Maine woods, would soon capture Quebec, and he wanted his schooners at the mouth of the St. Lawrence to scoop up fleeing vessels that "may come down and fall into our Hands."

The officers and men would get one-third the value of their captures, as before, but this time Washington did not exempt military stores, which should have made the prizes much more valuable to their captors.

Last, Washington warned Broughton not to annoy the Canadians, an admonition that had also been part of his orders to Arnold. The commander-in-chief did not want to alienate a populace that he hoped would join the Americans in their fight for liberty. If Broughton did meet any Canadian vessel not working for the British army, he was to "treat such Vessel with all Kindness and by no Means suffer them to be injured or molested."

Nearly identical orders went to Selman, save that Selman was told he would be under Broughton's authority. Broughton, for his part, was to consult with Selman as to where they should cruise and for how long.

While Glover and Moylan were keeping headquarters updated on the progress of the schooners, Reed and Washington were getting information from other sources as well, and what they were hearing suggested that the vessels were not as far along as their agents in Beverly implied. Reports from the front lines that six transports had just sailed unmolested into Boston Harbor made the general and his secretary even more impatient.

On October 17 their anxiety and frustration boiled over, and Reed sent a scathing letter to Glover:

> We learn with a good deal of Concern that there is no Probability of the Vessels being got away for several Days, & that in all Appearance, the Remainder of the Vessels besides Capt Broughton & Capt Sellman will not be ready these two Weeks to which the long Delay already & frequent Disappointment makes us give some Credit. The General is much dissatisfied & cannot but think a Desire to secure particular Friends or particular Interests does not mingle in the Management of these Vessels. The number of Workmen, we are told, is inconsiderable, and in short it is said in plain terms, that it will be made a Jobb of.

This was a serious accusation, suggesting that Glover was doling out work to his friends to the detriment of the schedule. Adding to suspicions at headquarters was the appearance that Glover had ignored specific instructions to fit out one of the ships at Newburyport and had chosen instead a fourth Marblehead vessel, though that decision may have been made before Reed's orders for Newburyport arrived. Glover was now told that if the third and fourth ships fitting out in Beverly, those staying in local waters, could not be made ready in five days, he must go to Newburyport and outfit one there.

Whoever was supplying Reed with his information also told him about Broughton's practice of returning to port each evening and allowing the crew to spend the night ashore. "We are told that our Vessels make a Practice of running in every Night when they have been out & the Men come on shore. This must be Rectified," Reed wrote. This last, though true, was an unfair accusation to lay in Glover's lap, as Glover had no authority over the operation of the *Hannah*; his orders were merely to find vessels and fit them out. Reed does not seem to have criticized Broughton, who was the one who truly deserved a rebuke and who had in fact done nothing in the previous week but nurse his cold.

On October 19 Glover and Moylan wrote to Reed to tell him that Broughton and Selman would be ready to sail the next day, but Selman's ship still needed a surgeon. They hoped Reed would send one quickly, "as we believe it will be difficult to prevail on the Capt & crew to go without one." They made no mention of Reed's angry letter. Possibly Glover had not yet received it or was too upset to reply.

The next day Reed wrote back in a much calmer tone, mollified perhaps that the St. Lawrence–bound ships would be under way at last. Along with notice that a surgeon was on his way, he suggested the men "fix upon some particular Colour for a Flag, and a Signal, by which our Vessels may know one another." On that head Reed had a suggestion. "What do you think of a Flag with a White Ground, a Tree in the Middle, the Motto (*Appeal to Heaven*). This is the Flag of our Floating Batteries."

As early as July the Americans had been flying flags with various but similar configurations. In its final form the flag consisted of a white field with a pine tree in the middle—a symbol long used in Massachusetts flags—and below it the motto Reed now suggested. This flag had been adopted for use aboard the floating batteries Washington had set up in the Charles River. Since it was already a naval ensign of sorts, Reed thought it might work for the new fleet.

But Broughton and Selman did not fly the *Appeal to Heaven* flag for the best of reasons—they sailed before Reed's instruction arrived. "The Schooners Commanded by Captains Broughton and Sillman Saild this morning," Glover and Moylan wrote, "as they had none but their old Colors, we appointed them a signal, that they may Know each other by, & be known to their friends—the ensign to the Main topping Lift." The date was October 22.

Stephen Moylan visited both captains aboard their ships just before they cast off and insisted on seeing the sealed orders they had been issued, each with the words "Not to be opened till out of sight of land" written across the front. Moylan inspected the orders, found the seals unbroken, and returned them. "[T]he horrors of death in all its forms would not have operated to have broke a seal or denyed a duty," Selman later wrote.

Washington's first vessel, *Hannah*, had retained her civilian name during her brief commission. Now, in keeping with the more officially sanctioned nature of the enterprise, the newly commissioned ships were given names more fitting to a Continental fleet. It is unclear when or by whom the names were chosen, but they were designed to honor and perhaps curry favor with the rebellion's civilian leadership. Broughton's schooner *Speedwell* became *Hancock*, after the president of the Continental Congress, and Selman's *Eliza* was rechristened *Franklin*, after Congress's oldest and most renowned member.

There was no doubt great relief at headquarters in Cambridge when word arrived that the schooners had sailed for the St. Lawrence at last. Washington was desperately eager to put his plan into action and to reap the potential rewards of stationing armed vessels in the middle of the busy shipping lanes of the St. Lawrence River. He had no way of knowing, of course, what an utter debacle it would be.

Harrison *and* Washington

"Your Conduct in fitting out the Vessels is much approved by his Excellency who is particularly pleased with your Dispatch." Joseph Reed wrote those words to Captain Ephraim Bowen on October 20, 1775, just three days after excoriating Glover for his perceived favoritism. Things in Plymouth seemed to be going well. The refit of the schooner *Triton*, now renamed the *Harrison*, was under way, and work would soon begin on Sion Martindale's *Endeavour*. Unfortunately, a good deal of the "dispatch" that Bowen was showing was little more than wishful thinking. He had been on the job less than a week and had not yet had time to prove that Plymouth could be just as great a source of aggravation as Beverly.

Aggravation was starting to make an appearance, however, and Reed touched on that. Benjamin Wormwell, part owner of the *Endeavour*, had decided that he wanted six shillings per ton per month for his share rather than the five shillings, four pence that the owners of Washington's other leased vessels were receiving. Reed told Bowen to find another ship if Wormwell would not relent, adding that Bowen could go to Rhode Island for guns if necessary. The prior warning against doing business on Bowen's home turf had only been issued, Reed now wrote, because "we have been very unfortunate in sending Persons to do Business where their Connections lay"— another clear reference to John Glover.

Martindale's grandiose visions continued to worry Reed. "I cautioned him against an extravagant Outset," Reed wrote, "but I fear his former Ideas upon the Subject are insuperable. There certainly can be no occasion for such a Number of Guns, unless he means to go without Powder for them."

Reed also informed Bowen that he would be sending as captain of the *Harrison* a man named William Coit, thirty-two years old, a lawyer from New London, Connecticut. Coit was currently serving as a captain in the 6th Connecticut Regiment, though earlier in life he had sailed as master of a merchant vessel. Coit's company had helped cover the retreat from Bunker Hill.

William Coit was tall and portly and carried himself like a soldier. He was also liberal in outlook and enjoyed certain eccentricities. According to one biographer, Coit always wore a scarlet cloak, which earned him the nickname "the Great Red Dragon." Perhaps his most striking attribute, however, was his sense of humor, which would happily be preserved in various documents.

Reed finished his letter with the usual admonition for speed. "Pray forward both Vessels as soon as possible, & in your next let me know when Martingale's Vessel will be ready." In a postscript he added, "By all Means caution Capt Martingale against a large Outset—The Design is to intercept the Enemy's Supplies, not to look out for the Enemy's Armed Vessels."

On October 22, one day after he had hoped to send *Harrison* off to sea and the day the *Franklin* and *Hancock* set sail for Canada, Bowen was still struggling to get his vessels fitted out. The weather was hindering his efforts, with a cold, driving rain holding up the work of shipwrights and riggers. Despite that, Bowen thought Martindale's vessel would be ready by October 28. Wormwell, happily, had agreed to accept the same rate of hire as everyone else and had headed off to Cambridge to "Sollicit a First or Second Lieuts Birth," a position Martindale hoped he would be granted given his familiarity with the ship.

Reed's warnings notwithstanding, Martindale was undertaking an elaborate refit of his vessel. The first major alteration was to her name. In Martindale's original instructions, the ship he was to command was to be named *Eagle,* but at some point the name was changed to *Washington.* Martindale must have pushed for the name change, because it would not have come from the commander-in-chief. Though General Washington unhesitatingly used similar flattery on members of Congress, he was far too concerned with maintaining his air of humility to name a ship for himself. Martindale, by contrast, was happy to let others know how important he was and what great deeds he would do.

The *Washington,* like all the ships in the general's growing fleet, had been hired as a schooner, but by the time Martindale was done with her she had become a brig or brigantine. Given the interchangeability of those terms in the eighteenth century it is hard to know exactly what rig she carried, but it was considerably more complicated than a schooner. Rather than the simple jib, gaff foresail, gaff mainsail, and square fore and main topsails of Washington's armed schooners, she would carry, at a minimum, a square foresail, square fore topsail, and square fore topgallant sail, and likely smaller studdingsails to set outboard of those. Nearly every sail would have to be purchased or made new. Her simple schooner foremast, basically one big stick, would have to be exchanged for a shorter foremast, above which would be attached a fore topmast and above that a fore topgallant mast, all of which required considerably more complex rigging.

William Watson's accounts convey a sense of the work and expense involved. Entries included "one top Gallant yard, one fore top Sail yard, one fore yard, one Sparr for fore top mast, one Sparr for ditto," along with "Stell yards," which might have been an abbreviation for studding-sail yards. The new spars and sails required attendant blocks (pulleys) and rigging. Each square sail was controlled by at least sixteen pieces of rigging, most of which involved blocks of some kind. Six-inch blocks, nine-inch blocks, twelve-inch blocks, six snatch blocks, thirty seven-inch blocks, double blocks, triple blocks, bulls eyes, and deadeyes all went into *Washington*'s elaborate new rig.

If she was being converted into a true brig, the same would have been done to the mainmast. There does not, however, seem to be a record for more yards on the mainmast, save for a "Crotchick" or crojack yard, a lower yard to which no sail was attached. This probably meant that *Washington* was a brigantine with a fore-and-aft mainsail and at least one square sail on the mainmast, not a true brig.

There is no mention in correspondence between Bowen, Watson, and Reed about the appropriateness of this change. Quite possibly neither Washington nor Reed fully appreciated the implications of converting a schooner to a brigantine. Even after the work of converting *Washington* had begun, Reed wrote to Moylan and Glover in Beverly to tell them that in Plymouth "a large Schooner Carrying 10 Carriage Guns" was fitting out and would be ready in a few days. Reed does not seem to have understood Martindale's plans, but those plans undoubtedly caused the long delay in getting *Washington* to sea.

On Monday, October 23, Bowen recorded in his Journal, "Set the Carpenters to Work on the Brig also the Rigers." They had a lot of work to do.

CHAPTER *18* *Congress Pays a Visit*

ON SEPTEMBER 29, more than a week before Washington notified them of his plan to arm schooners, the Continental Congress had decided to send a delegation to Cambridge "to confer with General Washington . . . touching the most effectual method of continuing, supporting and regulating a continental army." John Hancock informed the commander-in-chief that Congress had "appointed three of their Members, Vizt Mr Lynch, Doctor Franklin, & Mr Harrison to wait on you."

Benjamin Franklin was the most august member of Congress and had more international experience than any other delegate. He was probably the most famous man in America. Benjamin Harrison, a delegate from Virginia, was a longtime associate of Washington, the two men having served together in the Virginia House of Burgesses and as fellow delegates to the Continental Congress before Washington's departure to take command of the army. Thomas Lynch, from South Carolina, was and would continue to be an active member of Congress until being disabled by a stroke four months after visiting Cambridge.

Washington received Hancock's notice some days after dispatching his letter of October 5 informing Congress that he had "directed 3 Vessels to be equipped." In a return letter to Hancock he described the delegates' pending visit as "An Event which has given me the highest Satisfaction." He had recently sought his officers' opinions regarding the best way to maintain the army through the coming winter, and now he would be able to include the delegates in those considerations. In the days before their arrival, Washington's fleet expanded from three to six vessels, and it was likely no coincidence that the first Plymouth ship was renamed *Harrison* or that a later vessel would carry the name *Lynch*.

The delegation arrived at the camp in Cambridge on October 15 and three days later began five days of meetings with General Washington and representatives of the New England colonies. The discussions were wide-ranging and touched on pay and rations for officers and men; changes to the rules that regulated the army; the best method of procuring provisions; the size of the army and its various regiments and companies; whether a certain British prisoner, Ensign Moland, should be allowed to stay with his friends in Pennsylvania; and sundry other details.

The larger meetings finished on October 22—the day the *Hancock* and *Franklin* sailed for Canada—but Washington met privately with the congressmen for two more days. Though not the primary focus of the talks, maritime affairs were discussed. Prize money was one issue. The delegation endorsed the compromise Washington had settled on, allowing the ships' crews just a third of their prizes, not a half, but including military stores in the total.

On the penultimate day of meetings Washington posed his most direct question regarding naval action. "Six Vessels (armed) are now fitted out & fitting upon the best Terms to intercept the Enemys Supplies, will this be agreeable to the Congress?" The delegates approved the scheme and assured Washington they would recommend it to the Congress as a whole.

Not until November 30 would Congress officially act on the delegates' recommendation, resolving that "The Congress approve the General's fitting out armed vessels to intercept the enemy's supplies." Three and a half months after the commander-in-chief had launched his surreptitious war on supplies and *matériel*, he would receive official sanction to do so. By then it was a mere formality. Congress was deep into naval affairs, and Washington's fleet, which once might have been a point of serious political contention, had become a matter casually disposed of.

On October 24, the last day of the delegates' meeting with Washington, the matter of a "Court for the Tryal & Condemnation of Vessels taken from the Enemy" was discussed. This was no formality but an important issue for the commander-in-chief, who had thus far been burdened with having to decide the fate of captured ships himself. This was not only a distracting task but a politically risky one, as the capture of Langdon's *Unity* and the resulting mutiny had shown. The delegates assured Washington that Congress would recommend to the government of Massachusetts that prize courts be established, but the issue was shunted aside when the delegates returned to Philadelphia. Long after Washington had approval for his ships, he would still be pleading for courts to adjudicate their prizes.

"Mischievous Violators of the rights of Humanity"

The morning of October 22 was crisp and cold under clear blue skies. Along the low-lying shores of Beverly and Salem Neck, the last autumn leaves clung to oak and maple trees, and the sea rippled under a light southwest wind. On the Beverly waterfront the smell of wood smoke mingled with the ubiquitous odors of tar and the brackish harbor.

Men swarmed the decks of the schooners *Hancock* and *Franklin,* casting off the gaskets that held the foresails and mainsails between boom and gaff and stretching out peak and throat halyards. With seventy men on board each ship there was muscle enough to make the work easy, but so many hands would make for tight quarters once the vessels were under way. Adding to the clutter on each ship's deck were four 4-pounder carriage guns snugged up behind newly cut gunports. Ten swivel guns perched on the rails of each vessel.

The southwesterly breeze was perfect for lifting the small men-of-war off the docks and wafting them out to sea. With a word from Captain Nicholson Broughton, *Hancock*'s sails were hoisted and her lines let go, and she turned her bow to the east. Just astern of her followed Captain John Selman in command of *Franklin.* The schooners worked their way through the tricky channel that had almost been the undoing of *Nautilus* and stood out past Salem Neck to the outer harbor. They sailed east with the Massachusetts shoreline a mile to larboard, leaving to starboard the rocky hump of Marblehead and a smattering of small islands in the blue sea. The two captains knew them all as well as they knew the houses on their Marblehead streets.

Beyond, the open Atlantic stretched away before them, an unbroken horizon between the ships and their first landfall at Nova Scotia en route to the mouth of the St. Lawrence.

The seas were clear of enemy vessels. The *Nautilus,* which just a week before had been patrolling between Boston Harbor and Thacher Island, off Gloucester, was now anchored in the shadow of Bunker Hill—a floating battery on the front lines of the siege of Boston—leaving the way open for the Yankee men-of-war.

Hancock and *Franklin* plunged on for Canada, "running their eastings down" in the old sailors' parlance. Sailing a comfortable broad reach with the wind over their starboard quarters, they left the familiar coast of Massachusetts under the horizon. But it was late in the season, and they were on the North Atlantic, and it was too much to hope that the weather would remain favorable for long.

It did not. The wind backed through south toward east, and soon the schooners were making heavy work of it, close-hauled under shortened canvas, fighting their way through rising seas. As conditions deteriorated, life on board the crowded schooners must have become correspondingly more unpleasant, the men laboring on pitching decks or crowded below in the modified fish holds, their clothes soaked through from rain and boarding seas, their meals served cold because the seas were too rough to risk a galley fire.

For five or six days the schooners worked their way across the Gulf of Maine, making good a speed of around three knots as they struggled to cross the seven hundred nautical miles to the Cabot Strait, the entrance to the Gulf of St. Lawrence and the St. Lawrence River. Off the southwestern coast of Nova Scotia they crossed a shoal known as Brown's Bank. The seas were running high, breaking over the shallow bottom. At one point green water crashed over the deck of the *Franklin*, the force of the blow twisting the vessel. "I shipped a sea which racked the *Franklin*," Selman would later write, "and set her leaking."

The corkscrew action opened up the seams between the vessel's planks. The men worked furiously at the pumps, but *Franklin* could not be kept afloat if the leaks were not addressed.

The *Franklin* limped into Country Harbour, *Hancock* by her side. They were a hundred miles northeast of Halifax and two hundred miles short of Cape North, the northeastern point of Nova Scotia, which they would have to round on their way to the St. Lawrence River. There they managed to caulk the leaks in *Franklin*'s hull, perhaps by running the schooner aground in the upper reaches of the long inlet and waiting until low tide left her high and dry.

However it was done, by October 29 Washington's schooners were under way again, and on that day they took their first prizes. Those captures were not the North Country brigs loaded with ordnance, however. In fact, they were far from it.

The vessels were the schooners *Prince William* and *Mary*, two small Canadian merchantmen loaded with fish and oil. Broughton and Selman boarded the vessels and after examining their papers decided that the schooners were bound for Boston, thus making them legitimate prizes. The two captains then helped themselves to an eclectic assortment of items needed on board their own schooners. Broughton commandeered from the *Prince William* three cod lines, a dozen cod hooks, a cod lead, and six quarts of molasses, and from the *Mary* he took a hogshead of salt and six pounds of sugar. Selman confiscated one and half gallons of molasses and an empty three-gallon jug from the *Prince William*, and from the *Mary* he took a hogshead of salt, two more empty jugs, and seven pounds of sugar.

Lieutenant Edward Homan, second officer aboard *Franklin*, was made prize master of the *Mary*, while *Prince William* was put under the command of the *Hancock*'s second officer, Lieutenant John Devereux. The two ships were ordered to sail for Beverly. Devereux had been one of the officers on board *Hannah* who had received reward money from Langdon for retaking *Unity*. It was more than he would get for Broughton's latest endeavors.

In his attempts to justify *Unity* as a legitimate prize, Broughton had shown a tendency to overlook facts when they stood between him and profit. Washington no doubt considered Broughton's arguments on that occasion an anomaly, or he would not have trusted command of what he considered his little fleet's most vital mission to the man. But his Excellency was wrong. Broughton, apparently driven by avarice, was willing to call anything he could capture a prize, no matter how flimsy the evidence, and Selman seemed happy to acquiesce.

This character flaw, combined with Broughton's willingness to ignore orders and his unfortunate habit of stumbling upon ships owned by men who were leaders in the American cause, would spell trouble for his and Selman's Canadian adventures.

With the *Prince William* and *Mary* off to Massachusetts, Broughton and Selman continued their journey, but the wind turned easterly and the weather deteriorated, and they found it hard to make their easting. "[B]y unfavorable Winds & weather we have been able to make but little head," Broughton wrote to Washington a few days later, in a letter that would be sent with the next prize.

On October 31 the schooners spied a sail to the northward and turned in pursuit, but "the Wind Springing up sudingly to a heavy gale," their quarry hauled his wind and raced north for Whitehead Harbour, some twenty miles east of Country Harbour, the Americans still on his heels.

Broughton and Selman finally made the capture behind Whitehead Harbour's sheltering headlands. The vessel was the sloop *Phoebe*, loaded with fish and oil like the *Prince William* and *Mary* and by all appearances a simple Canadian merchantman, the sort of vessel Broughton's orders called for him to treat "with all Kindness and by no Means suffer them to be injured or molested."

Upon interrogating the *Phoebe*'s captain, James Hawkins, Broughton discovered that the sloop had taken provisions from Halifax to Quebec the previous spring and had also carried provisions from Louisbourg, on Cape Breton Island, to the West Indies. This last Broughton felt was a violation of the Continental Association, which called for a ban on importing and exporting goods to and from Britain, though how he came to that conclusion is unclear. During the interview, Hawkins, probably missing the significance of what he was saying, admitted that *Phoebe*'s owner had not yet decided if he would send her to Boston that fall.

Any talk of the ship going to Boston was enough reason in Broughton's opinion to consider her a prize. His report to Washington floridly declaimed that "The smallest Intention of going to that Den of Mischievous Violators of the rights of Humanity, must carry in the bosom of it as we conceive the Idea of Friendliness to their infernal Intentions." Broughton's words seemed designed as much to prove his own patriotic bona fides to a skeptical commander-in-chief as to explain why *Phoebe* was a legitimate capture.

Hawkins also informed Broughton that around the middle of September he had seen a ship and a brigantine bound up the St. Lawrence, though he did not speak either of them. Broughton's report seemed to imply that these vessels must have been the elusive North Country brigs that he and Selman had been sent to hunt.

Hawkins lastly told Broughton and Selman that a large brigantine was loading coal at Spanish River, now called Little River, on Cape Breton

Island, which Broughton called "the Island of Loisburg." There were reportedly "three or four Score Boston Men" digging coal there for the use of the ministerial army in Boston.

Once again Broughton and Selman helped themselves to the captured vessel's cargo, even before she had been adjudicated a legitimate prize. Broughton took a barrel of pork and one and a half barrels of "flower" plus ninety-two pounds of tobacco and some bread. Selman took much the same, neglecting only the tobacco.

The *Phoebe* was sent on to Beverly but her captain, James Hawkins, was detained. Broughton ordered *Phoebe*'s prize master, Sergeant Benjamin Doak from *Franklin*'s crew, to deliver her papers along with Broughton's letter to Washington. "[W]e shall hoist Sail directly," Broughton assured his Excellency, "the wind breasing rather favorably & pursue our Course."

By "our Course," Washington might reasonably have assumed that Broughton meant to round Cape North and stand for the mouth of the St. Lawrence River. He had, after all, been "directed to make all possible Dispatch for the River St. Lawrence." It was his primary mission. "No Acct yet of the Armd Vessels sent to St Lawrence," Washington wrote to Hancock on November 8. "I think they will meet with the Stores Inward, or outward Bound." Having not yet received any of Broughton's correspondence, Washington remained optimistic about his schooners' chances.

While Broughton and Selman were capturing their dubious prizes, a small convoy was working its way across the Gulf of St. Lawrence. It consisted of "the *Jacob* and *Elizabeth* Brigs, laden with Arms, Ammunition, Cloathing &c. for the King's Army under General Carleton," who was commanding in Quebec. The *Elizabeth* alone carried "10,000 stands of arms, cloathing for 10,000 men, 500 barrels of gunpowder, and a large quantity of ball." It is not certain that these were the two brigs of which Congress had been informed, but the descriptions are strikingly similar. And even if they were not, they were exactly the sort of prizes Washington hoped to grab.

There was one crucial difference between these brigs and the North Country brigs "of no force" that Broughton and Selman had been sent to find; the *Jacob* and *Elizabeth* had protection in the form of the twenty-gun man-of-war *Lizard*, which had been ordered to convoy *Jacob* from

Spithead in England to Quebec. The brig's cargo was simply too valuable to be transported without escort. *Elizabeth* had sailed alone, but instructions had been sent by the British Admiralty to the commander of any man-of-war bound for America that "in case he falls in at Sea with *Elizabeth* Store Ship bound to Quebec he do take her under convoy and see her safe into the River St. Lawrence." At some point *Lizard* and *Jacob* did fall in with *Elizabeth*, and the three vessels continued on to Quebec.

The twenty-gun *Lizard* might well have been too powerful for Broughton and Selman's schooners, but on October 26 the man-of-war lost *Jacob* in the fog and was unable to find her again. *Lizard* and *Elizabeth* continued on to Quebec, while the heavily laden, spectacularly valuable, completely unarmed *Jacob* sailed on alone.

Even if they had sailed there directly, Broughton and Selman might not have reached the mouth of the St. Lawrence in time to intercept the brigs. When the *Elizabeth* arrived at Quebec, however, Governor Guy Carleton "would not suffer the stores to be landed" for fear they would be captured by the invading Americans, "but ordered the ship to sail immediately for England." *Elizabeth* weighed anchor and headed home, still fully laden. Broughton and Selman had an entirely unexpected second chance to capture her, and they missed that one, too.

In fact, they did not even try. The only logical place to intercept military cargoes bound in or out of Quebec was the mouth of the St. Lawrence, but the two captains had no intention of going there. As *Elizabeth* and *Jacob* were passing by just to the north, the Marblehead men were making other plans.

His Excellency's hopes notwithstanding, by the time Broughton and Selman sent *Phoebe* to Beverly they were completely ignoring Washington's directions. What's more, they seemed either unaware or unconcerned that they were doing so. In his next letter to Washington, written four days after taking the *Phoebe*, Broughton informed the commander-in-chief that "We attempted for some time after our last, to get to Spanish River, in order to take the Brigantine loading with Coal." This had nothing to do with the mission they had been ordered to perform, but Broughton wrote as if he assumed Washington would approve of his conduct.

And it would only get worse.

"It cannot be displeasing to the General"

Bowen had hoped to have the *Harrison* under way on October 21, the day before Broughton and Selman sailed for Canada. By the 24th, however, he was still waiting for Captain Coit to arrive. What's more, the small collection of guns available at Plymouth would not be nearly enough to satisfy Sion Martindale's appetite for ordnance. Giving up on Coit, Bowen set out for Bristol, Rhode Island, armed with a letter from Reed to the Bristol Committee informing them that it "will much oblige the General, & promote the publick Service" if they could furnish Bowen with any guns they had to spare.

Incredibly, despite the enormous amount of work still needed to get *Washington* to sea, Sion Martindale went to Rhode Island with Bowen. William Watson would later tell Reed that Martindale and Bowen had both gone to Bristol to look for cannon, but Bowen never mentioned Martindale's presence or his participation in any of the negotiations to secure guns.

The weather was cold but clear as Bowen and Martindale made their way to Bristol. Bowen arrived there on the evening of October 25, but where Martindale went or what he did is unclear. Quite likely he went off to visit friends and family, just the sort of thing that caused Reed and Washington so much frustration with Marbleheaders.

Ephraim Bowen, at least, went right to work and "Waited on the Committee," who told him that the guns he had understood to be in Bristol belonged to Captain Simeon Potter, who was free to do with them as he would. Bowen visited Potter the next day and found that the old man had ten 4-pounders and ten swivel guns on hand, not as powerful an array as Martindale would have liked, though sufficient for the purpose he was supposed to serve. But Potter, whose business sense remained ascendant over patriotic fervor, would not lend or lease the guns but would only sell them for the goodly price of a thousand dollars for the ten, swivels not included.

Bowen, not surprisingly, thought the price too high and took his leave. He went south to the headquarters of the Rhode Island militia, a couple of miles north of Newport. There General Esek Hopkins, brother of Congressman Stephen Hopkins and future commodore of the Continental Navy, showed Bowen several cannon that would serve his purpose. Hopkins was willing to give up the guns but told Bowen he needed an order from Lieutenant Governor Cooke before he could release them.

Once again Bowen climbed into his sulky and headed to Bristol, where he made Potter a counteroffer, one which the old man could refuse and did. Bowen then continued on to Providence to speak with Nickolas Cooke, lieutenant governor of Rhode Island.

All the next day Bowen waited to speak with Cooke, only to be told by the lieutenant governor to come back in the morning after the Rhode Island Assembly had had a chance to discuss the matter. No doubt chafing at the delay and fretting over the pace of progress back in Plymouth, Bowen cooled his heels until the following morning. Finally Cooke presented Bowen with an order for Hopkins to provide ten 4-pounder carriage guns. Unfortunately, Rhode Island had no swivels to spare.

The entire proceeding was devolving into a convoluted mess. Bowen wanted swivels at least as much as he wanted carriage guns, since swivels could be used against an enemy's crew while doing little damage to the enemy's ship, an important consideration when your object is to take prizes, not sink them. To make Bowen's life even more unpleasant, the good weather came to an end and a cold rain began to pour down in torrents. He waited until 2 P.M. for the downpour to stop, and when it did not he left Providence anyway, driving his sulky through the mud and ruts and soaking rain.

After a miserable three-hour trip Bowen arrived again in Bristol and again called on Potter, this time to make an offer for the swivel guns alone. Potter, however, "would not Sell Without the Carriage Guns."

With dark coming on and the rain coming down, Bowen found a room for the night. At nine o'clock that evening he received a note from Potter offering his ten swivel guns, "Most of which is already Swiveled," for twenty dollars per pair. But of course Bowen would also have to buy the ten carriage guns, "Each Gun European made & proved & is reckend much Better than N Engd Cast Cannon," along with ten cartridges, two hundred shot, sponges, ladles, wormers, formers, leather and wood cartridge boxes, and powder horns, the whole package for eight hundred dollars.

Bowen was unimpressed. The next morning he had his horse brought around and headed for Newport to see Esek Hopkins again. First, however, he called again on Potter and "Made him One More offer of 220£

for his Guns which he Accepted after some time." One wonders what Bowen might have said to coax the hard-driving Potter to a price less than a quarter of his original offer.

Buying carriage guns from Potter that he could have obtained for free from the Rhode Island militia was still a tough call for Bowen. He explained to Reed that while he could have "got the Guns off Rhode Island, considerable Cheaper," he could "get no Swivels with them which was the Reason that I bot these."

A 4-pounder gun, though small by ordnance standards, was still a substantial piece of hardware, six feet long and weighing more than half a ton. Transporting ten of them overland on wet, muddy roads would be difficult and expensive. Luckily, nearly half the journey from Bristol to Plymouth, some forty-three miles across the lower part of Massachusetts, could be covered by a boat sailing inland on Mt. Hope Bay and then northeast up the Taunton River to the head of navigation in Taunton.

Bowen was aware that his five days in Rhode Island might be construed as exactly the sort of dawdling Reed had warned against. He wasted no time getting the guns loaded aboard a boat. Writing to Reed, Bowen assured him that "as I have used the Utmost dispatch Possible, I think it cannot be displeasing to the General." Certainly, if Bowen's journal is accurate, any time he wasted was no fault of his.

Bowen paid the boatman five dollars and got his receipt. The boat was not able to sail until nine o'clock that evening, no doubt due to tides, so Bowen headed for Taunton in his sulky to be there when it arrived. He reached Taunton before noon the next day, but the wind was blowing downriver and the boat was not yet there. Bowen waited all afternoon but the wind did not shift and the boat did not appear.

The next day Bowen, who by now must have been nearly frantic for all the delay, hired a pilot and sent him downriver to find the boat. The pilot found it at Swansea, in the river's lower reaches, only eight miles from Bristol. Luckily the wind shifted, and the boat made it to Taunton by two o'clock that afternoon. Bowen had already arranged for wagons to carry the ordnance the remaining twenty-five miles or so to Plymouth. No further time was wasted as the guns were transferred from the boat to the wagons, and with a shout from the teamsters the *Washington*'s battery rolled slowly east.

When Bowen arrived back at Plymouth on November 1, he had spent more than a week procuring guns to satisfy Sion Martindale's inflated sense of mission. Arriving four hours ahead of the wagon train, he found good news and bad waiting for him. The good news was that *Harrison*'s fitting out was complete, Coit and his crew had arrived from Cambridge, and the vessel had weighed anchor and stood out to sea. The bad news was that she was hard aground.

CHAPTER *19* *"For Gods Sake hurry off the Vessels"*

THE ALLURE OF heavily laden North Country brigs in the offing was foremost among George Washington's maritime ambitions through the second half of October, but it was not his only focus. Washington could see a parade of sail entering Boston Harbor with British supplies and provisions, and he was anxious to get *Hawk* and *Two Brothers*—the second pair of schooners undergoing refit in Beverly—off to sea. Joseph Reed wrote to Stephen Moylan, "For Gods Sake hurry off the Vessels that are to cruise. Transports with out Convoy arrive every Day at Boston."

Nicholson Broughton and John Selman had not yet sailed when Reed penned his angry letter to John Glover accusing him of "a Desire to secure particular Friends or particular Interests." Near the end of that letter he dashed off an order, more an afterthought, that would prove critical in the management of Washington's fleet: "Capt Manley is to have one of the Vessels left for the Coast about Cape Ann."

Captain John Manley is an enigmatic figure, and as with many about whom little is known, a lot has been made up. The stories often told about him include that he was a Marbleheader though born on Tor Bay in England, that he served in some capacity in the Royal Navy before turning to the merchant service, and that he went by the name John Russell in Marblehead and John Manley elsewhere.

In fact, Manley was most likely born in Boston around 1733 and sailed as a merchant seaman and captain from that city until the outbreak of the Revolution. In 1763 he married Hannah Cheevers. They had a son, also named John, who died at the age of eight months, and then a second, again named John, who survived his father. The senior John Manley was forty-two years old when he was tapped by Washington for command. Joseph Reed would later say of General Israel Putnam, "we give him credit for a Part of Manly's Success, as he brought him to us."

Whatever his background, Manley would prove to be exactly the sort of officer Washington was looking for—active, aggressive, ambitious, and unafraid.

The first mention of Manley in connection with Washington's fleet comes in a note from Reed to Glover and Moylan concerning command of the schooner *Two Brothers*, the name of which had been changed to *Lee* in honor of General Charles Lee, or Richard Henry Lee, or both. John Glover had suggested that his son, Lieutenant John Glover Jr., who had sailed as first officer aboard the *Hannah*, be posted as *Lee*'s captain. "Captain Glover will have the seventh Vessel fitted out," Reed wrote, "but the General fears he is too young. He has agreed to be second in Command under Manley for a little Time."

After *Hancock* and *Franklin* sailed, Moylan and Glover remained in Beverly, doing battle not with the British but with the shipwrights, riggers, sailmakers, and chandlers on whom they depended to get the second pair of schooners off. Moylan wrote to Reed, "I wish with all my soul that these two vessells were dispatchd."

Certainly Moylan wanted the schooners cruising for the good they could do the American cause. Additionally, however, he was eager to get back to Cambridge to visit with his old friends Thomas Lynch and Benjamin Harrison, part of the congressional delegation meeting with Washington, and "to be introduced to Doctor Franklin, for whom I have many years a vast veneration." In the end, the delegation would be finished and gone long before the schooners were.

The fourth schooner, *Hawk*, would become the *Warren*, named for the hero of Bunker Hill, Dr. Joseph Warren. Though she was one of two schooners named for Massachusetts men (if one excludes Franklin, who was born in Boston), *Warren* would be manned by New Hampshire troops from General John Sullivan's brigade. Her captain, Winborn Adams, was also from New Hampshire. The original plan had been for Manley to patrol off Cape Ann, but that area was in Adams's home waters. "As Adams is well Acquainted with the Coast farther Eastward than Cape Ann," Reed wrote, "it may perhaps not be amiss for him to go there."

Around this time Glover showed Moylan the angry letter Reed had written him. For nearly a month Moylan and Glover had worked side by side, focused on the same mission, struggling with the same legion difficulties. Most correspondence from headquarters had been addressed to them jointly, and they had formed a bond of mutual respect and no doubt friendship. Moylan wrote back to Reed in Glover's defense.

"Col. Glover showed me a Letter of yours which has mortified him much," Moylan wrote.

> I realy & sincerly believe he has the cause much at heart, & that he has don his best, (in the fitting out these four last vessells), for the publick service you Cannot Conceive the difficulty the trouble & the delay that there is in procureing the thousand things necessary for one of these vessels.

Moylan, whose civilian business was on the Philadelphia waterfront, center of commerce in the largest city in America, was accustomed to finding what he needed when he needed it. But now he and Glover were having to search all over Marblehead, Beverly, Salem, and Danvers "for every Little thing that is wanting."

Moylan included in his litany of complaints and justifications "the Jobbing of the Carpenters, who are sure the Idlest Scoundrels in nature." He would have happily fired them all, he said, except that there were none to take their places. Nor was Moylan impressed with their religious fervor, which seemed most manifest when they were looking for a day off. "[S]uch religious rascalls are they, that we Coud not prevail on them to work on the Sabbath. I have stuck very close to them since, & what by Scolding & Crying Shame for their torylike disposition in retarding the work, I think they mend something."

Those arguments aside, Moylan was not blind to the inherent drawbacks of Glover overseeing work in his hometown. While rejecting Reed's suggestion of favoritism and his implication of corruption on Glover's part, the Philadelphia merchant did see other issues at play. "[T]here is one reason, & I think a Substantial one, why a person born in the same town or neighborhood should not be employed on publick affairs of this nature in that town or neighborhood," he wrote. Without mentioning Glover by name, he continued in this ostensibly hypothetical vein:

> [T]he Spirit of equality which reigns thro' this Country, will make him affraid of exerting that authority Necessary [for] the expediteing the busi-

ness, he must shake eve[ry] Man by the hand, & desire, beg, & pray, do brother, do my freind, do such a thing, whereas a few hearty damns from a person who did not Care a damn for them would have a much better effect, this I know by experience.

Despite the myriad problems, by the fourth week of October *Lee* and *Warren* were nearly ready for sea, and Moylan and Glover alerted Reed to have the crews stand ready to march from Cambridge in preparation for embarking on October 26. They suggested that Reed alert the men as soon as possible so that "they may prepare what Necessarys they may have occasion for, & not delay in Looking out for them here." The two men were catching on to the ways of ships' crews. They understood, for instance, that Marblehead men could not march from Cambridge to Beverly without taking a detour along the way. "[A]s the Marblehead Gentry Will go home," they wrote, "it will be best to send them of[f] tomorrow [Monday], & we shall Stand a better Chance of being able to Collect them on Thursday." They added, "the Captains of both schooners should be here to Superintend the Work."

At the end of the note to Reed, the men included a list of requests that illustrated the scavenger-hunt challenges of provisioning a ship for sea: "Please to send the following articles immediatly 40 Spears 300 Sorted Swivel Shot, & some Match rope 2 Signal Flaggs, 50 lb Chocolate 50 lb Coffee 112 lb Sugar & Small firkin of butter."

Winborn Adams and his crew were still in Cambridge on Thursday, October 26, the day they were to have embarked onboard the *Warren*. Reed hoped to have them marching for Beverly the next morning. The *Warren* was all but ready, "her guns provision &c on board," Moylan wrote, "& I know there will be many things wanting which we Cannot possibly think of untill he Comes."

Meanwhile, John Manley was on board the *Lee* but had no crew. "Capt. Manley's vessell is all ready, we now wait the Collecting together of his hopefull Crew to send him off." Moylan told Manley he was to set sail "if there are even 30 onboard to morrow morning & the wind proves fair."

Broughton and Selman's ships had sailed with seventy men each, but the second two Beverly schooners, though essentially the same size as the first two (*Franklin* was in fact the smallest of the four), would ship only fifty men apiece. Prize crews from *Lee* and *Warren* could easily rejoin their ships, which would be cruising locally, whereas crews sent from Canada could not. Then too, Moylan and Glover may have concluded that it was ridiculous and unnecessary to cram seventy men on board small ships. Perhaps both reasons came into play.

Moylan was also encountering problems with John Glover's son. Reed had instructed the young man to take with him to Beverly the items his father and Moylan had requested. John Glover Jr. showed up with everything from spears to chocolate but failed to deliver "the Most Material Article, which is the 300 Swivel shot." To Moylan's annoyance, Glover told him there was no swivel shot to be had, though there were plenty of four-ounce bullets, which, if young Glover "had one ounce of Sense," Moylan wrote, "he must have Known would answer all the purposes."

Perhaps more irritating, John Jr. was trying to game the system to get a friend of his appointed to an officer's berth on *Lee*. Thinking that headquarters would not approve another officer without a proportional increase in the size of the crew, Glover asked that an additional twenty men be added to the ship's company. John Glover Sr. "did not chuse to interfere," so Moylan told Glover the Younger that "he may have his friend if he pleasd, who with 50 more[,] officers included, is all I would suffer to go on board." Any more than that would be "an incumberance on board one of these small vessells," and more money than headquarters would care to pay.

The end of October brought two major changes in the administration of Washington's fleet. The first was the appointment of agents in Marblehead and Beverly to organize provisions for the ships and to oversee the disposal of any prizes sent into those towns or Salem. Though Glover and Moylan's original instructions had called for them to find men suitable for the positions, they had not done so until then. While William Watson in Plymouth was bearing much of the load for Ephraim Bowen, Glover and Moylan had been going it alone. Finally they would receive some help.

This was not the prize court that Washington hoped Congress would appoint, and the agents could not relieve the commander-in-chief of the responsibility of adjudicating prizes, but they would see to the day-to-day operations of the fleet, thus relieving headquarters of a significant headache. The agent appointed for Marblehead was the senior John Glover's older brother, Jonathan Glover. In Beverly, where most of the fleet's activity would take place, the agent was William Bartlett, a local merchant and, happily for Washington, an active and intelligent man.

The other shake-up, one that went well beyond Washington's fleet, was the resignation of Joseph Reed. Reed had dropped everything to accompany Washington to Cambridge, but his former law practice had at last caught up with him. A number of the cases in which he was involved were coming to trial and he did not feel, ethically or professionally, he could ignore them.

His loss was a heavy blow to Washington, who had come to trust and rely on his secretary. Joseph Reed "moved upon so large a Scale as to comprehend at one view, the diversity of matter which comes before me," Washington wrote, "so as to afford that ready assistance which every Man in my Situation must stand, more or less, in need of."

In their ongoing correspondence after Reed's departure, Washington never stopped trying to convince the young lawyer to return to the commander-in-chief's "family." Less than three weeks after Reed left, Washington wrote to him, "judge you therefore how much I wish'd for your return, especially as the Armed Vessels, & the capitol change (in the state of the Army) about to take place [enlistments would run out in December], have added an additional weight to a burthen, before too great for me to stand under." In his private letters, Washington was not always as stoic and uncomplaining as his popular image would suggest.

On October 28, two days before Reed left for Philadelphia, another departure took place which was regarded at headquarters with relief and pleasure. Captain John Manley set off to sea.

"Yankeys & Punkings"

On November 2, two days after capturing the sloop *Phoebe*, *Hancock* and *Franklin* clawed their way off the rocky coast of Nova Scotia. Strong easterly winds and midautumn storms drove surf onto the steep shore, white water crashing against the rocks and cliffs, the tall pines that straggled down to the ledges whipping in the wind.

The stiff headwinds prevented *Hancock* and *Franklin* from rounding Cape North, at the northeast end of Cape Breton Island, or even from reaching Spanish River, where the *Phoebe*'s captain had reported a brigantine loading with coal for the British in Boston. "[T]he wind being contrary & blowing up a heavy storm we were oblig'd to give over our Design," Broughton reported to Washington, "we then stood for this Place where the Storm had hardly yet ceased'd."

"This Place" was the Strait of Canso, the narrow strip of water separating Nova Scotia from Cape Breton Island. Windbound, Broughton assured Washington that "no Vessel passes this season to Boston Halifax or to any part of American from Quebec but must pass within gun Shot of us." It was a ridiculous claim. Perhaps Broughton hoped that the land-lubber Washington would be unaware of sixty-mile-wide Cabot Strait, about a hundred and fifty miles northeast of Canso. The only reasonable place to intercept shipping from Quebec was the mouth of the St. Lawrence River, where Washington had ordered him to go.

Standing into the strait, the Americans came across a sloop that had likewise ducked in there to hide from the screaming wind behind the rugged cliffs of Cape Breton Island. She was the *Warren* (a merchant-man, not Washington's armed vessel), and her captain and owner was a man named John Denny from New Haven, Connecticut. Also on board was a passenger named Buddington who owned most of the cargo the *Warren* carried. They were bound from Gaspee, on the New Brunswick shore of the Gulf of St. Lawrence, to Nantucket.

Broughton decided to test Denny and Buddington's loyalty through a bizarre subterfuge. When he and Selman first spoke to the men, they "used the words Yankeys & Punkings [pumpkins, a common British pejorative for Americans] with apparent Jering, & asked after the King's Troops." Broughton reported that Denny and Buddington "answer'd as men well affected to the Ministry would," which is hardly surprising. When a man sees two armed vessels pointing their cannons at him, he will tend to agree with whatever the commander of the armed vessels has to say.

When Broughton revealed the truth of the matter to Denny and Bud-dington, the doubtlessly confused men further implicated themselves in Broughton's eyes because "they did not make such Apologies as true sons of Liberty strongly attachd to the Interist; but had mistaken their Company might naturally be expected to do."

That was proof enough for Broughton and Selman, who had already demonstrated that they needed little proof indeed before deciding a ship was a legitimate prize. They felt "bound to send the Vessel Cargo &

her papers" to Washington for his decision. They liberated more food from the *Warren*, removed Denny and Buddington, placed Captain Hawkins of the *Phoebe* as a prisoner on board, and sent her off with a prize crew and correspondence to the commander-in-chief. Broughton's report assured Washington that "immediately upon the wind suiting we endeavour to conform to the Spirit of your Excellency's Orders." They would bend that "Spirit" to their own ends, however, though Broughton did not say as much to Washington.

The easterly wind that had prevented the schooners from weathering Cape North would have been fair to push them through the twenty-mile Strait of Canso and into the Gulf of St. Lawrence had Broughton been so inclined. But soon the wind backed into the north and held the vessels windbound on the southern shore of Nova Scotia. While they rode at their anchors at a place Selman called "Plaster Paris," another vessel entered the strait and came to anchor. Broughton ordered Selman in the *Franklin* to take possession of the newcomer and bring her up to where the Americans were anchored.

In doing so, the *Franklin*'s mainmast carried away, the heavy spar tearing up running gear and standing rigging as it crashed to the deck, leaving a tangle of broken gear and splintered wood. The crew stripped the usable rigging and sails from the shattered mast and pulled the stump from its step in the keelson. Then men from both *Franklin* and *Hancock* landed on the wooded, swampy shore in search of a suitable tree for a new mast.

The men walked three-quarters of a mile into the forest and cut down five trees before they found one that would work. They dragged this log, which could not have been less than three feet in diameter and sixty feet long, across ground Selman described as a morass to a place where it could be shaped into a spar.

Making and stepping a new mainmast would have been no easy task on the dock at Beverly, but it had to be considerably more challenging in the wilderness. The men must have used axes, adzes, and planes to shape the raw tree into a finished mast that they floated out to the schooner. They then must have set up sheers on the deck, swayed the mast on board, attached the shrouds, backstays, crosstrees, and mast cap, stepped the mast, rigged the boom and gaff, bent the sails, and sent up the topmast. Still, according to Selman, they were only "detained several days" by the task. Doing all that in the forest of Nova Scotia in so short a time is proof enough that those Marblehead sailors were thorough-going seamen.

Franklin was ready for sea on November 13, and that same day the Americans scooped up another prize. She was the *Speedwell,* commanded by Francis Cory and owned by Jacob Greene and Company of Rhode Island. Once again, despite all evidence to the contrary, Broughton and Selman construed her to be a legitimate prize. Once again they were wrong.

The weather continued stormy and cold, and the men crowded aboard the schooners were on short rations despite the food liberated from captured vessels. The crews were getting restless, eager for action or for anything other than lying at anchor in the Strait of Canso. While still in the strait, the Americans stopped two merchantmen from the island of Jersey off the coast of France, loaded with lumber. Even Broughton and Selman could not construe these ships as legitimate prizes, though they did get from them information that piqued their interest.

The Jerseymen had on board pilots who were "aquainted with the Island St. Johns," now known as Prince Edward Island, just north of Nova Scotia in the Gulf of St. Lawrence. The pilots informed Broughton and Selman that "a number of cannon was there in the fortress and recruiting going on for Quebeck." Broughton considered this significant, though it had nothing to do with the mission he and Selman had been sent to Canada to pursue.

The commodore called his officers together for a council of war. Somewhere to the west of them, General Richard Montgomery and Colonel Benedict Arnold were maneuvering to take Quebec in a pincer movement, while the British were trying desperately to organize a defense from limited resources. The ships' officers decided they "should do essential service by breaking up a nest of recruits intended to be sent against Montgomery."

With that they set sail for the island of St. John, their original orders from the commander-in-chief now completely forgotten.

General George Washington was named commander-in-chief of the Continental Army in June 1775. This 1776 oil-on-canvas portrait by Charles Willson Peale shows the forty-four-year-old Washington in the familiar blue-and-buff uniform that he wore throughout the Revolution. (Courtesy Brooklyn Museum of Art and The Bridgeman Art Library International)

General Thomas Gage as portrayed by John Singleton Copley in 1768. Commander of the British army in America in 1775, Gage was more than ten years Washington's senior and considerably more experienced in military affairs. After nearly twenty years in America, he had a realistic appreciation of his army's delicate situation in Boston even before the battle of Lexington and Concord. He was replaced by General William Howe before the year was out. (Courtesy Yale Center for British Art, Paul Mellon Collection; The Bridgeman Art Library International)

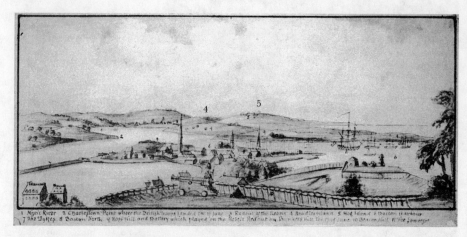

Boston's north end and surrounding hills and islands as seen by the besieged British in 1775. The hilly islands in the center, labeled numbers 4 and 5, are Noddles and Hog islands, where rebel forces burned hay and skirmished with British troops in May 1775. The anchored ship is the *Somerset*, one of the British ships of the line that proved too unwieldy to pursue Washington's nimble schooners through coastal waters. (Courtesy Library of Congress)

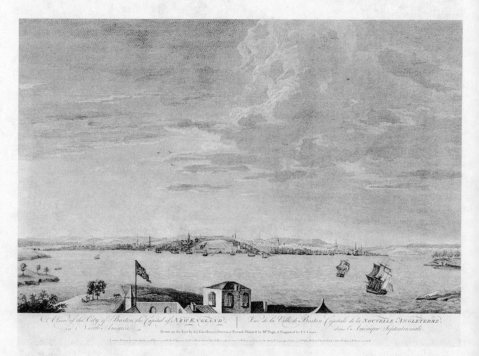

Boston as Washington saw it from Cambridge, looking across the Charles River. The spires of the many churches in the city and the hills that surround Boston on all sides are clearly visible. The open space in the city facing the viewer is Boston Common, where Gage's redcoats pitched their tents and drilled. (Courtesy Library of Congress)

Burnham Tavern is a museum today, but in 1775 it was the central gathering spot for the people of Machias, a small settlement in far eastern Maine, then a district of Massachusetts. When Icabod Jones and Midshipman James Moore arrived in Machias in May 1775 to take on a cargo of firewood and lumber for the British troops in Boston, local patriots gathered at the tavern to plan their resistance. (author photo)

The view eastward today from the head of Beverly Harbor. The tricky shallows and mudflats, such as those in the foreground, helped secure the harbor from British attack and are no doubt responsible for the dredging equipment on the barge to the left. The condominiums beyond the barge sit on Tuck's Point, which defines the easternmost extent of the inner harbor. On the horizon over the end of the point is Great Misery Island. The spit of land in the middle distance to the right is the end of Salem Neck, and on the horizon above it is Baker's Island. (author photo)

John Glover was a member of Marblehead's "codfish aristocracy" and one of the driving forces behind the creation of Washington's schooner fleet. His seafaring troops would ferry Washington's army across the East River during the night of August 29, 1776, in the retreat from the disastrous Battle of Long Island, and across the Delaware River on Christmas night, 1776, for the pivotal attack on Trenton. Glover and his Marbleheaders would participate in some of the fiercest fighting of the war. (Courtesy New York Public Library)

BRIG. GEN. GLOVER

Glover's stately Marblehead home, still a private residence today, befitted his standing as a well-to-do merchant and shipowner, militia officer, and influential member of Marblehead society prior to the American Revolution. (author photo)

Joseph Reed, a Philadelphia lawyer who joined Washington's "family" as the general's secretary, shouldered much of the burden of organizing and running the schooner fleet. Reed was so competent in that and other affairs that after his departure in October 1775 Washington never stopped entreating him to return, which, the following year, he did. (Courtesy National Park Service, Independence Hall Library, Philadelphia)

William Bartlett was a prominent merchant in Beverly, Massachusetts, when he was asked to serve as the Beverly agent for Washington's fleet. He was by far the most active of the several agents, Beverly being the primary port for fitting out the armed schooners and the most secure depository for prizes. (Courtesy Beverly Historical Society and Museum, Beverly, Massachusetts)

A British drawing of Boston and environs showing the disposition of Howe's army in March 1776. North is toward the upper right corner. Noddles and Hog islands are clearly visible to the right, and Dorchester Neck is on the lower left. Off the end of Dorchester Neck's downward crook is fortified Castle Island, to the west and northwest of which mudflats extend almost to Boston itself. The only land access to the city is over the narrow neck on its left. Jutting toward Boston from the top of the drawing is the peninsula on which Charlestown and Bunker's Hill are situated. The village of Cambridge is at the top, left of center. Numerous islands and tricky channels made Boston (and the entire coast of New England) hazardous for mariners who did not possess local knowledge. (Courtesy National Maritime Museum, Greenwich, England)

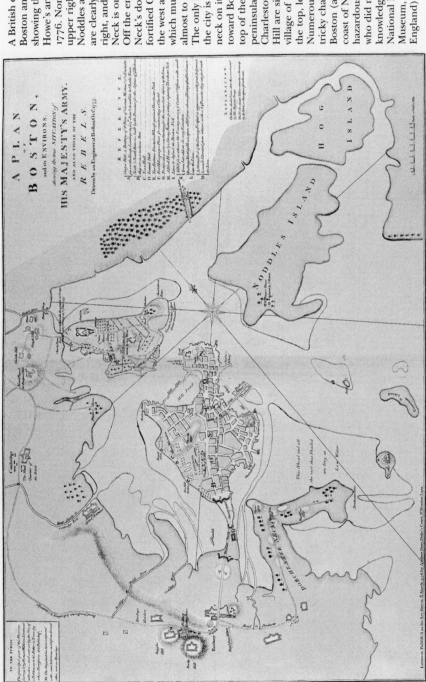

Two of Washington's schooners, *Franklin* and *Lynch*, attack the stragglers of a British merchant convoy bound into Boston. In 1776, under the command of John Manley, the schooners began to hunt as a wolf pack rather than individually. (Courtesy The Mariner's Museum, Newport News, Virginia)

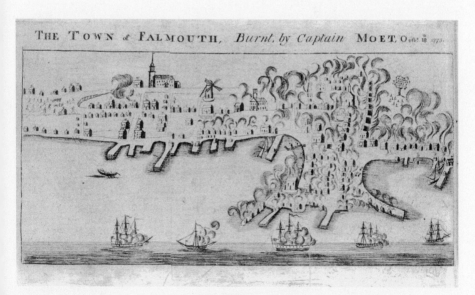

THE TOWN of FALMOUTH, *Burnt, by Captain* MOET, O ct. 18 1775.

Though somewhat cartoonish, this illustration captures the extent of the damage done to Falmouth, Maine, on October 18, 1775, by Lieutenant Henry Mowatt. The destruction of Falmouth was British Admiral Samuel Graves's most aggressive attempt to bring the rebels to heel, but it had the opposite effect, winning more Americans to the rebels' side. (Courtesy Library of Congress)

Marblehead and Beverly have long competed for the honor of "Birthplace of the American Navy," but both claims are open to question. (author photos)

CHAPTER *20* Lee's *Autumn Cruise*

THE SKIES WERE clear and blue, the rich blue of autumn, and the air bracing but not frigid when Captain John Manley cast off from Glover's Wharf in Beverly and let the schooner *Lee* drift out into open water. The decks of the seventy-two-ton schooner were crowded, as were those of all Washington's fleet, no doubt an odd sight to the man on the quarterdeck. Men-of-war always carried outsized crews, whereas merchant captains such as John Manley or Nicholson Broughton were accustomed to seeing no more than five or six men on a vessel the size of *Lee*.

The wind was from the northwest, fair for leaving the harbor. Manley worked the schooner down the narrow channel, setting sail as he went— foresail, fore staysail, jib, mainsail, and the square topsail on the foremast—with the wide Atlantic, his hunting ground, stretching out before him. At the peak of the main gaff a new flag rippled forward in the breeze, showing a green pine tree and the words "Appeal to Heaven" against a white field.

With Winborn Adams tasked to cruise to the northward, Manley set a course toward the southeast, slowly crossing the approaches to Boston Harbor, his lookouts' eyes turned seaward in the hope of spotting gray topsails coming up over the horizon, a glimpse of some unescorted transport sailing straight into their arms. There was one in particular for which Manley's crew kept a weather eye. Reports from Boston indicated that a transport carrying 1,200 barrels of gunpowder was missing. The British feared it had fallen into American hands, but the Americans knew better. If it had not sunk it was out there somewhere, and Manley had been instructed to look out for it—"a glorious prize indeed," Moylan noted.

The winds were light and the weather fair for the next couple of days, but the hunting was poor, and the long-watched-for powder ship never materialized. After a few days of unproductive cruising, Manley continued to the south, standing into Plymouth Harbor on November 1. As he passed the low-lying sandy islands that shielded Plymouth from Cape Cod Bay, he may have enjoyed the amusing sight of the schooner *Harrison* hard aground.

Not until the following day did *Harrison* once again float free. By then the wind had swung into the east and was blowing a fresh gale, and the two men-of-war lay windbound at anchor.

With the departure of Joseph Reed, Stephen Moylan had assumed the post of secretary pro tem for Washington, though his other duties kept him from bringing the kind of unwavering focus to the job that Reed had maintained. Still, he took the post seriously and was soon firing off letters filled with all the urgency and anxiety that had previously marked Reed's letters to him. He was not pleased to hear that Manley was anchored in Plymouth. "I hope *Lee* is out again," he wrote to William Watson.

It had certainly occurred to Washington and Moylan that the schooners were getting a late start, and no doubt they regretted not having organized their fleet earlier. "The Chance of taking Prizes must soon be over for the Advance of the Season," Moylan continued, "therefore the Cruizers should now be in port as little as possible, which you will please to urge to the Gentlemen who command them."

Moylan, more than Washington and Reed, must have understood the realities of keeping the sea or even getting out of a harbor in the stormy fall and winter seasons. But all he had seen thus far from Washington's captains was Nicholson Broughton's less-than-energetic performance in command of *Hannah*, so he understandably felt that vigorous prodding was in order. He did not yet know that John Manley was made of sterner stuff.

Even before Moylan wrote those words to Watson, both Manley and Coit were under way. By November 4 the wind, though still strong, had backed into the north northwest. In the early morning hours Manley was able to run out the channel from Plymouth to Cape Cod Bay, broad reaching with the wind over his larboard quarter, the white Appeal to Heaven ensign snapping at his main gaff. Six hours later, Captain William Coit followed astern.

The two hunters stood out from shore, their bluff bows banging into the chop and flinging spray aft along their raised quarterdecks. Before them was the wide expanse of the bay and the open ocean beyond, a field of deep blue serrated by cresting white water kicked up by the wind.

But the seas were not empty, far from it. Transports, merchant ships, and fishermen—British and American, Tory and Whig—were crowded along the eighty miles of coastline from Cape Cod to Portsmouth, New Hampshire. It was the most active theater in the war, and Washington's ships were sailing to the sound of guns.

Well to the north of *Lee* and *Harrison*, the British frigate *Cerberus* patrolled the waters off the mouth of the Piscataqua River, which formed the border between New Hampshire and the district of Maine. *Cerberus*, named after the three-headed dog of Greek mythology, was the ship that had carried the three generals—Howe, Clinton, and Burgoyne—from England, an irony not lost on wags of the period. Now she was patrolling the New England coast and made a dangerous enemy—fast, powerful, and well commanded.

On November 5, however, she fell victim to the Royal Navy's greatest threat in those waters, navigation. "[A]t 8 standing in for Piscataqua harbor Struck on the Wales Back," the ship's journal recorded, "hoisted the Long Boat out and towed her off."

Before she went aground, her lookouts had spotted a sloop in the distance, and Captain John Symons had dispatched two of the ship's boats, her pinnace and cutter, to chase the quarry down. Five and a half hours later the boats were back with the sloop *Ranger*, her hold full of firewood, as a prize. It was a valuable cargo for the British. The misery and suffering in Boston had only become more acute as the siege dragged on and the weather grew cold. A letter from Boston to England reported, "The inhabitants and troops literally starving with cold. They had taken the pews out of all the places of worship for fuel; had pulled down empty houses, &c., and were then digging up the wharves for firing."

The *Ranger* and her master, William McGlathry, had already been victims of the war for *matériel* being waged in the waters off Massachusetts. *Ranger* had been captured by the British during the summer and taken into Boston, where McGlathry had been forced to sell his cargo of firewood. In order to secure his and his vessel's release, McGlathry had accepted a pass from Admiral Graves to sail to the eastward for another load of wood for Boston. Once free of British hands, however, he had continued to haul wood to Newburyport, Salem, and Marblehead.

As summer turned to fall and the conflict on the water heated up, McGlathry had applied to the Committee of Safety in Salem for a certificate showing that he was supplying the Americans and not the British with wood. Now he was covered on both sides—he had a pass from Graves showing that he worked for the British and a certificate from Timothy Pickering of Salem proving his loyalty to America. Pickering actually encouraged this ruse, telling McGlathry to "retain the pass; that in case he met with a man of war he might destroy his other papers, & use the pass at Boston to save his vessel from condemnation."

Presumably, when McGlathry saw that he would not escape *Cerberus*'s boats, he tossed his American papers overboard, leaving only his pass from Admiral Graves. But Symons, *Cerberus*'s captain, was skeptical. He removed *Ranger*'s American crew save for her master, then placed a midshipman, two marines, four of the *Cerberus*'s sailors, and a pilot from *Canceaux* on board and sent the prize off to Boston. Unfortunately for them, the *Lee* was cruising in their path.

Manley stopped the sloop as she was running for the safety of Graves's fleet in Boston's inner harbor. After determining her status, he put his own prize crew aboard and sent her instead into Marblehead. Stephen Moylan instructed Jonathan Glover, the new prize agent in Marblehead, to "dispose of the wood &c on board on the best terms" and then to lay up the sloop herself until it could be determined whether she was a prize or a recapture.

Like so many of the prizes taken by Washington's fleet, *Ranger* turned into a headache. With ships carrying multiple papers, and with owners and masters of various and sometimes ambiguous loyalties, little about prize taking was clear-cut. Exasperated by questions of how much prize money was due the crew of the *Lee* for *Ranger*'s recapture, Moylan wrote to Jonathan Glover that he, Manley, and McGlathry should work it out "in Such a Manner as the General shall not have any further trouble about her."

A deal was struck, but a few weeks later Timothy Pickering waded into the issue. Prefacing his letter to Washington with "'This with real pain I ask your Excellency's attention (engaged as it is in affairs of such vast importance)," he went on to explain how Glover's demand for one-quarter of the cargo was unfair considering the circumstances of *Ranger*'s recapture. Eventually the matter was settled, but the saga underscored why Washington was so eager for Congress to establish prize courts and so take that particular cup from his hands.

The loss of a shipload of wood was a blow to the British, but it was not the only loss that hit home. A few weeks later, on hearing of the *Ranger*'s retaking, Captain Symons wrote to Admiral Graves complaining of the loss of his men. *Cerberus* was already shorthanded, and Symons had recently sent a number of his crew to the hospital, "four of whom are invalids and totally unfit for Service from old Age and other Infirmities." The loss of the seven-man prize crew would "render the effective Men now on board very short indeed." It was hard for the British military in North America to replace supplies and provisions lost to Washington's fleet, but it was harder still to replace soldiers and sailors.

To add to Symons's troubles, he discovered that the *Cerberus* had lost her false keel from the mainmast aft to the sternpost when she had run aground off the Piscataqua and had sustained further damage upon running aground again in the approaches to Boston Harbor. "Both these Accidents have been entirely through the Blunders of the Pilot," he told Graves.

On the morning Manley captured *Ranger*, His Majesty's armed schooner *Hinchinbrook* was cruising the waters of Cape Cod Bay, with Boston Lighthouse fifteen miles to the west northwest. At 6 A.M. she spotted a schooner and gave chase, crowding on sail and firing away with her 4-pounder carriage guns. But the wind began to fade as the day wore on, and soon the Yankee had the legs on the British schooner, drawing away and out of range.

The *Hinchinbrook*'s journal recorded, "Saw a Number of men on board her & she had three ports of a side." Since the Massachusetts General Court had authorized the creation of privateers only a few days earlier, this armed schooner was almost certainly either *Harrison* or *Lee*, most likely the latter.

Manley bore off to the northward, making again for Beverly and the approaches to Boston (Admiral Graves would write that "*Hinchinbrook* . . . chaced a Pyrate into Salem"). That evening he followed his prize, the *Ranger*, into Marblehead and came to anchor. The weather had been alternately fair and miserable, with vicious storms and freezing rain and spray, and Manley probably saw no point in wearing out his men battling the elements all night when there was no hope of finding a prize in the dark.

Lee resumed her hunt the next morning, cruising the waters around Cape Ann. A cold, driving rain was falling, but the men hauled away on sheets and halyards stiff with ice and set sail for the sea lanes that would put them in the path of ships inbound to Boston. They spent the night cruising around Cape Ann and the next day gave chase to a large ship but were unable to overhaul her.

Later that day, November 8, lookouts on board *Lee* spotted a schooner that appeared to be making for Boston. When *Lee* gave chase, the schooner crowded on sail and headed for shore in an effort to escape. As it stood in toward Marblehead Neck, a cadre of men from Beverly watched the action with more than passing interest.

The men of Beverly had already done a bit of freelancing in the naval line. A few days earlier, two sloops battered by autumn storms had come to anchor in the lee of Great Misery Island, about three miles east of Beverly. "Two Resolute People," William Bartlett reported to Washington, climbed into a boat and made for the vessels. One sloop set sail immediately and escaped, but the other, called the *North Briton*, was "much Torn to peaces in the Gail of Wind." The "resolute people" took her as a prize and sailed her into Beverly.

Bartlett, as prize agent at Beverly, was delighted at first, but his delight faded when it became clear that the captors did not think themselves under his authority. Washington ordered Bartlett to take an accurate inventory of everything on board the *North Briton*, but when he tried, the sloop's captors refused to allow it. Bartlett wrote to Washington seeking advice, "As I am Willing and Desirus to Live in peace with all men."

A few days later, when men from Beverly saw the schooner racing away from *Lee* and toward them, they saw a chance for another prize. Climbing into a boat, they pulled for the fleeing vessel, drew alongside, and swarmed aboard her. She turned out to be the *Two Sisters* out of Ireland, bound for Boston with "Beef, Tongues, Butter, Potatoes and Eggs (all much wanted for the Butchering assassins there)," as the *Boston Gazette* reported.

As with the *North Briton*, the *Two Sisters'* captors refused to recognize Bartlett as prize agent. The added twist this time was that John Manley also claimed her as a prize. Again Bartlett asked for Washington's help, but Washington, who was at that moment attempting to raise an entire army before his current troops' enlistments expired at the end of the year, had other things to worry about. This, he reminded Congress, was exactly why he wanted prize courts established.

Washington, via Moylan, suggested that Bartlett turn over the whole mess to the Massachusetts Committee of Safety, which in the end Bartlett did. John Manley was apparently angry enough over the incident that he threatened to use the force at his command to take the *Two Sisters* back, or at least there was official concern that he might. Bartlett assured Washington "as to Capt. Manly Using any Voiolent measures to take possession of the schooner from Ireland he has not & Shall Advise him by Your Excellency's Orders not too."

In the end *Two Sisters* would be judged a legitimate prize for Manley and the men of *Lee*, but by then another capture had made them by far the most famous sailors in the thirteen colonies.

The Prizes of Hancock *and* Franklin

On November 7, as Manley and the *Lee* were sailing from Beverly Harbor to continue their hunt, the schooners *Prince William* and *Mary*, captured by Broughton and Selman, arrived there from Nova Scotia. Even Ashley Bowen knew right away that they were not legitimate prizes. "Captain Broughton and Selman have sent two of our own vessels into Beverly," he wrote in his journal.

The next day, the day Manley chased the *Two Sisters* into Beverly, the *Phoebe* arrived under the command of her prize captain, Sergeant Benjamin Doak. Washington was about to receive his first indication of what his captains in Canada were up to.

One of the decisions Washington had reached with the three-man Congressional delegation a few weeks prior was that crews of unarmed merchant vessels would not be treated as prisoners of war. The crews from the *Prince William* and *Mary* were accordingly discharged on condition they could obtain a bondsman's assurance that they would not leave the Marblehead area, "least they give information to the Enemy of the Destination of Captains Broughton and Sellman."

The schooners themselves would be laid up in port until their disposition could be decided. A few days later Washington wrote another in his series of pleas to John Hancock and Congress: "Should not a Court be established by Authority of Congress, to take Cognizance of the Prizes made by Continental Vessels?" Unsure whether the front-door approach through Hancock would get results, he tried Congress's back door too. "I should be very glad if Congress would, without delay, appoint some mode by which an examination into the captures made by our armed vessels may be had," he wrote to his friend Richard Henry Lee, "as we are rather groping in the dark till this happens."

Both Washington and the Continental Congress were new to the ways of naval warfare, and they did not yet realize that prize courts were as crucial to the system as ships and guns. But Washington was figuring it out.

Overwhelmed as they were, Washington and his staff had little time to deal with captured vessels. Not until December 2 was Moylan able to examine *Phoebe*'s papers and determine that "it does not appear, that Captain Broughton has good Reasons for making Seizure of her." A few days before, a letter had arrived for Washington from Nicholas Cooke of Rhode Island, assuring the commander-in-chief that James Aborn, owner of the *Phoebe*, was a "Friend to the Liberties of his Country." That same day Washington ordered the vessel released.

On December 19 it was finally decided that neither the *Prince William* nor the *Mary*, Broughton and Selman's first two prizes, were legitimate captures. Washington sent orders to Jonathan Glover in Marblehead to deliver the vessels to their owners.

The *Warren*, whose captain, John Denny, and the man named Buddington, owner of the cargo, had been condemned for not objecting to Broughton's calling Americans "pumpkins," never made it to Beverly. She was blown south and made landfall at last in Stonington, Connecticut. Moylan wrote to the Stonington Committee of Safety to ask that they look into the case and determine the legitimacy of the prize.

The Stonington Committee did not pass the buck as other committees of safety routinely did, but neither did they race to comply. Not until January 8, 1776, long after Broughton and Selman were out of the picture, did they make their decision. The committee carefully questioned all the people on board the *Warren* concerning the character of Denny and Buddington, "who, for some Reasons weare suspected of being tory-istical." They did not find the men guilty of any unpatriotic deeds or motives and restored the vessel and cargo to their rightful owners.

During his short career, Broughton had managed to capture a vessel owned by a member of the Continental Congress, and he would, before he was done, take a brig owned by one of Salem's most ardent patriots. But the *Speedwell,* the fifth prize taken in Nova Scotia, would be his crowning achievement.

Speedwell arrived at Cape Ann in late November. After examining her papers, Robert Hanson Harrison, another of Washington's secretaries, wrote to William Bartlett that Washington did not consider the vessel a prize and that "he does not wish to have any Thing to do with her. . . . It appears that the Vessel belongs to General Greene and he will dispose of her as he shall think proper." Broughton had captured a sloop owned by one of the brightest rising stars in Washington's officer corps, General Nathanael Greene.

Not only did Broughton and Selman fail to enrich themselves and their men with prize money, the Committee of Safety in Gloucester would later decide that the two men should pay over a hundred pounds to the *Speedwell*'s owners for loss of cargo and damage to the vessel.

As November drew to a close, Washington had only the vaguest idea what Broughton and Selman were up to, despite their having been given explicit instructions on how to carry out a mission that was his highest priority. He had only two rather odd letters from the commodore—letters that suggested a willful disregard of orders—and five ships sent in as prizes, not one of them legitimate. His correspondence with Hancock made clear that he was growing concerned.

If he had known what Broughton and Selman were really up to, he would have been apoplectic.

CHAPTER *21* *"The blundering Captn Coit"*

RETURNING TO Plymouth from Rhode Island with his hard-won cannon, Ephraim Bowen was certainly unhappy to find the *Harrison* aground. He was probably even less happy to discover that this was the second time she had gone aground since his departure.

Captain William Coit and his crew of fifty had marched from Cambridge on October 24, arriving in Plymouth sometime after Bowen had given up waiting for them and left for Bristol. Coit found the *Harrison*, his new command, floating at the dock, fitted out with four 4-pounders and ten swivels. Her sides were painted black and her bottom tallowed, likely with sulfur mixed in as an antifouling agent, to give her the extra turn of speed that was required for her business.

She carried long oars, or sweeps, to move her in light air, a precaution that would ultimately be her salvation. The square topsails of her fore- and mainmasts were an addition that signaled her transformation from merchantman to man-of-war, as was the "Appeal to Heaven" flag at her main gaff. She was ready for sea, while nearby, carpenters and riggers swarmed over the *Washington*. Despite the attention, Martindale's vessel still had a long way to go.

The *Harrison* may have been fitted out, but Coit was not overly impressed with what he saw. Despite the recommendations of supposedly knowledgeable and disinterested Plymouth mariners, he found her "old & weak," but he was still willing to take her in harm's way. With fresh breezes out of the northwest, Coit cast off and set sail, his scarlet cloak snapping around his legs. Standing by his shoulder, aft on the quarterdeck, was a local pilot taken on board to navigate *Harrison* through the tricky sandbars around Plymouth Harbor. But the navigation proved too tricky even for an expert. The schooner had sailed no more than half a mile when she drove her bow deep into a sandbar, thanks to the "Stupidity & Unskilfulness of the Pilot."

Coit dashed off a note to Reed informing him of the accident and pointing out *Harrison*'s deficiencies. At the time Reed was negotiating with Major Benjamin Tupper, who had captured a schooner and a brig at Martha's Vineyard. Reed hoped to have Tupper take the vessels to Plymouth and fit them out as additions to Washington's fleet. Reed told Coit he could have one of those provided he could, with no loss of time, shift his guns and crew into her. But, he added, "we rather wish you should proceed in the *Harrison* as she is fitted out and sails well."

Reed wrote to Ephraim Bowen as well, mentioning the accident and stating pointedly, "We wonder we did not hear from you or Martindale by the Return of this Messenger." But of course Bowen and Martindale were still in Rhode Island, where Bowen, at least, was conducting the army's business as expeditiously as he could.

William Watson sent a note to Reed on October 30 saying that Captain Coit in the *Harrison* would be ready to sail that afternoon. He also said the *Washington* would sail in two or three days "provided Capts Martendal & Bowen can procure the Cannon & get them from Bristol in season." This was the first Reed had heard of the two men having left for Rhode Island.

The nasty weather that plagued Ephraim Bowen on his journey also kept the *Harrison* in harbor for a few days. Not until October 31 or November 1 did she once again get under way, standing boldly out to sea. Coit on his quarterdeck was likely anticipating the devastation he would wreak upon British shipping when once again the *Harrison* ran hard aground. It was in that compromised position that Ephraim Bowen found Coit upon his return to Plymouth ahead of *Washington*'s guns. Even more embarrassing, it was where John Manley found him when *Lee* ducked into Plymouth after cruising from Beverly.

By the next day *Harrison* was floating again, but now strong gales and driving rain, followed by easterly winds, kept her and *Lee* bottled up in harbor. The rain also slowed work on *Washington*, which in any event was going much slower than anyone had imagined. Watson had predicted she would be ready to sail in the first few days of the month, but on November 2 Martindale wrote to Reed that he imagined he "Shall be Ready to sail this day week at Fartherest."

Martindale's vision had not dimmed. "[I]n regard to the Vessel She Is very Suitable for the Business & think that A hundred or Eighty Men at Least is no more then a Common Complement," he informed Reed, "as I Flatter myself I shall be Able to Give a Good Acco of her." Along with the eighty men, Martindale asked for "A Drum and Fifer as the Other Priverteers are Equipped with them."

The letter was received not by Joseph Reed, who had returned to Philadelphia, but by Stephen Moylan, who reiterated to Watson that the commander-in-chief was concerned about Martindale's ambitious plans. "[T]he Intention of fitting out these Vessels, is not to attack the Armed, but to take the unarmed Vessels, which Captain Martindale seems to have lost Sight of." He informed Watson that the cartridges for *Washington*'s guns were being made up, and that eighty men from Nathanael Greene's Rhode Island regiment would be sent to man the ship. "I don't know the use of a Drum & Fife on Board, nor do I imagine that any of the other Vessels have got them," he added, "but if it will give Captain Martindale any Pleasure he shall be indulged with them."

The growing cold and deteriorating weather were causing increased anxiety in Cambridge. Washington decided against fitting out the two vessels captured at Martha's Vineyard because of the "advancing Season of the Year & the difficulty in procuring Cannon." With a third of their fleet apparently freelancing in Canada, Washington and his aides were anxious that their other commissioned ships snatch up all the prizes they could while the season permitted. Moylan expressed his hope that Manley in *Lee* and Coit in *Harrison* had sailed from Plymouth.

By the time Moylan penned those lines, both vessels had indeed managed to get to sea. Coit weighed anchor for the third time and stood for the entrance to Plymouth Harbor, and for the third time he ran the *Harrison* aground. He had apparently learned not to hit the bottom so hard, however, and by evening the schooner was floating again and had cleared the sandy shores of Plymouth to make her way into the open water of Cape Cod Bay.

Not long after the *Harrison* had left Plymouth astern, her lookouts spotted two small vessels in the offing. Coit closed on them, his 4-pounders loaded and ready behind their newly cut gunports. The vessels turned out to be the sloop *Polly* and the schooner *Industry* (both popular ship names in the latter half of the eighteenth century). Both were from Nova Scotia, bound for Boston, and both were loaded with exactly the sorts of things so desperately needed in the besieged city.

Polly carried twenty cords of firewood, seven horned cattle, eight sheep, and fifteen hogs along with potatoes, turnips, hay, fish, cheese, butter, and sundry fowl. *Industry* carried another twenty cords of wood along with livestock and vegetables. As with so many of the prizes taken by Washington's fleet, the captured goods made a nice addition to the Americans' supplies but, more to the point, were a dire loss to the British in Boston.

According to one account, Coit did not miss the opportunity to have some fun. "Capt. Coit (a humorous genius)," wrote a correspondent in Roxbury, "made the prisoners land on the same rock our ancestors first trode when they landed in America, where they gave three cheers, and wished success to American arms."

Harrison's lieutenant, Henry Champion, was dispatched to Cambridge to carry the good news to headquarters. Unfortunately he managed to quash any enthusiasm Washington might have felt by accidentally spilling candle wax on a letter the commander-in-chief was about to send to Joseph Reed. "I had just finished my Letter when a blundering Lieutt, of the blundering Captn Coit, who just blunderd upon two Vessels for Nova Scotia . . . pickd up a Candle, & sprinkled it with Grease." This was certainly an unfair characterization of the first captain in his fleet to make an unambiguous capture of two enemy supply vessels. Washington added, "but these are [the] kind of Blunders which one can easily excuse."

Unfortunately, Coit's brief cruise revealed a problem with *Harrison* that went beyond age and weakness. "Capt Coits mainmast Proves too rotten for the Service," Bowen reported the day Coit returned with his prizes, adding that he had "got another making so don't expect he will Sail again until tomorrow night."

Having had a sea trial in *Harrison*, Coit thought even less of her, and he expressed his opinion in his inimitable style to his friend Major Samuel B. Webb, aide-de-camp to General Israel Putnam:

> To see me strutting about on the quarter-deck of my schooner!—for she has a quarter-deck—Ah, and more than that too—4 four pounders, brought into this country by the company of Lords Say and Seal, to Saybrook when they first came [1635]. A pair of cohorns that Noah had in the Ark; one of which lacks a touch-hole, having hardened steel drove therein, that she might not be of service to Sir Edmund Andros

[1687]—Six swivels, the first that were landed at Plymouth, and never fired since.

Coit was being disingenuous about the cohorn's touch-hole. It might at one point have been without one, but an October 12 bill for *Harrison* includes the item "Drilling new touch hole in Cowhorn."

The guns, Coit told Webb, were his plague, but the ship herself was his comfort:

My schooner is used to the business, for she was launched in the spring of 1761, and has served two regular apprenticeships to sailing, and sails quick, being *used to it*. Her accommodations are fine; five of us in the cabin, and when there, are obliged to stow spoon fashion. Besides she has a chimney in it, and the smoke serves for bedding, victuals, drink and choking. She has one mast too, which is her foremast; she had a main-mast, but it was put in so long ago, that it has rotted off in the hounds. She has a deck, too. When it was first made it was new; and because it was ashamed of being old, the first time we made use of a clawed handspike, it broke a hole through; notwithstanding, the wench knew it was directly over the magazine.

Coit suggested that if peace came, the ship should be given to the Royal Society, and he promised to eat a red-hot gridiron if they had ever seen a curiosity to equal her. He told Webb she would do very well as long as they were going after unarmed vessels, but "if obliged to fire both guns of a side at a time, it would split her open from her gunwale to her keelson." (According to Coit's friend Joseph Williams, Coit promised Washington that, if given a fourteen-gun ship, "he will Answer his Expec-tations, or he will Stand at North Pole to All Eternity." The statement was "a high Expression," Williams said in a letter to a mutual friend, "but you know it to be his Language.")

While *Harrison* was getting her new mast fitted and *Washington* was having her bottom cleaned, the crew for Martindale's ship was rousted out of camp and sent off to Plymouth. Dr. John Manvide, a French sur-geon who had volunteered to sail aboard *Washington*, wrote in his jour-nal, "On the 8 November we left Prospect Hill at 4 o'clock in the afternoon with 80 men, arms and baggage to go to Plymouth, where the Brig was." They arrived at Plymouth three days later only to find their ship not even close to being ready for sea.

On November 13 *Harrison* sailed on her second cruise, but *Washington* was still fitting out. Two days had been lost to driving rain, which stopped any work from taking place. On the third Sunday in November Bowen wrote in his journal, "Nothing done, could get no Carp^{rs} to Work." The Plymouth carpenters seemed to have caught the same religious fervor that prevented the Beverly men from working on Sundays.

Well over a month after work on *Washington* had begun and two weeks after *Harrison* was ready for sea, Moylan wrote to Watson beseeching, "shall we ever hear of Captain Martindale's Departure?" But the brigantine was at last close to sailing. "I expected long before this, to have Capt Martindale Out on his Cruise," Bowen wrote to headquarters, "but the Weather is extremely bad, for a Fortnight past we have not been able to do any thing of consequence."

By November 17 the guns, water, and provisions were all stowed in *Washington*'s hold, her crew was on board, and she was ready to sail. The next day Ephraim Bowen left Plymouth and rode north to Cambridge. His work with Washington's fleet was done.

The Charlottetown Raid

While William Coit, John Manley, and Winborn Adams were still a week from getting their ships to sea, and Sion Martindale was certain he would be getting under way at any time, Nicholson Broughton and John Selman were lying at anchor in the Strait of Canso contemplating their next move.

The intelligence provided by the pilots off the Jersey vessels concerning St. John's Island (now Prince Edward Island) was correct, at least to a point. The old fort at Charlottetown did indeed have cannons, and a recruiting party sent to the island the previous summer by General Gage had indeed rounded up a few men for the defense of Quebec. But that recruiting effort had ended long before the Americans got wind of it.

The talkative pilots were set on board the *Hancock* and *Franklin* and ordered to navigate the schooners through the strait. As incentive they were advised that if they ran the schooners aground, "death to them would be inevitable." The wind hauled around southerly, fair for the Americans to run north through the narrow strait past plunging cliffs and shorelines covered in tall, virgin pine, Nova Scotia to the west, Cape

Breton Island to the east. They made the transit without mishap, the pilots behaving "true and honest," and forged north through St. George's Bay.

From there they could have ridden the southerly wind north to the mouth of the St. Lawrence River, where they had been ordered to go, but that seems not even to have been considered. Broughton and Selman had abandoned any pretense of following even the spirit of Washington's orders. They were acting entirely on their own.

Instead the two schooners bore off to the west through the Northumberland Strait, between Nova Scotia and St. John's Island. On November 17 they stood into Hillsborough Bay on the island's southeast coast. Charlottetown, the capital of St. John's Island, was situated at the head of the bay. With men in the forechains heaving the lead lines and calling depths back to the quarterdeck, the raiders felt their way toward the town.

Charlottetown was a small settlement, home to around 425 people at the time. It had been made the capital of St. John's in 1765, and three years later the land was surveyed and a town of five hundred building lots laid out. Governor Walter Patterson had arrived in 1770 to assume political control of the island, and for the next five years things were relatively peaceful.

As it happened, Governor Patterson missed one of the most significant events in the island's history. The previous August he had sailed for England on an extended leave, and the administration of the island had fallen to Phillip Callbeck, the oldest member of the local council, who referred to himself as "commander in Chief of the Island St John." Second in command was Thomas Wright, a justice of the peace and one of the men who had surveyed and laid out Charlottetown. They would soon have reason to regret their governor's absence.

The *Hancock* and *Franklin* came to anchor a mile and a half from the shore. Boats were swayed over the schooners' sides, and armed shore parties clambered down the boarding ladders and settled on thwarts. Armed with pistols, cutlasses, tomahawks, and muskets, the Marbleheaders prepared to storm ashore and take possession of the town.

Unfortunately the schooners carried one boat apiece, and those two were ridiculously small for men-of-war, thirteen or fourteen feet long and able to accommodate only six men at a time. Most naval vessels of the time carried a number of boats, including a launch large enough to land troops sufficient for just the sort of action Broughton and Selman were staging. But the crowded conditions of the schooners likely precluded carrying more or larger boats, and Glover and Moylan had certainly not anticipated the sort of invasion now being launched against the surprised village of Charlottetown.

The six men Selman loaded into his boat included the pilot, who could hardly be counted on to fight for the American cause. Broughton loaded six into his boat as well, and they set off. Selman pulled to the northward while Broughton headed southwest, their plan being to trap the town's defenders between two "columns" of five men each.

The arrival of the "two large Schooners belonging to Marblehead" caused a certain amount of consternation in the town, particularly as no one knew what they were up to. "Not having heard that the Rebellious Colony's had fitted out Privateers, I Judged them to be Pirates," Callbeck wrote, and "by their Conduct they were actually such."

When it became apparent that the newcomers' intentions were hostile, panic spread through Charlottetown. Riders were sent off to warn the island's other communities and no doubt to call for men to march to the town's aid. Callbeck, as acting governor, took it upon himself to defend his community. Luckily for Broughton, Selman, and their anemic landing party, however, the "commander in Chief of the Island St John" had no troops to command. "In order to preserve the Town from being burn'd," Callbeck later reported, "I determin'd (not having force of any Kind to make Resistance:) to face them singly."

When Selman's boat pulled up to the town landing, Callbeck and Wright were on shore to greet him with "a very Civil reception." The pilot in Selman's boat gave Selman a sign indicating which of the men was the acting governor. Selman and his armed sailors swarmed ashore and grabbed Callbeck as well as John Budd, the Clerk of the Court. Callbeck asked to be allowed to go to his home before being confined, but Selman refused, and, according to Callbeck, "one of the party insultingly without any provocation struck him." Callbeck and his clerk were taken out to the *Franklin* and held on board the anchored ship.

The only detailed accounts of what happened next come from the pens of Callbeck, Wright, and Budd, who might be expected to harbor resentment and bias and perhaps to have shaded their stories. Certainly their rhetoric was calculated to inspire outrage. Callbeck's report to Lord Dartmouth, the American Secretary in London, was likely written in the hope of extracting some compensation for his loss. It began, "persecuted allmost to ruin in the Service of my Sovereign, I shall take the liberty to trouble Your Lordship with a tale of woe, which can best be felt by a Heart like Yours."

Nearly forty years after the event, when Selman wrote an account of his cruise with Broughton, he somehow failed to mention the worst of the Marbleheaders' behavior. Nonetheless, if Callbeck's, Wright's, and Budd's accounts are true—and other sources suggest that they are—the Americans' behavior was outrageous indeed. Even those aspects of the raid that are not in dispute are enough to condemn Broughton and Selman for a barbarous assault.

Having taken possession of Charlottetown without opposition, the American captains began to improvise a plan. Selman sent a message to Callbeck aboard the *Franklin* demanding keys to the town's storehouses. Callbeck sent the keys back with his clerk, along with a request that he, Callbeck, "might attend and open the doors of such places as the Captains choose to inspect."

But Selman was not interested in Callbeck's help. He and Broughton opened one of the storehouses and found it filled with woolen goods and sundry other items. Commodore Broughton called his officers to another council of war to decide if those articles were there to aid the recruiting effort, and, not surprisingly, the officers decided that they were. According to Selman, the articles in the storehouse "were taken and sent on board Broughton's vessel and mine."

Having emptied the storehouses, the Americans proceeded to loot Callbeck's home. In an account of the attack written to George Washington, the Charlottetown men reported:

> [T]hey went into Mr Callbeck's dwelling house where they examined all his private papers and broke the Bed chamber's Closets and cellar doors open though they had all the Keys. In Mrs Callbeck's bed room they broke open her drawers and Trunks scatter'd her Cloaths about read her Letters from her mother and Sister's, took the Bed and window curtains, also the Bed & bedding, and they or some of the party took Mrs Callbecks Rings Bracelets Buckles and Trinkets, also some of their Cloaths. After

which they took the parlour window Curtains looking Glasses Carpets and
several articles of plate.

Having finished upstairs, the Marbleheaders moved on to the pantry,
where they took vinegar, oil, candles, sweetmeats, ham, and bacon as
well as wine, porter, rum, and sundry other bottles and casks, save for
one barrel of wine "which they stove the head in and drank the whole
out." They then moved on to the councilman's office, taking furniture,
clothing, and shoes as well as the fifty-nine-ounce silver seal of the province and Governor Patterson's commission.

Callbeck's report to Lord Dartmouth was considerably more lurid
and sensational than the account he sent to Washington. In his letter to
Dartmouth he wrote, "These unfeeling Monsters, not satiated with their
flagitious Depredations of the whole of my Property, & the common
Rights of Mankind, blood-thirstily sought Mrs Callbeck for the purpose
(to use their own Words:) of cutting her throat, because she is the
Daughter of a Mr Coffin at Boston, who is remarkable for his attatch-
ment to Government."

Callbeck could not know this firsthand, of course, because he was
locked up aboard *Franklin* at the time, and the pregnant Mrs. Ann Coffin Callbeck was at the family farm four miles away and never encountered the Americans. Perhaps the Marbleheaders who stood guard over
the acting governor were taunting him, but it is unlikely that Broughton
at his worst would have countenanced the murder of a young woman,
regardless of whose daughter she was.

Having finished with Callbeck's house, the Marbleheaders broke into
the unoccupied home of Governor Patterson and looted it in the same
fashion. Around that time Selman learned that Thomas Wright, as justice of the peace, was the man who had actually sworn in the recruits for
Quebec. "[T]o keep pace with their barbarity Captain Selmon order'd
his party to go in and to take Mr Wright from the arms of his Wife and
Sister," Wright himself reported to Washington, "and insultingly smiled
at the Tears and Lamentations of Women who were in the greatest
distress."

Wright was bundled off to the *Franklin*, where he joined Callbeck. The
two men raised a howl of protest at the treatment they were receiving,
certain the Americans could not have orders to do what they were doing.

By way of justifying their actions, Broughton and Selman read Washington's instructions to Callbeck and Wright, which served only to prove how self-deluded they had become, a fact the prisoners picked up on immediately. As Callbeck and Wright later pointed out to Washington, "they were not directed to go to the Island, and . . . your Excellency had particularly cautioned them not to abuse private property."

The two Canadians continued to argue their case, pointing out that Broughton and Selman were not "in any respect conformed to their instructions." They begged to be returned to their families, but the Americans would not relent, making clear, rather, that their intention was to take the men off as prisoners. Selman would later claim that they were taken for possible exchange should Montgomery or some other high-ranking American officer be taken prisoner at Quebec, but that has the feel of a rationale made up long after the fact.

Finally Callbeck and Wright asked to be allowed to spend the night ashore. Selman was opposed to the idea, but Broughton allowed it. It was likely during their night at home that they surveyed and inventoried the damage and pilfering that had taken place. To Selman's surprise, the two men returned the following morning and gave themselves up as prisoners.

At some point during the raid, the Americans inspected the cannons at the fort. Much as they would have liked to deliver the guns to the ordnance-starved Continental Army, it was not logistically feasible. The cannon barrels could not have weighed less than a ton apiece, and the Americans had only their little fourteen-foot boats in which to move them. What's more, with the alarm spreading around the island, they felt their hold on the town was tenuous. In the end they settled for spiking the guns and leaving them there.

The morning after arriving off Charlottetown, the two schooners weighed anchor and headed back the way they had come, their holds stuffed with loot and their prisoners secured. Callbeck estimated the value of the stolen property at "the amount of two thousand pounds sterling."

On November 20 the *Franklin* and *Hancock* once again anchored off Canso. Wright and Callbeck saw this as their last chance. From Canso it would be easy to get back to Charlottetown, but if they were carried to the American colonies they would have little chance of returning before spring. They appealed to Broughton and Selman, pointing out that Mrs. Callbeck was "left destitute of every support, also between 70 and 80 people who [were] lately arrived on the Island and depended on Mr Callbeck for their support during the Winter will in all probability starve." They also pointed out once more that the captains had not only exceeded but ignored their orders and "should be blamed by the Government."

Broughton and Selman were unmoved. Wright told Selman, "if we come acrost a Brittish Frigate I will have you hung to the yard arm," but threats had no more effect than appeals for sympathy.

Also anchored at Canso were several merchant vessels, and Broughton and Selman ordered the ships' masters to report on board the *Hancock* with their papers. After examining the cargo and destination of each vessel, they determined that one, the *Lively*, bound from England to Charlottetown with forty tubs of butter, was a legitimate prize. The others were let go, but only after Broughton and Selman took the opportunity to spread some disinformation. They told the merchant captains that the New England schooners had taken twenty-two prizes so far and that a twenty-two-gun American ship was patrolling between Canso and St. John's Island.

Hancock and *Franklin* had been under way nearly a month. The weather was cold, the ships were crowded, and food was running low. The men were no doubt worn down from battling the constant storms that swept over their small vessels. It was time to head for home.

CHAPTER 22 *Convoys and Cruisers*

ON NOVEMBER 8 the *Charming Nancy*, bearing a company of artillery for Boston, made landfall off Cape Ann. She had sailed from England two months earlier in a small convoy with the ordnance storeships *Williamson, Nancy,* and *Juno,* under the protection of the forty-four-gun *Phoenix.* In the manner of convoys, however, the ships had become increasingly scattered as they fought their way across the stormy Atlantic. *Charming Nancy* had not seen *Phoenix* since October 21.

The weather was terrible, "Dirty rainy Mornng with a Very cold wind from the Northward," as *Charming Nancy* felt her way toward the rocky coast in poor visibility. Finally, as the weather cleared, the transport's captain made the long climb to the head of the ship's main topmast. From there he was able to see the low gray shoreline of Massachusetts and the two lighthouses at Cape Ann and Thacher Island.

He soon saw more than that. "[S]aw two sail ahead, but could not be certain what they were," the ship's journal recorded. A vast amount of shipping was moving through the area, and the *Charming Nancy*'s master was certainly aware that the waters in which he was sailing might be crawling with armed American vessels, cruising for prizes like the ship he commanded.

Even more valuable than *Charming Nancy* was the ordnance storeship *Williamson,* which had managed to remain with *Charming Nancy* for the entire crossing and was now exchanging signals with her. *Charming Nancy* was carrying the men of an artillery company, but *Williamson* was carrying ordnance stores, guns, gunpowder, shot, flints, muskets, and other items that were desperately needed in Washington's camp. The other two ordnance storeships, *Juno* and *Nancy,* carrying cargoes similar to *Williamson*'s, had not been seen for weeks.

With strange sails in the offing, the men of the *Charming Nancy* made ready to defend themselves. "Our 4 Pieces of Cannon were loaded with

Grape shot, and order'd our Men to be ready on the 1st Notice in Case they should offer to attack us." There was no doubt a sense of relief aboard the transport when the distant sails altered course away from the ordnance vessels, but still the men stood to their guns, "Hammocks lashed on the Quarter Deck . . . match lighted, ten Rounds of Cartridges Each Man, & the 2 Companys with their Arms on Each side of the Deck." Later that evening two more vessels could be seen making for Boston. One they thought they recognized as their escort, the *Phoenix*, which they had not seen for eighteen days.

As evening came on, lookouts aboard *Charming Nancy* saw yet another sail, one that caused real alarm on the transport's crowded decks. "Saw a large schooner and as we supposed belonging to the Provintials bear down on us." *Charming Nancy* put up her helm and closed with the unarmed *Williamson* to protect the ordnance brig's valuable cargo.

Had the merchant captains known for certain who the schooner was, they might have been even more alarmed. She was the *Lee*, under John Manley's command, cruising the waters around Cape Ann. Ashley Bowen reported that Manley had sailed on November 7 and had "chased a large ship from Cape Ann above the Graves [ledges in the outer approaches to Boston Harbor] before she gave over the chase."

If Manley had known that the *Williamson* was stuffed with exactly the cargo Washington most dreamed of, he would no doubt have been more aggressive in his pursuit. But all he saw were two vessels, each bigger and, in the case of *Charming Nancy*, more powerful than his own. He broke off the chase and headed for open water.

While *Charming Nancy* and *Williamson* were struggling to make their way down the coast to safety, the *Phoenix* came to anchor in Boston Harbor, and her captain, Hyde Parker, reported to Admiral Graves. The admiral was not happy to learn that the valuable convoy from England had been scattered and that the vessels, particularly the ordnance transports, were arriving piecemeal and without protection. Feeling that ships "droping in singly and unaquainted might be in Danger of the Rebel Cruizers," he dispatched the twenty-gun frigate *Mercury* to cruise for the remnants of the fleet and see them safely into Boston.

Working his way down the treacherous New England coast, *Charming Nancy*'s master decided as night came on to lay to under bare poles for fear of running aground in the dark. The next morning he got under way again, his bow turned toward Boston Harbor, the crew and passengers still under arms and ready to defend their ship and the *Williamson*. Around 8:30 A.M. a boat approached with a pilot Admiral Graves had sent to take them into Boston.

By eleven o'clock that morning the ships were anchored in Nantasket Roads, the wind having failed, but they were not yet out of danger. Once the wind filled in again they weighed anchor and set sail but were met by a boat from one of the men-of-war, which alerted them to the presence of "above 40 Whale boats waiting behind the Hills with 400 Rebels to attack us." Happily they could see the frigate *Mercury* in the distance, so they lay to and "all got under Arms in Order for the Attack," until the man-of-war could come up with them and escort them the rest of the way to Boston.

With *Mercury* close by, *Charming Nancy* and *Williamson* stood toward Boston. The whaleboats dispersed at the sight of the frigate, and from *Charming Nancy*'s deck they could see "only a few Stragling boats."

That day, November 9, was one of intense activity in the seas off the coast of Massachusetts. Ashley Bowen noted, "This morning passed three ships for Boston. Some rain. At noon passed twenty-eight sail more for Boston." Back on September 21 the twenty-gun frigate *Lively* had been ordered to escort a convoy of ships to Penobscot Bay, Maine, to load desperately needed firewood. Now, a month and a half later, they were back, twenty-one ships in all, a crowd of gray sails covering the horizon, standing in past the scattering of islands in Boston Harbor, their holds crammed with firewood from forests to the east.

It was just the sort of sight that drove George Washington to distraction. After all the aggravation he had endured fitting out his vessels, this massive fleet was sailing unmolested right up to the Boston docks. That day Washington's secretary, Robert Hanson Harrison, wrote to John Glover with further prodding from the commander-in-chief: "There are many Transports from England & Ireland arriving every Day at Boston: should any of the armed Vessels be in your Port, you will please to order them out to Sea immediately."

Hoping to motivate his captains by appealing to the piratical avarice that Washington now understood formed a large part of the Yankee sailor's character, Harrison added, "Every Hour they remain in Port may be a Loss to them of a good Prize."

In fact the convoy had not passed Cape Ann unnoticed. Jonathan Glover, Washington's Marblehead agent, wrote that "Capt Manly was Doging the fleet of Ships that whent into Boston Last Night But was kept of By the *Lively*, Ship of war." Despite the seemingly easy pickings, the well-handled frigate managed to keep the American schooner at bay.

Late that afternoon the *Charming Nancy* and the *Williamson* worked their way into Boston's crowded harbor and came to anchor. Sixty days out of England, they were safe at last amid the men-of-war of the North American Squadron.

One question at least was answered for them. "One of the Ships we saw Yesterday Evening was the *Phenix*," the *Charming Nancy*'s journal recorded, "& the other the *Juno*, An Ordnance Storeship." With the *Williamson* now arrived under *Charming Nancy*'s protection, two of the three ordnance storeships with their hugely valuable cargoes were accounted for.

The *Nancy*, however, was still at sea.

"Our Rascally privateers-men"

As November dragged on, Washington grew exasperated with his fleet. Nearly three months had passed since he had come around to the idea of arming vessels and had set that scheme in motion, and thus far he had little to show beyond a near-constant stream of aggravation. He was learning as well about the touchy, defensive nature of sailors before the mast. He wrote to Joseph Reed, "Our Rascally privateers-men, go on at the old rate, Mutinying if they can not do as they please. those at Plymouth, Beverly, & Portsmouth, have done nothing worth mentioning in the Prize way & no Accts are yet recd from those further Eastward."

In Canada, where another of Washington's initiatives was unfolding, the situation was more fluid. Richard Montgomery had advanced from New York across Lake Champlain to the St. Lawrence River and was surrounding Montreal. Meanwhile, 150 miles downriver, Benedict Arnold had reached the walls of Quebec after a heroic march through the Maine woods only to find his column too decimated by starvation and desertion to launch an effective attack. Now Arnold was camped outside the walled city, waiting for Montgomery to reinforce him.

Ever restless to move things forward, Washington issued an order on November 16 that would change the entire situation around Boston. He instructed twenty-five-year-old artillery colonel Henry Knox to proceed to New York to procure what artillery could be had there. That done, Knox was to "go to General Schuyler & Get the remainder from Ticonderoga, Crown point [a fortification on the western shore of Champlain], or St Johns [at the northern end of Champlain]." Those words initiated what was—along with Arnold's march to Quebec—one of the epic missions of the American Revolution, and Henry Knox would prove his worth by dragging the big guns over the frozen countryside from Ticonderoga all the way to Framingham and then Cambridge, where they would be turned on their former owners.

In Plymouth, William Coit's men were helping to reinforce Washington's view of Yankee seamen. William Watson, the Plymouth agent, wrote to Stephen Moylan that "Capt Coit has had much difficulty, & is greatly perplexed with an uneasy sett of fellows, who have got sowerd by the severity of the season & are longing for the Leeks & Onions of Connecticut."

It was certainly true that the weather had been miserable that fall, a steady diet of rain and brutal cold. "The Severe cold weather has very much retarded our geting these Vessels to Sea," Watson reported. Around the same time Samuel Graves wrote to Philip Stephens, Secretary of the British Admiralty, "We have had a remarkably wet Autumn, and lately so much blowing Weather, that I fear the Ships coming from England will be roughly handled."

Given the conditions, it is a mark in favor of Coit's men that they did finally put to sea in a ship of dubious integrity. Watson assured Moylan that Coit "has through his difficultys conducted well, I think no man co'd have managed better."

Captain Coit's *Harrison* got under way again on November 23, and, incredibly, Martindale's *Washington* was with her. More than a month after Ephraim Bowen had begun the conversion of the schooner *Endeavour* into the brigantine *Washington*, her yards and square sails were rigged, her ten carriage guns were finally mounted, her eighty Connecticut sailor-soldiers were on board, the fifer and drummer were ensconced, and Captain Sion Martindale was finally off to sea.

A fresh breeze was blowing under overcast skies and the air was mild as *Washington* cleared Plymouth Harbor and stood into Cape Cod Bay. "We had not gone 3 leagues beyond the bay when we saw a frigate and a transport which were waiting for us," Surgeon Manvide recorded in his journal. After giving the vessels a good look, Martindale decided they were too much for his brigantine, so, according to Manvide, "we reversed our course."

Around one o'clock in the afternoon, *Washington* met up with Coit and *Harrison.* The two vessels joined forces and turned in pursuit of the enemy, hoping they would be enough to overpower the frigate, but their bold stand did not last long. "[T]hey were three altogether and they seemed determined to defeat us and make us prisoners," Manvide wrote, a detectable note of panic in his words. The frigate was likely the twenty-eight-gun *Tartar*, which by herself was more than a match for the two Americans. She was escorting a convoy into Boston, but Captain Medows turned and went in pursuit of the Plymouth ships, leaving his sheep long enough to drive off the prowling wolves.

Washington and *Harrison* put up their helms and raced for the safety of rebel-held Cape Cod. Coit had written humorously about *Harrison* sailing fast because she was used to it, but he may have been only half kidding. The schooner showed a good turn of speed. "Capt Coit proceeded much faster than we did," Manvide noted, though one might have expected *Washington*, with her clean bottom and spread of square sails, to have the heels on the schooner.

Through the remaining daylight hours and into the night the ships raced for land. It was 3:30 A.M. before *Washington* came to anchor, her men waiting to see what morning light would reveal of the frigate in their wake. But when the sun came up over the low, sandy end of Cape Cod, it revealed only Captain Coit's *Harrison*, anchored six miles away.

Martindale weighed anchor and got under way. Manvide's journal entry of that morning read, "God alone knows what will happen," and if that is any indication of how the others felt, morale was not running high. In a light wind *Washington* made her way slowly toward Plymouth Harbor, where she once again came to anchor. The ship's boat went ashore, to what end is unclear, and that seems to have been the extent of Martindale's activity for the day. For someone who had told Moylan that he needed an elaborate vessel because "I Flatter myself I shall be Able to Give a Good Acco of her," Martindale seemed in no great hurry to show what he could do.

Now that he was actually at sea and not just talking about it, Sion Martindale seemed to exhibit a certain backwardness. Not so the "blundering" Captain Coit. Rather than lurking around Plymouth, Coit weighed anchor and headed northwest toward Boston, putting himself in the way of shipping coming into Boston but also right under the guns of the British navy cruisers stationed there.

The wind was light out of the south southwest, and *Harrison* stood to the north with the breeze easy over her larboard quarter. As the schooner passed Point Allerton on the Hull peninsula, Coit must have seen the sloop-of-war *Raven*, the armed transport *Empress of Russia*, the powerful frigate *Phoenix*, and other vessels lying in Nantasket Roads, the anchorage just north of Point Allerton. His Majesty's ships made an unnerving sight for a lightly armed schooner, but Coit saw opportunity as well. Fine on the larboard bow was Boston Lighthouse, America's oldest lighthouse, marking the southern approaches to Boston since 1716. Near the lighthouse on Little Brewster Island were two British transports lying at anchor.

It would have been perfectly reasonable for any captain to bear off to the north and head for the horizon in the face of those men-of-war, but Coit was more bold than that. Calculating that he could snatch the transports and be gone before the armed vessels in Nantasket Roads could get under way, he ordered the *Harrison*'s boats cleared away and the boarding parties told off and then stood on past the mouth of the Roads.

The captain of one of the transports, a brig loaded with forage, saw *Harrison* approaching and guessed what the schooner was and what her intentions might be. The transport's crew tumbled up on deck and on orders from the quick-thinking captain "cut his jeers, Topsail Halliards &c"—that is, cut the lines that would have allowed the captors to set the brig's sails. *Harrison* likely hove to and sent a boat across to take the brig and get her under way. As the Yankee boat pulled for the transport, the transport's master ordered his men into their own boats, and they pulled for safety, leaving the disabled brig to the enemy.

All this activity finally attracted the attention of the men-of-war in Nantasket Roads, a couple of miles away. "At 1 saw a Schooner engaging [a] Transport without the Light House and took her but the People had got away in boats," the *Raven*'s journal recorded.

Captain Hyde Parker of the frigate *Phoenix* knew he could not get his ship under way in time to stop the rebel, so he turned out and armed his boats' crews and sent them pulling for the lighthouse. He then passed orders for *Raven* to get under way, and *Raven* "Slipt both Cables and made Sail after her." The *Raven*'s captain, John Stanhope, crowded on sail, sending up the topgallant yards and setting those sails and then flashing out studdingsails to starboard and larboard. The *Empress of Russia* did likewise.

Coit's men were no doubt dismayed upon boarding the transport to find the jeers and halyards lying in frayed heaps on the deck. It would have required no more than half an hour's work to get the lines rove off again, but the men could see *Raven* and *Empress of Russia* coming for them, studdingsails set on either side, and *Phoenix*'s boats pulling hard in their direction. They knew their time had run out.

The *Harrison*'s boarding party climbed back into their boat and returned to the schooner, leaving behind the prize they had so briefly held. One report suggested that they first dumped burning coals on the deck of the master's cabin in hope of setting the transport alight, but if they did so, it did not work. The *Harrison* spun around and raced for safety, *Raven* and *Empress of Russia* following with their great spreads of canvas set to the light wind. The men from *Phoenix*'s boats boarded the disabled transport brig and took her in to Nantasket Roads.

Coit ran off toward the south, the fast-sailing *Harrison* quickly opening up a lead on her pursuers. For three hours *Raven* pressed the chase, but the wind began to die away, and soon both vessels were barely making steerageway. *Harrison*, which carried those oars so beloved of John Adams, now put them to good use. "[T]he wind dieing away," the *Raven*'s master's log read, "the privateer got off with oars." Around 4:00 P.M. *Raven* gave up the chase and worked her way back to the lighthouse, where she came to anchor.

The next morning one of *Phoenix*'s boats approached the *Raven* with a report that a ship had been taken by the rebels. The *Raven*'s captain, John Stanhope, "saw a Ship to the Et wd [eastward] supposed it to be her." Once again he set all plain sail and studdingsails and went in pursuit. Seeing another British man-of-war in the offing, he made the signal for an enemy in sight while firing six shots at a schooner he most likely supposed was *Harrison*.

It was not. The frigate *Cerberus* sent a boat to *Raven* to explain that the ship *Raven* was pursuing was H.M.S. *Nautilus*, sailing in company with *Fowey*, and the schooner he was firing on was *Hinchinbrook*. *Fowey* was escorting a convoy into Boston, and the other vessels had been sent by Admiral Graves to cruise for the *Nancy*. The admiral hoped "the Ordnance Brig was safe but heartily wished she was in." Coit, in the *Harrison*, was nowhere to be seen.

In the end, Coit's bold action won him nothing but the grudging admiration of the British military. Major General William Howe, writing to Lord Dartmouth, called Coit's attack "A remarkable Instance of daring spirit."

CHAPTER *23* *"Hard gales and Squally"*

THE ORDNANCE BRIG *Nancy*, like all the ships plunging through the stormy waters off the Massachusetts coast in the first week of November, was fighting a string of driving gales that swept rain and snow before them. Admiral Graves would later describe the weather that week as "so tempestuous that it was impossible for any Ship, all things considered, to keep her Station on the Bay." *Nancy* seemed to be having a particularly hard time of it.

On the same day when *Charming Nancy* made landfall at Cape Ann and started her run south for Boston with the *Williamson* under her wing, *Nancy*, under shortened canvas, had been blown twenty-five miles southeast of Cape Cod. As the sun came up that morning, November 8, it revealed moderating weather, with clear skies and fresh breezes that curled the tops of the blue waves white. The wind was out of the northeast, making it extremely difficult for the heavily laden merchantman to work her way around the tip of the cape and on to Boston Harbor.

Also in the area was the frigate *Cerberus*. In the middle of October Admiral Graves had ordered *Cerberus*'s captain, John Symons, to cruise between Casco Bay, in the district of Maine, and Cape Ann to "protect his Majesty's faithful Subjects trading according to law, and to distress and annoy the Rebels by all means in your Power." Symons had been ordered to remain at sea for a month. His time nearly up, he was no doubt eager to get his battered ship back to Boston.

Like *Nancy*, *Cerberus* had been driven south of Cape Cod by the gale-force winds. At six in the morning on November 8, she saw two vessels in the offing and closed with them. A few hours later, the ship's journal recorded, "Spoke a Brig from London to Boston wt Stores." The brig was *Nancy*. *Cerberus* took the two vessels under her protection.

The little ad hoc convoy continued through the day, beating against the wind and getting only ten miles closer to Cape Cod. Not until the following day did the weather moderate enough for Symons to send the frigate's cutter across to the two vessels. "I immediately sent them signals and took Charge of them," he later wrote. As night came on, Symons heaved to his frigate rather than blunder through the dark with land so close by, and he signaled the others to do likewise.

The weather continued to deteriorate, "hard gales and Squally." By ten o'clock in the morning the frigate was under way again with *Nancy* and the other vessel in company. That day they met up with another ship, this one bound from Liverpool with coal, and she too joined them. They were able to make good only another seven miles but managed at least to get north of Cape Cod before heaving to once again.

The storm showed no sign of abating. Forced to clew up and stow her topsails, *Cerberus* lay to with a balanced mizzen sail. By six the next morning the man-of-war found herself lashed by "Violent hard gusts of wind and rain."

The frigate's age and her long time at sea began to tell. Symons ordered the courses, the lowest sails, reefed and set, and the ship began to claw her way back out to sea, struggling for sea room and to keep from being driven onto the nearby shore. Under the relentless pressure of the wind, however, the frigate's fore staysail blew apart. The fore topmast staysail was pulled from the netting in which it was stowed and "went all to Pieces before we could save it."

An hour later the reef points, the thin lines that bound up the mainsail, gave way and the sail split, the torn bits of canvas blowing off to leeward. A wave slammed into the stern section and tore off the rudder coat, which was meant to prevent water from flooding in where the rudder entered the hull. The sea poured into the gunroom where the officers lived and flooded the bread lockers. Several of the chainplates that helped support the masts were broken, and the ship began to leak copiously from the strain.

And at some point in the middle of this chaos, *Nancy* disappeared.

Four days after her fellow ordnance storeships *Juno* and *Williamson* dropped anchor in Boston Harbor, *Nancy* was still nowhere to be seen. General William Howe was getting worried. *Nancy* was not just another supply ship. She carried *matériel* of great importance to the army in Boston, and perhaps of even greater concern, her cargo was exactly what the Americans needed to maintain their war effort. The activities of

Washington's armed vessels had certainly not gone unnoticed. In writing to Dartmouth about his concerns for *Nancy*, Howe pointed out, "the Rebels Cruisers are ever watchful and take the advantage of their [the British transports'] Weakness or Necessities, wherein they have already been too successful."

Howe made his concerns known to Admiral Graves, who wrote back explaining that he had ordered Henry Mowat, who had returned a few weeks before from burning Falmouth, "to put to Sea immediately" in the six-gun sloop-of-war *Canceaux* and "to look for the Brig *Nancy*, and have given direction to set her on fire if found in Cape Anne Harbour and she cannot be cut out." It had occurred to the British that *Nancy* might now be an American prize. Rumors were already circulating that the Americans were aware of *Nancy* and her cargo and were vigorously searching for her.

Canceaux, however, was too short of water to get under way, and the weather was too rough for them to take more on board. The sloop was forced to lie at anchor in Nantasket Roads until the wind and seas moderated enough for water to be sent out.

By November 15, *Canceaux* was watered and under way. With every passing day, anxiety for *Nancy*'s safety mounted. Graves was determined "upon using every means to prevent her falling into the hands of the Enemy." A few days after *Canceaux* sailed, he ordered the schooner *Hinchinbrook* and the sloop-of-war *Nautilus* to join the hunt. *Lively* had only recently returned from Maine and was taking on wood, water, and provisions, but Graves intended to send her out as soon as she was ready. *Fowey* and *Tartar* were escorting convoys to Boston, but once they arrived they too would be sent out again.

Nancy could not have been more than a hundred miles from Boston, just a day's sail in good weather, when she parted company with *Phoenix*, but more than a week later she still had not been heard from. Her captain, Robert Hunter, had likely worked the ship farther out to sea to keep from being driven ashore by the storms that were pounding the area. Admiral Graves "heartily wished she was in" but felt somewhat reassured knowing so many of his vessels were out searching for her.

On Monday, November 27, the twenty-gun frigate *Mercury* fell in with the *Nancy*, now fifteen miles east of Cape Ann. "[S]poke the *Nancy* Brig with Ordnance Stores," the *Mercury*'s journal recorded, "Ordered her to keep Company . . . took her under Convoy."

The two ships sailed for Boston with the wind blowing hard and squalls of rain and snow sweeping their decks. *Nancy* continued to struggle through the stormy seas. Whether due to poor seamanship, a poorly loaded cargo, or inherent unseaworthiness, she seemed even less able than most clumsy merchantmen to batter her way across Massachusetts Bay.

Alexander Graeme, captain of the *Mercury*, made every effort to keep the deep-laded brig with him. "[A]t 2 P.M. fird 2 Guns and made the Signal for Brig to Windward to bear up and run out she did not mind at ¼ past repeated the signal but to no purpose." Soon after, likely in the night, *Mercury* lost contact with *Nancy*.

Two days later *Nancy* was still trying to work her way into Boston Harbor. The winds were from the south and west, right on the nose for a ship off Cape Ann trying to make westing. With reefed topsails braced hard up, the clumsy brig plunged on close-hauled, making virtually no progress as she sailed tack on tack. She was close, maybe twenty miles from Nantasket Roads, and there was perhaps a sense on board that the long nightmare passage, which had started in England nearly two and a half months before, was about to end. Certainly Captain Hunter must have been glad when he saw what he took to be a pilotboat pulling for his vessel, carrying someone with local knowledge to steer *Nancy* into safe harbor.

And he was right. But not in any way he imagined.

"This instance of Divine favour"

The waters through which *Nancy* sailed were crowded with shipping, even that late in the season. Transports in and out of Boston, men-of-war, American merchant ships, and fishing vessels from Marblehead, Beverly, and Salem passed through the area daily. "Three ships for Boston," Ashley Bowen recorded one day, and then the next, "Passed for Boston 3 ships. 2 or 3 cruisers out of Boston. The *Lively* off Cape Ann." And again the next day, "Passed five ships for Boston. Some cruisers out of Boston."

Some of those ships were genuine privateers, privately owned vessels armed at their owners' expense and cruising for British merchant ships under a Massachusetts-issued letter of marque and reprisal. On November 1 the Massachusetts House of Representatives had enacted the "Act for Authorizing Privateers and Creating Courts of Admiralty." This and similar actions by other colonies and the Continental Congress would set off a wave of privateering. For the rest of the war, privateers would be a mixed blessing, posing a serious hazard to British shipping but draining the resources of the Continental Navy.

Two of the ships prowling the area, however, were not privateers. They were Washington's schooners *Lee* and *Warren*, ships in the hire of, manned by, and under orders from the Army of the United Colonies. Despite that fact, many people, including on occasion George Washington himself, referred to them as privateers.

Earlier in the month Richard Henry Lee had written to Washington to ask about the availability of armed vessels to sail to the Delaware River and protect the approaches to Philadelphia. Washington had replied that a few of the individual colonies had ships, though none of any consequence. As to his own fleet, he pointed out that the "vessels are all manned by officers and soldiers, except perhaps a master and pilots." As the army was being completely restructured, it was possible that in the process the ships would be decommissioned. After all the frustrations and disappointments he had suffered, a note of resignation crept into Washington's letter. "[H]ow far, as they are upon the old establishment, which has not more than a month to exist, they can be ordered off this station, I will not undertake to say, but suppose they might be engagued anew."

As it was, Washington told Lee, two of his six ships had sailed for Canada "upon the Cruise directed by Congress; the rest ply about Cape Cod and Cape Ann, as yet with little purpose." The commander-in-chief's enthusiasm was at a low ebb, but he was about to have his faith restored.

Warren, under the command of Winborn Adams, had sailed from Beverly at the end of October and almost immediately had captured a sloop loaded with wood and thought to be bound for Boston. The sloop was sent into Portsmouth but was soon after released, as she was not a legitimate prize. On November 25, however, Adams was more fortunate, capturing the schooner *Rainbow*, which was indeed bound for Boston with a hold full of potatoes and turnips.

Like Adams in *Warren*, John Manley in *Lee* was keeping to sea as much as possible in that rough, freezing weather. Ashley Bowen noted that *Lee* sailed in and out of Beverly and hovered around Cape Ann but took no prizes.

On November 26 Lieutenant Colonel Loammi Baldwin, who had long been keeping watch on maritime comings and goings in Boston, sent a note to Washington with the information that "the officers in Boston (in particular the Admiral) was under great concern about a Brigg from England laden with all sorts of Ordinance Stores . . . their chief dependance seems placed on her Cargo."

More detailed reports filtered in from other sources. That same day Stephen Moylan wrote to William Bartlett in Beverly:

> We have information upon which we can depend, that a brigg Laden with 100 Gs of Brass cannon, a number of Mortars & other Military Stores, is now Missing from Boston, the Vessell which Convoyed her was arrived a fortnight past, it is apprehended She has fallen into our hands, if true it would be the most fortunate Circumstance that could happen for the publick good as well as the Captors, if Sir either of the armed vessells are in port, it is his Excellencys express orders that they put to Sea as soon as possible & keep a sharp Look out for the Brigg who is without any force, if taken there will be a Noble dividend to make.

Neither Manley nor Adams needed to be told to get their vessels to sea. It is not clear whether or not they received the alert regarding *Nancy*, but both were active captains who maintained their patrol of the sea lanes despite brutal weather.

On November 28, John Manley was tacking back and forth off Cape Ann, putting his schooner in the way of ships inbound to Boston. The day before he had managed to snatch up a prize, the sloop *Polly*, carrying Spanish milled dollars and turnips. (If nothing else, Manley and Adams were greatly frustrating British turnip lovers in Boston.) The weather was miserable. "Raw cold," Ashley Bowen reported. "This night much rain and wind at SSE."

November 29 was warmer, with mist and fog blowing in patches offshore. Manley in *Lee* was inshore, watching the approaches to Nantasket

Roads. He was no doubt grateful for the break in the weather, but he would soon have reason to be more grateful still, because *Lee* and *Nancy* were sailing converging courses.

After months of bashing around the Atlantic, *Nancy*'s master, Robert Hunter, finally saw his chance to make port. *Nancy* was standing into shore when Manley caught sight of her. The excitement must have been palpable on board *Lee* at the vision of a prize so heavily laden and vulnerable. The Yankee captain hove to and got the *Lee*'s boat alongside. Eight of his men armed with pistols and cutlasses took their places on the thwarts and sternsheets and pulled for the heavy brig, which, incredibly, seemed to be waiting for them.

Hunter, standing on *Nancy*'s quarterdeck, did not perceive his danger. Like most merchant captains he hoped to pick up a pilot to steer his ship into Boston. As the boat pulled toward *Nancy*, Hunter called out to the Americans requesting pilotage, which Manley's men assured him they would provide. The boat swooped to *Nancy*'s side and tied off, and the eight men climbed the boarding ladder to the deck. "[N]o sooner had they got on board," a contemporary account read, "than they drew their hangers and pistols, and insisted on carrying her into Portsmouth instead of Boston."

Nancy, the most valuable prize conceivable, was taken with no resistance and likely no small degree of astonishment on the part of her crew. Portsmouth, however, was not the destination. Even if Manley had not yet heard of *Nancy*, it could not have taken him long to realize what he had. His only concern was to get his prize to the nearest American port, and that was Gloucester, on Cape Ann Harbor.

The two ships got under way and stood for Gloucester. One report, apparently erroneous, suggested that Manley crossed paths that day with a second ordnance ship en route to Boston. In writing to Joseph Reed, Washington noted that Manley, "unluckily miss'd the greatest prize in the world; their whole ordnance, the ship containing it being just ahead, but he could not have got both." This rumor was repeated in other correspondence, one writer saying "Capt Manly would have taken her also, but 2 Men of Warr appearg in site, he thought it most prudent to secure what he had got."

It is unclear which ship this other might have been. There seems to be no record of the arrival of *Baltick Merchant*, which sailed with *Nancy* and was carrying a good portion of the artillery company's guns, but neither is there any record of concern for her failure to arrive, as there is with *Nancy*, suggesting that she did in fact make it safely into Boston long before *Nancy* went missing. The other ordnance vessels of the convoy were all accounted for. But it is certainly true that the British men-of-war *Fowey*, *Canceaux*, and others were hovering around Cape Ann, making it something of a miracle that Manley was able to get his prize into safe harbor before she could be retaken.

Once *Lee* and *Nancy* were anchored, Manley dispatched a messenger to Washington with the good news, along with the invoice of the brig's cargo. The messenger arrived in Cambridge to find Washington at his headquarters entertaining members of his inner circle. Among them was the wife of Dr. John Morgan, who had taken over as director general of hospitals after the arrest of Benjamin Church. Observing the scene, Mrs. Morgan wrote, "What delighted me excessively was seeing the pleasure which shown in every countenance, particularly General Gates's: he was in ecstacy. And as General Washington was reading the invoice there was scare an article he did not comment upon, and with so much warmth as diverted everyone present."

Ecstasy was no doubt the right word to describe the feelings of Washington, Gates, and the other members of the Continental command as they read the list of goods carried in *Nancy*'s hold. The prodigious haul included 2,000 muskets with bayonets (a weapon the Continental Army sorely lacked in the early days of the war), scabbards, and steel ramrods. To accompany the muskets were 2,000 cartridge boxes with belts and frogs. Fifty-three kegs held 105,250 flints for various makes of muskets.

Also included were more than 3,000 twelve-pound cannon balls and more than 4,000 six-pounders, as well as 150 carcass shells to set buildings aflame. To carry it all there were seven ammunition wagons.

The list of smaller items went on and on. Though seemingly of little significance, they were essential to the business of warfare and extremely difficult to procure in the United Colonies. Thus the generals felt considerable glee upon reading of "Callipers, one pair brass, one pair of iron ditto" and "Empty paper cartridges, twelve pounders, 10,000 in the three quarter ton vats" and "Empty flannel cartridges. Heavy, 24 pounders, 1500 in a case."

There were also "Harnesses, horse, thills with cart saddles, 80," "Spare spunge, and rammer heads . . . Muscovy lanthorns thirteen; tin ditto, ten; dark ditto, fifteen," along with camp kettles and frying pans, hand-spikes, tarred marlin, sheepskins, white rope, spikes, nails, weights and scales, olive and train oil, portfires, empty shells, fixed fuses, cured paper, and dozens of other things.

One item seemed to catch the imagination of everyone who surveyed the list: "One brass mortar of 13 inches, with a complete mortar bed." Of all that wildly valuable cargo, the squat, massive gun, a highly specialized weapon of limited usefulness, seemed to many the most wonderful thing of all.

"Generall Gates," wrote one correspondent from Cambridge, "says was he to have made out an Invoice for our purpose, he would not had add'd one artic[l]e more." The idea that *Nancy*'s cargo perfectly matched the fantasy invoice of the military leaders became a popular comment, often repeated. It was not far from the truth.

In reporting the brig's capture to John Hancock, Washington made no mention of Manley's having missed a second ordnance ship. Only in writing to his friend and confidant Reed did he mention this minor disappointment. Not that the commander-in-chief was ungrateful. In his letter to Reed he continued, "we must be thankful, as I truly am, for this instance of Divine favor; for nothing surely came more apropos."

CHAPTER **24** *"[U]niversal joy ran through the whole"*

NEWS OF *Nancy*'s capture raced through the Army of the United Colonies. "Your favor of the 27th came safe to Hand at a Time when we were all flush'd with the agreeable account of Captain Manley's having taken a Prize of the utmost Consequence," Stephen Moylan wrote to Joshua Wentworth in Portsmouth. The good word buzzed though the camp at Cambridge and beyond. Ashley Bowen noted in his journal, "This day two years a grand Town Meeting was held at the Old South Meeting House on the TEA affair at BOSTON, and this day Captain John Manley hath another sort of tea at Cape Ann."

No sooner had Washington heard the news than he began to disseminate it. Copies of the *Nancy*'s inventory were sent with letters announcing the capture. The first letter, of course, was to John Hancock and the Continental Congress, who of late had received little good news from the commander-in-chief concerning the state of the army and none regarding his fleet. "Last evening," Washington wrote, "I received the agreeable account of the Schooner *Lee*, Comanded by Captain Manly haveing taken & Carried in to Cape Ann a Large Brigantine bound from London to Boston Loaden with Military Stores, the Inventory of which I have the pleasure to inclose you."

It was a wonderfully understated announcement for so monumental an event, but then Washington was not an ostentatious man. In this case he did not have to be. The inventory said it all. Washington ended the letter to Hancock with, "I sincerely Congratulate you on this very great acquisition."

Washington, who wrote expansively about his military affairs to a number of correspondents, had thus far been largely silent concerning the establishment of his fleet. With the capture of *Nancy* he set about to correct that oversight. To William Ramsey he wrote, "I fitted out at the Continental Expense, several Privateers; chiefly with [the] design to Intercept their Fresh Provision Vessels," and then went on to describe the capture of the ordnance brig. He wrote in a similar vein to Benedict Arnold and others, informing them at last of the creation of his fleet now that there was news worth imparting.

Washington wrote to Joseph Reed on the night of *Nancy*'s capture and sent his friend another copy of the inventory. (A third went out to Philip Schuyler at Albany.) Reed had endured with Washington all the aggravations of creating the fleet and had shouldered a good part of the burden. Washington was no doubt pleased to let his former secretary know that the effort had yielded a return.

His Excellency's first concern, of course, was protecting the valuable cargo from recapture. "[T]hat no part of it may slip through my fingers," he wrote, "(for I have no doubt as this capture was made in sight of the other vessel, or of there being some bold push to recover it) I instantly upon receiving the account, ordered four companies down to protect the stores."

Along with the four companies of regular troops, Washington ordered John Glover and William Palfrey, an aide-de-camp to General Lee, to ride for Gloucester and "assemble the minute men in the neighborhood of Cape Ann" to cover the removal of the cargo. The officers were also to press into service any teams of horses and wagons in the area.

An army of soldiers, dockworkers, and teamsters descended on Gloucester to guard *Nancy*, unload her cargo, and forward it to the camp at Cambridge. All or part of fifteen militia companies arrived at Cape Ann Harbor. Orders were sent to William Bartlett to forward a thousand pounds of beef and a thousand pounds of bread to feed the men guarding the prize. Twice as much would eventually be needed.

By December 2 the wagon train of *matériel* began to roll into Cambridge. The excitement that attended the news of *Nancy*'s capture was nothing compared with that of actually seeing the contents of her hold. Word raced through the camp. Lieutenant Joseph Hodgkins wrote, "Part of the famos Prise has arived at Cambridge from Cap ann." Stephen Moylan's letter to Joseph Reed gives a good sense of the carnival atmosphere:

I wrote you last Thursday and would have given a good deal that you was here last Saturday when the stores arrived at camp; such universal joy ran through the whole as if each grasped victory at hand: to crown the glorious scene there intervened one truly ludicrous, which was old PUT [General Israel Putnam] mounted on the large mortar which was fixed in its bed for the occasion, with a bottle of rum in his hand, standing parson to christen, while godfather Mifflin [Colonel Thomas Mifflin] gave it the name of CONGRESS. The huzzas on the occasion I dare say were heard through all the territories of our most gracious sovereign in the Province.

William Tudor wrote to John Adams to fill him in on the detail of *Nancy*'s cargo. "The loss must be very great to the Enemy, but the Acquisition is immense to us," he said. He had been told that it would have taken eighteen months for the Americans to assemble an equal supply of ordnance stores, if they could have been had at all. If all the engineers in the army had been consulted, he told Adams, "they could not have made out a compleater Invoice of Military Stores." Tudor went on to remind Adams that Manley had once been the congressman's client during Adams's career as a lawyer.

Every day more and more supplies bumped over the frozen, rutted roads from Gloucester to Cambridge. In Salem, William Palfrey gathered the baggage wagons and gun carriages that had been shipped broken down in *Nancy*'s hold, assembled them, and sent word to Glover to forward the harnesses so that British wagons could be used to haul British goods to the Americans. Palfrey was concerned that his absence from Cambridge would anger General Lee. He wrote to Washington that "the Agents have so much on their hands that is impossible for them to go through the Business without some assistance & I beg Sir you would be so obliging as to mention the matter to Genl Lee."

By the second week in December *Nancy*'s hold was sufficiently empty to risk moving her from Gloucester to Beverly. Washington had never been comfortable with the ship anchored at Cape Ann, which he called "a very open Harbour and accessible to large ships." The commander-in-chief felt certain the British would attempt to retake the brig. In fact, on November 26 Admiral Graves had given orders to all of his ships in Boston Harbor to "go into Cape Anne and Marblehead Harbours, and if possible destroy or cut out every Vessel they find there," though he admitted to General Howe that they had little hope of success.

Graves's doubts notwithstanding, Beverly was a much more difficult harbor to attack, a fact that *Nautilus*, for one, had discovered to her detriment. On December 9, with the skies overcast, the weather blessedly mild, and the wind out of the north, *Nancy* made the run of twelve or so miles from Gloucester to Beverly, coming safely to anchor where Washington's navy had come to life.

Beverly resident William Bartlett saw to the sale and disposal of the cargo, handling the myriad receipts, bills, and requests scrawled across hundreds of bits of paper. It would take two months before everything was emptied from *Nancy*'s hold and all the military stores were hauled to the army in Cambridge. Among the many hundreds of pages in Bartlett's papers is one notation that gives a sense of the extraordinary value of her cargo: "[P]roceeds of the Sales of the ~~ship~~ Brig^{tne} Nancy & cargo . . . £20'541..15..3¾"—i.e., 20,541 pounds, 15 shillings, and 3¾ pence.

The British Loss

George Washington would have rested easier had he known that the British remained ignorant of *Nancy*'s capture for a full week after it took place. A majority of the brig's cargo was already in Cambridge and the mortar already christened *Congress* by Old Put before the British even heard rumors of their loss. As late as December 4 Francis Hutcheson, a Tory, wrote from Boston, "We have been these three weeks under great Anxiety for the arrival of a Brig with thee Morters wi[th] Shels and other Ordnance Stores."

Even as Hutcheson was writing that, Graves wrote to Philip Stephens reporting the stories he had heard about the loss of the ordnance brig. This bad news was delivered with all the reasons why none of it was his fault. "The Tempestuous Weather we have lately had ruins all the Ships cruizing on the Coast at this Season," he began. "It is however necessary to keep Ships out, though at a great risque" to protect the storeships and transports. However, "notwithstanding our utmost Endeavors to the contrary, I fear the *Nancy* Brig laden with Ordnance Stores is taken. It is reported she was carried into Cape Anne."

Graves was making excuses, to be sure, but that does not mean he was wrong. The wintry North Atlantic was doling out a terrific beating to his ships, but he had still dispatched all that he could to search for *Nancy*.

The admiral continued in the same vein, allotting blame in every direction, including a fair share to the Admiralty. "It is much lamented that a Cargo of such Consequence should be sent from England in a Vessel destitute of Arms even to protect her from a Row Boat," he wrote—perhaps hyperbolically, or perhaps in reference to a rumor that *Nancy* had in fact been taken by a rowboat. "An Officer with a Party of Men on board would have saved the vessel."

That last was probably not true. *Nancy* could not have carried enough men to match Manley's large crew, though a strong resistance might have driven off a less determined attacker. Graves also placed the blame on *Nancy*'s master, Robert Hunter, voicing the old complaint of navy men concerning merchant captains' inability to maintain station in convoy. He suggested all ordnance in the future be sent out "In good ships of force, well-appointed, and constantly have an officer on board, for the ignorance and obstinacy of masters of merchant ships in disobeying signals will ever prevent a convoy keeping together."

Graves saw another possible explanation for the *Nancy*'s loss: "I greatly fear . . . that the pilot, (who I hear is an American) has either betrayed the master or enticed him to go in with the promise of great rewards." Such an explanation made sense given that *Nancy* was so close to Boston for so long and under the convoy of two different men-of-war, yet still managed to be taken. There is, however, no evidence to suggest that either Hunter or the pilot purposely turned her over to Washington's schooner. Still, the rumor persisted. Lord Sandwich wrote to American Secretary George Germain that the brig's capture was "most probably owning to the treachery of the master."

The significance of the *Nancy*'s capture was not lost on Lord Sandwich. "The loss of the ordnance storeship is a fatal event," he told Germain. The British ministry, which had never given any thought to the possibility of American sea power, was now feeling its sting.

The first public notice in England of *Nancy*'s capture was published in the *London Chronicle* in early January 1776. In that same issue it was reported that General John Burgoyne had returned from Boston and had "opened the eyes of the Ministry, both with respect to the personal courage of the Americans, and the number of well disciplined troops our armies will have to beat."

The Washington at Sea

On November 24, the day William Coit made his daring raid on the transports anchored near Boston Lighthouse and five days before Manley captured *Nancy*, the brigantine *Washington* was lurking uselessly around Plymouth Harbor. The next day Martindale headed out to sea but remained within a few miles of Plymouth, not the most likely place to encounter British transports. *Washington* stopped two vessels that proved to be legitimate American merchant ships and chased a third, a packet boat she could not catch.

Martindale sent the ship's boat off with a lieutenant in command to expand the area of patrol. The boat crew boarded a couple of vessels bound for Plymouth with cargoes of wood but found no legitimate prizes.

Washington herself was only three miles offshore when her lookouts once again spotted one of Admiral Graves's cruisers, a frigate that, according to Manvide, "apparently wanted to give us battle." In what was now a familiar maneuver, Martindale hauled his wind and raced for the safety of Plymouth Harbor. "We returned to the same anchorage which we had left in the morning," Manvide wrote. There they remained, hoping Coit in *Harrison* would join them.

The waters off Beverly and Marblehead were squarely in the middle of the track that transports bound from England to Boston could be expected to follow. Not so Plymouth, which was thirty miles by sea from the approaches to Boston Harbor. William Coit understood that finding prizes meant leaving Plymouth. Sion Martindale, on the other hand, had not strayed more than ten miles from *Washington*'s homeport since getting under way.

The next day Martindale and crew put to sea again, but their luck with the weather ran out. The light winds and pleasant late-autumn days they had been enjoying were swept away by a fierce storm that barreled in from the west, carrying "Strong gales, wth Snow and Sleet." In Nantasket Roads, the *Cerberus*, *Fowey*, and *Empress of Russia* were driven aground on Centurion Rock. The *Washington*, unable to get back to port, spent a miserable night at sea, pounded by wind and waves, her decks glazed with sleet and freezing spray.

The next day the brigantine limped back to Plymouth and anchored at the mouth of the harbor, where she remained all day, buffeted by chop from the strong westerlies and blanketed by a series of snowstorms. She remained at anchor the next day but sent her longboat out to investigate a strange sail seen passing. At one o'clock in the afternoon the longboat was back with an eighty-ton sloop, the *Britannia*, bound from Nova Scotia to Boston with "wood, hay, cheese, potatoes, turnips, cabbage, hens, turkeys, geese and ducks and other goods."

It was the first prize taken by *Washington*, and Manvide pronounced it "of very little value." Nonetheless, he and Martindale took the opportunity to go ashore and consult with William Watson over the disposal of the prize.

On November 28, the day before John Manley would redeem all of George Washington's hopes in one stroke, Martindale put to sea again, tacking against a northwesterly wind to work his way into the shipping lanes where he might find a prize and "Give a Good Acco" of his finely fitted vessel. The brigantine managed to get about nine miles from Plymouth, her men all the time fearing that they would encounter "the same vessels of our mortal enemy."

As night approached and the weather continued to deteriorate, *Washington* once again headed for Plymouth. She came to anchor and spent another miserable night pounded by storms and swept by "Strong winds, rain and snow."

By the following morning the Connecticut soldiers who manned the *Washington* had had enough. "As we were about to get under way and make for Cape Hand [Ann] our crew mutinied unanimously," Manvide recorded. The *Washington*'s lieutenant, Moses Turner, was dispatched to headquarters in Cambridge with a letter from William Watson explaining the situation. Watson informed the commander-in-chief that the crew of the *Washington* "have agreed to do no Duty on board sd Vessel, & say that they Inlisted to Serve in the Army & not as marines."

Watson went on to explain that Martindale had done everything he could to make things easy for his men but they appeared to be "a sett of the most unprincipled, abandoned fellows [I] ever saw." This, Watson said, was what might be expected "from Fellows drawn promiscuously from the army for this Business, but that if people were Inlisted for the purpose of privateering much might be expected of them."

It was December 1 when word of the *Washington*'s mutiny reached Cambridge. In light of the fantastic score Manley had just made, General Washington had little patience for such insubordination as Martindale's crew were displaying. The commander-in-chief ordered that "such as are unwilling to proceed to Cruize with him, be immediately sent to Camp to join their respective Regiments." After all the trouble and expense of fitting out the *Washington*, the commander-in-chief wanted Martindale's ship hunting the enemy at sea, regardless of who was manning or commanding her. "[I]f Capt Martindale Cannot get hands to go with him, you must put in Captain Coit or any one else that Can as being detained in Port now may be of the utmost Prejudice to the American Cause."

Moylan reminded Watson of *Nancy*'s "imense value" and pointed out that "his Crew will Make their fortunes by Manley's activity." He ended the letter with the plea, "in fine get her out, Let the expence be what it will, & put what Captain & Crew you think the best for the good of the Service onboard of her."

When Watson received Moylan's letter he went to work, determined to get *Washington* to sea the next day, one way or another. He went on board the *Washington* to find out why the crew refused to do their duty (though one wonders why he had not done so already). It turned out that the men were simply cold and uncomfortable. The mutiny was "principally owing to their want of Cloathing, & after Supplying them with what they wanted, the whole Crew to a man gave three Cheers & declared their readiness to go to Sea next morning."

There were other factors as well that led to the men's change of heart. "The warm weather at that time & the news of Capt Manlys good success had a very happy Influence on the minds of the People," Watson wrote.

The aggravation emanating from Plymouth, and the scant and dubious news received from Canada, were tempering the satisfaction Washington derived from Manley's taking of *Nancy*. After months of dealing with Yankee seamen he was less impressed than ever. He wrote to John Hancock, "the plague trouble & vexation I have had with the Crews of all the armed vessels, is inexpressable, I do believe there is not on earth, a more disorderly Set, every time they Come into port, we hear of Nothing but mutinous Complaints, Manlys Success has Lately, & but Lately quieted his people."

The sailors, however, were not the only malcontents. In that same letter Washington informed Hancock that he had been forced to call out the militia to aid in putting down a mutiny by Connecticut troops who were determined to go home immediately at the end of their enlistment, before they could be replaced. And though the sailors were without question vexatious, as sailors were wont to be, theirs was arguably the tougher lot. Serving in a shore-based regiment with little to do but try to keep warm and stave off boredom was a far cry from standing a four-hour watch on the deck of a small schooner, lashed by boarding seas and freezing rain, and then trying to sleep in soaked clothes after a meal served cold because the weather was too rough to light the galley fires. On top of that, Washington's sailors were the only troops in the Boston area who were in any immediate danger of coming to grips with the enemy.

On Sunday, December 3, *Washington* set her sails to light and variable winds and stood north out of Plymouth, heading at last for the good hunting around Cape Ann. The weather was fine and the crew warm in their new clothing, and there was likely a spirit of optimism on board as the men contemplated matching the riches that the *Lee*'s crew would soon enjoy. Four men had been left behind in Plymouth due to illness. Perhaps they cursed their luck. They would not do so for long.

Washington cruised north, finally getting more than ten miles from Plymouth. As the day wore on, the weather began to deteriorate, with strong gales and squalls rolling through, but the brigantine kept the sea.

She was not alone. Boston and its approaches were under near constant patrol by the various men-of-war under Graves's command, which moved in and out of Nantasket Roads to sweep the area from Cape Ann to Cape Cod. About twelve leagues, or thirty-six miles, from Cape Ann, His Majesty's frigate *Fowey* of twenty guns was lying to under a backed main topsail.

Earlier that day *Fowey* had seen "a Brigg standing to the Northward," which was most likely the *Washington*. It was blowing hard then, and the frigate set her topsails double reefed, tacked, and went in pursuit. For two hours she chased the brig with the wind rising all the time, until Captain George Montagu ordered a third reef in the fore and main topsails and the mizzen topsail handed. Finally, with Cape Ann bearing northwest and about eighteen miles away, he "laid Maintopsail to the Mast" and gave up the chase.

Later that day the frigate *Lively* came up with the *Fowey*. She was of similar size and also cruising the approaches to Boston for the rebel's armed vessels. After exchanging news and intelligence, the two ships parted company to continue their search.

At 4:45 P.M., lookouts on *Fowey* again spotted a brig to leeward, and this time she was without doubt the *Washington*. The frigate "bore away And gave Chase," setting the fore topsail, which had been handed, and shaking out the reefs. The two vessels raced away to the south, the larger *Fowey* gaining with every mile made good. In just forty-five minutes the frigate had the brigantine within range of her guns. Montagu ordered the third reef out of the main topsail and began blasting away with the *Fowey*'s 6-pounders. He fired eight shots before Martindale decided that it was pointless to run and hove to.

The seas were likely running too high to risk sending a boat across, so Montagu "close reef'd the Topsails and handed them and lay to as did the Brigg." The *Lively* had sailed off, but the sound of guns brought her back. *Fowey*'s journal recorded, "at 10 his Majesty's ship *Lively* Came up to us."

All through the dark night the two frigates lay to under bare poles with the hapless *Washington* under their heavy guns. Manvide, unfortunately, had stopped keeping his journal two days earlier, so what was said or felt aboard the *Washington* during those long hours as she pitched and rolled with the frigates nearby is unknown. Nothing good, one would imagine.

At 6:30 in the morning, *Fowey* "hoisted the Cutter out And sent her on Board the Brigg, which proved the *Washington* of 6, Six Pounder & four fours, having 10 Swivells & Seventy four Men." Those were the guns, of course, which Ephraim Bowen had gone to such lengths to procure from Rhode Island. For all the time and expense that had gone into converting the schooner into a brigantine, for all Martindale's grandiose visions, the *Washington* surrendered without firing a shot, having taken only one prize, the little sloop *Britannia* loaded with farm produce. And she had been taken by *Washington*'s longboat while Martindale lay at anchor in Plymouth Harbor.

In the end, Sion Martindale did achieve one bit of notoriety. He was the first man ever to surrender an American man-of-war to the British navy.

CHAPTER 25 *"His people are contentd"*

AFTER HIS bold but ultimately fruitless attack of November 24 on British shipping near Boston Lighthouse, William Coit ran south toward his cruising grounds off Plymouth. In his wake were the *Raven, Phoenix, Hinchinbrook*, and all the other men-of-war he had left in confusion.

But not all of Graves's cruisers were at Nantasket Roads, and as Coit stood toward Cape Cod he was sighted by the frigate *Mercury*, which took up the chase. Once again *Harrison* proved herself a fast ship as the two vessels raced south. *Mercury* cut the Yankee off from Plymouth, so Coit kept on, ducking safely into Barnstable.

Once at anchor there, Coit dispatched Lieutenant Henry Champion to Cambridge with a report of their latest action. The "blundering" Champion, who on his previous visit to headquarters had spilled grease on Washington's letter to Joseph Reed, arrived on November 30 to find Washington's staff flushed with excitement over Manley's capture of *Nancy* the day before.

Among other news, Champion brought word that *Harrison* was, in Coit's opinion, "so Old & Crazy as to be unfit for the Service She is imply'd in."

Moylan sent Champion back to the agent in Plymouth, William Watson, with a letter from headquarters. If *Harrison* could not be made fit for sea, and if another vessel could be fitted out in six to eight days using the guns and stores from *Harrison*, then that should be done. However, Moylan wrote, the "Mutinous Spirit which reigns thro' the Marines & Sailors makes the General dispair of your being able to effect this or any purpose, so that I believe it may be best to give the Affair up, & not put the Publick to an unnecessary expence."

Washington left the decision to Watson but advised that if *Harrison* could not be fitted out and crewed with "Men willing to go in her, within the abovementioned time, you are to Lay the Schooner up." A careful inventory of stores and ammunition was to be made and Coit was to "make what dispatch he Can to Camp with the Men under his Command."

But William Coit, who celebrated his thirty-third birthday at Barnstable, seemed to have developed a love/hate relationship with his vessel. Old and crazy as she might be, she was also fast, and he was not willing to give her up. On November 29, the day before Champion reached Cambridge and the day Manley captured *Nancy*, *Harrison* worked her way out of Barnstable and stood north, resuming her patrol of the southern reaches of Cape Cod Bay. There her lookouts spotted a northbound schooner, which was made to heave to.

She proved to be the *Thomas* out of Fayal in the Azores, and she was owned by Richard Derby of Salem, a patriot of unassailable credentials, though his name likely meant nothing to Coit. The previous spring Derby, at the request of the Massachusetts government, had raced to London aboard his schooner *Quero* with news of the fighting at Lexington and Concord, so that the American version of events would be the first to reach England.

Thomas's master assured Coit that he was bound for Salem, but Coit was dubious and took the schooner as a prize. The two vessels continued north. Closer to Boston they sighted another schooner, a fishing vessel by the looks of her, but Coit stopped that one as well. As it happened, the innocuous-looking schooner contained a cargo of great value to the British: five Tory pilots who were cruising the sea lanes on the lookout for inbound vessels they could guide through the channels into Boston. Coit must have instantly recognized the value of depriving the British of their service. He imprisoned the pilots and took the schooner as a prize.

Soon after, with strong gales sweeping across Cape Cod, *Harrison* and her prizes stood into the sheltered harbor at Plymouth. *Harrison*'s speed had kept her out of trouble several times already, and Coit wanted to maintain that edge. He had the schooner hauled on the ways and her bottom graved, which meant that flaming torches were held up to the hull bottom to melt the tallow that had been applied there. In this process the tallow and any growth adhering to it would slough off. Other minor repairs were made as well, including one to the chimney of *Har-*

rison's cookstove, which Coit had complained so filled the vessel with smoke.

William Watson reported to Moylan that Coit "will be ready in two days, & is determined to take another cruise in her—His people are contentd & behave well." But despite that happy scenario, Coit's career as one of Washington's captains was sailing rapidly downhill. As late as December 1, Washington was ready to put Coit in command of the much-lauded brigantine *Washington* if Martindale could not get her to sea. But sometime after the end of Coit's cruise from Barnstable, things changed.

The capture of Richard Derby's schooner did not help Coit's cause. On December 5, Moylan wrote to Watson that "Captain Darby informs me that Captain Coit has unjustly seized on a Schooner, Named the *Thomas*." The letter went on to instruct that the schooner be returned and castigated Coit in an unprecedented manner:

> it is his Excellency's Commands that she [*Thomas*] be immediately delivered up to him, & that Captain Coit pay for any Thing that the Schooner may be robb'd of. It is not the Intention of the Continent to interupt good Citizens in their Trade. That was not the Intent of fitting out these armed Vessels at the Continental Expense. This Captain Coit would know well, if he consulted the Instruction given him.

The tone and insinuation of the letter were surprisingly harsh. After all, even John Manley had made the mistake of capturing a prize that was judged illegitimate. Perhaps Derby's standing and influence had something to do with it, or perhaps Washington was venting his mounting frustration with all his captains. Nicholson Broughton and John Selman had just returned from Canada, and Washington was just beginning to fathom the depths of their failure.

Still, Coit continued in command of *Harrison* at least through the first half of December. On December 13, ten days after the *Washington*'s capture, rumors began to circulate through headquarters that one of the fleet had been taken. Moylan wrote to Watson, "There runs a Report about Camp that one of our little Fleet is taken & carried into Boston. We shall be uneasy until we hear from Martindale as he is the one suspected"—correctly, as it turned out. Moylan added, "if Coit and he are safe, let us know as soon and possible." This would suggest that the Great

Red Dragon was still a captain as of that date, and perhaps even cruising with *Harrison*, though apparently with little success.

Concord

John Manley did not bask in the glory of his magnificent capture. On December 1—soon after *Nancy* was safely anchored in Cape Ann, word sent to Cambridge, and his prize crew collected—he weighed the *Lee*'s anchor and once again stood out to sea. That he did not linger to enjoy the considerable adulation he could expect says quite a bit about the man's character.

The day was cold and raw as the schooner bore away before the northwest wind, her men likely more motivated than they had ever been. It was not long before the lookouts spotted another likely target, a full-rigged ship of around 250 tons trying to work her way into Boston against the contrary winds.

Manley brought the ship to and boarded her. She proved to be the *Concord*, from Greenock, Scotland, and had been battering her way across the Atlantic for nearly three months. In her hold she carried "350 chaldrons of coal, and a quantity of bale goods." General William Howe, lamenting the boon she would be to the Americans, later wrote that she was "loaded with woolen Goods, and every Article necessary for Cloathing . . . which must afford great Relief to their most essential Wants."

Nancy was a hard act to follow, but *Concord* was an excellent prize. Her cargo of coal was desperately needed in Boston, and the clothing was most welcome in Cambridge.

Lee escorted the much larger *Concord* to Marblehead, where they arrived on the morning of December 3, just about the time Sion Martindale in *Washington* was leaving Plymouth for his final cruise. Captor and prize stood off the mouth of Marblehead Harbor, and Manley sent *Concord*'s invoice ashore to Jonathan Glover, the prize agent there, along with a number of letters that had been found on board.

Glover ordered *Concord* around to the more secure harbor of Beverly, but the prize, "as She was Turning in, got a ground on the Barr." Though she suffered no damage on the soft bottom of Beverly Harbor, *Concord* was stuck fast.

The papers taken from the prize were forwarded to headquarters in Cambridge, where they presented Washington with a new quandary. As the commander-in-chief explained to John Hancock, "it is mention'd in the Letters found on board that this Cargo was for the use of the Army, but on Strict examination I find it is realy the property of the Shippers & the person to whom Consigned."

Washington's instructions to his captains were to cruise for ships "in the Service of the ministerial Army." *Concord*'s cargo was privately owned and consigned to a private citizen, Tory though he might be. It was not, technically, an army cargo. On the other hand, a shipload of coal and warm clothing would be a great relief to the people of Boston, civilians and military alike, and it was just that sort of relief that Washington hoped to prevent with his ships.

The question of a privately owned cargo as a legitimate prize had not come up before. By the time *Concord* was taken, however, the war for *matériel* was in full swing, and Washington was tired of fine distinctions. The same day Washington wrote of the problem to Congress, Moylan wrote to Jonathan Glover and William Bartlett that "His Excellency has no doubt, but as the Enemy are seizing & making prizes of our Vessels every day, that Reprisals should be made." Hopes of a short war or the king interceding with Parliament on America's behalf had largely faded, rendering concerns about the political implications of American vessels making captures at sea a thing of the past.

But Washington would not authorize the capture of private property without the approval of Congress. Once again he was forced to confront an issue of prize adjudication that was beyond his authority, and he took the opportunity to remind Congress again of the need for prize courts. "It is Some time Since I recommended to the Congress, that they woud institute a Court for the trial of Prizes made by the Continental Armed vessells, which I hope would have 'ere now taken into their consideration, otherwise I shoud again take the Liberty of urgeing it in the most pressing manner."

This issue was becoming a genuine crisis for Washington, with cargoes piling up, crews clamoring for prize money, and captured vessels crowding the ports of Beverly and Plymouth. What's more, with enlistments soon up, Washington was in the process of recruiting and organizing an entirely new army, and he had no time for adjudicating prizes.

Still hoping for inside help to prod Congress into action, he raised the issue again with Richard Henry Lee:

> I must beg of you my good Sir to use your Influence in having a Court of Admiralty, or some power appointed, to hear and determine all matters relative to Captures—you cannot conceive how I am plagued on this head, and how impossible it is for me to hear and determine upon matters of this sort . . . at any rate my time will not allow me to be a competent judge of this business.

Stephen Moylan informed Glover and Bartlett that, as long as the *Concord* could be kept safe from recapture, her cargo should remain untouched until they heard from Congress. It was too late for that, however. *Concord* was hard aground and would not come off unless she was significantly lightened. Even before Moylan wrote his instructions, William Palfrey, still in Salem to oversee the transport of *Nancy*'s cargo, informed him, "we have been busily employ'd in getting her [*Concord*'s] Cargo into small Craft, in order to get her off the Ground."

By December 5, *Concord* was unloaded save for the coal and warped alongside the dock at Beverly. The dry goods were safely warehoused in Salem, but Palfrey wrote Washington concerning "a large Quantity of Potatoes on board the Ship & Sloop [possibly the *Polly*] which if not speedily dispos'd of will perish & be of no Service to any one."

A few days later Washington again wrote to Hancock with new information regarding *Concord* and her owner. "I am Credibly informed that James Anderson the Consignee & part owner of the Ship *Concord* & Cargo, is not only unfriendly to American Liberty, but actually in arms against us, being Captain of the Scotch Company at Boston." If Anderson was actively fighting Americans, part of the "ministerial Army," that would settle the issue. Washington concluded the letter with a statement that essentially sealed the fate of Anderson's ship and cargo: "there are many Articles on board So absolutely necessary, for the Army, that whether She is Made a prize of, or not, we must have them."

Some of *Concord*'s cargo was liberated before any decision could be made by Congress. As early as December 11, William Bartlett wrote to Washington acknowledging a letter from the commander-in-chief and promising to forward *Concord*'s cargo to headquarters as fast as possible. Bartlett's chief problem was "the Roads being Very bad the Teamers

think the Price Stipulated by Our General Court not sufficient." To overcome this work stoppage by the teamsters, Bartlett asked if Washington
would be willing to pay them more.

Though *Nancy* was being picked clean, not all of her cargo was fair
game either. Three casks of porter found on board were apparently the
property of her captain, Robert Hunter, and these were purchased from
him and sent on to Washington's headquarters, as was "one BLL of
Lemons what was Remaining Sound out of the Ship *Concord.*"

When Congress finally considered whether *Concord* and her cargo
constituted a legitimate prize, the correspondence found on board the
ship undermined whatever case Anderson might have had. "There were
a vast number of letters," Moylan wrote to Joseph Reed, "and what is
really extraordinary not one of them that does not breathe enmity, death
and destruction to this fair land, G-d them."

On December 22, before Washington's plea to Richard Henry Lee
even reached Philadelphia, Hancock sent Washington the expected
reply. Though Congress had taken no position on the legitimacy
of Anderson's ship and cargo as a prize, Hancock informed the
commander-in-chief that Congress "approves your taking such articles
found on board the *Concord,* as are necessary for the army," regardless
of how the case might ultimately be adjudicated.

Hancock also included another bit of welcome news. On November
25 Congress had approved a report concerning Washington's first
request for "establishing proper Courts." This was the request the
commander-in-chief had made back on November 8 after Coit's capture
of the *Polly* and *Industry.*

The wide-ranging report underscored how far Congress had come
from considering naval action "the maddest idea in the world." The committee concluded that many American vessels engaged in lawful trade
had "in a lawless manner, without even the semblance of just authority,
been seized by his majesty's ships of war and carried into the harbor of
Boston." After enumerating a list of maritime atrocities already well
known to Washington and anyone else in New England, the report in
its first article authorized the seizure and forfeiture of all "frigates,
sloops, cutters and armed vessels" that might fall into colonial hands.

More to the point, the second article authorized the seizure of any
transport carrying any supplies whatsoever for the British army or navy.

234 GEORGE WASHINGTON'S SECRET NAVY

The article, however, authorized forfeiture of only the cargo, not the ship, unless the ship was owned by an American who was supplying the British army, in which case both ship and cargo were liable. The report also established that no master of any vessel could cruise for prizes without obtaining "a commission from the Congress" or someone appointed by Congress for the purpose, thus establishing the institution of privateering at a national, not just colonial, level. This, of course, would have to be reconciled with the colonies, which were or soon would be issuing privateering licenses of their own.

Most satisfying to Washington, the report's fourth article called on the various colonial legislatures "as soon as possible, to erect courts of Justice, or give jurisdiction to the courts now in being for the purpose of determining concerning the captures to be made as aforesaid." The commander-in-chief did not have his prize courts yet—the colonies still had to create them—but he was one step closer.

Hancock's reply also included a copy of a Congressional resolution of December 19 in answer to Washington's question about *Concord*. That resolution amended the second article of the November 25 report to read that any vessel carrying "goods, wares or merchandizes, for the use of such [British] fleet and army,"—whether American-owned or not— "shall be liable to seizure, and, with their cargoes, shall be confiscated." Though Congress would not condemn Anderson's ship, they made it legal for a prize court to do so. *Concord* would remain in American hands.

CHAPTER **26** *"And a Privateering we will go, my Boys"*

JOHN MANLEY was America's first naval hero and one of the first men to be made famous by the American Revolution. Though he is little remembered today, his name was once celebrated throughout the colonies. As the year 1775 wound down, his notoriety radiated outward from Massachusetts, and his exploits were recounted in newspapers and correspondence across the nascent country. "Manley is truly our hero of the sea," Moylan wrote to Joseph Reed. A letter from Beverly printed in the *Pennsylvania Packet* begins, "You have no doubt heard of Captain Manly, who goes in a privateer out of this harbour, because his name is famous, and as many towns contend for the honour of his birth as there did for that of Homer's." Arguments over the place of Manley's birth would suggest that then, as now, his origins were enigmatic.

In 1776 a broadside ballad titled *Manly: A Favorite New Song in the American Fleet* circulated through the colonies. Written anonymously by "a SAILOR," the verses romped along with all the patriotic silliness so beloved by Revolutionary War "balladeers":

> Brave MANLY he is stout, and his men have proved true
> By taking of those English Ships, he makes their Jacks to rue;
> To our Ports he sends their Ships and Men, let's give a hearty Cheer
> To Him and all those valiant Souls who go in Privateers
> And a Privateering we will go, my Boys, my Boys,
> And a Privateering we will go.

The ballad continued in that vein for another nine stanzas. The broadside's woodcut printing was topped by a picture of Manley, sword under his arm. One hopes for Manley's sake it was not a close likeness.

Manley, of course, was not a privateer but an officer in the Continental Army. Privateering fever, however, swept Massachusetts once that colony's General Court finally authorized citizens to fit out private men-of-war. Five privateers were commissioned during December in Salem, Gloucester, and Newburyport. The speed with which these privately owned and operated vessels put to sea, when contrasted with the time and effort Washington expended to put a like number into service, spoke to the huge potential profit to be made from privateering. The big hurdles experienced by Moylan, Glover, and Bowen apparently shrank when enough money could be seen on the other side.

But Manley remained the most successful sea raider of all. His fame rested not just on *Nancy* and *Concord*, though those two would have been enough. He spent as much time at sea and took as many prizes as he could, lining his crew's pockets while serving the American cause. He gave his men little time or reason to mutiny or desert.

On December 9 *Lee* was cruising about fifteen miles offshore when the gray topsails of a ship hove up over the horizon. Manley may well have fixed her in his telescope, gauged her potential strength, and decided she was too much to take in a headlong attack. In that he was right. She was the 300-ton transport *Jenny* from London under Captain William Foster. She carried a crew of eighteen, well provided with small arms, and mounted two 6-pounders, which could have given *Lee*'s thin sides a beating and if well served would have been a match for the schooner's four 4-pounders.

Opting for guile rather than force, Manley disguised *Lee* as "one of the King's Armed Schooners," likely through the simple expedient of flying British colors, a ruse that was universally considered legitimate provided he hoisted the proper colors before attacking. He closed with the *Jenny*, and Foster, suspecting nothing, took no action to defend his ship. Then, with the transport under the muzzles of his guns, Manley hauled down the British flag and raised the white "Appeal to Heaven" ensign to the peak of the main gaff in its place.

Realizing his mistake too late, Foster threw some of his small arms and his important papers overboard, including his pocket book with the signals by which British merchant ships communicated with naval vessels, an important piece of intelligence lost to the Americans. Word of Foster's actions infuriated Washington and those at headquarters. Moylan wrote to Bartlett, "It was very unlucky that the Captain of the Ship threw his Papers overboard. He deserves to be severely punished, if it is true that this was done after he was made a Prize of. In any other War but the present he would suffer Death for such an action." If Foster jettisoned the papers after striking his colors he did indeed violate accepted conventions of naval warfare, though it is not certain he did so. Moylan went on to say that it was essential to show that "Americans are humane as well as brave," and Foster should be treated with "all possible Tenderness."

Unfortunately for Foster's effort to foil American intelligence gathering, his pocket book did not sink. Possibly it was wrapped in a waterproof cloth that rendered it buoyant, because a few days later the book washed ashore in Massachusetts and was promptly delivered to headquarters.

Jenny was a valuable prize. She had on board coal and a hundred butts of porter, both of which would have done much to warm the residents of Boston, as well as forty live hogs. After installing a prize crew on the transport, Manley continued to cruise the bay.

Soon another sail was sighted, and once again *Lee* ran her quarry down. This proved to be *Little Hannah* from Antigua, carrying 139 hogsheads of rum, one hundred cases of Geneva, and a number of such luxury items as "one Box of Pickles one Keg of Sweetmeats one Box of wine Two cases of wine one BBL of Tea & Loaf Sugar one BLL of Oranges."

Manley escorted both prizes into Beverly that same day. As it happened, the fine treats found on board *Little Hannah* were much wanted at headquarters in Cambridge. Washington and his staff were anticipating the imminent arrival of Martha Washington for an extended visit with her husband. Moylan instructed Bartlett, "you will please to pick up such things on board as you think will be acceptable to her & send them as soon as possible." Moylan reminded Bartlett to pay for any items taken.

Moylan also expressed concern over rumors reaching Cambridge that crowds of people—both civilians and men from the armed schooners— were flocking aboard the prizes. He feared that looting was taking place and passed along Washington's orders that no one but agents and officers were to board the captured vessels. "Agents will be blamed & held accountable" for embezzlement, he told Bartlett, "so you see the necessity of being strict in enforcing this order." He concluded, "pray when are you to send the Porter &c We want it much."

A few days later Washington received a more detailed account of the looting, and Moylan shot another letter to Bartlett. "[T]he General was Much Surprised at the Rapacity of the Crews in stripping the Prizes of every little Thing they could lay their hands upon," Moylan wrote. Bartlett was instructed to round up everything that had been stolen, and the cost of what could not be found was to be deducted from the "pilagers" share or, if they were unknown, from the share of the entire crew.

At headquarters, Manley's continued success was considered a fulfillment of and justification for Washington's original vision for his little fleet. Moylan wrote to Watson, by way of nudging the Plymouth vessels to greater action, "Captain Manly's good Fortune seems to Stick to him. . . . This shows of what vast Advantage to the Cause these Vessels would be, if the Commanders were all as attentive to their Duty and Interest as Manly is."

And Manley's good fortune did not wane. In the third week of December he took a sloop from Virginia called *Betsey*, which was carrying a load of "Indian Corn, Potatoes & Oats for the Army in Boston." Manley escorted his prize to Marblehead, arriving late on December 16. Ashley Bowen wrote on the 17th, "This morning I find Captain Manley and his prize sloop in our harbor." That same day, Manley took his prize around to the more secure harbor at Beverly.

Betsey's cargo had been sent courtesy of Lord Dunmore, the deposed Royal governor of Virginia who, from shipboard in the Chesapeake, was leading his own minor resistance to the rebellion. But more important than the cargo was a trove of letters to Lord Howe in Boston concerning ways in which the rebellion might be put down in the South. "Lord Dunmores Schemes are fully Laid open in these Letters," Washington wrote to Hancock. The papers also included letters from Patrick Tonyn, the governor of East Florida, and other British officials in the southern colonies. Also aboard *Betsey* was Moses Kirkland, a loyalist who was traveling to Boston to confer with Howe on strategies to subdue the southern colonies.

The letters were too important to send by way of a regular courier, so Washington sent them to Congress in the care of Pennsylvania Captain James Chambers. Kirkland was secured for later transport to Philadelphia. Washington wrote to Hancock, "indeed these papers are of So great Consequence, that I think this, but little inferior to any prize, our famous Manly, has taken."

The corn and oats, however, required more wrangling. Major Thomas Mifflin, the army's quartermaster general, wanted them but was unwilling to match the high price Bartlett could command in Beverley. Since Bartlett was obligated to Manley and his crew to obtain the highest price he could get, he would not sell. Moylan wrote back informing Bartlett that the corn and oats had to be sent to headquarters, as the need was great. Mifflin would match the price offered in Beverly.

The crews of the ships *Jenny* and *Little Hannah* were taken to Cambridge under guard and remained there for the time. Moylan asked that Bartlett forward their baggage, "for they are in a very dirty condition."

John Manley took *Betsey* with less than two weeks remaining in 1775 and in the enlistment of his men, who had joined the army and ended up going to sea. *Lee* took no more prizes in December. For Manley and his crew, the first year of the American Revolution was over.

The Final Cruise of Broughton and Selman

Far to the northeast, Nicholson Broughton and John Selman continued to run amok. By early December, Washington's only news of his captains was from the string of prizes straggling into Massachusetts, each of which was proving an illegitimate capture. The commander-in-chief had lost control of his captains and had all but given up hope.

It was late November when *Hancock* and *Franklin* made their way back along the coast of Nova Scotia, heading for home. With them was the *Lively*, which they had taken as a prize while she was anchored at Canso.

Near Barrington, on the southwest coast of Nova Scotia, they took their last prize. She was the brig *Kingston Packet*, loaded with fish for the West Indies. Once again Broughton and Selman showed their remarkable propensity for capturing just the wrong vessel. *Kingston Packet* was owned by the highly connected Richard Derby of Salem, the same

Richard Derby whose schooner *Thomas* had been taken by the unfortunate William Coit. As near neighbors of Derby, Broughton and Selman must have known that his patriotism was unassailable. But as his was an American-owned vessel bound to the British West Indies, they considered it in violation of the Continental Association and took it.

The four vessels made their way west across the Gulf of Maine, bound for Beverly. Rather than sail directly there, however, they made landfall first at the town of Winter Harbor, now known as Fortunes Rocks, south of Biddeford Pool, Maine. There they dropped anchor around December 1. The prizes *Lively* and *Kingston Packet* were left at Winter Harbor while a number of prisoners, including those taken at Charlottetown—Phillip Callbeck and Thomas Wright—as well as the captain of the *Lively*, a man named Higgens, were marched to Cambridge under guard.

Why Broughton had the prisoners march from Winter Harbor to Cambridge is not entirely clear. Certainly the schooners were crowded and low on food, and even a few men sent ashore would have provided some relief. But Winter Harbor and Beverly were only about sixty miles apart by sea, no more than a one-day sail. Broughton probably wasted more time than that by sidetracking to Winter Harbor in the first place. Perhaps the commodore was having second thoughts about the legitimacy of his excursion to St. John and wanted to meet with Washington before Callbeck and Wright were able to tell their side of the tale.

Even before the captains had reached Beverly, however, Washington was harboring deep misgivings. His last word from Broughton had been the bizarre letter in which the commodore described tricking Denny and Buddington by calling Americans "pumpkins," then assured his commander-in-chief that no vessel could get past him while he was stationed in the Strait of Canso. His Excellency sensed that his captains were off the leash. He wrote to Hancock to warn him of pending failure, saying that "by the Last Accounts from the Armed Schooners Sent to the River St Lawrence, I fear we have but little to expect from them." Washington understood that lying at the Strait of Canso was not the same as patrolling the mouth of the St. Lawrence River, and added, "if they chose a proper Station, all the vessells Comeing down that river must fall into their hands."

As Washington was writing those words, the *Hancock* and *Franklin* let go their anchors in Beverly Harbor. "This morning arrived Captains Broughton and Selman from a cruise to the Isle St. John in the Gulf of St. Lawrence," Ashley Bowen recorded. Word of the captains' doings apparently spread fast. The ever-informed Bowen added, "We hear they have brought the Lieutenant-Governor of St. John with them."

The day before, Callbeck, Wright, and Higgins had passed through Portsmouth on their way to Cambridge. There is no indication whether they or Broughton and Selman were first to get their story to Washington, but certainly the Canadians met a warmer reception than the Americans.

Callbeck and Wright had long before guessed that the attack on Charlottetown was unauthorized, and their interview with Washington confirmed it. Sometime later, Wright informed Lord Dartmouth, "From the reception we met with at Head Quarters, in Cambridge, and particularly from Generl Washington, I have reason to believe that these Transactions were not intended," but rather were done in revenge for Callbeck and Wright's recruiting efforts.

Wright added, "of this they [Broughton and Selman] accused us with to the General," which would imply that Broughton and Selman had met with Washington before the Canadians arrived in Cambridge. Or perhaps they all met at the same time, which would have made for a lively conference indeed.

Certainly when Washington heard what Callbeck and Wright had to say, he had heard enough. To John Hancock, Washington wrote:

> my fears that Broughton & Sillman would not effect any good purpose were too well founded, they are returned, & brought with them three of the principal inhabitants of the Island of St Johns. Mr. Collbuck is president of the Council, acted as Governor they brought the Governors Commission, the Province Seal &a &a. as the Captains Acted without any Warrent for Such Conduct, I have thought it but justice to discharge these Gentlemen, whose famillys were Left in the utmost distress.

Washington was not alone in siding with the Canadians. James Warren wrote in his diary, "Capt Broughton with another Privateer . . . return having infamously covered the ignomincy of their return with the Pretence of serving some gentleman belonging to the Island of St John . . . who he said were enlisting men against the Colonies." Stephen Moylan wrote to John Glover, "I beg you will be attentive to Mr Callbeck's goods, Let him have every thing that he was so cruelly pillaged of."

To further add to Washington's irritation, he was still plagued by issues surrounding Broughton and Selman's ostensible prizes. The root of the problem, as with all the prizes, was that Congress had yet to institute prize courts—though they had authorized the colonies to do so—and there was still no recognized means by which the legitimacy of prizes could be determined.

Richard Derby's brig *Kingston Packet* had been sailed from Winter Harbor to Salem, Derby's home. The Salem Committee of Safety appealed to Washington to decide the vessel's fate, but Moylan wrote to the committee, "His Excellency cannot be a Competent judge of such matters, if he was, he has not time to attend to them." Moylan instructed the committee to make a decision and assured them that "whatever you determine on will Meet with the General's approbation."

The committee, however, wanted none of it. A number of local merchants were using their ships as Derby was, and different communities had adopted differing views of such activity. The committee therefore felt the question should be "determined by Judges whose Jurisdiction is General."

For Washington and Moylan, that was the last straw. Moylan wrote to John Glover ordering him to "Manage the matter, so as Head Quarters may hear no more of her." Glover did just that. "The two vessels sent into Winter Harbor were very unjustly taken," Moylan would later write, "and are delivered up to their respective owners." *Kingston Packet* was released, as was the schooner *Lively*, in which Callbeck and Wright and the other prisoners took passage back to Canada.

The mission to intercept the North Country brigs, the mission for which Washington had such hope and which helped legitimize his fleet and create the American navy, came to nothing in the end but headache and expense. The only good it did the Americans was to cause considerable alarm to the British. Francis Legge, Governor of Nova Scotia, declared martial law in the wake of Broughton and Selman's depredations. "My Reason for urging this Measure, is, that the Americans have fitted out Vessels of War, and have lately been cruising in these seas."

Legge's action stands as testament to the correctness of Washington's strategic thinking. With his little and sometimes dysfunctional fleet, his Excellency had shown that even if the British in Boston did not want to come out and fight he could carry the fight to them and that American military power could be projected beyond the entrenchments surrounding the city.

CHAPTER 27 *A New Army*

WASHINGTON'S SCHOONERS continued to prowl the waters off the Massachusetts coast through the end of 1775. From Beverly, Portsmouth, and Plymouth, the small ships with their 4-pounder guns and outsized crews stood out onto the gray, freezing waters of the North Atlantic, placing themselves in the way of shipping moving into Boston Harbor and the frigates and sloops of the British navy.

None but John Manley enjoyed any luck. Winborn Adams in *Warren* took only one prize by December 24, the schooner *Rainbow*, and he had the misfortune to take her just a few days before Manley captured the ordnance brig *Nancy*, which made *Rainbow* look paltry. On December 1 Stephen Moylan wrote to Joshua Wentworth, the prize agent at Portsmouth, explaining that the excitement of *Nancy*'s capture "made us look over the Potatoes & Turnips of Captain Adams; but now being a little cool, I assure you I do not think Adams' *bon Fortune* so despicable, though of little Value to us, It is depriving the Enemy of what to them would be of Consequence."

Adams enjoyed little *bon fortune* after that. *Warren*'s sails were in bad shape and her swivel guns in poor condition, though to his credit he continued to cruise while Moylan and William Bartlett struggled to find replacements.

A snowstorm swept through New England on Christmas Eve day, blanketing *Lee*, *Hancock*, and *Franklin* as they rode at anchor in Marblehead. But Winborn Adams in *Warren* stayed at sea despite the snow and in doing so finally met with some small measure of success. Though the visibility was poor, the *Warren*'s men spotted a sloop inbound for Boston and forced her to heave to. She proved to be the *Sally*, out of Lisbon, with a cargo of two pipes (i.e., large barrels) and 126 casks of wine and a crew of British man-of-war sailors.

Sally was owned by Peter Barberie of Perth Amboy, New Jersey, a man who was "looked upon as friendly" to the American cause. She had been bound into New York with her cargo when a tender from the frigate *Niger* picked her up off Sandy Hook, New Jersey. An officer and five of the frigate's men had been put on board to take the sloop to Boston, where they stood right into the cordon of armed vessels Washington had fitted out.

Warren and her prize rode out the night at sea, and the next day Adams escorted *Sally* into Marblehead. The weather on the heels of the snowstorm was unseasonably pleasant. *Lee* and *Hancock* stood out to sea, their men showing a Protestant Yankee's traditional disregard for the Christmas holiday but hoping for a gift nonetheless. Though they would have been delighted to capture a ship stuffed with coal, they were disappointed even in that. The recaptured sloop *Sally* was Winborn Adams's second and final prize and the last capture of Washington's fleet in 1775.

As the first year of the war wound to a close, Washington had more on his mind than the disposition of his schooners. Foremost was the fact that his army would be leaving soon, and he was not at all certain of gathering sufficient men to replace them. This, of course, was a problem he had been wrestling with since early November. The enlistments of most of the men would expire around the end of the year. For months the commander-in-chief had been struggling to assemble what was essentially an entirely new army before the old one dissolved.

While Washington recognized the great danger of undertaking such a task in the face of the enemy, others saw only opportunity for advancement and a few perks. "Such a dearth of Publick Spirit, & want of Virtue," Washington complained to Joseph Reed near the end of November, "such stock jobbing, and fertility in all the low Arts to obtain advantages, of one kind or another, in this great change of Military arrangement I never saw before." Washington had at that point enlisted only 3,500 men, and to secure even that inadequate number he had had to offer generous furloughs. The Connecticut troops would not stay for any consideration.

"[S]uch a dirty, mercenary Spirit prevades the whole, I should not be at all surprizd at any disaster that may happen." Washington knew that

246 GEORGE WASHINGTON'S SECRET NAVY

to fill the lines he would have to bring in minutemen and militia units, which would only corrode the discipline he had labored so hard to establish. Though he had learned to avoid expressing his disdain for New Englanders openly, the sentiment showed clearly in his correspondence.

Washington was not the only one concerned. Anyone who intended to stay with the army through the next campaigning season had reason to worry. "Our men inlist very slow and our Enemy have got a Reinforsement of five Regiments," wrote Lieutenant Joseph Hodgkins of Ipswich, Massachusetts, "and if the New Army is not Reased [raised] in season I hope I & all my townsmen shall have virtue anofe to stay all winter."

Building a new army occupied most of Washington's thought and energy through December. The task was crucial, and the commander-in-chief resented any distractions. His regular pleas to Congress to establish prize courts for his fleet were made largely to spare himself from having to waste precious time on such minutia, particularly as he did not consider himself a qualified judge in such matters.

By the middle of the month, Washington wrote Reed that "only 5917 Men are engaged for the Insuing Campaign." He had been told that more would join and were only holding out to see what bonuses or other inducements might be offered, but he was skeptical.

From Canada the news was good. After a brutal march through the wilderness of Maine, Benedict Arnold and his band of around six hundred men had arrived at Quebec and, though much weakened, would be linking up with Richard Montgomery, who had captured St. Johns, a British fort at the north end of Lake Champlain, and Montreal. Henry Knox wrote from Fort George, on the south shore of Lake George, that "I returnd from Ticonderoga to this place on the 15th instant & brought with me the Cannon &c. . . . It is not easy to conceive the difficulties we have had getting them over the lake."

Around this time Washington was confronted with yet another distraction. The previous month Ethan Allen, the fiery leader of the Green Mountain Boys, who had helped capture Fort Ticonderoga the previous May, had himself been captured by the British in an ill-advised and unauthorized attempt to take Montreal ahead of Montgomery. Allen was now a prisoner in Canada, and Washington intended to apply to General William Howe for a prisoner exchange. But now there was another

American officer in British hands for whom Washington had to make such an arrangement. "I am Much affriad I Shall have a Like proposal to Make for Captain Martindale," Washington wrote to Hancock, "of the Armed Brigantine *Washington*, & his men, who it is reported was taken a few days past." Washington added, "We Cannot expect to be allways Successfull."

On December 18 Washington wrote to Howe protesting that Allen "has been thrown into Irons & Suffers all the hardships inflicted upon common Felons." Washington informed Howe that if such was true, the same treatment would be meted out to Brigadier General Richard Preston, a British officer captured in the Canadian campaign. Washington went on to add that Americans had the highest regard for the name Howe and were not happy to see it "at the head of the Catalogue of the Instruments, employed by a wicked ministry for their destruction." He did not mention Sion Martindale or his men.

If the letter was intended to put Howe in a cooperative mood, it failed. Howe replied that he had no authority over Canada and had never heard of Allen but was certain General Guy Carleton, the commander there, "has not forfeited his past pretensions to decency & humanity." Howe added that he was sorry to "find cause to resent a sentence in the conclusion of your letter big with Invective against my Superiors, and insulting to myself, which Should obstruct any farther intercourse between us." Howe did not address the issue of a prisoner exchange.

In fact, by the time Howe replied to Washington, Sion Martindale and most of his men were long gone, shipped off to England for trial in the hold of the frigate *Tartar*, which had sailed on December 16. The British were not ready to consider Americans captured aboard armed vessels as legitimate prisoners of war, and Admiral Graves wrote to Secretary of the Navy Philip Stephens that he had no commission to "try persons Guilty of Acts of Rebellion or High Treason Committed on the High Seas." Remaining in Boston from Martindale's crew were two unfortunate sailors who had deserted from the *Glasgow* and *Swan* and joined the rebel side and two Englishmen whom Graves described as "Prisoners" of the Americans, and who had now joined the crew of the *Fowey*.

By the end of the month, Washington received word that Martindale and his men, along with Ethan Allen, were already gone. "[T]his may account for General Howes Silence on the Subject of an Exchange of Prisoners," he wrote to Hancock.

But there was more to it than that. When Howe wrote to Dartmouth concerning Washington's proposed prisoner exchange, he told the American Secretary that he would not "enter upon such a measure without the King's orders." Howe also understood the psychological advantage that could be gained from causing the *Washington*'s crew to disappear without a trace, the chilling effect such a thing could have on others inclined to take the war to sea. Expressing those thoughts to Dartmouth, Howe acknowledged that the naval war being waged by Washington's schooners "will hurt us more effectually than any thing they can do by Land during our Stay at this Place." Here was tacit confirmation from the man most qualified to give it that Washington's navy had been exactly the right strategy for the siege of Boston.

Year's End

By the end of December Washington could report that 9,650 men had enlisted in the newly established army. Many were new to the service, and many who had joined the army in 1775 had left. The latter included nearly all the men in George Washington's navy. Morale had never been particularly high among those recruited for sea service. Between the bitter cold North Atlantic and the powerful men-of-war of the British fleet, the work was harder and more dangerous than any other duty on the Continental Line. While some of the men, particularly the crew of the *Lee*, had earned significant prize money, their riches were on paper only. Congress's long delay in establishing prize courts and the further delay engendered by turning the responsibility over to the colonies meant that not one penny had been doled out to the men.

Like the ships' companies, the schooners' captains continued to serve through the end of the year. But Washington was just as dissatisfied with them—Manley excepted—as he was with the foremast sailors, and he intended to clean house.

With army enlistments expiring at the end of the year, Washington seems simply to have let the clock run out on Captain William Coit. Though it is not saying much, Coit was Washington's most successful captain after John Manley, but the commander-in-chief had never been pleased with him. Possibly Washington found Coit's insouciant manner annoying. He had said little about Coit other than to call him "blundering," a characterization that was unfair at the time and appeared even more so given the boldness and judgment Coit had since displayed, qualities much lacking in other captains. Nevertheless, Coit was gone by the end of the year, and Moylan wrote to Joseph Reed, "Coit I look upon as a mere blubber."

Reed, apparently, did not have so low an opinion of Coit. In writing to Samuel Webb, a mutual friend (it was to Webb that Coit had penned his amusing description of *Harrison*), Reed asked, "What is become of Coit? I expected he would have disputed the Lauril with Manly."

In January 1776 the colony of Connecticut authorized the construction of a small frigate named the *Oliver Cromwell*. Coit may have gotten wind that this was going to happen and so did not dispute his lost command of *Harrison*, hoping instead for the larger ship from his home colony. In any event, he was given command of the *Cromwell* in July, but the following month she was damaged by lightning, and he was able only to sail her to New London, where delays in fitting out and problems with crew desertions kept her in port. Coit was dismissed from the command in April of 1777 and became a captain of privateers.

Four and a half years later Coit participated in the defense of New London when Benedict Arnold, by then a brigadier general in the British army, attacked and burned the town. Coit was captured and spent time on one of the hellish prison ships in New York. He died in 1802 at age sixty during a visit to his daughter near Wilmington, North Carolina, and was buried there. Despite Washington and Moylan's dismissal of him, and as insignificant as the prize might have been, the Great Red Dragon was still the first captain in the armed service of America to capture a ship flying the British flag. It was a point of pride he enjoyed the rest of his life.

Nicholson Broughton and John Selman continued to cruise throughout the month of December, sailing out of Beverly. On December 22 Bowen reported, "Sailed Captain Broughton on a cruise," and both he and Selman are mentioned again later in the month. A list of *Hancock* and *Franklin*'s expenses show Broughton and Selman still officially listed as captains of their ships through January 3, 1776.

As December drew to a close, Broughton and Selman decided to square things with Washington. "This year being nearly up Commodore Broughton and myself went to Head-Quarters at Cambridge to see the

General," Selman wrote. Washington did not invite them in but rather met them on the steps of his headquarters, which might have been the men's first indication that this interview would not go well.

"[W]e let his Excellency understand we had called to see him touching the cruise," Selman wrote. "[H]e appeared not pleased—he wanted not to hear anything about it." Cutting off the men in mid-explanation, Washington turned to Selman and asked if he would be willing to stand again as an army officer in John Glover's regiment, a none-too-subtle way of telling Selman his days as a ship captain were over. Selman said he would not be willing to do that. Washington then asked the same question of Broughton, and Broughton, too, answered, "I will not stand."

And that was the end of the naval careers of Nicholson Broughton and John Selman. On January 2, 1776, Stephen Moylan wrote to Joseph Reed that Broughton and Selman "are indolent and inactive souls. Their time was out yesterday, and from frequent rubs they got from me (under the General's wings) they feel sore, and decline serving longer." Selman sat out the war, but Broughton did end up rejoining the army and fighting with the land forces.

As December 1775 turned into January 1776, with no indication at all of the monumental events that would take place that year, Washington's ships floated abandoned in their respective harbors. Ashley Bowen noted, "Our four cruisers are all hauled up at Beverly." Stephen Moylan wrote to Joseph Reed, "I am just informed all the vessels are now in port, the officers and men quitted them; what a pity as vessels are every day arriving."

As with his army, George Washington would have to build his navy anew.

"[E]very assistance the Fleet can afford shall be chearfully given."

The autumn and early winter of 1775 had been a trial for Admiral Samuel Graves, and Graves was not a man to endure trials in silence. The weather was fierce, and his ships were suffering from a lack of manpower, supplies, and an adequate shipyard—the closest being Halifax. General Howe was not at all happy with the way things were going on the naval front and made his feelings clear, though always with a polite formality. The general's dissatisfaction only made the admiral dig his heels deeper still.

Even before *Nancy* was taken, Howe "expressed his Apprehensions for the Safety of the Vessels expected with Stores." He suggested to Graves that frigates be stationed at Marblehead and Cape Ann to cut off the use of those ports to Washington's cruisers, which were quickly evolving from nuisance to genuine threat.

Graves replied with studied insincerity: "Your Excellency can make no request or proposal for the good of His Majestys Service that I will not readily attend to, and heartily assist to carry into execution," he wrote, then explained why he could neither assist nor execute Howe's plan. The admiral had been informed of a battery of twelve cannon including two 18-pounders at Marblehead and a partial fortification at Cape Ann. The danger was too great that his ships would become windbound under the enemy's guns. At Cape Ann, Graves explained, "the outer Road [harbor] is foul, narrow and greatly exposed," and the same was true of Marblehead.

It was "indeed beyond dispute," the admiral conceded, that the Americans had several small vessels cruising Massachusetts Bay for transports. But in Graves's opinion the rebel schooners with their 4-pounder guns actually had the advantage over the British men-of-war, being more nimble sailers and "being light vessels, draw little Water, and the whole Country their Friends, can lie under the Land, and, upon observing a Vessel or two unguarded, dart upon them suddenly, and carry them off even in sight of the King's Ships." In this he had a point.

Graves offered a counter suggestion. Perhaps Howe should use his troops to destroy Marblehead and Cape Ann. "[T]hree hundred Soldiers, with two good Frigates," could take the battery at Marblehead, and with the aid of artillery could burn the town. A thousand men could take and hold Cape Ann. Graves knew perfectly well that Howe was in no position to do either. Howe had already made it clear to his superiors in London that he did not have the men or supplies to hold Boston and also mount an offensive elsewhere. The suggestion was as disingenuous as his offer to "heartily assist" in any way.

Armies of the eighteenth century did not often fight during the winter months, so little was expected of Howe during that bitter cold December. The navy, however, enjoyed no such reprieve. Graves took pains to remind his superiors how difficult it was to keep the sea in such conditions. "Their Lordships well know the Situation of this Coast in the Winter," he wrote to Philip Stephens. "the prevailing Winds S E and N W, hard Gales each way, and with the former thick Weather, Rain, Snow, and Ice, without a friendly Port to push for except Boston, the Entrance of which is narrow and dangerous."

Certainly Graves's arguments were valid, but more than a few observers felt the real problem was an old and inactive admiral in command of the North American Squadron. Francis Hutcheson, a loyalist in Boston, wrote metaphorically, "the White flag at the fore top Mast head [Graves was a Vice Admiral of the White, and his flag flew at the top of *Preston*'s foremast] is Old, Durty, and unfit for Service, if the Ministry Expects it shou'd fly with Luster they must send a *New One* Clean and Ferm."

The long-simmering friction between Graves and Howe only grew worse as the year wore on and the situation in Boston deteriorated. One unnamed correspondent suggested that the antipathy between the men "originated with their wives; both of whom led their husbands." According to the writer, Graves obstructed every attempt Howe made to supply the garrison by sea, and the admiral "quarrelled with the General, the army, with all his own officers except his hangers-on." He went on to observe that "though there are near twenty pendants flying in this harbour, I cannot find that there is one vessel cruising in the bay." While this writer may have had a particular bias against Graves (he may have been an army officer), he was not the only one to note that Graves's ships were often at anchor and protected by booms. It is certainly true that the admiral enjoyed little success and that the transports that did arrive did so mostly out of luck or a want of activity on the part of Washington's captains.

One of the few successes Graves enjoyed was the capture of the brigantine *Washington*, and the admiral was quick to spot an opportunity and act on it. His plan—audacious for a man accused of inactivity—was to man the prize with seventy British sailors and send her back to sea before word of her capture spread, a British wolf in Continental sheep's clothing. Washington's unsuspecting men-of-war would allow her to close with them, and then she would overwhelm them with her guns and men.

Graves ordered Lieutenant George Dawson to take command of the *Washington*, but when the lieutenant examined the ship he found her to be in such bad condition that he "thought it highly dangerous to venture so many Lives in her." This would seem incredible given the labor and money Sion Martindale and William Watson had just poured into her. Graves, though he did not know her recent history, was skeptical. "The Admiral vexed at this Dissappointment," he wrote, "and almost Doubting the truth of the many verbal Reports made to him of her Disability, ordered three Captains to take their Carpenters with them and report her Condition under their Hands."

The captains and carpenters confirmed Dawson's estimate. The carpenters found "The whole of the Timbers under the Deck—Rotten and totally decayed. The Main Beam and foremost Beam decayed. The Main Deck totally decayed." The bowsprit was broken in two places, the main boom as well, the ceiling planking bad, and in general "the Hull in the present State is not fit for Sea." Sometime later, Graves himself visited the ship and confirmed the truth of the survey.

That much damage and rot could not have occurred between early November, when *Washington* sailed from Plymouth, and early December when Lieutenant Dawson took charge of her in Boston. This begs the question, what was Martindale thinking when he called her "Very Suitable for the Business?" Further, how could Watson and the carpenters at Plymouth not notice these problems when they set about refitting her as a man-of-war? There seems to be no good answer to this mystery. The saga of the armed brigantine *Washington* is, even in the context the amateur American army of the American Revolution, a singular example of mismanagement, poor decision making, and sheer idiocy.

By mid-December the depredations of Washington's fleet, and particularly the capture of *Nancy*, were increasingly alarming to General Howe. He wrote to Lord Dartmouth suggesting that stores be sent from England in men-of-war with their lower-deck guns removed, or at least in "Vessels of sufficient Force to defend themselves against these Pirates."

Once again the general pressed the admiral to provide more protection for incoming supply vessels, and once again Graves answered that he could do no more than station ships off Cape Ann, Marblehead, and Cape Cod and hope for the best. Graves suggested again that the problem could be solved if the army were to capture the rebel ports. "If your Excellency thinks it advisable to attempt seizing the Peninsula of Cape Ann," he wrote unhelpfully, "every assistance the Fleet can afford shall be chearfully given."

Howe did not respond. A letter from an officer in Boston, printed in a London newspaper and thick with sarcasm, compliments Graves on his "utmost prudence," the admiral having "orderd the ships of war in this harbour to be secured with bombs [booms] all around, to prevent their being boarded and taken by the Rebel whale-boats." The writer imagined that Parliament would thank Graves for "so effectually preserving his Majesty's ships."

Just about the time Washington's fleet was being laid up for the winter, Graves finally decided to take positive steps to prevent their sailing. On December 27 *Fowey* made sail and stood for Cat Island off the mouth of Marblehead Harbor. Graves explained in a letter to Philip Stephens that by stationing *Fowey* there he hoped to "keep in many of the Cruizers belonging to Salem, Beverley and Marblehead Harbours." The admiral once again recited his litany of troubles, including the "Badness of the Weather this Fall, on a very dangerous Coast," and explained that he had done everything in his power to protect the transports arriving at Boston, "however unsuccessfully."

Ashley Bowen noted *Fowey*'s arrival. The frigate staged a theater of sound and fury, firing at passing vessels to little effect. Despite *Fowey*'s presence, Bowen wrote, "Captain Manley passed for Beverly to haul up."

The following day *Fowey* was under way, her journal noting "at 8 saw 5 rebel Privateers in the Eastern Channel, weighed and gave them Chace, after firing several 6 pounders at them they took shelter in Cape Ann." Since Washington had only four vessels in the area, and some of those had already been laid up, this would suggest some of the ships *Fowey* was chasing were indeed privateers, a few of the growing number of privately owned vessels hunting the seas for British prizes.

On December 29 Ashley Bowen wrote in his journal, "This day raw cold. Passed a cruiser to Beverly. The *Fowey* took no notice of her."

If Graves was looking to save his command by deploying *Fowey* to Marblehead and sending off a steady stream of excuses to Whitehall, he was too late by far. Unbeknownst to him, the Admiralty had the previous September decided to recall him to England. On December 30 the ax fell, with Rear Admiral Molyneux Shuldham arriving aboard the fifty-gun *Chatham* to take Graves's place.

Shuldham's arrival and his own dismissal took Graves entirely by surprise. Shuldham was Graves's junior and had not even achieved flag rank when Graves had been appointed to command the North American Squadron. Graves was shocked to see that Shuldham's orders were dated September 29, when the Admiralty had until nearly that date been sending Graves letters approving of his conduct. Shuldham's arrival was Graves's "first and only notice or intimation, either from the Admiralty or any part of Government, of having given dissatisfaction," though indeed his friend the Earl of Sandwich, First Lord of the Admiralty, had been dropping hints for months regarding Graves's inactivity.

Despite his shock and outrage, Graves, by his own account, "betrayed no Emotion or Resentment either at the thing itself or the manner of it, concealing all indignation, and was manly enough to avoid even taking the least notice of the hardness of his Usage."

With one day left in 1775, Graves was out and Shuldham was in. A little more than twenty-four hours would bring a new year and with it a new nation and an entirely new war.

CHAPTER 28 *A New Year*

"Head Quarters, Cambridge, January 1st 1776
Parole The Congress Countersign, America.
     This day giving commencement to the new-army, which, in every point of View is entirely Continental; The General flatters himself, that a Laudable Spirit of emulation, will now take place, and pervade the whole of it."

Thus began the first general orders issued by George Washington for the year 1776.

January 1 brought various and conflicting emotions to the American camps surrounding Boston. Literally thousands of soldiers packed their gear and headed for home, while five thousand militiamen took their places, holding the line until more troops could be recruited into the ranks of the Continental Army. Engineer Jeduthan Baldwin noted in his journal, "the Old Troops went of & left the lines bair in Some parts, cold."

A new army required a new flag, and on January 1 one was raised for the first time in Cambridge. Called the Union Flag or the Grand Union Flag, it consisted of the British Union Jack in the upper left corner against a field of thirteen red and white or sometimes red, white, and blue stripes. This would remain the official flag of the United Colonies until it was superseded later that year by the Stars and Stripes.

The raising of the Grand Union Flag was cause for celebration, and the event was marked by cheering from the American lines so loud it could be heard in Boston. But that enthusiasm would soon be dampened, and the goodwill of the men would turn to anger and a renewed dedication to the American cause.

The previous October King George had opened Parliament with a speech addressing the "present situation of America." Until news of his address reached America, many colonists still held out hope that the king remained a friend to Americans and that Parliament alone was the oppressor, but the king's address destroyed all such illusions.

The king told Parliament that the protestations of loyalty he had received from the colonies were a mere diversion "whilst they were preparing for a general revolt." He reported that despite the moderation and kindness with which he had treated the colonies, the "rebellious war now levied is become more general, and is manifestly carried on for the purpose of establishing an independent empire." The king announced that he had increased his naval and land forces to deal with the rebellion and, more ominously, had made treaties with foreign governments to help put down the insurrection.

"When the unhappy and deluded multitude . . . shall become sensible of their error," King George concluded, "I shall be ready to receive the misled with tenderness and mercy." He promised to give certain persons authority to grant pardons to whomever they saw fit and to accept the submission of any province or colony.

The text of the speech arrived in Boston in late 1775, and copies were sent out to the American lines by the British on January 1. The words marked a turning point in the war.

Ironically, the British cooped up in Boston thought the king's proclamation had produced the opposite effect. Soon after copies of the speech were sent out from the city, the soldiers and loyalists huddled there heard the cheering for the Grand Union Flag and took it to be cheering for the sovereign's words. Washington wrote of the incident to Joseph Reed, noting that "we gave great Joy to them (the red Coats I mean)." The cheering, he explained, "was receivd in Boston as a token of the deep Impression the Speech had made upon Us, and as a signal of Submission—so we learn by a person out of Boston last Night—by this time I presume they begin to think it strange that we have not made a formal surrender of our Lines."

As of January 1 the Continental Army still did not have all the men Washington desired or needed, but there were enough, with militia, to make him reasonably confident of countering any British offensive, and more were arriving every day.

The commander-in-chief was keenly aware of the extraordinary and unprecedented nature of what he had accomplished. On January 4 he wrote to John Hancock and the Continental Congress:

> It is not in the pages of History perhaps, to furnish a case like ours; to
> maintain a post within Musket Shot of the Enemy for Six months together,
> without [powder] and at the same time to disband one Army and recruit
> another, within that distance, of Twenty odd British regiments, is more
> probably than ever was attempted; But if we succeed as well in the last, as
> we have in heretofore in the first, I shall think it the most fortunate event
> of my whole life.

Washington omitted the word "powder," leaving its place in the sentence
blank. Powder was still so scarce in the American camp that he did not
dare write it for fear the letter might fall into British hands. But clearly
he was sanguine enough about his recruiting efforts not to mind if Lord
Howe got wind of them.

Though the army and the flag and the king's proclamation were new,
the strategic situation was unchanged. British and Americans still faced
one another in stalemate, neither one in a situation to mount an offensive. If anything, the Americans were in a worse position than they had
been at the end of 1775. The previous year Washington had at least
had his little fleet at sea, the only American force in the Massachusetts
theater able to carry the fight to the enemy. Now even his fleet was
immobile.

Washington was eager for a fight, as he had been since soon after
arriving in Cambridge the previous July. On September 8 he had peti-
tioned his general officers on the idea of launching an offensive against
Boston, thinking that "a Surprize [attack] did not appear to me wholly
impracticable, though hazardous." His generals, however, voted unanimously against the proposal.

In early October the idea was floated again, this time through a
"sense-of-Congress" resolution transmitted to Washington by the visiting committee of conference comprising Benjamin Franklin, Benjamin
Harrison, and Thomas Lynch. If Washington believed an attack could
be successfully carried out before the last day of December, when the
army's recruitments were up, Congress felt it should be done. Once
again Washington polled his general officers, and once again they felt
that the time was not right.

By December Washington was pretty much resigned to the stalemate.
Powder was low, his troops were going home, and he was struggling to

replace them. It was hardly an auspicious time for a major offensive. "I have no doubt that you . . . are wondering," he wrote to a friend, "how it happens that two Armies almost in Stones throw of each other should keep so long from Action—I can account for it in a few words—there Situation is such (being on two Peninsula's very strongly fortified and surrounded by Ships of War and Floating Batteries) that we cannot get to them and they do not choose to come to us."

Congress revisited the notion of an attack later in December. The discussion had always hinged in part on whether an attack should be made if it would cause the destruction of the town. After considerable debate, Congress resolved that if Washington and his council of generals felt such an attack would meet with success, they should launch it even if "the town and the property in it may thereby be destroyed." On December 22 the Congress communicated that resolution to the commander-in-chief.

Washington received the news in early January and in reply assured Congress that he would launch an attack "the first moment I see a probability of success." But that moment had not arrived, and the general went on to repeat that "circumstances, & not a want of inclination, are the cause of the delay."

No one was more eager to get at the enemy or more frustrated by the stalemate around Boston than General Washington. Sending Benedict Arnold off to Quebec, ordering Philip Schuyler and Richard Montgomery to move against Montreal, dispatching Henry Knox to collect the cannon at Fort Ticonderoga, and establishing an armed fleet were all means of getting things moving in the military line and, one might argue, indulging in a little vicarious warfare.

Happily for Washington, he did not have to wait long before the deck was shuffled again.

"The arch-rebels formed their scheme long ago"

The siege of Boston became a strategy by default. With neither side in a position to launch an offensive against the other, Washington's only military option was to starve the British out of Boston. The American command entertained no thought that doing so would end the war or even accomplish much of anything toward that goal, but there was nothing else to do.

The irony of the situation was that the British wanted to leave Boston. The troops had been sent there initially to suppress the growing insurrection in the city, not because Boston was an ideal location to quarter an army. It was in fact a terrible place to do so, and the British military commanders had recognized as much from the beginning. The proper beachhead for the British army in the colonies was New York City.

New York had several advantages. The wide Hudson and East rivers allowed naval access to every part of the city, making it impossible for the Americans to hem in the British as they could in Boston. The Hudson River provided easy access to Lake George, Lake Champlain, and ultimately the St. Lawrence and Canada. The British had long felt that controlling that waterway would effectively cut off New England from the rest of the colonies, making it easier to quash the rebellion. And New York was thought to harbor the most loyalist population in America.

Thomas Gage had raised that point back in July 1775. Writing to the Earl of Dartmouth, he pointed out that Boston was where "the arch-rebels formed their scheme long ago. This circumstance brought the troops first here which is the most disadvantageous place for all operations. . . . Was this army in New York, that province might to all appearances be more easily reduced."

The following month Gage reiterated to Dartmouth how poor a location Boston was, "and the more it is considered, the worse it is found to be." Once more he pointed out that the rebellion was now general and not confined to Massachusetts, making New York City the proper place for the army.

Dartmouth, the ministers in London, and the king agreed with this assessment. Dartmouth wrote to William Howe, who would supplant Gage, informing him of the government's opinion that the army should be shifted to New York immediately and not remain in Boston through the winter of 1775.

That letter was written on September 5 but did not reach Howe in Boston until two months later, and by then it was too late. Howe did not have enough tonnage of shipping to remove "the troops, the artillery, the stores of all denominations, the well-disposed inhabitants with their effects and such merchandise as it may be thought prudent to remove." If every vessel in port were employed, there would still be a deficiency of 11,602 tons. If the army were split and moved in two embarkations, it would leave both halves vulnerable to attack, particularly as the garrison in Boston would be depending on the timely return of the transports in a season when the weather could well prevent their returning at all.

Life was generally miserable for the garrison in Boston. Fuel was scarce. Houses and wharfs, particularly those belonging to Whigs, were torn down and burned. Rations were scarce and irregular, fresh provisions all but unheard of. Smallpox broke out, though luckily it amounted to no more than a minor epidemic. Though the officers staged balls and theatrical productions in Faneuil Hall, boredom stalked them relentlessly through the winter months. But they were not in any danger from the enemy.

"We are not in the least apprehension of an attack upon this place from the rebels by surprise or otherwise," Howe wrote to Dartmouth. "[O]n the contrary, it were to be wished they would attempt so rash a step and quit those strong entrenchments to which alone they may attribute their present security."

Howe may have seen the Americans' entrenchments as the primary obstacle to a British offensive, but he did not dismiss the threat posed by the Continental Army. In mid-January he wrote to Dartmouth, "Neither is their army by any means to be despised, having in it many European soldiers and all or most of the young men of spirit in the country who are exceedingly diligent and attentive to their military profession."

Lord Howe and General Washington found themselves of the same mind. Each understood the other was too strongly entrenched to attack, and each wished the other would ignore that fact and launch an attack anyway. And so, by unspoken mutual understanding, the stalemate continued.

The Continental Navy

The Boston battlefield may have been frozen and Washington's fleet tied to the docks in Beverly and Plymouth, but in Philadelphia the establishment of the Navy of the United Colonies was forging ahead. On

October 13 the Congress had finally authorized the fitting out of two small men-of-war at the Continental expense, one "to carry ten carriage guns" and the second of undetermined size and armament. A committee consisting of Silas Deane, John Langdon, and Christopher Gadsden had been appointed to prepare an estimate of that expense and lay it before Congress.

On October 30 the committee had reported, and their suggestions showed how much interest in naval affairs had grown in the few weeks since Congress had first considered the matter. They recommended that the resolution of the 13th be carried out "with all possible expedition," that the ten-gun vessel be made ready, and that the second vessel be of fourteen guns. The committee went on to suggest that "two other vessels be fitted out with all expedition; the one not exceeding 20 Guns, the other not exceeding 36 Guns."

Deane, Langdon, and Gadsden had upped the ante considerably. The vessels they described were not small ships like Washington's, meant to hunt down unarmed transports, but genuine men-of-war, as big as most of the ships Graves had prowling the approaches to Boston. To help plan the increasingly ambitious fleet, Congress decided to add four more members to the committee of three. Those picked to form what would be known as the Naval Committee included Congress's earliest and most vocal advocates for the establishment of a navy: Stephen Hopkins, Joseph Hewes, Richard Henry Lee, and John Adams.

The committee "immediately procured a Room in a public house in the City, and agreed to meet every Evening at six o Clock in order to dispatch this Business with all possible celerity." Once these delegates were given the reins of naval affairs, matters developed quickly, and the Naval Committee assumed a much more expansive view of its mandate.

On November 2 Congress resolved that the committee be authorized to draw up to one thousand dollars from the treasury and "to agree with such officers and seamen, as are proper to man and command such vessels." The men serving on Continental vessels would get one-half the value of any man-of-war captured and one-third the value of any transport. A resolution of November 11 specified that two battalions of marines be enlisted for service on the men-of-war and that no one should be entered into the marine corps who was not also a sailor or at least well acquainted with shipboard operations. Given the new navy's difficulties finding mariners to serve as sailors, however, it seems unlikely they found many to serve as marines.

A week after the committee was formed, John Adams wrote to his friend Elbridge Gerry, a Marblehead patriot and one of the leaders of the Revolutionary movement in Massachusetts, asking him to look into the availability of ships to purchase and mariners to man them. Though he had often portrayed himself as an authority on naval matters, Adams admitted to Gerry that "It is very odd that I . . . who have never thought much of old Ocean, or the Dominion of it, should be necessitated to make such Enquiries." But Adams was now thinking quite a bit about "old ocean," even asking Gerry to look into where men-of-war might be built from the keel up "in Case a Measure of that Kind Should be thought of." Adams fired off a similar letter to James Warren.

The Naval Committee wasted little time carrying out their first order of business, the purchase of ships. By mid-November four vessels were tied to the waterfront wharves of Philadelphia merchants Willing & Morris and James Cuthbert, undergoing a transformation from merchantmen to ships of the Continental Navy.

The largest of the four was the *Black Prince*, which was renamed *Alfred* after Alfred the Great of England, "the founder of the greatest Navy that ever existed." She was the flagship of the squadron, ship-rigged (square-rigged on all three masts) and carrying around thirty-two guns. Next in line was the *Sally*, which became *Columbus* "after the Discover[er] of this quarter of the Globe." Also ship-rigged, she carried about twenty-eight guns.

The other two vessels were brigs. One, another *Sally*, was renamed *Cabot* "for the Discoverer of this northern Part of the Continent." She mounted some fourteen guns. Last was the *Defiance*, which, despite already having an appropriate name, was renamed *Andrew Doria*, an incorrect spelling of the name of "the Great Genoese Admiral." Also joining the fleet was the Rhode Island sloop *Katy*, Congress's original vessel of "ten carriage guns," which had already seen so much action in the few short months since she had been commissioned. *Katy* was renamed *Providence* after the town from which she sailed, the hometown of Stephen Hopkins.

The men charged with converting the merchantmen to men-of-war in Philadelphia ran into many of the same supply problems John Glover and Stephen Moylan had encountered in Beverly. This came as a surprise to Moylan, a Philadelphian, who had once claimed that he would have had few problems outfitting Washington's schooners there. "How often have I exclaimed at the delays attending the fitting out our Beverly Fleet," he responded to Reed, who had written him of the headaches with the Philadelphia fleet. "I find this country [Massachusetts] should not bear so much blame as both of us have laid at its door." He added that he wished "the scheme of fitting both fleets out was adopted some months earlier," a sentiment Washington certainly shared with regard to his own vessels.

The Naval Committee also selected officers for the nascent fleet, and their choices were remarkable even by eighteenth-century standards of regionalism and nepotism. As "first captain," also given the title of admiral, the committee selected fifty-seven-year-old Esek Hopkins, the general in the Rhode Island militia to whom Ephraim Bowen had appealed for guns. Hopkins was a former privateersman and the younger brother of committee member Stephen Hopkins. Commanding the flagship *Alfred* was committee member Silas Deane's brother-in-law Dudley Saltonstall. Command of the *Columbus* went to Abraham Whipple, former captain of *Katy* and the man who had led the attack on HMS *Gaspee* in 1772. Whipple was certainly among the most qualified Americans for a naval command, but being both a prominent Rhode Islander and husband to the niece of Stephen and Esek Hopkins no doubt helped his cause.

The captain of the brig *Cabot* was John Burroughs Hopkins, Esek Hopkins's son. Command of the *Andrew Doria* went to the only non–New Englander, Nicholas Biddle of Philadelphia. Biddle would go on to distinguish himself in naval service, but he likely owed his appointment largely to the influence and connections of his prominent family. First officer on board the *Alfred* was a young Scotsman named John Paul, who had added Jones to his name years before to hide his identity after killing a mutinous seaman. On December 3, nearly a month before it would be raised in Washington's camp at Cambridge, Jones hoisted the new flag of the United Colonies, the Grand Union Flag, to the *Alfred's* gaff. It was the first time that flag had ever been flown.

By purchasing and fitting out four ships the Naval Committee had done as directed, but the committee members did not stop there. On

November 23 they presented for consideration of Congress a draft of the "Rules for the Regulation of the Navy of the United Colonies." Largely the work of John Adams, the rules were based on those of the British navy.

Adams's rules, as befitted a Boston lawyer, were extensive and comprehensive, touching on virtually every aspect of the operations of a man-of-war from how often divine services were to be performed (twice a day unless bad weather or some other circumstance intervened) to the daily food and drink allowance for each man on board (including half a pint of rum per man, every day). Behavior in battle, behavior on shipboard, punishments for various transgressions, the wages of officers and men, and more were covered.

The rules also included more of John Adams's characteristic micromanagement. The document specified that "The cooper shall make buckets with covers and cradles," and "All ships furnished with fishing tackle, being in such places where fish is to be had, the Captain is to employ some of the company in fishing." The rules also made clear that "there shall be supplied, once a year, a proportion of canvas for puddingbags, after the rate of one ell for every sixteen men." The rules were discussed, amended, and finally approved by Congress on November 28.

All this was accomplished before Congress made a formal decision to create a navy. That debate, centered on the motion from the Rhode Island delegation, had been postponed again and again. Proponents of the navy, recognizing that opposition was still strong, chose not to confront the issue head-on. Instead they eased Congress into a naval policy with one minor expedient measure after another, like easing the proverbial frog into the frying pan.

In mid-November Samuel Ward of Rhode Island wrote, "Our instructions for an American fleet have been long on the table. When it was first presented, it was looked upon as perfectly chimerical; but gentlemen now consider it in a very different light." Ward felt the motion should be brought forward again, but after sounding out some of his fellow delegates he realized that Congress was still not ready.

When the motion was finally reconsidered on December 11, the debate was almost a formality. Congress had begun the construction of a fleet, had chosen officers, and had established the rules and regulations for the service. They had given their blessing to Washington's naval endeavors and had authorized privateering and prize courts in the colonies. Incrementally, and almost invisibly, the proponents of a navy had created one.

When Congress as a whole resolved "That a Committee be appointed to devise ways and means for furnishing these colonies with a naval armament," the navy was formally established. The new committee to oversee naval affairs, the Marine Committee, consisted of a delegate from each colony. Samuel Adams replaced his cousin John as the Massachusetts representative, but a number of others who had sat on the Naval Committee, including Richard Henry Lee and Christopher Gadsden, now joined the Marine Committee.

The Naval Committee continued to meet into the second week of December. John Adams recalled those evening meetings, a gathering of collegial, like-minded men, as "the pleasantest part of my Labours for the four Years I spent in Congress." In his autobiography he left a detailed portrait of those gatherings, sequestered in their private tavern room on cold, dark winter nights in Philadelphia:

> Mr. Lee, Mr. Gadsden, were sensible Men, and very chearful: but Governor Hopkins of Rhode Island, above seventy Years of Age kept us all alive. Upon Business his Experience and Judgement were very Usefull. But when the Business of the Evening was over, he kept Us in Conversation till Eleven and sometimes twelve O Clock. His Custom was to drink nothing all day nor till Eight O Clock, in the Evening, and then his Beveredge was Jamaica Spirit and Water. It gave him Wit, Humour, Anecdotes, Science and Learning. He had read Greek, Roman and British History: and was familiar with English Poetry particularly Pope, Tompson and Milton. And the flow of his Soul made all his readings our own, and seemed to bring to recollection in all of Us all We had ever read. I could neither eat nor drink in those days. The other Gentlemen were very temperate. Hopkins never drank to excess, but all he drank was immediately not only converted into Wit, Sense, Knowledge and good humor, but inspired Us all with similar qualities.

On January 4, 1776, the first ships of the Continental Navy cast off from the wharf along the Philadelphia waterfront and ghosted onto the ice-choked Delaware River. In addition to the Grand Union Flag, *Alfred* was likely flying a flag presented to Esek Hopkins by Christopher Gadsden. Now known as the "Gadsden Flag," it consisted of a yellow field bearing a coiled rattlesnake and the words "Don't Tread on Me."

The small fleet braced its yards to a light wind and dropped a few miles downriver before dark and then tied up to the wharves on Liberty Island. The next morning they found themselves frozen solid in the ice, and there they would remain until January 17.

The Continental fleet added another layer to an already complicated naval picture. Under the auspices of various government and private organizations or with no authority at all, more and more armed vessels were putting out from American ports in search of British shipping. Nearly all the colonies had either established naval forces already or soon would. Privateers under the command and ownership of entrepreneurs swarmed out of the seaports of New England.

And there still remained the Revolution's first armed vessels, Washington's navy.

CHAPTER 29 *A New Fleet*

DESPITE THE disappointments and frustrations General Washington's fleet had caused him, the new year brought no lessening of his enthusiasm for naval warfare. Quite possibly the aggravations of his armed schooners paled when compared with those of the army. What's more, armed vessels remained his only means of actively engaging the enemy. Whatever the commander-in-chief's state of mind, he was ready to get his fleet back to sea.

Of the six original captains, only John Manley remained. That was fine with Stephen Moylan, who did not hide his disdain for the others, and most likely Washington felt the same way. Certainly his Excellency had been wholly unequivocal in his dismissal of Nicholson Broughton and John Selman and nearly as much so with William Coit. Winborn Adams chose not to continue in command of *Warren*, and the British navy had captured Sion Martindale and shipped him off to England. Nearly all the sailors had left their ships. The fleet reforming under the new Continental Army would be a virtual tabula rasa.

John Manley preferred the *Hancock* of the four vessels then at Beverly, and he assumed command of her on January 1. On that day he ordered various sundries to suit the vessel more to his liking. Along with several pieces of navigational equipment, "Two Four hour Glasses," and "One Speaking Trumpet," he purchased "Two China Mugs, Several Coffee Cups, One Coffee Mill, One two Gallon China Bowl," and "one new Beaver Hatt."

Washington issued a commission to Manley as "Captain and Commander of the schooner *Hancock*," something he had not done in the past. In his earlier instructions he had simply directed his army captains to "take the Command of a Detachment of said Army and proceed on Board" their ships. This new commission represented a higher level of formality in the establishment of his fleet.

It also reflected Washington's desire to maintain sole authority over his little ships. In creating a navy, Congress had drafted a boilerplate commission for officers, and a number of those blank commissions had been sent in a packet of Congressional correspondence to the commander-in-chief so that he might use them when commissioning captains. The Congressional commissions, however, made the captains answerable to Congress and to the commander-in-chief of the naval forces (at that time Esek Hopkins), as well as to Washington, and General Washington did not care to relinquish that much control.

Instead, the commission he issued to Manley and would issue to his other captains was his own creation and kept authority in his hands. "By virtue of the powers & authorities to me given by the Honorable Congress," the commission began, "I do hereby Constitute & appoint you Captain and Commander." It was the same authority he had tacitly assumed in creating his fleet in the first place, and since no one in Congress had objected, he felt free to claim it more explicitly now. The commission instructed Manley to obey all orders that "shall be given herein by the Honorable Continental Congress, myself or any future Commander in Chief of said Army." Washington could not avoid the overarching authority of Congress, but he would not have Esek Hopkins or any other naval officer interfering with his army's fleet.

Also on January 1 Washington appointed William Burke, who had served as master of *Warren* under Winborn Adams, to succeed Adams as captain, and he appointed an agent for the Continental vessels at Gloucester. There had previously been no agent there, though the armed schooners had often been forced to seek refuge in Gloucester's Cape Ann Harbor.

The agent was Winthrop Sargent, and Stephen Moylan sent him his instructions. They differed from those received by the other continental agents in just one material respect, the caveat that, "As the Harbour of Cape Anne, is not looked upon as safe to lay up any Prizes or their Cargoes, you must as soon as possible have such as may be brought in there, sent up to Beverly." The Americans did not know that Admiral Graves, at least, considered Cape Ann Harbor unassailable.

In late 1775 Congress had finally authorized the colonies either to establish prize courts or to adjudicate prizes in existing courts, and Washington was eager for rulings on the captured ships accumulating in Beverly and Plymouth. The schooners' sailors, having received none of their promised prize money, could hardly be blamed for their discontent. What's more, the captains of the captured vessels were caught in a legal limbo, forced to remain in Massachusetts under parole until the fate of their ships could be decided.

On January 3 Washington sent copies of the Congressional orders regarding prize courts to Jonathan Glover in Marblehead, William Bartlett in Beverly, and William Watson in Plymouth, along with orders to libel, or adjudicate, the prizes in the courts of admiralty established by the Colony of Massachusetts. "[Y]ou mus[t] use all your diligence that the trial be brought to as Speedy an issue, as possible, in order that a distribution be made to the Captors," he wrote.

The agents began immediately to move the ships through the courts, and almost as quickly they hit another snag. Because the Massachusetts law establishing admiralty courts did not entirely agree with the resolutions of Congress, the colony could not try vessels that fell under Congressional authority. To correct the problem the Massachusetts General Court amended their laws to conform to the resolutions of Congress, but that did not happen until February 20. The prizes were eventually adjudicated in April and sold in May, long after Washington had left the Massachusetts theater.

In Marblehead and Beverly, military affairs continued apace. On January 1 Ashley Bowen wrote, "Our men coming home from Cambridge and Beverly [Washington had stationed troops in Beverly] as the times are out for the last year. The *Fowey* lay as per last." The following day recruiters were marching through the streets to the roll of drums, raising men for the new army. "James Mugford Junior beat up for recruits for John Glover's men for the thirteen United Colonies," Bowen noted.

John Glover's 21st Massachusetts Provincial Regiment had been disbanded at the end of the year and a new regiment, the 14th Continental, formed in its place. On January 3 Glover himself was in Marblehead to "beat up for the 13 United Colonies and the 14th Regiment." Since the start of the war, Washington had been inundated with requests from seaport towns to have troops stationed there for their protection, as they saw themselves vulnerable to British seaborne attack. In refusing these requests, Washington had explained that he lacked enough men both to surround Boston and to garrison other towns. One of the few exceptions to this rule was Beverly, where part of the 21st and now the 14th were stationed. Washington's concern, of course, was not so much the town as his schooner fleet and their prizes.

Through the first weeks of January the schooners remained tied to wharves along the Beverly waterfront while John Glover and William Bartlett saw to their fitting out for further cruises. The weather turned warm, with rain and a January thaw, a reprieve from the bitter cold. Stephen Moylan rode out from Cambridge on January 3 to see that preparations were being made on the ships and "to try and get some of them to sea while the weather continues mild." Moylan feared that the presence of *Fowey* off Cat Island would prevent the schooners from getting out.

No sooner had Moylan completed his inspection and left than John Derby, who had loaned John Glover the cannons for the schooner *Lee*, arrived to demand the guns back. John and his brother Richard Derby were fitting out privateers and needed the guns for their own vessels. Despite his genuine patriotism, Richard Derby had reason to resent Washington's fleet. Two of his ships had been captured by Washington's schooners, and though they had both been released, the attendant trouble and expense had been considerable.

Bartlett tried to bargain with Derby, asking that the guns be left aboard the *Lee* for one more cruise, but Derby "Utterly Refused," a clearly flustered Bartlett wrote, "and insists upon having off them imediatly." Glover and Bartlett rode after Moylan, hoping to catch him and let the commander-in-chief's right-hand man deal with the standoff, but they could not overtake him.

A few days later Moylan responded to Bartlett's note, advising him to buy Derby's guns if Derby would sell. If not "he must give them to him." Moylan added, "be alert in fitting the Vessels out, &."

As *Hancock* and *Warren* were the only vessels with captains, they were farthest along in their fitting out. By January 9 *Hancock* was well provisioned, her hold stuffed with beef, potatoes, rice, water, molasses, rum, cordwood, and all the sundries needed to keep a ship at sea. A new square sail was being built. But the weather had turned colder, with the wind blowing a gale from the northwest, and *Hancock* remained tied to the dock.

John Glover rode to Cambridge to report to Moylan on the vessels' progress. Both Manley and Burke had managed to recruit officers and men in "a sufficient Number for these Small vessells." As to guns, if Derby's could not be purchased, Moylan wrote, Bartlett was to take the ordnance from the vessels that were not yet ready for sea. There were also four guns available from the prizes *Nancy* and *Concord*, and Moylan believed "four as good as six for the Purpose these Vessels are fitted out." Indeed, *Lee* had originally been fitted out with four 4-pounders, though Manley may have added two more while she was under his command.

One vessel, the *Harrison*, remained in Plymouth, and like the Beverly ships she was tied to the dock and deserted. But Washington wanted her out to sea as well. Moylan wrote to William Watson on January 7 ordering him to "examine into the Condition of Captain Coit's Schooner." Coit had repeatedly disparaged the vessel, leading Moylan to think she might not be seaworthy. If she was, Watson was to "look out for some Person qualified to take Command of her" and have that person assemble a crew. But if she was unseaworthy, and if another schooner, "remarkable for sailing," could be found along with a "clever Set of Officers & Men," then Watson should fit that ship with the *Harrison*'s gear and send her off to sea.

A week later Watson sent his reply. After "strict enquiry" into *Harrison*'s condition he was told "(tho she be not very well accomodated for the officers) is an excellent Sailor; & is sufficiently strong." Coit had found much humor in the tiny officers' quarters, but his assessment of *Harrison*'s seaworthiness was quite different from that of Watson's surveyor. Here was another example, as with the brigantine *Washington*, of two or more presumably knowledgeable men reaching very different conclusions regarding a ship's condition.

With that positive assessment and an estimate of at least £100 to outfit a new ship, even using the guns and equipment from *Harrison*, Watson recommended sending Coit's old ship back to sea.

The man who carried Watson's letter to headquarters was Watson's choice to command *Harrison*. Captain Charles Dyar had sailed with Coit, and Watson felt "his character is high as a good officer, & as an active, smart sailor." Dyar was not much at public speaking, however, and Watson warned Washington that he would not "at first interview appear to your Excellency, to advantage, he is no orator & seems rather softly."

Dyar's lack of oratory skills did not seem to bother Washington. Perhaps a soft-spoken, tongue-tied man was even a relief after William Coit. His Excellency agreed to give Dyar command of *Harrison* and to enlist a crew for a six-month term. Dyar recommended that *Harrison* be fitted out with a square sail and some other light sails. Washington left this to Watson's discretion but, eager to get the schooner to sea, suggested that Dyar cruise with the sails he had while the new ones were made up.

Watson felt that there would be no problem recruiting good men for her crew as long as they could enlist for six months rather than a year and as long as the apparently popular Dyar remained in command. "Our people are very fond of knowing their officers," Watson wrote. That much Washington knew. He had learned it to his chagrin early on.

The Armies Look South

Vice Admiral Molyneux Shuldham had been having a rather hard time since first hoisting his flag aboard the fifty-gun ship *Chatham* in Portsmouth, England, on October 3, 1775. Shuldham was under orders to proceed to Boston on board *Chatham* and succeed Samuel Graves "in the Command of His Majesty's Ships and Vessels employ'd and to be employ'd in North America." Two days later the ship unmoored and made sail for America with a favorable wind from the west northwest, but before she could clear the harbor the wind backed into the southwest, and *Chatham* was forced to return to her mooring and wait for another fair breeze.

The delayed departure gave Shuldham a chance to complain to the Secretary of the Admiralty, Philip Stephens, about his accommodations. Anchored at Spithead, the newly minted admiral wrote that he found his apartment on board the ship "so very unfit for an Officer of my Rank that I am sure there is not a Man on board her who is not furnished with a more Warm and comfortable Lodging."

Four days later Shuldham reiterated his complaint that "the *Chatham* is the worst and Oldest of any of the Fifty Gun-ships upon that Service," and particularly unfit as she would be "his constant residence" while in Boston. He requested that the ship *Vigilant,* also at Portsmouth, a sixty-four-gun ship only two years old, be fitted out and sent to him in the spring. Shuldham preferred *Vigilant* because "she is the most Floaty Ship of her Class in the Harbour."

For the time being, however, Shuldham had no choice but to endure the *Chatham*, which finally got under way in late October. There was no letup in the harsh weather, and the ship endured sixty days of punishment in her voyage to Boston. "[T]he Voyage was almost a constant Succession of Storms and contrary Winds," he wrote to Stephens, "attended with the most severe Weather I ever felt, which has so Shatter'd the *Chatham* that she must remain unfit for any Sea Service 'till she is Chaulked and repaired."

Shuldham learned firsthand the truth of what Graves had been alleging the past three months. The weather throughout the fall and winter had indeed been brutal, and shipping had suffered considerably. As one captain of a British transport wrote to the ship's owners after his arrival in Boston, "The sea continually washed over us, and froze so excessively hard, that, had it not been for our masts, we might have been taken for an island of ice."

The foul weather was a greater enemy to British resupply than all the armed vessels the Americans could muster. Early in 1776 a British officer was dispatched to the West Indies to see if he could locate any of the supply ships that had been sent to Boston but had not arrived. In Antigua he found thirty-seven of them. Unable to reach Boston, they had run for the West Indies island for shelter and were languishing there in various states of disrepair.

When *Chatham* finally came to anchor in Boston, Shuldham learned about the grim strategic situation he had inherited. He wrote to Stephens, "I was much concerned to hear on my Arrival of the Number of small Arm'd Vessels fitted out by the Rebels, and which had taken many unarmed Ones of Ours bringing Stores and Supplies to this place." The admiral began laying the groundwork for future excuses, pointing out that even though Graves had stationed his men-of-war "in all the most likely places to intercept them," the rebels had been "too early Suffer'd to take possession of all the Harbours, Creeks and Rivers on this Coast," which provided them effective bases of operations. His point, essentially, was that if he could not stop the depredations of the rebels' cruisers, it was because Graves, General Thomas Gage, and General William Howe had not done their jobs.

Shuldham recommended that all future stores and supplies be sent out in armed vessels. That would solve two problems. The transports would be able to protect themselves, and the extra men needed on board an armed ship could be left in Boston to fill out the crews of the men-of-war, which had been woefully short of their complements since the outbreak of fighting.

Boston, Shuldham found, was a town making preparations. Howe was preparing to shift his army to New York as soon as possible. Indeed, it was hoped back in London that he had already done so. Shuldham had been ordered to make his way to Boston "or whereever else you might hear Vice Admiral Graves to be." But Howe still did not have transports enough to move the army in one embarkation. On January 16 he wrote to the Earl of Dartmouth, "[T]hat no time may be lost in transporting the army from hence to New York, I shall continue to take up all proper vessels that can be got." Until transports were sent from England, however, he would never have enough.

With provisions in Boston as short as ever and supply ships falling prey to weather, Washington's cruisers, and now privateers, it was time to become more proactive in feeding the garrison. Howe ordered two transports with 175 marines aboard, in the company of the twenty-gun frigate *Scarborough*, to Savannah, Georgia. There, he hoped, the Royal governor, with the marines at his back, would be able to load the ships with rice and other provisions.

At the same time, preparations were under way for a British offensive against a totally unforeseen target. With the northern theater huddled in stalemate and winter quarters, the king and his cabinet in London (like George Washington) were eager to find some other means of prosecuting the war. The British government believed, not unreasonably, that the southern colonies were more fundamentally loyal than New England and that the South, being more dependent on trade, would not hold out for long against an assault. Based in part on the commonly held but erroneous belief that a fifth column of loyalists would rise up to join an invasion, the cabinet decided to launch a seaborne assault on Charleston, South Carolina.

Organization of the southern command had begun in October. On October 22, Dartmouth wrote to Howe in Boston that Sir Henry Clinton had been tapped to command the attack on Charleston. Those instructions arrived in Boston with Admiral Shuldham on December 30.

Shuldham did not assume command of the fleet immediately upon his arrival, and it was left to Graves to organize the naval side of the campaign. He and Howe began to make arrangements to transport Clinton and two companies of light infantry and some Highlanders south to meet troops that would be sailing from England. The twenty-gun frigate *Mercury* and the fourteen-gun sloop-of-war *Falcon* were made ready for the voyage, along with two transports.

On January 6 Graves ordered Alexander Graeme, captain of *Mercury*, "to receive Major General Clinton, his retinue and Servants and such Officers as the General may desire." In all, Clinton's party amounted to eleven men, a lot to house in the officers' quarters of a twenty-gun ship, which were hardly roomy to begin with. Always on the lookout for the army's comfort, Graves ordered "Cots to be made for them and Births built with Old Canvas and Deals to accommodate them in the best manner you can."

George Washington was careful to keep informed of developments in Boston, and these preparations did not escape his notice. He wrote to John Hancock on January 4 that "a very Intelligent Gentleman" from Boston told him of "a Fleet now getting ready under the Convoy of the *Scarborough*." Washington did not know where this gathering threat would strike, but he had an idea.

Howe was not alone in understanding that his army had to leave Boston and that New York was the proper base for British operations. Washington had figured that out as well. He wrote to Hancock that some believed the convoy was bound for Newport, Rhode Island, "but generally thought in Boston, that it is meant for Long-Island; and it is probable It will be followed by more Troops." To Connecticut governor Jonathan Trumbull he wrote that "there is great reason to believe that this Armament, if not immediately designed against the City of New-York is nevertheless intended for Long Island." He added, "It is a matter of the utmost importance to prevent the Enemy from possessing themselves of the city of New York."

General Charles Lee, Washington's second in command and the man many considered the Continental Army's best officer, likewise understood the need to keep New York out of British hands. "The consequences of the Enemy's possessing themselves of New York," he wrote to Washington, "have appear'd to me so terrible that I have scarcely been able to sleep." Lee urged Washington to send him to Connecticut to raise a body of troops for the defense of the city, which Washington did after first clarifying with John Adams, who was then in Massachusetts, that New York fell within the limits of his command.

A few weeks later, when word reached Washington that Clinton had sailed from Boston, it reinforced his belief and concern that New York was the target. Washington thought Howe was moving his troops piecemeal to the city, unaware, of course, that Howe deemed such a move too risky. By the end of January 1776, both British and American commanders had turned their attention to New York. Both sides understood that this would soon be the new theater of the war, but no one knew when.

"Sailed Manley in schooner"

While *Harrison* in Plymouth was being outfitted for her next cruise, *Hancock* and *Warren* in Beverly were also readying for sea. On January 17, Bartlett received word from Washington's secretary, Robert Hanson Harrison, that four of the sailors from the prize *Concord* had been granted permission to ship out as crew aboard the schooners. For safety's sake, however, Washington indicated that he "would not wish that great a Number of them should be in one vessel."

Weather and a lack of guns and sailors were obstacles to be overcome or waited out before the schooners could put to sea. But a potentially more difficult problem lurked just off the entrance to Marblehead, three nautical miles south of Beverly's outer harbor. That was the twenty-four-gun frigate *Fowey*, under the command of Captain George Montagu, the ship that a month before had captured Sion Martindale and the brigantine *Washington*.

The locals were keeping a wary eye on the frigate. Ashley Bowen's journal noted nearly every move the British man-of-war made, from cutting wood on Cat Island to sending her longboat to sound the channel.

But *Fowey*, powerful as she was, was not the ideal ship to stop traffic in and out of Beverly. Her size and her square rig made her difficult to get under way, which meant that she could not react quickly when an enemy vessel suddenly appeared. Though a frigate was nimble compared with ponderous ships of the line, still she was not weatherly enough to maneuver easily through the confined waters and among the many hazards to navigation off Beverly, Salem, and Marblehead.

Fowey had arrived on December 29 and soon after moored near Cat Island in a spot that left plenty of sea room all around. Montagu no doubt remembered the mauling *Nautilus* had received after venturing too close to Beverly the previous summer.

For two weeks the ship rarely moved, only shifting her moorings once in a while. Montagu struck the topgallant masts and yards, depriving the ship of her uppermost sails—a common enough practice during the winter months when fierce storms might be expected. The *Fowey*'s crew were put to work hanging sails out to dry, "drawing and knotting yarns, making platts, etc."—busywork, essentially. The longboat was sent to collect more ballast. The frigate never cleared for action. The ship's log shows an almost leisurely existence on board.

Two weeks after arriving at Cat Island, Montagu struck the frigate's topmasts and topsail yards, on which were set the topsails, the primary driving sails. With only her lower masts left in place, *Fowey* was rendered practically immobile.

A greater threat to the Americans was the schooner *Halifax*, of six guns and ten swivels, commanded by George Dawson, which joined *Fowey* on January 3. *Halifax* was a match for Washington's schooners both in firepower and maneuverability, and she put those traits to work. On January 16 her log recorded, "at Noon Standing to wards the No[rth] shore to prevent the Rebel Vessels getting out of Beverley Harbour . . . PM got all Clear for Action Boat Empd during the Night rowing Guard."

Warren was ready for sea on January 17. The wind was light in the morning, with snow, hail, and thick fog. In the afternoon Burke judged the conditions right for slipping past the cordon of British men-of-war, and at 5 P.M. he dropped down the river and stood into the outer harbor, where the *Halifax* was lying in wait.

At the sight of the big schooner, the British cruiser took off in pursuit, blasting away with her deck guns. The wind by then was blowing a fresh gale from the north northwest, and Burke crowded on canvas to get to open water, returning *Halifax*'s fire as he did so. "[S]he soon got past us after firing seven shott at us," the master's log of *Halifax* recorded, "and Not being aquainted wt the passage she got safe out to sea."

With night coming on, Dawson did not dare drive his schooner through the tricky, dangerous waters of the bay. Local knowledge and the right weather conditions allowed *Warren* to get out to sea and resume the hunt. It must have been clear enough to Burke that *Fowey*, with her topmasts struck, was not going anywhere. Ashley Bowen wrote simply, "Tis said Burke sailed from Beverly."

The following day *Halifax* remained at anchor close to Beverly, where the frigate feared to sail. Around noon, in clear weather and a fresh breeze, a schooner was spotted on the east side of the bay. *Halifax* got under way at once, giving chase and firing at her as she closed. Probably still fearing for his schooner in the tricky approaches to Beverly, Dawson loaded the yawlboat with an armed crew and sent them tearing off under sail.

The schooner, either by accident or as a means of escape for her crew, ran aground. The yawlboat came up with her and boat crew boarded the abandoned ship, but the chase had been seen from shore. Locals grabbed up small arms and peppered the British sailors with gunfire as they worked to get their prize floating again. Finally the *Halifax*'s men "brought her off Notwithstanding the feiring of the Rebels from the Beach."

She turned out to be no more than an innocuous fishing schooner, but Dawson kept her as a tender to *Halifax*, a minor consolation after missing the most coveted prize, one of Washington's armed schooners.

Two days later, on January 20, George Montagu, captain of *Fowey*, came on board the *Halifax*. Montagu was likely frustrated by his frigate's limitations and eager to join the action. Soon after, the *Halifax*'s new tender and boats from *Halifax* and *Fowey* drove another schooner ashore, but this time "the Rebels coming down and feiring on our Boats Prevented them from destroying her."

The schooner escaped, but in any event she was not the schooner the British were after. The day before Ashley Bowen had written in his journal, "Sailed Manley in schooner . . . on a cruise." Bowen apparently did not know the name of Manley's new command, but he did know that Washington's navy was once again at sea.

CHAPTER *30* *Commodore of the Fleet*

WITH *HANCOCK* and *Warren* under way, attention turned to the remaining two schooners in Beverly, *Franklin* and *Lee*, which were not far behind. Captains had been selected for those ships shortly after William Burke was picked for *Warren*. *Franklin* would be commanded by Samuel Tucker, a Marblehead captain, and *Lee* by Daniel Waters, a native of the town of Malden, four miles northeast of Cambridge.

Stephen Moylan wrote to George Washington from Beverly requesting commissions for the new captains. Robert Hanson Harrison, filling in for Moylan at headquarters, sent the commissions for Tucker and Waters on January 20, the day after Manley sailed. Though Burke was the first captain to get his ship under way, for some reason his commission would not be issued until February. When it came, it was identical with the others', keeping control of the fleet in General Washington's hands and away from the commander of the Continental navy.

Harrison also sent Washington's instructions for the captains. These did not differ greatly from those issued to Nicholson Broughton nearly five months earlier except in the handling of prizes. Broughton's instructions had called for prize masters to take captured vessels into port and "notify me by Express immediately of such Capture, with all Particulars and there to wait my farther Direction." The new instructions directed captains to deliver their captures into the care of the port's prize agent, an office that had not existed in September 1775. Washington would no longer involve himself directly. With full Congressional approval for his naval activities he no longer needed to hide or obfuscate them.

The clause covering recaptures was missing from the new instructions. That too was now the agent's business. The instructions concluded with a harsh admonition reflecting Washington's dissatisfaction with his earlier captains. "As it was very apparent," the section began,

—that the ill Success which attended the Major part of the Armed Vessels in the former Cruzes was owing to the want of Industry & the inactivety of the Officers who Commanded You will therefore take Notice, that a fondness to be on Shore—indolence or activity will meat with there Just deserts—for if it appears, that the Captain or any of the Officers do not exert themselves & do all that they possibly Can for there own & the publick good—they shall be dismissd the Service—& renderd incapable of Serveing there Country in any Honourable Station hereafter—in the Army or Navy.

If the prize money offered "For your encouragment and that of the other Officers & men" was a small carrot, that final paragraph was a large stick. Broughton and Selman, who had made as big a hash of their assignments as one could imagine, had nonetheless been offered the chance to rejoin their army units. No longer. From now on, incompetence or even a perceived lack of exertion would result in dismissal from the service with no chance of serving again. Washington still held fond hopes for his fleet and wanted captains who could fulfill those hopes.

To that end, the commander-in-chief was happy to hear from Moylan in Beverly that the vessels were nearly ready for sea. "His Excellency is much pleased that our fleet is likely to get out again," Harrison wrote to Moylan, "& wishes your return as soon as you have dispatched them." Moylan had become nearly as invaluable to the commander-in-chief at headquarters as Joseph Reed had once been.

On January 23, *Fowey* hove up her anchors and made sail for the first time since mooring off Cat Island on December 30. The frigate sailed about a mile and a quarter east and came to anchor again off Bakers Island, where Captain Montagu hoped to find a supply of drinking water, which had run short on Cat Island. About that time Montagu dispatched the *Halifax* back to Boston with a letter informing Admiral Graves (who had not yet relinquished command to Molyneux Shuldham) that he could not put a stop "to the Insolence of the Privateers" without more force.

As if to prove the point, Samuel Tucker in *Franklin* slipped out of Beverly soon after *Fowey* shifted to Baker Island, clearing Salem Neck and dropping anchor in Marblehead. Once darkness fell, *Franklin* weighed her anchor and stood for the open ocean. The next day Daniel Waters in *Lee* did the same.

The new orders under which the captains sailed contained one other clause not found in Washington's instructions to his earlier captains. Number six read, "As Captain Manly is appointed Comodore of the four Schooners now fitted out . . . you are to obey him as Such in all Cases." Hoping that John Manley could inspire and lead others to replicate his success, Washington made him commodore of the fleet. Washington wrote to Hancock, "I have for his great vigilance & Industry appointed him Commodore of our Little Squadron & he now hoists his Flag aboard the Schooner Hancock."

Less than a week later, Manley would demonstrate once again why he warranted his promotion.

The General Gage

For four days after clearing Beverly, John Manley cruised the approaches to Boston without success, but that would change. The sea lanes were filling with greater numbers of transports sent from England and Canada to relieve the troops and civilians battened down in the city. Despite the increasing presence of privateers, enough shipping was getting through that General Howe, on January 19, ordered a halt to the practice of tearing down houses and wharves for firewood, which had been going on for months.

There is no record of where Manley cruised in those first four days, but by January 25 he was ready to enter the lion's den. The weather was fair and cold and the wind offshore from the north northwest, good conditions for hunting. In the early morning hours he set his course for the main channel into Boston. By 8 A.M. he was only a few miles southeast of Boston Lighthouse and just outside the mouth of Nantasket Roads, where British men-of-war rode at anchor. It was from there that Captain William Coit had staged his daring but ultimately futile raid the previous November 24, but Manley was a luckier man.

Also standing for Boston was a merchantman from Whitehaven, England, with a load of potatoes and sea coal. Her name was *Happy Return*, which would prove to be a double misnomer. *Hancock* closed with the transport, guns run out, the "Appeal to Heaven" flag snapping at the main gaff. Manley no doubt hailed her with his new speaking trumpet, and she surrendered without resistance.

The capture of *Happy Return* took place, it was later pointed out, "within two miles of the *Renown*, man-of-war [a fifty-gun fourth rate], then in Nantasket Road, who did not offer the least assistance, though the wind was off shore." *Renown* was likely not the only British man-of-war to watch the capture. The fifty-gun *Centurion* and the *Nautilus*, which had already grappled with Washington's schooners, were also in the area. But, like *Fowey* off Marblehead, those ships could not get under way at a moment's notice. The incident points not to lethargy on the part of the Royal Navy but to the fact that big, square-rigged men-of-war were the wrong ships with which to go after nimble schooners.

Manley sent a boarding party across to *Happy Return*, and the transport's crew and captain, James Hall, were taken on board the *Hancock*. A prize crew boarded the merchantman with orders to sail her into Plymouth. Plymouth was not Manley's homeport, but neither was it guarded by *Fowey* and *Halifax*, which were patrolling the waters off Beverly. Plymouth was also an easier run in the prevailing wind and did not require working upwind past Nantasket Roads. Darting into the lion's den was one thing, but taunting the lion was another.

So *Hancock* and her prize put up their helms and shaped a course southeast toward Plymouth with the wind well astern. By 9 A.M. they had covered about five miles and were off the town of Cohassett when the *Hancock*'s lookouts spotted another sail. She proved to be the *Norfolk*, also a transport ship and likewise out of Whitehaven. Like *Happy Return*, she surrendered with no resistance.

Manley removed the captain and crew from *Norfolk* and put a prize crew on board her as well. Washington's schooners had put to sea the previous autumn with crews of fifty to seventy men, but that had been deemed excessive. Now they were manned with some thirty sailors before the mast, and placing prize crews on two vessels left Manley only sixteen men on the *Hancock*. That was more than enough to sail the ship but not nearly enough to sail and work the guns efficiently. Thus, there would be trouble if *Hancock* was forced to engage the enemy, which of course is exactly what happened.

Just as the prize crew was getting *Norfolk* under way for Plymouth, three more vessels hove into view. Two were small provision vessels from

Halifax, but convoying them was "a schooner of eight carriage guns, with many swivels and full of men." She was the tender *General Gage*, a vessel that would have been more powerful than *Hancock* even if the latter had been fully manned.

As Manley's prizes raced for Plymouth and the *General Gage*'s charges raced for Boston, the two schooners closed with one another. Carriage guns, swivel guns, and small arms lashed out as the ships exchanged fire, circling for advantage. The *General Gage*'s captain, with his superior numbers, might well have tried to run alongside *Hancock* and board, but Manley kept off and maintained a barrage of iron.

William Watson later told Washington that the shorthanded Manley "receivd considerable assistance from his prisoners, more particularly from the Captains, who did as much as they dared do in such circumstances." Watson presumably heard that from Manley himself, though why the prisoners would want to help their captors is unclear. Perhaps they were currying favor, secretly sympathized with the American cause, or were annoyed that the Royal Navy had done nothing to help them.

For half an hour the two ships fired into each other. The *Hancock*'s rigging was cut up and one man, the gunner, suffered a mild chest wound. There is no record of damage to the *General Gage*, but the British schooner's captain must have thought he was getting the worst of it, as he finally put up his helm and ran for Boston. Manley did not follow. According to one report, *Hancock* had only six cartridges left.

By six o'clock that night, *Hancock* and her two prizes were safely at anchor in Plymouth Harbor alongside the *Harrison*. The Plymouth schooner had yet to sail, though nothing was "wanting for the *Harrison* but a Guner & a few Quire of cartridge paper."

Also at anchor was the seventy-five-ton sloop *Yankee*, commanded by Corban Barnes. *Yankee* was a privateer sailing out of Plymouth, one of the growing number of privately armed vessels hunting the enemy.

William Watson had not seen Manley since *Lee* had last called at Plymouth the previous autumn. He immediately took charge of the prizes and sent the captured documents off to Washington with a report of the action. "I congradulate your Excellency on this reitterated instance of Commodore Manlys success," he wrote, "and wish sincerely, that all the servants of the american Republic were equally industri[ous] with Manly."

A few days later, Watson wrote again to correct a few omissions in his first hasty report. He now reported that Manley might have taken the *General Gage*'s convoy "had it not been for the cowardice of one of our Continental armed Vessels, who was very near them, but dared not engage." Washington, of course, was furious that one of his captains could behave in such a manner. Moylan wrote back to Watson demanding an inquiry and requesting that he "Let the General know which of the schooners it was."

Nothing ever came of the issue, which would suggest that Watson had once again garbled his information. If there was a second armed vessel—and none appears in any of the accounts of the fight (which are all secondhand)—it might have been a privateer, not one of Washington's armed vessels. Privateers were under no obligation to fight anyone they did not care to fight. This helped them minimize risk and maximize profit but limited their military usefulness.

From the *Hancock*'s tiny great cabin, John Manley also wrote to Washington, reporting on his success and the fight with the *General Gage* and using the opportunity to request a larger vessel. Washington wrote back praising Manley's "Conduct in engageing the eight Gun Schooner, with So few hands as you went out with, your attention in Secureing Your prizes, & your general good behavior." He assured Manley that he would have "Comand of a Stronger vessell of War" as soon as one could be had, but that he should continue to cruise in *Hancock* until then and hopefully "inspire the Captains of the other Armed schooners under your Command with Some of your activity & Industry."

In the same letter Washington informed Manley of having instructed the other captains that "they are to be under your Comand, as Comodore." It has been suggested that this was the first Manley had heard of his advancement, though it would seem unlike the commander-in-chief to promote an officer without bothering to inform him until well after the fact. More likely Washington had notified Manley early in January that he would be in overall command of the fleet.

The morning after Manley's arrival in Plymouth, January 26, a cold front descended on the region. "This day smart cold," Ashley Bowen reported from Marblehead, and for the next four days his journal entry began with that same phrase. Harbors began to freeze over. Watson wrote to Washington near the end of January, "Commodore Manly is now in our harbor, has been puzzeled with the Ice, (with which we are now blocked up) but has received no damage." *Harrison* was more than puzzled by the freeze. "Capt. Dyar is now in the Ice, has lost a anchor & cable, but we hope to find them again, we are now cutting the ice & hope to get him out without further damage."

Eager as John Manley undoubtedly was to be cruising again, the ice held him fast in Plymouth Harbor until the month of January was nearly out.

Captains Ayres, Tucker, and Waters

It was a measure of the faith Washington still had in his little fleet that he wished to replace the captured *Washington* with another armed schooner. That ship would be named *Lynch* after the third congressmen in the delegation that had visited headquarters the previous October.

The man selected to command *Lynch* was John Ayres, and his first lieutenant was Marbleheader John Roche. By the end of January a suitable ship had been located in Manchester, about halfway between Beverly and Gloucester, frozen fast in the ice.

At the request of Lieutenant Roche, twenty-one men from John Glover's 14th Continental Regiment were selected "for assistance to bring up a Schoonr from Manchester lately taken into the Continental Service." By January 28, Ayres, Roche, and the Marblehead troops were in Manchester, housed in a nearby tavern and ready to begin the task of getting the ice-bound schooner to Beverly.

Ayres hired eight local men to help chop the vessel out of the ice. It was slow going, and considerable work had to be done just to ready the schooner for the short jaunt down the coast. On February 6 Ayres put a carpenter and five assistants to work on *Lynch*. The next day she was ready to go.

February 7 was bitter cold, with the wind blowing from the northwest and squalls rolling through the area. *Lynch* pounded into the freezing chop on a starboard tack for the six-mile reach along the coast from Manchester to Beverly. But weather was not Ayres's only concern. Just as the other Beverly schooners had to run past *Fowey* to get out of the harbor, *Lynch* would have to run past the frigate to get in.

Fowey had been on the move, patrolling from Marblehead to Cape Ann, but by February 7 she was once again moored by Baker's Island. Ayres kept north of her, to windward, as he raced for Beverly. *Fowey*'s log read, "fired 17 Nine Pdrs at a Rebel Privateer running in thro' Bakers Island Channell." Knowing he would never catch the schooner, Montagu contented himself with hurling round shot at her as she passed.

Once in Beverly, *Lynch* was tied to Glover's wharf and began her conversion from fishing schooner to man-of-war. Material poured in over her bulwarks: steering sail booms, deadeyes, scrub brooms, crosstrees, square sails, planks, grindstones, ensign staffs, rigging, handspikes, and on and on. As usual, the work took longer than expected. Not until the last week of February was *Lynch* provisioned with "40 Galls W[est] I[ndian] Rum, 10 Barrs Beef, 86 lb Rice," and sundry other stores. So much time was lost freeing *Lynch* from the ice and getting her fitted out and provisioned that by the time she was able to assist General Washington in the siege of Boston the siege was all but over.

While *Lynch* was tied up in Beverly, the *Franklin* and the *Lee* cruised the waters off Cape Ann, lookouts scanning the horizon. Samuel Tucker and Daniel Waters had decided to keep company during their cruise. Two ships could cover twice the area of one and could help one another in case of trouble.

It was hard sailing, with snow falling heavily on January 26 and bitter cold enveloping the region. The harbor at Marblehead froze over. Offshore, ice from wind-driven spray built up on the schooners' decks and coated the rigging as *Lee* and *Franklin* beat back and forth, hunting British transports. "Tedious cold," Ashley Bowen wrote.

Finally, on January 29, they met with some luck. Cruising halfway between Cape Ann and Boston Lighthouse, the two schooners crossed paths with a westbound sloop. When the sloop was made to heave to and her papers examined, she proved to be the *Rainbow*, Samuel Perkins, master. Her cargo consisted of "45 Cords of wood about 10 Bushels of Potatoes 2 Busshels of Turnips a quantity of Spruce (for beer) . . . also a peice of Vension a quarter of Veal & a Goose."

Perkins claimed that he was bound from Damariscotta, in the district of Maine, to Newburyport or Salem, and he produced as proof a certificate from the Committee of Safety of Newcastle (adjoining

Damariscotta). But Tucker was skeptical, since Perkins had somehow managed to sail right past both of his supposed destinations and seemed to be heading for Boston. He put a few of the *Franklin*'s hands aboard and sent *Rainbow* into Cape Ann.

Franklin and *Lee* followed in *Rainbow*'s wake, but the seas were not as free of threats as they had been. *Fowey*, like a bear waking from hibernation, was on the move again. "[A]t 10 sway'd up the Topgall't Masts," her log recorded—illustrating just how ponderous it was for a ship such as *Fowey* to get under way—"claped a slip Bouy on the small Bower [anchor] Cable & sliped it, hove up the best Bower [larger anchor] and gave chase to 4 Privateers to the Westward."

The weather began to deteriorate as *Fowey* chased the *Franklin* and *Lee*, "fresh gales with sleet," according to *Fowey*'s log, "½ past 1 A.M. the Privateers took shelter in Cape Ann Harbor." Tucker and Waters did not remain there long. After delivering *Rainbow* to the authorities at Gloucester, they once again weighed anchor and stood out to sea.

The hunting was still good. On February 2 they stopped a brig named the *Henry & Esther* "Laden with wood, 150 Butts of water, & 40 Suits of Bedding . . . one of the transports in the Ministerial Service." A prize crew took the vessel to Annisquam Harbor on the northern coast of the Cape Ann peninsula. Under clear skies and a moderate gale, Tucker and Waters headed south and west around Cape Ann, making for the approaches to Boston and keeping the shelter of Gloucester and Beverly at their backs.

Once again the two schooners sailed under the guns of *Fowey* as she patrolled the waters around Baker's Island, but Captain Montagu had perhaps learned the day before how pointless it was to try to run the fast schooners to ground. The *Fowey*'s log recorded, "fired 5 Guns & several swivells, at some Rebel schooners," and that was all the effort he made before Tucker and Waters ducked back safely into Cape Ann Harbor.

There the two captains learned that their first prize, *Rainbow*, had been sent on her way. Her captain, Samuel Perkins, had produced his certificate from Newcastle when questioned by a member of the local committee of safety and had given his solemn oath that he was bound for Salem, and that was enough to secure his release. Later, after *Rainbow* was captured by *Fowey* with suspicious ease and sent into Boston, questions would arise as to whether Perkins was a patriot, a loyalist, or playing both sides. Those questions would never be answered with certainty, underscoring once again the ambiguities in the rules of engagement.

As spring came on and the weather turned more favorable for shipping, however, opportunities for prize-taking would only increase. And after months and months of stasis, the changing season would also bring a seismic change in the prosecution of the war.

CHAPTER *31*   "*[A] Stroke well aim'd*"

BY MID-JANUARY the naval war for *matériel* was under way again, but in Cambridge Washington felt that the opportunity to launch an attack against the enemy in Boston had already passed. There was no money in the arms chest and little gunpowder in the storehouses. Recruitment had slowed, and many who had joined had failed to report to camp. The army was greatly in need of muskets, as new recruits were refusing to bring weapons from home unless paid an allowance for their use and guaranteed the right to bear the arms home again when their enlistments were up.

Worse yet, many of the troops from the old army had taken their muskets home with them despite Washington's precautions and threats aimed at preventing just that. "[W]e have not, at this time 100 Guns in the Stores," Washington wrote to Joseph Reed, "of all that have been taken in the Prize Ship." Departing troops had managed to undo nearly all the benefit accrued from John Manley's capture of the *Nancy*.

The endless parade of problems, the grinding winter, and military inactivity were taking a toll on the commander-in-chief's optimism. Writing to his friend and confidant Reed, he vented his frustrations. "This Letter discloses some Interesting truths," he admitted, adding that he would be uneasy until he knew Reed had received it and it had not fallen into the wrong hands. "Could I have foreseen the difficulties which have come upon us . . . all the Generals upon Earth should not have convinced me of the propriety of delaying an Attack upon Boston till this time." He often thought he would be happier if he had "taken my Musket upon my Shoulder & entered the Ranks," or, if he could have justified such a thing, "retir'd to the back Country, & livd in a Wig-wam."

In theory Washington could have resigned. As a practical matter, his honor would never have allowed it. And for all his private complaining, it is unlikely he would have wanted anyone but himself at the head of the army.

On January 16 another council of general officers was held at headquarters, this time with John Adams and James Warren joining the military men. Washington "laid before the Council a State of the Regiments of the Continental Army, the consequent Weakness of the Lines and in His Judgement, the indispensable necessity of making a Bold attempt to Conquer the Ministerial Troops in Boston."

Perhaps shamed by the presence of civilians, the council for the first time "agreed unanimously" that an attack should be made "as soon as Practicable," without actually committing to any specific plan. The council suggested that Washington request thirteen regiments of militia from Massachusetts and the neighboring colonies to augment the troops of the Continental Army. In effect, the decision to take decisive action against the enemy was again put off for another day.

The month of January brought little change to the strategic situation around Boston save for one development in the Americans' favor. On January 18 the hulking, portly Colonel Henry Knox arrived at Cambridge to report the completion of his mission to Ticonderoga. Twenty miles away, at Framingham, lay the train of artillery that he and his men, through an extraordinary effort, had hauled across the frozen countryside from Lake Champlain in northern New York. This impressive battery consisted of forty-three heavy cannon—12- and 18-pounders—plus one 24-pounder, eight mortars, and a number of smaller guns.

Washington saw in this newly arrived ordnance an opportunity. South of Boston was Dorchester Neck, a stretch of high ground that, if fortified, would command the city and more importantly the harbor, making it untenable for any British ship to remain at anchor there. As early as July of the previous year it had been suggested that Dorchester Heights be fortified, but Washington had rejected the idea for lack of artillery. Now that was no longer a problem. And thanks to John Manley and the *Nancy*, the Americans had shells to accompany Henry Knox's mortars.

On February 11 Washington made an inspection of Dorchester Heights with Knox, generals John Thomas and Joseph Spencer, and engineering officers Rufus Putnam and Richard Gridley. Five days later he convened another council of war.

Once again Washington suggested an assault on Boston. The requested militia units had come in or were coming in. The garrison in Boston amounted to no more than five thousand men, according to the latest intelligence, but would be receiving reinforcements shortly. "[A] Stroke well aim'd at this critical juncture," Washington argued, "might put a final end to the War, and restore peace & tranquility."

Whether he actually believed that or was hoping his generals would is unclear, but Washington was eager to mount an attack. He was conscious of "the Eyes of the whole Continent fixed with anxious Expectation of hearing of some great Event." He knew it was up to him to provide such an event, but he was unable to do so. The reasons he could not attack—a lack of gunpowder and a shortage of men—were military secrets. Ignorant of those facts, people might conclude that the commander-in-chief's backwardness prevented offensive action.

The other members of the council were more measured in their consideration, perhaps because their reputations were not so much on the line. Once again they rejected the idea of an all-out attack, even though they had approved it in concept the month before. The generals believed correctly that Howe had more than 5,000 troops (he actually had 8,906 officers and men). Less than half the militia Washington had requested had arrived. An assault should be preceded by a bombardment of the town, and there was insufficient powder for such a thing.

The council did decide to take one step, however. "Resolved . . . preparations should be made to take possession of Dorchester Hill, with a view of drawing out the Enemy."

Hancock *and* Hope

On January 30 John Manley managed to free *Hancock* from the ice of Plymouth Harbor. With the skies clear and the wind blowing fresh, *Hancock*'s crew swayed away on the halyards to set the fore-and-aft sails, and the schooner stood out into open water.

Sailing with *Hancock* was the privateer sloop *Yankee* commanded by Corban Barnes. "Manly & the yankee Barnes now under sail bound on a cruise," William Watson wrote to Washington that day. That was likely a first, a Continental armed vessel and a privately armed vessel sailing in company. Adjudicating any prize taken by both of them would have been a nightmare, though presumably Manley and Barnes discussed that before sailing together. Manley no doubt saw the pairing as a way of expanding his range and firepower with no expense to the Continent, the essence of the attraction of privateers, but he would have no authority over Barnes.

The captains would not get to test the practicality of their alliance, however. As they stood out of Plymouth Harbor with the whitecaps of Cape Cod Bay stretching out before them, they sailed into the path of a British man-of-war.

That vessel was the brig *Hope*, a former merchantman named *Sea Nymph* that had been taken by *Mercury* and carried into Boston. There she was fitted out by Admiral Graves specifically to hunt down Washington's ships. "The *Hope* Brig is perhaps one of the best fitted and appointed Vessels of her Size in the Kings Service," Graves wrote to Philip Stephens. "She mounts eight 4 Pounders, and six 3 Pounders besides Swivels; I have given her a Corporal and nine Marines to complete her 50 Men."

Hope was ideal for going after Washington's schooners. She was far better armed and manned than any of the Continental vessels and was probably as fast a sailer. While not as nimble as a schooner, she was not nearly so ponderous as the great men-of-war, which could do little other than ride at anchor at Nantasket Roads or, like *Fowey*, shift anchorages now and again. "I hope she will soon do Execution with the Enemies Privateers," Graves concluded.

When Graves said "enemies privateers," he had John Manley in mind. Manley would have been gratified to learn that his name was known and despised in Boston. British Lieutenant Colonel Stephen Kemble, for example, on hearing a report concerning a rebel ship, wrote that it was "said to be that same Manley commanding, who has done so much Mischief on the Coast, by taking our Merchant Ships."

Hope's captain, Lieutenant George Dawson, received orders to "Cruize against the Rebels within the Bay of Boston." At 8 A.M. on January 30, eight bells in the morning watch, as *Hancock* and *Yankee* were getting under way to the south, Dawson "Got up T-G-yds [topgallant yards] Weighd & Came to Sail." The armed brig bore away before the fresh breeze, making ten knots as she raced along the coast south of Boston. By noon she had passed Plymouth Harbor. The tip of Cape Cod was nine miles to the north northeast and the weather was starting to deteriorate when a sail was spotted in the distance. "Made Sail & Give Chace," the *Hope*'s log read.

The sail was *Hancock, Yankee* having apparently sailed off. Manley might at first have seen the brig knocking around Cape Cod Bay as a potential prize, but once she began to crack on sail and come after him in bold pursuit, he must have quickly realized she was no unarmed merchantman. He put up his helm and raced north, His Majesty's brig *Hope* right in his wake.

The wind was blowing from the south southwest, and *Hancock* had the wind over her larboard beam as she raced northwest along the coast. The wind had been perfect for getting out of Plymouth but was foul for getting back in, so Manley bypassed that safe haven and continued north, working his way closer to the coast.

Hope was on a good point of sail, and it is likely that she began to overhaul *Hancock* as the two vessels raced toward Boston. At some point Manley abandoned the idea of outrunning the brig, if indeed he had ever harbored such a hope. At 4 P.M., with night coming on, he swung *Hancock* to the west, close-hauled, standing into the North River and the harbor at Scituate, and drove the schooner hard aground.

Dawson brought the *Hope* within gunshot of the stranded vessel, which he now knew for certain was "one of the Rebel armd Schooners." He came to anchor and opened up with the brig's broadsides, pouring round shot into the immobile *Hancock*. The schooner's guns would not bear on *Hope*, and Manley's men could do nothing but endure the pounding.

Manley himself was ill and remained below in his cabin. A cannonball from one of *Hope*'s guns smashed through the stern section and passed six inches from Manley where he lay. A slight change in the gun's elevation and Dawson would have enjoyed a hero's reception in Boston.

Later reports suggested that *Hope* fired "not less than 400 times upon the privateer," which would seem an exaggeration, though apparently 130 balls were collected on shore the following day. Around 7 P.M. the tide lifted *Hancock* off the sand and her crew attempted to work her up the river, but once again they ran aground and stuck fast. Still caught under the brig's guns and facing the real possibility of capture, Manley ordered the *Hancock* scuttled. Water poured into the grounded hull, and the ship settled further into the sand.

The weather continued to worsen, a fresh gale driving snow before it. Around 8 P.M. Dawson left off firing into the darkness, tucked a second reef in his topsails, and sent down the topgallant yards he had sent up that morning. *Hope* spent an anxious night with her anchor dragging, despite veering nearly 150 yards of cable.

While *Hope* was fighting the storm at anchor, Manley and his crew made their way ashore and summoned help from the local militia. During the night breastworks were hastily constructed on both shores of the river and a few pieces of field artillery trundled into place.

Dawn came with a break in the weather and the Americans ready to defend their armed schooner, which Dawson on board *Hope* intended to finish off. "Hoisted the Boats out and Sent them Mand & Armd to Endavour to Set her on fire," *Hope*'s journal read. Through a barrage of small-arms and artillery fire, *Hope*'s men rowed to where *Hancock* lay on the sandbar and boarded the abandoned vessel.

They found the schooner half sunk, nearly full of water, and so far gone that it seemed she would never sail again. In that condition they had no hope of burning her. What's more, the constant fire from shore made things acutely uncomfortable for the British sailors on *Hancock*'s deck. They removed a swivel gun and a red ensign and left *Hancock* on the bar, "the Privateer being effectually disabled from ever cruizing again," Dawson later reported.

The action at the mouth of the North River had been nearly a repeat of the defense of *Hannah* against *Nautilus* in Beverly the previous autumn—and with similar results. Rumors of *Hancock*'s demise were greatly exaggerated. She was soon refloated and taken around to Scituate for repairs.

For Washington's fleet, going to sea was becoming an increasingly dangerous proposition. Taking command of the North American Squadron from Samuel Graves at the end of January, Molyneux Shuldham, now a vice admiral, pursued a more aggressive course against the American fleet and the privateers. *Hope, Fowey, Lively, Nautilus,* and other men-of-war were kept constantly patrolling the approaches to Boston and Cape Cod Bay. On February 22 William Watson wrote from Plymouth, "The *Harrison* Capt. Dyer returned last night from her second unsuccessful cruize. our enemies are very vigilant, and in good weather, are seen every day from this shore."

The point was driven home the next day when *Harrison* and the privateer *Yankee* stood out of Plymouth Harbor only to find *Hope* once again lurking around Cape Cod Bay. "Saw two Sail, Running out of Plymouth Harbr," the *Hope*'s log recorded, "found them to be a Sloop and Schooner Rebel Arm'd Vessels."

Dawson closed with the rebels, but this time the American ships did not race for the safety of Plymouth. With two vessels against Dawson's one, Charles Dyar and Corban Barnes decided that the odds favored them.

The fight took place so close to shore that William Watson could see the entire drama from the window of his parlor. For three hours the vessels traded shot, the Americans no doubt relying on their number and maneuverability, the *Hope* leaning on her heavier firepower and her larger and better-trained crew.

In the end it appeared that neither the rebels nor the Royal Navy had the edge. By 6 P.M. the fight was over, though who broke it off is unclear. William Watson observed, "Dawson . . . was obligd to sheer off . . . and was seen stopping the shott holes when he bore away."

The *Hope*'s log, on the other hand, recorded, "Engaged, them and Drove them into Plymouth." Despite that laconic description, the rebels had managed to dole out a beating to *Hope*. The lower yard on her mainmast was damaged and one of the main shrouds and much of the running rigging shot away.

Twice in the course of a month, Washington's captains had stood up to and driven off ships of the vaunted British navy—first Manley against the *General Gage* and then Dyar against *Hope*. Dyar could not have taken on the brig alone. Watson wrote to Joseph Trumbull, "Capt Barnes of the *Yankee* deserves the thanks of the public, who rescued the *Harrison* from destruction." But privateers such as Barnes were simply another aspect of the developing picture; the Americans were growing more bold and aggressive in taking the fight to sea.

There is no record of damage done to *Harrison* and *Yankee*, but at least some of *Hope*'s gunfire must have hit home. For *Harrison* it was a moot point. Even before word of the fight reached headquarters, it was decided to put the schooner out of commission. She was in such disrepair and would have required so much work to make her seaworthy that she was judged not worth the effort. A letter to Watson informed him of the decision and advised him to take care of "every article belonging to the Continent on board." Of the contradictory assessments of *Harrison*'s condition, William Coit's proved correct.

Washington's fleet had taken a few notable prizes in January, but February proved a disappointment. *Harrison* had taken no prizes in the month, and now she was condemned. *Lynch* was still fitting out, and *Warren*, *Franklin*, and *Lee* had had no luck. Even John Manley had been sidelined by the *Hope*, the *Hancock* standing in need of repair before she could cruise again.

For months the schooner fleet had been Washington's only means of fighting the enemy around Boston. But that was about to change.

The End of the Siege

The night of Monday, March 4, was set as the time that Dorchester Heights would be fortified. To distract the enemy, beginning on March 2 General Washington opened up on Boston with a barrage of shells and round shot. Reluctant though he was to expend precious powder and shells, particularly on a diversionary tactic, he was staking a great deal on this plan. After eight months of virtual inactivity, this was his first major offensive. Placing artillery on Dorchester Heights would make the city untenable for the British, but Washington's real hope was that it would finally force General Howe to come out of the city and fight.

The British and Loyalists in the city were shocked when the long-silent batteries suddenly opened up, raining exploding shells among the closely packed wooden houses. A Salem ship's captain taken prisoner by the British escaped and reported to Washington that the "Bombardment and Cannonade caused a good deal of Surprize and alarm in Town, as many of the Soldiery said they never heard or thought we had Mortars or Shells." The soldiery must have forgotten about the ordnance brig *Nancy*. Certainly after *Nancy* was taken there had been considerable comment about how her cargo would be used against her former owners.

The mortar fire did little damage to the city, however. Firing mortars was a demanding task requiring trained artillerists, which the Americans lacked. On the first night the neophyte gunners managed to burst two thirteen-inch mortars and one ten-inch gun. One of the thirteen-inch guns was the mighty *Congress*, "the Brass one taken in the Ordnance Brigg" and once the pride of the American lines.

The next night the shelling resumed, and again the night after that. Howe later reported to Dartmouth that the Americans "threw some shells . . . without doing any personal damage and but little to the buildings." Six British soldiers were wounded. The gunfire was answered with a fusillade from the British lines, their guns blasting out blindly in the night "at such a distance as to be very uncertain in the execution." Only two Americans were killed by British guns over the three nights, a lieutenant who had a leg shot off and a private killed by an exploding shell.

Any injury done to the British in Boston was a secondary consideration. The gunfire was merely cover for the real work of fortifying Dorchester Heights, which began on the night of March 4.

Leading the troops on Dorchester Heights was General John Thomas, a Massachusetts physician who was well liked and respected at headquarters. Just after dark, as the gunfire commenced, Thomas and his men, about two thousand strong, moved out. A "full bright moon" illuminated the landscape, and the night was "remarkably mild and pleasant."

Leading the way was a covering party of about eight hundred men, who took possession of the heights with no resistance and indeed without the British having any inkling what they were up to. The covering party was followed shortly by the main force of twelve hundred men led by General Thomas. With them were wagons pulled by three hundred teams and filled with entrenching tools, hay, and fascines—bundles of sticks that would form a base for the earthworks and which the army had been furiously manufacturing in advance of that night.

Hay piled up along the ridge formed a screen from the enemy, and under the direction of engineering officers Richard Gridley and Rufus Putnam, fortifications were raised on the ground previously marked out. With pickaxes and shovels the men began entrenching earth frozen eighteen inches deep, heaping dirt over the fascines and raising the walls of the forts. A Connecticut officer recalled, "in one hour's time we had a fort enclosed, with fascines placed in shandelears; and we immediatly employed as many men at intrenching as could be advantageously, used for that purpose."

Around 4 A.M. a relief party took over the exhausting labor from the men who had begun the entrenchments. By dawn the Americans had built three forts strong enough to withstand enemy shot atop a rise much higher than Bunker Hill, with a commanding view of the city and harbor. It was March 5, the sixth anniversary of the Boston Massacre.

When the sun came up, the British troops in Boston looked south and were shocked at what the enemy had wrought overnight. General Howe paid an inadvertent compliment to the extraordinary effort of the Americans when he wrote to Dartmouth, "It was discovered on the 5th in the morning that the enemy had thrown up three very extensive works with strong abbatis round them on the commanding hills on Dorchester Neck, which must have been the employment of at least 12,000 men."

If Howe had reason to be alarmed, Admiral Shuldham had even more. Artillery on Dorchester Neck could do little harm to the soldiers, but plunging fire from the heights could sink ships riding at anchor in the harbor. This, indeed, was Howe's major concern as well. If the fleet was driven off, the troops would be genuinely trapped, as would happen to Cornwallis at Yorktown nearly five years later.

Howe had only two options, fight or flight, and his honor and that of the British army would not allow flight to be the first choice. Shuldham wrote that the entrenchments on Dorchester Neck were "so alarming and I presume unexpected an Event . . . that General Howe Ordered an Attack to be made upon it that night."

Twenty-four hundred British troops were loaded onto transports and flat-bottomed boats to be conveyed to Castle William (on Castle Island, now joined to the mainland at City Point, South Boston), from where the attack would be launched against the heights. This was exactly what Washington had hoped for. The works had been strengthened throughout the day and were well manned by troops who expressed "a warm desire for the approach of the enemy." Barrels filled with earth and stones were arrayed along the edge of the heights to be rolled down on the tightly packed troops that would march up the slopes, Bunker Hill fashion, into the guns of the entrenched Americans.

But even a fight on Dorchester Heights, which promised every chance for an American victory, was not enough for Washington, who had waited so long for this moment. In a clever plan that Howe apparently did not anticipate, Washington ordered four thousand troops under the command of Israel Putnam to stand ready to embark in boats and launch an attack against Boston once Howe had committed troops to the assault against Dorchester Heights.

It would have made for a bloody day indeed, and the British would likely have had the worst of it, but it was not to be. "[T]he Wind blowing too fresh for the Boats to Row ahead the Expedition was laid aside," Shuldham wrote. Howe did not yet abandon his attack, however, merely postponing it until the next day. But the storm raged on, whipping itself into a frenzy of rain and hail that lasted through the daylight hours of March 6.

The storm afforded Washington's men two additional days to strengthen their defenses, a fact of which Howe was well aware. "The weather continuing boisterous," he wrote to Dartmouth, "gave the enemy time to improve their works, to bring up their cannon and to put themselves in such a state of defense that I could promise myself little success by attacking them." There was no doubt considerable relief among the king's officers and men when word passed that they would not be attacking Dorchester Heights after all. Rather, Lord Howe "judged it most advisable to prepare for the evacuation of the town."

The siege of Boston was over.

CHAPTER *32* "*It is with the greatest pleasure I inform you*"

LOADING BOSTON'S troops, loyalist civilians, and *matériel* on board transports would have been a difficult logistical task even in the best conditions. Doing so with too few transports, too few supplies, and as quickly as possible under the constant threat of attack from the enemy made the operation a chaotic nightmare for General Howe and Admiral Shuldham. "A thousand difficulties arose on account of the disproportion of transports for the conveyance of the troops, the well-affected inhabitants, their most valuable property, and the quantity of military stores to be carried away," Howe wrote.

The patriotic civilians in Boston were happy enough to see the British go, but their chief concern was that Howe would destroy the town on his way out. They had good reason for their fears, as Howe had made it clear he would do so if the Americans interfered with the embarkation of troops and stores. A delegation from Boston sent word to Washington informing him that Howe "has no intention of destroying the town, unless the troops under his command are molested" and asking that Washington send some assurance that the British troops would be left alone.

Washington replied that, as the note "was not obligatory upon General Howe," he could not make such a promise. There was, in fact, no formal communication at all between Howe and Washington during the British army's evacuation of the city, and neither man ever knew for certain what the other intended. But Howe wanted simply to get his troops and the loyalists safely out of Boston, and Washington wanted them to leave and not to burn the city on their way out the door. Each commander saw that it was in his best interest to leave the other alone. On March 13 Washington called a council of war. Even after a week of watch-

ing the preparations in Boston, the commander-in-chief could only spec-
ulate as to Howe's plans, but "he had reason to believe that the Troops
were about to evacuate the Town." The chief question then was where
the British would go. Washington told the council that "in all probability they were destin'd for New York, & would attempt to posses themselves of that City." Washington was correct. He had understood all along
that New York was the proper seat of operations for the British army in
America. What he did not appreciate was the disarray in which Howe
found himself and his desperate lack of provisions, for which Washington's fleet was in part responsible. Howe needed to regroup and secure
several months' worth of supplies before he could launch the next phase
of military operations. He explained his decision to Dartmouth, writing:

> I am justly sensible how much more conducive it would be to His Majesty's
> service if this army was in a situation to proceed immediately to New York,
> but the present condition of [the] troops crowded in transports with
> regard to conveniences, its inevitable dissortment of stores, and all the
> encumbrances with which [it is] clogged, effectually disable me from the
> exertion of this force in any offensive operations, although I should
> receive a supply of provisions before my departure from hence, which con-
> siderations I hope will lead His Majesty to approve of my determination.

"Halifax," he explained, "is the only place where the army can remain
until supplies arrive from Europe."

The quick evacuation and lack of transports meant that a lot had to
be left behind. When they could find no buyers, officers destroyed the
furniture they had purchased. Cannons for which there was no space
shipboard were spiked and thrown into the harbor along with their
ammunition. Howe would later write from Halifax, upon reading the
returns of what stores had been destroyed, that "in the ordnance branch
they have exceeded my expectations."

The previous summer General Gage had given a commission to
ardent Tory Crean Brush to receive and store the household goods of
anyone in Boston whose home was to be used to quarter British troops.
Now Howe commissioned Brush to "take into your possession all such
goods" that would be of use to the enemy. Brush went about his duties
with a vigor born of his hatred for the rebels, breaking into storehouses,
stripping them, and loading the plunder on board the storeships *Min-*

erva and *Elizabeth.* Soon soldiers and sailors were imitating his example, looting the city despite Howe's promise to hang any looters on the spot.

Unsure of Howe's plans, Washington continued to strengthen Dorchester Heights and to further encircle Boston with his lines. On the day he called his council of war, Washington wrote to John Hancock that the British, to his surprise, had not yet left the city. Still, he remained fairly certain they would, as a number of transports had already dropped down to Nantasket Roads. He likewise did not know whether the city would be destroyed, but "from the destruction they are making of sundry pieces of Furniture, of many of their Waggons, carts &c," it seemed unlikely, as that effort would be needless if they intended to put the whole town to the torch.

At the western end of Dorchester Neck, pointing like a finger at Boston, was a piece of high ground called Nook's Hill, which even more than Dorchester Heights commanded the city below. Washington had so far resisted fortifying it for fear the British would panic and do something rash. By March 16, however, he was ready to give Howe a little push. That night Continental troops occupied Nook's Hill and began to throw up earthworks as they had on Dorchester Heights. The British opened up with 24-pounders, firing on the works throughout the night to no effect. The Americans wielded picks and shovels and held their fire.

The next morning, American guns on Nook's Hill looked down on the Boston waterfront less than a mile away. Howe knew his time was up. He ordered the last of the men onto the transports, and the ships dropped down to the anchorage at Nantasket Roads.

"It is with the greatest pleasure I inform you," Washington wrote to Hancock on March 19, "that on Sunday last, the 17th Instant, about 9 O'Clock in the forenoon, The Ministerial Army evacuated the Town of Boston, and that the Forces of the United Colonies are now in actual possession thereof."

The city was not nearly as shattered as Washington had feared it would be. He happily informed Hancock that "Your house has receiv'd no damage worth mentioning." Hancock's furniture was "In tolerable Order," and even the family portraits were unmolested. During most of the siege, the house had been occupied by General Henry Clinton. It was lucky indeed that no harm had come to it since Clinton's departure.

Now Washington's thoughts turned entirely to New York. When it had first appeared that the British were abandoning Boston, he had sent a rifle battalion there to begin building a troop presence. As soon as the British evacuation became a near certainty, Washington sent another five regiments south. As long as Howe's ships remained at Nantasket Roads, however, Washington himself would remain in Cambridge. He informed Hancock that he would make the shift to New York once "all Suspicion of their return [to Boston] ceases."

Because of Washington's decision eight months earlier to arm a fleet of schooners, Shuldham's fleet would not be able simply to disappear over the horizon. Washington assured Hancock that he would "direct Commodore Manly and his little Squadron to dog them," keeping an eye on where the British fleet was bound and "picking up any of their Vessels that may chance to depart their Convoy."

The Wolf Pack

While Washington and his troops were sealing Howe's fate in Boston, the commodore and his little squadron were regrouping for the coming campaigning season. It was snowing on February 17 when John Manley took his schooner, newly repaired in Scituate after her run-in with *Hope*, back to Marblehead. "Anchored here the *Hancock* cruiser from the South Shore," Ashley Bowen wrote, "and this afternoon she sailed round to Beverly."

By the end of February five schooners were operating out of Beverly: *Hancock*, *Lee*, *Franklin*, *Warren*, and *Lynch*. They hunted the waters off Massachusetts and ran the gauntlet of *Fowey*, *Nautilus*, and *Hope* in and out of port, but they met with little luck in the way of prizes. Thanks to Admiral Shuldham, the seas were actively patrolled by British men-of-war, and Washington's fleet now had competition. The fourteen-gun brig *Yankee Hero*, a privateer out of Newburyport, was also cruising in Manley's area and managed to take the brigantine *Nelly*, inbound for Boston, on March 2.

Around the beginning of March, Commodore Manley changed his fleet's tactics. Washington had long advocated that each schooner be given an area to patrol, and this approach had been followed in a general way since the inception of the armed vessels. Now, however, rather than patrol individually, Manley decided that the fleet should hunt as a pack, generally four schooners at a time, depending on who was at sea.

That the neighborhood was getting dangerous may well have influenced Manley's decision. Both he and Charles Dyar of *Harrison* had grappled with the well-armed and well-manned *Hope*, and there were other, more powerful cruisers looking for Washington's fleet. It was not long before the wisdom of Manley's new approach revealed itself.

On March 3, *Hancock*, *Lee*, *Franklin*, and *Lynch* were cruising off Marblehead when the fleet's *bête noire*, *Hope*, and the armed schooner *Tryal* hove into sight. *Hope* was cruising to the south of the fleet. Her log recorded "at 1 [P.M.] Made Sail after the four Vessels to the No wd [northward] at 4 Came up with them [proved] to be Rebel arm'd Schooners."

Once again *Hope* found herself confronting Washington's fleet. Like *Harrison* and *Yankee* in Plymouth, the schooners opted to stand and fight, and this time there were four rather than two, with a combined firepower of sixteen 4-pounder guns, two 2-pounders, and twenty-six swivels to *Hope*'s eight 4-pounders, six 3-pounders, and ten swivels. *Tryal* likely carried four small carriage guns, but the British were still outnumbered and outgunned. If anyone had sufficient reason to put up his helm and run for safety it was *Hope*'s commander, Lieutenant George Dawson, but of course such a thing would be unthinkable for an officer of the Royal Navy confronting mere rebel schooners possessing no more than a two-to-one advantage.

The vessels closed to within range of their guns around 5:30, just as the sun was setting. They were close enough to shore that Ashley Bowen was able to watch the fight from the high ground surrounding Marblehead Harbor. "This evening," he wrote, "I saw a brig and a schooner engage four of the Continental schooners."

The fight was quick and sharp, with the wolf pack swarming around *Hope* and *Tryal* and pouring round shot into them. The Royal Navy brig's rigging was shot up and she took numerous hits between wind and water. One man was wounded. As with the earlier fight, there is no record of damage to the American vessels, but they likely did not escape unscathed.

After half an hour it was over. "Night came on, they parted," Bowen wrote. Who broke off first is unclear, but once it was over, neither side showed much interest in resuming. The *Hope*'s log read "at 6 P.M. . . . Schooners Boraway for Cape Ann Harbr Hauld our Wind to the East ward."

Cruising to the east was the frigate *Lively*, whose masthead lookouts witnessed the end of the fight. "4 Sail in Sight," her log read, "which we judged to be Privateers the *Hope* Brig & *Tryal* Schooner in Chace of them," which, if true, would indicate that the Americans were the ones to break off and run for safety, though *Hope*'s log makes no mention of a chase. If *Lively* had been able to join the fight, the outcome would have been different, but the action was over by the time she was close enough to observe it.

Three days later the wolf pack met with some luck. The ship *Susannah*, bound from London to Boston with "Coal, Porter & Krout," was unlucky enough to sail into the net Manley cast over the approaches to Boston. She struck to the fleet and was carried into Portsmouth, New Hampshire.

For the next few days British men-of-war continued to swarm over Manley's cruising grounds. The thirty-two-gun frigate *Niger* joined *Fowey* off Beverly, and *Hope* and *Lively* maintained their patrols. Manley's squadron managed to avoid them but could take no more prizes. Rumors of Continental troops fortifying Dorchester Heights began to filter into Marblehead, but nothing was known for certain.

Then, on March 8, Admiral Shuldham sent orders for His Majesty's sloop *Nautilus* to get under way immediately and make for Marblehead. Her mission this time was not to harass Washington's schooners but to carry recall orders to all British men-of-war in the neighborhood. With the decision made to evacuate Boston, Shuldham wanted his fleet ready to help in that effort. Washington's schooners could wait.

On the afternoon of March 8, Ashley Bowen watched *Nautilus* stand in around Marblehead Neck and make the signal for *Fowey* to return to Boston. "[I]mmediatly the *Fowey* came to sail," he wrote, "and stood over from Beverly shore and joined the other ship and both stood for Boston." It must have been a lovely sight for Bowen and all the patriots of Marblehead, Salem, and Beverly to see the hated *Fowey* disappear over the horizon. Life for Manley and his squadron suddenly became much safer and less complicated.

Two days later another large transport, the *Stakesby* of three hundred tons, was swept up by Manley's fleet. Like *Susannah*, *Stakesby* was carrying coal, cheese, porter, and sauerkraut, a source of ascorbic acid—vitamin C—used to combat scurvy in the British navy.

Night came on bitter cold with fog closing down visibility, poor conditions for a landfall as the fleet escorted the prize to Gloucester. About three miles from the harbor, the *Stakesby* piled up on the rocks, her hull shattering from the impact. Manley in *Hancock* hit the ledge as well. The shallower-draft schooner slid over into deeper water but only after having "Damaged his Vessel Verey Much." *Hancock* lost her bowsprit and likely suffered other damage, but she managed to limp into Gloucester. *Stakesby*, however, was not going anywhere.

Winthrop Sargent, the Continental agent in Gloucester, immediately organized a salvage party. Four days after *Stakesby* went aground he could report to Washington that he had saved "all the Sails & Most of the Rigen from the Ship," as well as cables, anchors, and about fifty casks of porter. But that was it. As the salvagers worked on the deck of the listing vessel, His Majesty's brig *Hope* came up over the horizon. With the evacuation of Boston under way, Shuldham had sent *Hope* out again to patrol for unsuspecting ships like *Stakesby* that she could escort into Boston.

"Saw a Vessel, on Shore on the East Point of Cape Ann, with a Number of the Rebels on bd," the *Hope*'s log read. Captain Dawson sent the brig's master and an armed boat crew to investigate. On seeing the man-of-war's boat approach, the salvagers abandoned *Stakesby* and pulled for Gloucester. The British boat crew boarded the stranded merchantman and assessed her condition. Then, with night coming on, they stove in what barrels of porter they could and set *Stakesby* on fire. The tide was out, leaving much of the ship exposed, and she burned down to the waterline. In the end, Sargent had managed to retrieve 42 casks of porter, some vinegar, two boats, the sails, anchors and cables, and three hogs.

The British Leave at Last

A few days after taking *Stakesby*, Samuel Tucker in *Franklin* and John Ayres in *Lynch* dropped anchor in Marblehead. Commodore Manley was not with them. It is likely that *Hancock* was still undergoing repairs after her run-in with the ledge off Gloucester. *Warren* and *Lee* might have been in port as well or out hunting for prizes. Over the next few days Tucker and Ayres dipped in and out of Marblehead but found no enemy transports in the offing.

In Nantasket Roads, the British fleet of men-of-war and transports was at last ready to go. It had taken some time for the hastily loaded ships to be made ready for the open ocean. Cargo had to be repositioned to put the vessels in proper trim, then secured, and the thousands of people stuffed aboard the ships had to be accommodated in some scant comfort. On the night of March 20, Howe ordered the destruction of Castle William, the last British-held stronghold in Massachusetts. The fire could be seen for miles, leading many in surrounding communities to believe that Boston itself had been put to the torch.

The next day Washington's wolf pack was once again at sea, now five schooners strong. They assembled at Cape Ann and cruised south, heading for the mass of shipping in Boston Harbor. As they made their way along the coast they overtook a merchant brig passing Marblehead in the early afternoon. She was one of those unfortunate vessels that had tried to reach Boston the previous fall, only to be blown clear to the West Indies. Now her master was hoping at long last to finish his voyage.

"Our five cruisers sailed from Cape Ann and gave her chase," the ever vigilant Ashley Bowen wrote. With Manley's fleet in his wake, the brig's captain crowded on sail and raced for the protection of the British navy at Nantasket Roads.

Like hounds after a fox, the schooners stood on as the brig headed for Boston. Around 3 P.M., lookouts at Boston Lighthouse saw what was taking place and ran up the signal that an attack was in the offing. The armed brig *Diligent* and the sloop *Savage* were ordered under way. "Slipp'd pr order," the *Diligent*'s log read, meaning that rather then weigh anchor they dropped the anchor cable overboard with a buoy attached, "as did the *Savage* & made Sail out of the road, saw 5 Rebel Privateers & an English brig."

Manley's fleet closed fast on the merchant brig as the six ships raced toward Boston. Soon they were within gunshot and began to fire on their fleeing prey. Perhaps hoping the navy would come to his rescue before

he was boarded, the brig's captain let his sails fly and came to a wallowing stop, surrendering as the Americans came up with him.

The gamble paid off. Before Manley could take possession of his
hard-won prize, *Diligent* and *Savage* hurtled out of Nantasket Roads with
studdingsails set aloft and alow. The situation presented Manley with
choices and judgments. Did he have time to take the prize before the
men-of-war closed with him? Should his five schooners take on these two
British men-of-war or was there too much chance of larger ships coming out after them?

Manley made his decision, choosing the better part of valor. He and
the others put their helms up and ran, *Diligent* and *Savage* following in
their wakes. The wind was from the northwest, making Plymouth an easier port to reach than Beverly or Cape Ann, so the fleet headed southeast with the British in full pursuit. *Diligent*'s boat, which was loaded with
supplies and towing astern, broke free and drifted off, but the armed
brig kept up the chase.

The British ships pursued the Americans for twenty miles until at last
darkness came on and they put up their helms and stood back for
Boston. The men of Washington's fleet must have been relieved to see
them go, but in Plymouth a general panic was just starting. Seeing the
fleet of schooners standing into the harbor, townspeople thought they
were under attack from the British. They lit signal fires on hilltops and
fired guns to warn the countryside, but the fires and guns were mistaken
for the work of an attacking force. Rather than spreading the word, the
signals only helped spread the panic. Messengers raced off to nearby
towns to call up the militia.

Not until first light was the truth revealed. "In the morning, to their
great joy," wrote a woman who heard the story from a friend in Plymouth, "[they] found that the fleet which had thrown them into such a
panic was Captain Manley with four other privateers, who were driven
into the harbor by a large man-of-war,—and so ended this mighty affair."

For some days the British fleet stood ready to get under way, awaiting
only a fair wind to do so. Finally, on March 25, Shuldham made the signal for a part of the fleet to weigh anchor and make sail. Josiah Quincy,
observing the British from Braintree at Washington's behest, watched
from 11 in the morning until 3 in the afternoon as more than fifty trans-

ports laboriously weighed, made sail, and stood for the open sea with two frigates sailing as escort.

Ashley Bowen watched the fleet pass Marblehead. "Sailed 55 sail of shipping from below Boston and steered to the Eastward," he wrote. The next morning some of the fleet were still in sight. From Gloucester, Winthrop Sargent saw them as well and reported the sighting to Washington.

On March 27 the rest of the fleet weighed and set sail. The journal of HMS *Chatham* recorded being "in Company with HM Ships *Centurion Lively Savage* & *Tryal* Schooner with Sixty Six Sail of Transports and other Vessels." Over one hundred ships were now making their way northeast to Halifax, jammed with troops, equipment, stores, personal goods, and refugees from the burgeoning war in America.

There is little record of the activities of Manley's fleet, but there can be no doubt that they dogged the convoy as Washington had ordered. Admiral Shuldham, however, was perfectly aware that Washington's schooners and various privateers were lying in wait for his transports, and he was careful to see that the ships were well covered by powerful escorts. Nor did the weather work in Manley's favor. The wind veered from north to southwest, allowing the convoy to maintain its course to Halifax, and though it blew a fresh gale at times, the weather was never so severe as to scatter the fleet and leave vulnerable transports unprotected by men-of-war. Washington's wolf pack was unable to snatch up a single straggler from the massive fleet moving northeast to Canada.

That is, until April 2. Having chased the British fleet into Canadian waters with no success, Manley in *Hancock*, in company with *Lee* and *Lynch*, hauled his wind and headed back for Massachusetts Bay. Forty-five miles east of Cape Ann, the little squadron spotted a heavily laden brig wallowing north. The three schooners cracked on sail and easily overtook the transport. Outpaced and outgunned though she was, the brig did not give up, but rather "made resistance," which might have meant that her master tried to run away or that the thirteen soldiers on board fired on the Americans with small arms or a few shots from carriage guns. But the gesture was futile in the face of a much stronger force.

At last the brig surrendered and a boarding party was sent across. The prize proved to be none other than the *Elizabeth*, the storeship on which

Crean Brush had loaded the property that had been voluntarily turned over to him as well as what he had shamelessly looted from Boston storehouses. The total value of the cargo was estimated at around £24,000.

Also on board were passengers, among them the infamous Crean Brush himself. Rather than a well-furnished Halifax exile, Brush found himself headed for a prison cell.

On April 7 Winthrop Sargent wrote to George Washington concerning the disposition of the prisoners taken on board *Elizabeth*, but by then Washington was gone. The American Revolution was moving to New York.

EPILOGUE: *Washington Rides South*

GEORGE WASHINGTON rode out of Cambridge on April 4, 1776, nine months and two days after riding in to take command of the army. Most of his troops had already marched to New York, but Washington would not leave until he was absolutely certain General Howe was gone.

The vast works that had been so laboriously constructed around Boston were left standing, but only a token force remained to man them. Washington and his generals felt that the town would never again be seriously threatened, and they were right. The British had had enough of Boston.

Washington left the aging, ailing General Artemus Ward in command. Ward, who had been commander-in-chief before Washington's appointment, had recently resigned his commission, fearing "his health would not allow him" to do his duty. He soon retracted the resignation, however, claiming that his leaving the army was too "disagreeable to some of the officers." Washington, who did not think much of Ward, was skeptical. "[W]ho those Officers are I have not heard," he wrote to Reed. "I have not enquired." But Ward would do for command of a largely inactive post. "I shall leave him till he can determine Yea or nay, to Command in this Quarter," Washington added.

Washington also left his ships. The five remaining schooners—*Hancock*, *Franklin*, *Lee*, *Warren*, and *Lynch*—were all sailing out of Beverly, and General Washington and his close assistants had managed through great personal effort to establish an infrastructure of agents and prize courts to support them. Much of that had been accomplished through the agency of John Glover, a member of Marblehead's codfish aristocracy, who had personally supplied facilities and equipment and whose connections had often smoothed the way to fitting the fleet for sea. Even so, the way had been far from smooth.

To re-create such a fleet in New York would have been nearly impossible, and Washington no doubt knew that he would have neither time nor energy for the effort during the coming campaign. The fleet had been created in part to carry the fight to the enemy when no other means existed. Once Howe moved on New York, as Washington was sure he would, there would be plenty of fighting on the ground.

The fleet in Massachusetts had enjoyed advantages that could not be replicated. Friendly and well-protected seaports with facilities to fit out or repair ships had been available within fifteen miles of the enemy's stronghold, and British transports bound for Boston had been forced to sail past those ports to reach safe harbor. The British fleet had been undermanned, equipped with the wrong sort of ships, and led by an inactive and uninspired admiral in Samuel Graves.

But that was all in the past. Only three months had gone by since the start of the new year, but it must have felt much longer than that to the commander-in-chief, because in that short time everything had changed.

The New War at Sea

One of the most dramatic changes was in the way the war was being fought at sea. When George Washington had quietly commissioned *Hannah* the previous August, there had been no armed vessels sailing under the authority of the Continental Congress. In fact, the very idea had been so controversial that Congress would not even discuss it. Understanding that, Washington had kept his fleet a secret as long as he realistically could.

By the time he rode away from Cambridge, the seas were bristling with American armed vessels. Rhode Island had once been the only colony with a navy, but by spring 1776 all the colonies (or, as they would soon be known, states) had established their own naval forces or soon would. Delaware Bay swarmed with row galleys built by Pennsylvania to protect the approaches to Philadelphia. Connecticut had commissioned the armed brigantine *Minerva* and was building the larger *Oliver Cromwell*, the small frigate that William Coit would take command of in July but would never get to sea. Maryland had a navy led by the *Defence*. While the British were evacuating Boston, *Defence* fought the Royal Navy sloop-of-war *Otter* in Maryland waters and recaptured the prizes she had taken.

The Continental Congress was practically bipolar in its approach to a navy, careening from a refusal even to consider one to wildly unrealistic expectations of the ships that could be built and what they could accomplish. Authorization to create a Continental Navy had come in late 1775, and the two ships and two brigs under the command of Esek Hopkins had been the first result. In January 1776 Hopkins's fleet had been ordered to the Chesapeake Bay to "search out and attack, take or destroy all the naval force of our enemies that you may find there." That done, they were to wipe out the British naval presence in North and South Carolina and then move on to Rhode Island and destroy the powerful squadron at Newport.

It was a quixotic mission, and Hopkins ignored it all. Relying on a clause that allowed him to "follow such courses as your best judgement shall suggest," he took his squadron instead to the Bahamas. On March 3, the second day of Washington's shelling of Boston in preparation for taking Dorchester Heights, Hopkins's fleet captured New Providence Island and the town of Nassau in the first joint navy and marine corps action in America's short history. They met with virtually no resistance.

The raid was a success. Hopkins captured seventy-one cannons—from 9-pounders to 32s—fifteen mortars, and twenty-four barrels of powder, though a sloop loaded with considerably more powder managed to slip away. On the return home, the squadron fell in with the British frigate *Glasgow* and her tender off Block Island on the night of April 6. The ships battled for three hours, firing away in the dark, until at last *Glasgow* managed to free herself and limp into Newport. Though the Americans battered the frigate so badly she had to be sent to Halifax for repairs, they failed to capture her despite their four-to-one advantage.

The next day the fleet made its way to New London, Connecticut, where the officers and men were welcomed as heroes. On April 9 George Washington, en route to New York, visited Hopkins aboard the flagship *Alfred*. Hopkins begged a short-term loan of two hundred men from Washington to fill out his ships' companies, to which Washington agreed.

Hopkins's status as a naval hero was short-lived, however. Questions soon arose as to why he had ignored every one of the orders issued by

Congress, why so much gunpowder had escaped capture at Nassau, and how four American vessels could fail to capture one British frigate. Hopkins managed to sink himself in the end by distributing his captured guns as he saw fit, without consulting Congress. He was eventually suspended and then dismissed from the service.

Hopkins's orders had called him "Commander-in-Chief of the Fleet of the United Colonies," but whether Congress considered him the naval equivalent of George Washington or meant the title to apply only to the immediate cruise is unclear. Most likely the Continental Congress was not entirely sure itself. But after that cruise, neither Hopkins nor anyone else would ever again hold such a title in the Continental Navy.

Even before Hopkins's fleet sailed from Philadelphia, Congress expanded its naval ambitions, ordering the construction of thirteen frigates to be built from the keel up. In November 1776, growing more ambitious still, the delegates ordered an eighteen-gun brig, five thirty-six-gun frigates, and three seventy-four-gun ships of the line despite the fact that money and resources for such a program did not exist. In the end only one of the seventy-fours was built. Named *America*, she was launched in 1782 and given to France, where she quickly fell apart. Four years later she was condemned and broken up.

Congress's naval expansion involved more than ship construction, however. In late March 1776, as Washington was preparing to move to New York, Congress authorized the capture of all British vessels, not just those operating in support of the British army or navy. Soon afterward they published their *Instructions to Privateers* establishing Congressional authorization for privateering, something that was already being done on the colonial level, and the number of privateers grew daily.

When Washington had started his secret navy, it was the only way he had of taking the war to sea. By the time he left Cambridge, his five schooners were just a small part of a large and still growing naval community. But he would not give up his ships.

"Commodore Manley declines"

Ironically, Washington was still no fan of the navy. He had come to realize after long deliberation that a seaborne force was a necessary adjunct to the siege of Boston, but he remained generally opposed to Congress's grander naval forays. He resented the Congressional attention and resources that were dedicated to Hopkins's fleet, and he felt—correctly as it turned out—that the frigates authorized by Congress represented a colossal waste of money and effort. But he was not ready to abandon the fleet that he himself had created.

Washington left orders and instructions for General Ward touching on a number of points regarding the regulation of the army remaining in Boston. Part of the instructions concerned the libeling, or adjudication, of prizes taken by the Continental armed vessels and the disposition of prisoners taken from the prizes. These instructions made clear that Washington intended his fleet to continue operating as before, sailing out of Massachusetts ports and snatching up British transports where and when they could.

On May 3 British navy secretary Philip Stephens in London received word from Admiral Molyneux Shuldham of the British evacuation of Boston. From that date on, no more ships were sent into the arms of Washington's cruisers in Massachusetts waters. But there were ships at sea as of that date that had cleared for Boston, and for the next few months Washington's fleet would continue to benefit from the month and a half it had taken for word of the evacuation to reach London.

Shuldham, well aware of this problem, left the fifty-gun *Renown* under the command of Francis Banks at Nantasket Roads "to intercept and send to this place [Halifax] the Ships with Supplies Ordered to Boston." To assist Banks, Shuldham ordered the fifty-gun *Centurion* as well as *Niger*, *Fowey*, and *Hope* to remain under Banks's command. Though the main British force was gone, Massachusetts Bay was still a dangerous place for Washington's ships.

In the spring of 1776, however, the biggest threat to Washington's fleet was not the British navy but rather low morale. Though the men of the fleet had always been prone to grumbling and discontent, the dissatisfaction now reached a breaking point. Nor were the men—officers and seamen alike—unjustified. By the beginning of April, prizes taken as far back as 1775 still had not been libeled, and the men had received none of the prize money they had been promised. The *Concord*, *Jenny*, *Little Hannah*, *Sally*, *Betsey*, and other captures were rotting at anchor in Beverly Harbor, their cargoes unloaded and in many cases already sold off. Nearly all the muskets taken in *Nancy* had been carted away by departing troops, the shells expended on the British in Boston, and the wonderful mortar *Congress* shattered, but still the men who had captured *Nancy* had seen not a shilling of prize money.

What's more, their wages were three months in arrears. Artemus Ward wrote to Washington that "the Men would not be induced to go out again unless they receive their pay." Since Ward had no money to give them, he instructed Colonel John Glover to replace departing sailors with men from his regiment, who were also owed several months' back wages.

On May 3, Ward wrote Washington with yet another problem. "Commodore Manley declines going on another cruise," he informed the general, "until he has a larger Ship." In fact, by that time Manley did have a larger ship, at least on paper. On April 17 the Continental Congress had voted that "John Manley and Isaac Cazneau were elected captains of the two frigates now building in Massachusetts bay."

With the naval buildup taking place, it was inevitable that Manley would be offered a command greater than the little schooner *Hancock*. As of April 1776, with Esek Hopkins and his captains still on their return voyage from their self-invented mission in the Bahamas, John Manley was America's first and only naval hero.

Soon after, Manley resigned from Washington's fleet and took command of the new frigate building in Newburyport, which was also named *Hancock*. For the rest of 1776 and into 1777 he labored to get the ship finished, manned, and out to sea.

Finally, in May 1777, *Hancock* managed to get under way. A month and a half later she was captured by the British frigate *Rainbow*, and Manley spent a year as a prisoner of war before being exchanged. With no Continental vessels available to command, he turned to privateering, in which he enjoyed limited success, and was twice more made a prisoner of war. In 1781 he took command of the frigate *Hague* and remained her captain until the end of the war. "Brave MANLY," as the broadside ballad so aptly called him, died in 1793.

The Fleet Goes On

Samuel Tucker became senior captain in the schooner fleet after Manley's departure, and General Ward appointed him to command the *Han-*

cock, which was the only vessel with crew enough to put to sea. On May 7, 1776, Tucker took two brigantines bound for Boston and sent them into Lynn, Massachusetts.

While *Hancock* was cruising, James Mugford, *Franklin*'s sailing master, took it upon himself to get *Franklin* ready for sea. Mugford was the one whom Ashley Bowen had observed back in January seeking recruits for John Glover's regiment. Now, under the authority of his master's warrant, he assumed command of the schooner.

Mugford took *Franklin* to sea on May 15, and two days later the schooner's lookouts spotted a sail on the horizon. Standing into Boston Harbor was the 300-ton transport *Hope*. She had a crew of eighteen men, and *Franklin* carried only twenty-one, but *Franklin*'s carriage guns, small though they were, convinced the *Hope*'s captain to surrender without a fight.

Hope, it turned out, was not just another transport full of coal and sauerkraut, and Mugford was probably wide-eyed when he read her manifest. She was an ordnance ship and carried a thousand carbines complete with bayonets, scabbards, steel rammers, cartridge boxes, and slings. She carried hundreds of entrenching tools, sandbags, wheelbarrows, gun carriages, and carpenters' tools. She carried an incredible fifteen hundred "cooper hooped, whole barrels" of gunpowder. Even with the swarms of American armed vessels putting to sea, no prize had been taken to equal her since Manley had taken *Nancy*.

Mugford opted to escort his valuable prize straight into Boston through a narrow channel past Pullen Point (now Winthrop), well to the north of the British ships in Nantasket Roads. In the process, however, *Hope* ran aground. Fearing she might be retaken, the Americans sent boats from Boston and hauled a majority of the cargo to safety before the ship refloated on the tide.

With the army in New York, the capture of *Hope* failed to garner the same frenzied attention that *Nancy* had enjoyed, but James Mugford found himself the new naval hero of Massachusetts. It was a status he would not enjoy long.

On May 19, two days after taking *Hope*, the *Franklin*, with the privateer schooner *Lady Washington* in company, left Boston for another cruise. Near Point Shirley (the southern extremity of what would become Winthrop) *Franklin* went aground and stuck fast. Seeing the stranded rebel schooner, Captain Banks of *Renown* sent boats from his ship and from the newly arrived *Experiment* to take Mugford's ship and carry her off.

It was 10 P.M. and full dark when five British boats, "Mann'd & Arm'd," descended on the *Franklin*. Though Mugford and his men were vastly outnumbered, they put up a terrific fight, holding off wave after wave of attacking British sailors. The *Renown*'s barge overturned, and a lieutenant, two seamen, and two marines drowned in the ensuing chaos. Not a man on board *Franklin* was injured or killed until moments before the British were forced to break off the fight. Then "The intrepid Captain Mugford fell . . . run through with a lance while he was cutting off the hands of the Pirates as they were attempting to board him."

The next day *Franklin* floated free, and her men set sail and carried Mugford's body around to Marblehead, where he was laid to rest on May 22. Ashley Bowen wrote, "This afternoon a grand funeral as James Mugford is buried. Seventy of Colonel Glover's regiment came and attended the funeral. Captain Tucker fired minute guns. A grand procession." James Mugford's naval career was one of the most glorious and certainly the briefest of any captain in the Continental service.

By the middle of May, *Lynch*, *Warren*, and *Lee* were also under way, bringing Washington's fleet back up to five vessels. On June 6, cruising off Cape Cod, the schooners captured the ship *Ann* from Glasgow. Crammed on board were ninety-five officers and soldiers of the 71st Highland regiment, bound to join General Howe in Boston. About thirty-five of the soldiers were put on board *Lynch*, which made for Plymouth, and the rest, still on board *Ann*, were carried into Marblehead.

Ann, the Americans discovered, was one of thirty-five troop transports carrying Highlanders to America, and others continued to arrive. Some were intercepted at sea by British men-of-war and redirected to Halifax. Twice Washington's schooners fell in with them only to be driven off by gunfire from the troops on board and the timely arrival of the frigates stationed in Nantasket Roads.

The British men-of-war and Washington's schooners continued their cat-and-mouse games into June. On June 12, Lieutenant Dawson in *Hope* was cruising the approaches to Boston when four of Washington's fleet came up with him. Dawson had doled out punishment to the schooners in the past and had also been at the receiving end of rough treatment.

This time, four-to-one odds did not look promising to him. He put up his helm and fled for safety. "Chaced by four Sail of Rebel Schooners," *Hope*'s log recorded. The brig had the heels on the schooners, and Dawson was able to come to anchor in Nantasket Roads that evening, having avoided yet another run-in with his old enemies.

By mid-June General Artemus Ward had had enough of the Royal Navy loitering in Boston Harbor. He ordered Colonel Asa Whitcomb of the 6th Continental Infantry to march five hundred men to North Quincy and construct a battery on Long Island, which overlooks Nantasket Roads from the northwest, "to annoy the Enemies Ships."

At 4:00 A.M. on the morning of June 14, the men on board the British men-of-war were greeted by the disconcerting sight of cannon leering at them over newly built earthworks on nearby Long Island. *Hope*'s log read, "at 5 the Rebels fired a Number of Shot and Shels at us which Occasioned the Men of War and Transports to Weigh and Come to Sail."

That was the end for the British navy in Nantasket Roads. Banks ordered Boston Lighthouse burned, and then the men-of-war and the various transports they had collected made sail and stood for Halifax. The last remnants of the British military presence in Boston were gone.

A few days after their leaving, three more transports with troops from the 71st Highland regiment sailed into the arms of the Americans and were captured.

"Removed at such a distance as his Excellency is"

After leaving Boston, General Washington tirelessly prepared his army and his defenses to meet the British whenever they should arrive at New York, which, as of mid-June, they still had not. Incredibly, with all he had to do in his new theater of operations, he continued to field questions regarding his fleet and to exert some long-distance control.

Bit by bit, however, the schooners were slipping from his hands. Artemus Ward now had the direct supervision of the fleet, and in May Congress appointed John Bradford, in Boston, to act as Continental marine agent for all naval ships including Washington's, thus superseding Jonathan Glover, William Bartlett, William Watson, and Winthrop Sargent. Not surprisingly this created far more problems than it solved, particularly as Bradford, though a confidant of John Hancock, was not an ideal choice for the position. Washington, of course, was dragged into the middle of the disputes that ensued between Bradford and Washington's agents.

Then, on June 29, the largest army ever assembled in North America landed on Staten Island, New York, under the command of General William Howe and prepared to overrun the American lines. Washington had bigger things to worry about than quibbles concerning jurisdiction over prizes. Touching on a dispute between Bradford and Jonathan Glover, Washington wrote, "Not conceiving myself Authorized, nor having the smallest inclination to interfere in any degree in the matter; it is referred to Congress."

On August 5 Congress resolved "That the Marine Committee [of Congress] be directed to order the ships and armed vessels, belonging to the continent, out on such cruizes as they shall think proper." This resolution was intended to remove control of naval affairs from Esek Hopkins, not to take charge of Washington's fleet, though in effect it did just that. The Marine Committee took authority over every man-of-war fitted out at Continental expense, including Washington's schooners.

By midsummer 1776 no more British transports were blundering into Boston, and Washington's fleet greatly expanded its cruising range in search of prizes. Sailing as far south as Virginia and as far north as Canada, the schooners continued to pick up British merchant vessels, all of which were now fair game.

In late August, *Warren* and *Lynch*, operating in company, fell in with the British frigate *Liverpool* about twenty miles out of Massachusetts Bay. The schooners split up and *Lynch* made her escape, but the frigate easily ran *Warren* down, taking her as a prize and making Captain William Burke and his crew prisoners of war. Incredibly, after a year of dodging British men-of-war, *Warren* was only the second of Washington's fleet to be taken by the enemy. Burke would later escape from prison and go on to serve as a captain in the Continental Navy.

General Howe launched his attack against Washington's forces on Long Island late in the day of August 26. Things went poorly from the start for the Americans. By the next day Howe had shattered Washington's lines and driven the Americans back to the East River. On the night of August 29–30, the seasoned mariners who made up John Glover's regiment of Marbleheaders manned the boats that carried Washington's army across the river to Manhattan, winning for the army the chance to fight again another day. From that point on and for months to come, George Washington's war would be one retreat after another as Howe pushed the Continental Army across New York and New Jersey.

With military disaster looming, Washington continued to receive correspondence asking that he intervene in sundry issues related to the schooner fleet. Finally, by the second week of September, he had heard enough. In answer to one such letter, Washington wrote via his secretary a succinct summary of his attitude and situation: "Removed at such a distance as his Excellency is and Involved in a multiplicity of Important business It is impossible for him to give decisions about or pay Attention to the Continental Armed Vessels at the Eastward."

Washington may have been done with the fleet, but the schooners continued to operate some time longer under the nominal authority of Artemus Ward and the supervision of John Bradford. In the second week of November, Samuel Tucker in *Hancock* and John Skimmer, who had taken command of *Franklin* after James Mugford's death, captured the brig *Lively*, bound for New York, her hull crammed with clothing for Howe's army.

Lively was sent into Boston. Her manifest revealed that she carried "665 dozen Men's Shoes, 41 doz. Women's Ditto . . . 247 dozen ruffled Shirts; 18 dozen plain ditto; 57 dozen Check ditto; 3052 yards Blanketing; 74 dozen Pladding Breeches," and on and on, an extraordinary haul, a boon to Washington's underequipped army and a blow to Howe, who needed those clothes for the coming winter. *Lively* joined *Nancy* and *Hope* among the three most significant prizes taken by Washington's schooners. She was the last major strike the fleet would make.

As November 1776 drew to an end and the weather deteriorated, Washington's ships remained at anchor in Boston Harbor with little chance of leaving. John Bradford reported to Hancock that "the men seem loth to go out on a cru[i]se this Season by reason the vessells are so uncomfortable."

The schooners were in various states of disrepair. *Lynch* had no guns, Ayres having thrown them overboard to escape a British frigate, and

Bradford described her as "dismantled . . . she remains in pay doing nothing." *Hancock*, he wrote, was "unfit to proceed again," and it would cost as much as she was worth to make her seaworthy. Bradford considered *Lee* "a good vessell," but her captain, Daniel Waters, "seems determined not to exert himself in the publick Cause. . . . [T]he Worthy Capt Skimmer has the worst vessell amoung the whole."

For the rest of 1776 and into 1777 the schooner fleet hung idle on their moorings in Boston Harbor. By mid-January 1777 John Bradford discharged the schooners *Hancock* and *Franklin*, "wch were unfit for the Service." Only *Lee* and *Lynch* now remained of Washington's fleet, sitting in harbor without captains or crew.

During the lull, Samuel Tucker and Daniel Waters traveled to Philadelphia to meet members of Congress and lobby for better commands. Their efforts paid off when, in March, both men were made captains in the Continental Navy. With no ships available to command, Waters signed on with John Manley aboard the frigate *Hancock*, serving as something akin to a sailing master. He was still aboard when *Hancock* was captured by the frigate *Rainbow*. Like Burke, Waters would survive prison and return to command a vessel for the Continental Navy.

Not until 1778 would Tucker receive a command, the frigate *Boston*. His first assignment was to convey John Adams to France, where the Congressman assumed his new post of ambassador. Tucker continued to command *Boston* until he was forced to surrender when the British took Charleston, South Carolina, in May 1780. Tucker, a prisoner, was soon exchanged and served as a privateer captain until the end of the war.

With Tucker and Waters joining the Continental Navy, John Skimmer was given command of *Lee*. John Ayres still had nominal command of *Lynch*, but when asked to carry dispatches to France he refused to go to sea unless *Lynch* carried at least twenty men and four guns "to support the dignity of his comissn."

Bradford, who had no love for Ayres, refused the demand and wrote, "we are luckely rid of him." Ayres, like most of his compatriots, ended up commissioned as a captain in the Continental Navy, though he seems never to have been given a man-of-war. He served in privateers and, ironically given his refusal to go to sea in the unarmed *Lynch*, commanded packet ships for Congress. He died in Bordeaux in 1778 while commanding the packet *General Arnold*.

Bradford gave command of *Lynch* to a captain named John Adams (no relation to the Congressman), who agreed to sail the schooner to France with a minimum crew and no guns. *Lynch* was now referred to as "the *Lynch* pacquet [packet]" as opposed to the "Continental Armed Vessel." Adams delivered his dispatches to France but on the voyage home was captured by one of England's most promising young captains, John Jervis of *Feudroyant*, who would go on to become Lord St. Vincent and one of the foremost admirals of the Napoleonic Wars.

On March 20, 1777, the last of Washington's schooners, the *Lee*, went to sea under the command of John Skimmer. Since *Lee* would have to travel far afield to find the sort of prizes that had once sailed right into Boston, she was fitted out with ten carriage guns, eighteen swivels, and a crew of fifty-four officers and men, enough to man several prizes with crews.

Skimmer took his command south to Bermuda, and after cruising there for a short while made his way north to Nova Scotia. He returned to Boston around the end of June, having covered thousands of miles and taken five prizes. Soon he was under way again, heading back into Canadian waters. Three months later he returned to Marblehead, having taken another three prizes. In the end, Skimmer proved the second most successful of all Washington's captains, taking more prizes than any but John Manley, though never one as valuable as *Nancy* or *Hope*. His second cruise was the longest continuous voyage of any of Washington's ships, and it was the last. Soon after Skimmer's return to Marblehead, John Bradford returned *Lee* to her owner. George Washington's navy was no more.

Power at Sea

In March 1776 General Howe had loaded his troops on board transports and with the protection of the British navy sailed off to Halifax. Three months later the fleet arrived in New York, literally out of the blue. One year after that, Howe again loaded his men on board ships and disappeared over the horizon, only to reappear at Philadelphia. If Washington had not known it before, he certainly learned over the first few years of the Revolution the absolute need for naval superiority when fighting a war beside the sea.

He also understood that America could never build a navy to counter that of Great Britain. Despite its naval ambitions, the Continental Congress could barely keep the army supplied with food, clothing, and ammunition. It was only with great difficulty that the thirteen frigates Congress ordered in March 1776 were constructed, and their contribution to the war effort amounted to almost nothing. In September 1777 the enemy brushed aside a fleet of gunboats built in Pennsylvania to guard the Delaware River. In August 1779 the Penobscot Expedition—an amphibious assault force sent to drive the British out of Penobscot Bay in the district of Maine—was annihilated by a superior British squadron. The American fleet included three Continental Navy men-of-war and sixteen armed vessels from Massachusetts, New Hampshire, and the privateer ranks—344 guns in all—making it the largest fleet assembled by the Americans during the war.

Perhaps the most successful American naval action was Benedict Arnold's fight to stop the British advance on Lake Champlain in October 1776. But even that was a success only because of the delay it caused to the British advance from Canada—a delay that enabled the Americans to win the Battle of Saratoga in 1777. Arnold's fleet was all but wiped out.

Washington had come to appreciate the need for sea power, but he did not believe America could provide it. In February 1778, however, the United States of America (the new country's official name since Congress's adoption of the Articles of Confederation on November 15, 1777) signed a treaty of cooperation with France—a treaty prompted in great part by America's victory at Saratoga—and for the first time Washington enjoyed the prospect of support from a real navy. In July of that year a powerful French squadron arrived on the coast of America. It was all that Washington could have wished for—ships that were powerful enough to take on the British navy but did not drain his own forces of money, men, or *matériel.*

With the arrival of the French, Washington began to think in terms of combined land-sea operations in ways he could not have done before. Through the remainder of 1778 and all of 1779, however, his efforts were thwarted by a number of factors, including the still-superior strength of the British navy in North America.

But Washington did not give up hope. In July 1780 he dispatched his aide, the Marquis de Lafayette, to Rhode Island to present plans for combined operations to the newly arrived French general, the Count de Rochambeau. In describing how Rochambeau's five thousand troops could best work in cooperation with his own army, Washington wrote first, "In any operation, and under all circumstances, a decisive naval superiority is to be considered as a fundamental principle, and the basis upon which every hope of success must ultimately depend."

More than a year would pass before all the elements finally came together. With General Charles Cornwallis cornered in Yorktown, Virginia, the French squadron was able to drive the British fleet from the mouth of the Chesapeake Bay and deny Cornwallis an escape by sea. His consequent surrender to Washington and Rochambeau's combined forces effectively ended the war. For that one brief, shining moment, the naval superiority that had been denied Washington for six long years was his. He did not waste the opportunity.

Birth of a Navy

An old saw suggests that success has a thousand parents but failure is an orphan. By those standards alone, America's first navy could be considered a ringing success. Any number of communities vie for the distinction of "Birthplace of the United States Navy." Machias, Maine, claims that title for Jeremiah O'Brien and Benjamin Foster's taking of the *Margaretta*. Whitehall, New York, known in 1775 as Skenesborough, claims the title for a couple of reasons, including the little fleet built there in the summer of 1776 by Benedict Arnold to oppose the British invasion south over Lake Champlain. And for their part in the creation of George Washington's navy, Marblehead and Beverly also aspire to the sobriquet.

Hannah, the first ship in Washington's fleet, was a Marblehead schooner. Her owner and the man who was instrumental in Washington's naval efforts, John Glover, was a Marbleheader, as were most of the officers and men who manned the fleet at the beginning. Clearly Marblehead deserves consideration as the birthplace of the American navy.

On the other hand, neither *Hannah* nor any of Washington's other schooners were fitted out in Marblehead. No sooner were they hired than they were taken around the corner to the safer port of Beverly. John Glover's wharf was not in Marblehead but on the Beverly waterfront. Nearly all prizes were sent to Beverly, and none of Washington's agents was more active than William Bartlett in Beverly. Certainly, then, Beverly too can claim to be the navy's birthplace.

For more than two hundred years the two towns have fired these arguments at one another like verbal artillery flying over poor Salem, which is caught between them.

But before one considers the primacy of either Marblehead or Beverly, one must ask if Washington's fleet really constituted the creation of the American navy at all. There is no question that Washington's schooners were the first armed vessels to put to sea in the risk and pay of Continental authority. But the authority under which they sailed was that of the commander-in-chief of the army, and even he did not really believe he was authorized to do what he was doing. The ships were officered by men with army commissions and manned by soldiers, albeit soldiers who had been sailors in civilian life. It was not a navy.

A true American navy could only come from the Continental Congress, the only legal entity representing the entire country-in-the-making, if indeed any Revolutionary government could be considered a legal entity. Congressional debate concerning a navy was sharp and loud precisely because members of Congress understood what a profound step it was. Creating a navy was tantamount to declaring sovereignty. When a navy was finally authorized, it came as part of a major realignment of the delegates' thinking with regard to the war and the colonies' fundamental relationship with England.

George Washington sent the first armed ships to sea, but he did not create the American navy, nor did he ever claim to. Quite the opposite. He was careful even after the creation of the Continental Navy to keep his own fleet separate. When Washington's captains were eventually given commissions in the Continental Navy, time served in the schooner fleet played no part in their seniority.

After Congress authorized the first ships of the Continental Navy in October 1775, the ships were fitted out in Philadelphia. Thus the city in which American independence was born can also validly claim to be the true "Birthplace of the United States Navy."

Washington's Naval Vision

Washington's idea of what an American navy could best do—capture British supplies at sea—was far more realistic than that of Congress, but even he probably did not appreciate all the implications of his strategy. Washington was thinking simply of providing for his men and depriving the British, two highly valid objectives. But raiding British commerce did more than that. It constituted a direct attack on the British merchant class, who exerted considerable influence in government. It drove up insurance rates, creating discontent with the war in London. It forced the British navy to divert resources to protect vulnerable but essential shipping. It struck the empire at its economic base.

Washington's armed schooners and the privateers that followed in their wake caused a ripple effect well beyond the shiploads of coal, porter, and sauerkraut of which they deprived the British army. Washington's ships cost very little compared with the larger ships of the Continental Navy, and privateers cost the government nothing at all, yet their impact on the war's outcome was certainly greater.

For all the headaches they caused, Washington's schooners were a success. They captured thirty-eight vessels that were deemed legitimate prizes. They forced Admiral Graves and later Admiral Shuldham to exhaust resources to protect British transports, and they hastened Howe's evacuation of Boston by making his supply problems that much more critical.

The capture of the ordnance brig *Nancy* was just the godsend Washington had envisioned when he first sent his ships to sea. It gave the American troops desperately needed war *matériel* and kept it from the enemy's hands. It gave the Americans a minor victory at a time of dreary stalemate. The capture of *Nancy* brought a much needed burst of hope and optimism to a camp in which spirits were flagging and boredom, hard weather, and discomfort were working their insidious effects. It made John Manley the first naval hero at a time when a hero was needed.

Sometimes Washington's gambles paid off and sometimes they did not. The creation of the fleet was a gamble indeed, early in his tenure, but in the end the new commander-in-chief looked like a visionary when Congress ordered him to find armed vessels to go after the Quebec-bound British ordnance brigs and he was able to reveal that he was three steps ahead of them.

George Washington the frontier soldier traveled a long road to embrace the need for American naval power and to understand its potential and limitations. When he realized what armed vessels could do, he deployed them with the same determination, practicality, and supple strategic vision that would help him lead his army to improbable victory eight years later. The Virginia farmer, oddly enough, was the man who first took the American Revolution to sea.

ACKNOWLEDGMENTS

WRITING IS generally thought of as a solitary task, and to be sure the part that involves putting words on paper is best accomplished alone with one's thoughts and writing implements. But the journey from idea to printed book involves many fellow travelers, and one of the great joys of my career has been getting to know and appreciate those who have helped me along the way.

This book has been no different. I owe thanks to many people. Michael Crawford at the Naval Historical Center was terrifically helpful from the beginning, directing me to research material and providing essential documents. Dr. Crawford and his staff are working toward the completion of the important series *Naval Documents of the American Revolution*, without which any work on the naval history of the War for Independence would be vastly more difficult.

Darren Brown, curator at the Beverly Historical Society and Museum, was a great help with the wealth of material in their collections, as was Karen MacInnis at the Marblehead Museum and Historical Society. Peter Drummey and all the people at the Massachusetts Historical Society also deserve thanks for their help. Thanks to James Kirby Martin for his help locating primary sources and to Ted Crackel and Phil Chase for their thoughts on George Washington's papers. The research librarians at the Curtis Memorial Library in Brunswick, Maine—Janet Fullerton, Linda Oliver, Mike Arnold, Paul Dostie, Marian Dalton, and Diana McFarland—are always helpful and efficient, and my work would be difficult indeed without them. The people at the Bowdoin College Library likewise deserve my sincere thanks—especially Pat Myshrall, who is so kind even when I egregiously ignore due dates. Thanks as well to Allison Eddyblouin and Brian Wyvill for their higher math skills (higher than mine, certainly).

Nat Sobel, my agent for nearly a decade and a half, continues to be a bedrock of support. Thanks as well to all the great people in his office, in particular Emily Russo and Adia Wright. The people at McGraw-Hill are the most wonderful, professional, competent, friendly publishing folks I have had the pleasure to work with. Heading that gang is Jon Eaton, a thorough, meticulous editor but also a man of great patience and humor. Nancy Dowling and Molly Mulhern have been continuously kind and helpful both with this book and with *Benedict Arnold's Navy*. Marisa L'Heureux gave this book its final polish and steered it to timely publication despite my best efforts to thwart her. In the publicity department, I am very much in debt to Ann Pryor for all her good work bringing my books to light.

And, of course, my thanks forever to Lisa, my wife, for all the sacrifices that go with being married to a writer and for all those times when I may be home in body, but my spirit is standing the quarterdeck of an armed schooner, plunging through the choppy seas of Cape Cod Bay in the wake of a British transport.

ENDNOTES

ABBREVIATIONS

AA—American Archives
BHS—Beverly Historical Society
DAR—Documents of the American Revolution
EIHC—Essex Institute Historical Collections
GWP/LC—George Washington Papers, Library of Congress
JCC—Journals of the Continental Congress
LC—Library of Congress
MarHS—Marblehead Historical Society
MHS—Massachusetts Historical Society
MHSP—Massachusetts Historical Society *Proceedings*
NDAR—Naval Documents of the American Revolution
PGW/RWS—Papers of George Wasington, Revolutionary War Series
PJA—Papers of John Adams
PRO/ADM—Public Records Office, Admiralty Records

PROLOGUE: A VERY DELIGHTFUL COUNTRY

vii **great horsemen of the age:** McCullough, *1776*, 47.

vii **noble and even majestic** and following: Thatcher, *Eyewitness*, 30.

viii **a very delightful Country:** Washington to Samuel Washington, PGW/RWS 1, 134.

viii Washington's tour of the lines: Batchelder, *Cambridge History*.

viii Descriptions of American Lines: Batchelder, *Cambridge History*; Fischer, *Paul Revere's Ride*; French, *First Year*; Frothingham, *Siege*; McCullough, *1776*; PGW/RWS 1.

ix **We wish you may have found** and following: Address from the Massachusetts Provincial Congress, PGW/RWS 1, 52.

ix Description of Camp: Emerson, *Diaries*, 80.

ix **tents and ten thousand simple hunting shirts:** Washington to Hancock, PGW/RWS 1, 87–88.

x Description of British lines: Ibid, 86.

CHAPTER 1: THE BRITISH COMMAND

1 Gage: Fischer, *Paul Revere's Ride*; French, *First Year*; Mackesy, *War for America.*

2 **Massachusetts Regulatory Act:** Middlekauff, *Glorious Cause.*

2 **too prevalent in America:** Gage to Barrington, quoted in Fischer, *Paul Revere's Ride,* 39.

2 **These People shew a Spirit:** Gage to Barrington, quoted in French, *First Year,* 258.

3 **If you think ten thousand Men sufficient:** Ibid, 15.

3 Gage's position and appointment of Howe, Clinton, and Burgoyne: French, *First Year*; Mackesy, *War for America*; Middlekauff, *Glorious Cause.*

"A corrupt Admiral without any shadow of capacity"

3 Graves: French, *First Year*; Fowler, *Rebels*; Miller, *Sea of Glory.*

3 **rose to his present rank:** Graves, *Conduct,* Gay Transcripts, MHS.

3 **a tough, boisterous man:** Belknap Journal, MHS.

3 **A curious Event** and following: Bolton, *Letters of Percy,* 60.

4 **both his fists,** description of fight: Hallowell to Gage, NDAR 1, 1140.

4 **the Admiral has had the worst of it:** Bolton, *Letters of Percy,* 60.

4 **In his own department:** *Extract of a Letter from Boston,* NDAR 1, 1183.

4 **A worthy General:** Eden to Germain, quoted in James, *British Navy.*

5 **she was so leaky:** Graves, *Conduct,* Gay Transcripts, MHS.

5 **a few Shipwrights:** Ibid.

5 **hiding the sails and rudders:** *Narrative of Graves,* NDAR 1, 524.

6 **The Fears of a few:** Graves to Stephens, NDAR 1, 326.

6 **handy Ships** and following: Graves to Stephens, NDAR 1, 356.

6 **her peacetime complement:** Graves, *Conduct,* Gay Transcripts, MHS.

6 **[T]he tars, not liking the employ:** *Essex Journal,* NDAR 1, 537.

"Very great Pains have been taken to starve the Troops"

7 **The whole country:** Gage to Dartmouth, DAR IX, XLVIII.

7 British taken by surprise: Bowler, *Logistics*; Mackesy, *War for America.*

7 **supply system:** Bowler, *Logistics,* 15.

7 **In the course of two days:** De Berniere to Gage, quoted in Fischer, *Paul Revere's Ride,* 263.

8 **Very great Pains:** Gage to Dartmouth, Carter, *Gage Correspondence,* 1, 408.

8 **eight tons of food per day:** Bowler, *Logistics,* 92.

8 military and civilian population: Frothingham, *Siege of Boston,* 19; *Letter from Cambridge, July 12, 1775,* AA 4, 2:1651.

8 **Very sickly:** *Letter from Cambridge,* Ibid.

8 conditions in Boston: French, *First Year*; Frothingham, *Siege of Boston.*

8 **How the times are changed:** *Sewell's Letter,* quoted in French, *First Year.*

CHAPTER 2: THE GREATEST EVENTS . . . IN THE PRESENT AGE

10 **Fly to the foot** and **We ask but for Peace:** AA 4,1:937.

11 **I rec^d notice** and beginnings of siege: French, *First Year.*

11 **between fifteen thousand and twenty thousand men strong:**
Washington's Return, July 19, 1775, and Ellery to Philadelphia
Committee of Correspondence, AA 4:2, 381.

11 **four thousand effectives:** French, *First Year.*

11 **greatest Events taking Place:** Emerson, *Diaries.*

11 **[T]his Congress, after solemn deliberation:** Warren to New Hampshire
Congress, AA 4:2, 378.

12 **to be conven'd** and following: Warren to Congress, JCC 2, 24.

12 **tremble at having an army:** JCC 2, 77, 78.

12 Congress establishes the army: French, *First Year*; Frothingham, *Siege of
Boston*; Middlekauff, *Glorious Cause.*

12 **our business:** JCC 2, 80n.

13 **in order that they be safely returned:** AA 4, 2:1833.

13 **made a motion:** quoted in French, *First Year,* 750.

13 **take into consideration:** JCC 2, 79.

13 **exercise the powers of Government:** JCC, 2, 84.

14 **five thousand barrels of flour:** Ibid.

The Choice for Command

14 **an honest Man:** Gerry to Massachusetts Delegates, PJA 3, 40.

14 **destitute of all Military Ability:** Warren to Adams, Ibid, 37.

15 **General Lee is a perfect original:** Journal of Dr. Belknap, MHSP Series
1, 4:79.

15 **General Lees Learning:** Diary and Autobiography of Adams, 3, 324.

15 **Every Post brought me Letters:** Ibid, 321.

15 **they seem to me to want a more Experienced direction:** Warren to
Adams, PJA 3, 4.

16 **officers of such great experience:** Adams to Gerry, Ibid, 26.

CHAPTER 3: NODDLES ISLAND

17 **hoisted the white ensign, etc:** *Journal of* Preston, NDAR 1, 546.

17 **knee-deep at low tide:** *Account of the Late Battle, New York Journal,* NDAR
1, 544.

17 **several tons of hay from another island:** French, *First Year,* 188.

18 **guardboats, etc:** *Graves to Gage,* NDAR 1, 523.

18 **six hundred American soldiers, etc:** Report to the Massachusetts
Committee of Safety, Ibid, 545.

18 **two o'clock in the afternoon, etc:** *Journal of* Preston, Ibid, 546.

18 **all boats mann'd, etc:** *Glasgow Journal,* NDAR 1, 547.

18 **greater concern to Graves, etc:** Graves to Stephens, NDAR 1, 622.

18 **tar, pitch, junk, lumber:** Graves to Stephens, DAR XI, 173.

19 **the island was blazing:** Ibid; *Glasgow Journal*, NDAR 1, 547; *Cerberus Journal*, NDAR 1, 554.

19 **the Bauls Sung like Bees:** *Farnsworth's Diary*, quoted in French, *First Year.*

19 **we heard they were upon Hog Island:** Ingall's Journal, MAHS.

19 Attack on *Diana*: *Account of the Late Battle*, NDAR 1, 544; *Report to the Massachusetts Committee of Safety*, Ibid, 545; *Extract of a Letter from the American Camp*, Ibid, 551; *Extract of a Letter Dated June 1*: Ibid, 584; Graves to Stephens, Ibid, 622.

20 **The sloop was disabled:** *Extract of a Letter from the American Camp*, NDAR, 1, 551.

20 **got out of the wreck:** *Extract of a Letter Dated June 1*: Ibid, 585.

21 **great part of the King's stores:** DAR XI, 173.

21 **They have lately amused themselves:** *Percy to Reveley*, Bolton, *Letters of Percy*, 55.

Firewood

21 **described as a drought:** Emerson's Journal, 81.

21 **coal:** Bowler, *Logistics and Failure*, 61.

22 **a six-month supply of provisions:** Ibid, 43.

22 **Great Difficulties now arose:** Graves, *Conduct*, NDAR 1, 524.

22 **The Barrack Mas^r is to Collect:** Howe, *Orderly Book*, 26.

22 **As Wood cannot be got:** Howe, *Orderly Book*, 77.

"The wilderness is impervious and vessels we have none"

22 **Population and description of Machias:** Inhabitants of Machias to Massachusetts Congress, AA 4, 2:708; Drisko, *Narrative*, 31.

23 **We dare not say** and following: Ibid.

23 **Supplying this Garrison with Wood:** Gage to Graves, NDAR 1, 337.

23 **having exerted himself:** Gage to Graves, NDAR 1, 518.

23 **an infamous Tory:** *Providence Gazette*, NDAR 1, 1124.

23 **a dog:** Warren to Samuel Adams, NDAR 1, 1059.

24 **His Majesty's schooner *Halifax*:** Nunn to Graves, NDAR 1, 117.

24 **has my permission to carry Twenty Barrels Pork:** Gage to Graves, NDAR 1, 337.

24 **an Armed Vessel's being sent:** Ibid, 518.

24 **Mr Ichabod Jones:** Graves, *Conduct*, NDAR 1, 538.

25 **manned with as good a crew:** Graves to Stephens, Graves *Conduct*, MSH.

25 **remain for their Protection, etc:** Graves to Moore, NDAR 1, 537.

CHAPTER 4: MACHIAS SONS OF LIBERTY

27 **required the signers** and following: Machias Committee to Massachusetts Provincial Congress, NDAR 1, 676.

27 Foster and O'Brien: Sherman, *O'Briens of Machias, Maine.*

28 Fight and taking of *Margaretta*: Machias Committee to Massachusetts Provincial Congress, NDAR 1, 676; Godfrey's Report, Ibid, 655; Cobb's Deposition, Ibid, 757; Flinn's Deposition, Ibid, 848.

28 **thirty Men in Arms:** Cobb's Deposition, Ibid, 757.

28 **the officers of the schooner:** Jones, *Historical Account*, 50.

29 **looked out of the Window:** Godfrey's Report, Ibid, 655.

29 **alarmed that they were pursued:** Cobb's Deposition, Ibid, 757.

29 **before their pursuers:** Godfrey's Report, Ibid, 655.

29 **he was determined to do his duty:** Machias Committee to Massachusetts Provincial Congress, NDAR 1, 676

29 **strike to the sons of Liberty:** Flinn's Deposition, Ibid, 848.

30 **desiring him to strike:** Godfrey's Report, Ibid, 655.

30 **he was not ready yet:** Ibid.

30 **Fire and be damn'd:** Machias Committee to Massachusetts Provincial Congress, NDAR 1, 677.

30 **smart engagement:** Ibid.

31 **The firing continued:** Godfrey's Report, NDAR, 655.

31 **were beat off from a brisk fire:** Ibid.

31 **made a Barricadoe:** Ibid.

The First Sea Fight of the War

31 **being well acquainted:** Godfrey's Report, NDAR, 655.

32 **guns, swords, axes:** Machias Committee to Massachusetts Provincial Congress, NDAR 1, 677.

32 **the 10th of said June:** Flinn's Deposition, Ibid, 848.

32 **it was in vain to Refuse:** Ibid.

32 **breast works of pine boards:** Machias Committee to Massachusetts Provincial Congress, NDAR 1, 677.

33 **brought her alongside:** Godfrey's Report, NDAR, 655.

33 **immediately weighed Anchor:** Ibid.

33 **a very dull sailor:** Machias Committee to Massachusetts Provincial Congress, NDAR 1, 677.

33 **[T]hey coming up with us very fast:** Godfrey's Report, NDAR, 655.

33 **strike to the Sons of Liberty:** Ibid, 656.

33 **Captain Moore imployed himself:** Joseph Wheaton to John Adams, quoted in Allan, *Naval History*, 10.

34 Killed and wounded: Machias Committee to Massachusetts Provincial Congress, NDAR 1, 677.

34 **he preferred Death:** Godfrey's Report, NDAR, 656.

34 **carried her up to Mechais:** Ibid.

35 **Captain Jeremiah Obrian and Captain Benjamin Foster:** Journal of Massachusetts Provincial Congress, Ibid, 758.

35 *Polly* **would be fitted out:** Machias Committee of Safety to the Massachusetts General Court, NDAR 2, 445. In this letter, the Machias Committee mentions "the sloop *Mechias Liberty,* sloop *Unity,* the *Margaretta.*" Since *Polly* is not mentioned, she must be the vessel that became *Machias Liberty.*

35 **the Pirate:** Ibid, 977.

35 **unaquainted with the disposition:** Graves to Stephens, Ibid, 1164.

35 **this is doing great Service:** Warren to Adams, Ibid, 1102.

36 **have been of very great:** Gage to Graves, Ibid, 685.

CHAPTER 5: "THE AMIABLE, GENEROUS AND BRAVE GEORGE WASHINGTON, ESQUIRE"

37 Washington's background and selection as commander-in-chief: Adams, *Autobiography*; Ellis, *His Excellency*; Flexner, *Washington*; French, *First Year*; Leckie, *Washington's War*; McCullough, *1776*; Stephenson, *Washington.*

38 **a committee to bring in a dra't:** JCC 2, 90.

38 **great experience and abilities:** Adams to Abigail Adams, Adams, *Familiar Letters,* 59.

39 **Oh that I were a soldier:** Ibid.

39 **I was struck with General Washington** and following: Abigail Adams to John Adams, Adams, *Familiar Letters,* 79.

40 Washington's uniform: Adams to Abigail Adams, Adams, *Familiar Letters,* 59.

40 Virginia Blues uniform: Elting, *Military Uniforms in America,* 20.

40 **blue coat:** Thatcher, *Eyewitness,* 30.

40 **New England Army:** Diary and Autobiography of Adams, 3, 321.

40 **that Congress would Adopt the Army:** Ibid, 322.

40 **Exertions, Sacrifices and general Merit** and following: Ibid, 321, 322.

41 Washington's election: JCC 2, 91.

41 **I assure you:** Washington to Martha Washington, PGW/RWS 1, 3.

41 Washington's attitude toward command: Ellis, *His Excellency*; Wiencek, *Imperfect God.*

41 **From the day I enter upon the command:** Rush, *Autobiography,* 113.

42 **it was utterly out of my power:** Washington to Martha Washington, PGW/RWS 1, 4.

Cambridge

42 Washington's departure: Adams to Abigail Adams, *Familiar Letters*, 70.

43 **retarded by necessary Attentions:** Washington to Hancock, PGW/RWS 1, 85.

43 Trip to Boston: French, *First Year*, 296–298; Frothingham, *Siege of Boston*, 214–216.

43 **turning out for various alarms:** Frothingham, *Siege of Boston*, 215

43 British cannonade: *Pennsylvania Gazette*, quoted in Batchelder, *Cambridge History*, 251.

43 **July 2. Rained:** Ingalls' Journal, MHS.

43 **nothing heppeng extrorderly:** Diary of James Stevens, quoted in French, *First Year*, 299n.

44 **geaneral Washington & Leas:** Wade and Lively, *Glorious Cause*, 25.

44 Washington's first visit to Boston: Flexner, *Washington*, 19.

44 The differing views of Washington and the people of Massachusetts: Fischer, *Washington's Crossing*; Higginbotham, *Washington Reconsidered*.

44 **the principles of democracy:** quoted in Fischer, *Washington's Crossing*, 19.

44 **an unaccountable kind of stupidity:** Washington to Lee, PGW/RWS 1, 372.

45 **curry favour with the men:** Ibid.

CHAPTER 6: NEW LORDS, NEW LAWS

46 **It is with inexpressible concern:** General Orders, PGW/RWS 1, 71.

46 **thrown up a strong Work:** Washington to Hancock, PGW/RWS 1, 98.

46 **dangerous situation:** Washington to Lee, PGW/RWS 1, 99.

46 British troop arrival and strength: PGW/RWS 1, 81, n.3.

47 **their new Landed Troops:** Washington to Lee, PGW/RWS 1, 99.

47 **Thousands are at work:** Emerson, *Diary*, 79.

47 **I have made a pretty good Slam:** Washington to Lee, PGW/RWS 1, 373.

48 **as we have been incessantly:** Washington to Samuel Washington, PGW/RWS 1, 135.

48 **I have the sincere Pleasure:** Washington to Hancock, PGW/RWS 1, 91.

48 **their Officers generally speaking:** Washington to Lund Washington, PGW/RWS 1, 336–7.

New Terrain

48 **I feel great distress:** JCC 2, 92.

49 **complete command:** Washington to Samuel Washington, PGW/RWS 1, 135.

50   Washington's nearly going to sea: Freeman, *Washington*; Flexner,
     Washington; Humphreys, *Life of Washington*; Stephenson and Dunn,
     Washington.
50   **offers several trifling objections:** Robert Jackson to Lawrence
     Washington, quoted in Freeman, *Washington*, 1, 195.
50   **apprentice to a tinker** and following: Joseph Ball to Mary Washington,
     quoted in Freeman, *Washington*, 1, 199.
51   **mentioning particularly, all Arrivals of Ships:** General Orders,
     PGW/RWS 1, 79.

CHAPTER 7: "WE HAVE THE UTMOST REASON TO EXPECT ANY ATTACK"

53   requests for a war chest, etc.: PGW/RWS 1, 85.
53   **distinguish the Commissioned Officers:** Ibid, 158.
53   **Provisions of all kinds cheap:** Reed, *Life and Correspondence*, 117.
53   **The great Scarcity of fresh Provisions:** Ibid, 116.
54   **report the Names of such Men:** Ibid, 118.
54   **I have ordered all the Whale Boats:** Ibid, 138.
54   **As the season is now advanced:** Washington to Congress, AA 4, 2:1710.
54   **[T]here is but one way out of the Town,** and following: Gage to
     Dartmouth, *Gage Correspondence*, 409.
54   **The Americans could sweep the countryside:** Bowler, *Logistics and
     Failure*, 63.
55   **Here we are still cooped up:** Percy, *Letters*, 58.

The Article of Powder

55   **We are so exceedingly destitute:** Washington to Congress, AA 4, 2:1626.
55   **prohibit the export of gunpowder:** *Order in Council, April 5, 1775*, AA 4,
     2:277.
55   Manufacture of powder, etc: French, *First Year*, 525.
56   **303½ barrels of gunpowder** and following: Washington to the
     Continental Congress, AA 4, 3:28.
56   **fill the cartridge boxes of every man:** Washington to Richard Henry
     Lee, PGW/RWG 1, 293.
56   **The General was so struck:** Quoted in French, *First Year*, 487.
56   **Our situation in the article of powder** and following: Washington to
     the Continental Congress, AA 4, 3:28.
57   **in strict confidence, to acquaint you:** Washington to Trumbull, AA 4,
     3:37.
57   **It is with indignation and shame:** *General Orders, August 4*, AA 4, 3:35.
57   **The enemy having more ammunition:** Reed to Pettit, Reed,
     Correspondence, 117.

Bermuda Powder

58 **One Harris is lately come from Bermuda:** Washington to Cooke, PGW/RWS 1, 221.

58 **winter in Newport in Rhode Island:** Graves, *Conduct*, Gay transcripts, MHS.

58 **charter two suitable vessels:** Resolution of Rhode Island General Assembly, quoted in Rider, *Valour Fore and Aft*, 19.

59 **employed by the Government:** *Instructions to Whipple*, NDAR 1, 670.

59 **We understand there are two armed Vessels:** Washington to Cooke, PGW/RWS 1, 221.

60 **[T]he Nature of the Business:** Cooke to Washington, NDAR 1, 1260.

60 **have come to a Resolution:** Cooke to Washington, AA 4, 3:631.

60 **I need not mention to you** and following: Washington to Cooke, PGW/RWG 1, 424.

60 **Capt. Whipple sailed on Tuesday:** Cooke to Washington, PGW/RWS 1, 463.

61 **His Station in the River is very necessary:** Cooke to Washington, PGW/RWS 1, 467.

61 Account of Bermuda Voyage: Cooke to Washington, PGW/RWS 1, 481, 493.

61 **[I]t is not in our power:** Washington to Cooke, PGW/RWS 1, 514.

Chapter 8: The Congressional Navy Cabal

62 **[t]he Congress is not yet:** Adams to Warren, *Warren-Adams Letters, Vol. 1*, 74.

62 **We ought to have had in our hands:** Ibid, 88.

63 **[a]s a considerable part of my time:** Adams, *Diary and Autobiography, Vol. 3*, 342.

63 **Gadsden had served as an officer in the British navy:** Adams to Gerry, NDAR 1, 628.

63 **He has several Times taken Pains:** Ibid.

64 **I thought it very happy:** Warren to Adams, *Warren-Adams Letters, Vol. 1*, 81.

The *Gaspee* Affair

65 Rhode Island's maritime history: Rider, *Valour Fore & Aft*; Sydney, *Colonial Rhode Island*; Arnold, *History of the State of Rhode Island*.

66 **At around noon on June 9:** Bowen, *Narrative of the Capture and Burning of the British Schooner* Gaspee in Bartlett, *A History of the Destruction*.

66 **Lindsey, according to the local press:** Bartlett, *A History of the Destruction*, 73.

66 **Tack on tack *Hannah* and *Gaspee* raced north,** and following: Bowen, *Narrative of the Capture* in Bartlett, *A History of the Destruction*.

"[T]o go and destroy that troublesome vessel"

68 **Mawney, who had hurried to the tavern** and following: Statement of Dr. John Mawney in Ibid.

69 **an illiterate seaman named Bartholomew Cheever:** Affidavit of Bartholomew Cheever in Ibid.

70 Attack and capture of *Gaspee*: from various accounts in Bartlett, *A History of the Destruction*.

The Royal Navy Reacts

74 Depredations of *Rose*: Rider, *Valour Fore & Aft*; Fowler, *Rebels Under Sail*.

74 **wise and pacifick measures** and following: Resolution of the Rhode Island General Assembly, AA 4, 3:231.

CHAPTER 9: "OUR WEAKNESS & THE ENEMY'S STRENGTH AT SEA"

76 **with fresh Provisions** and following: Washington to New York Provincial Congress, NDAR 1, 1093.

76 **the great distress they are in at Boston:** Washington to Nicholas Cooke, NDAR 1, 976.

76 **1900 Sheep** and following: Hutcheson to Haldimand, NDAR 1, 1179.

77 **a private in the 35th Regiment of Foot:** *Howe's Orderly Book*, 69.

77 **As to the furnishing of Vessells:** Washington to Committee of the General Court, NDAR 1, 1114.

78 **consider in what manner:** Journal of the Massachusetts House of Representatives, NDAR 1, 1200.

The Fishermen Soldiers of Marblehead

78 **we have only:** Washington to Lee, AA 4, 3:455.

79 **I can hardly look back:** Reed to Bradford, *Reed's Correspondence*, 1, 118.

79 **Our Lines of Defense:** Washington to Lund Washington, PGW/RWS 1, 336.

79 **The inactive state we lie in:** Washington to John Augustine Washington, AA 4, 3:685.

79 **Finding we had no great prospect:** Washington to Ramsay, PGW/RWS 1, 431.

79 John Glover and Marblehead history: Billias, *General John Glover*.

80 **Liberty to retail strong Liquors:** Quoted in Ibid, 18.

80 **This day wind at WSW:** Bowen *Journal* II, 432.

81 **Our men are enlisting very fast here:** Holyoke, *Family Letters*, 211.

81 **The fishermen are enlisting:** Ibid, 440.

81 **This morning at 3 o'clock:** Bowen *Journal* II, 444.

81 **21st Massachusetts:** Billias, *General John Glover*.

Hannah

82   *Hannah* history: *Troubled Waters*, Smith and Knight, *American Neptune*.
82   **three or four good Marblehead schooners:** Graves to Stevens, *Gay Transcripts*, MHS.
83   **prevent all kinds of illicit:** Graves to Burnaby, NDAR 2, 548.
83   **John Glover went off:** Bowen, *Journal*, II, 443.
83   **a certain parcle of upland:** Quoted in Article by Beverly Carlman, Beverly Historical Society.
83   **To Schoon *Hannah* Portledge Bill:** Glover, *Colony Ledger*, MarHS.
84   **This day fair weather:** Bowen, *Journal*, II, 453.
84   **To the hier of ditto Schoo:** Glover, *Colony Ledger*, MarHS.

Chapter 10: George Washington's Secret Navy

85   **full power and authority:** *Washington's Commission*, AA 4, 2:1850.
85   **And whereas all particulars:** Congress to Washington, AA 4, 2:1852.
85   **punctually to observe:** *Washington's Commission*, AA 4, 2:1850.
86   attitudes toward the creation of the navy: O'Connor, *Origins of the American Navy*.
86   **each colony, at their own expense:** JCC II, 189.
86   **long letter to Congress:** Washington to Congress, AA 4, 3:243.
86   Letters to others: AA 4, 3.

"The First Armed Vessell Fitted out in the Service of the United States"

87   Harbors of Marblehead and Beverly: Bowditch, *Chart*.
87   **two boxes of wax candles:** NDAR 1, 91, 93.
87   **harrass and impress:** *Massachusetts Spy*, NDAR 1, 91.
87   **some three thousand:** Stone, *History of Beverly*.
88   **Blacksmiths, shipwrights, cordwainers:** Beattie, *Washington's Fleet*.
88   **Broughton:** Billias, *Glover*.
88   **This afternoon as Captain Nick Broughton:** Bowen, *Journal*, 445.
88   **appointed to the Command:** Glover to Congress, NDAR 2, 1289n.
88   **take Command of a detachment:** Washington's Instructions to Broughton, NDAR 1, 1287–8.

"[T]he dayly Piratical Acts of Graves's Squadron"

90   Convoy to Boston: Journal of *Charming Nancy*, NDAR 2, 709.
90   **the *Savage* put back:** Graves to Philips, NDAR 2, 210.
90   **arrayed themselves in Arms:** Lords Commissioners to Graves, NDAR 2, 701.
91   **This is but a small Retaliation:** Tudor to Adams, PJA 3, 174.
92   **Whereas it is expedient His Majesty's Service:** Despatches of Shuldham, 7.

CHAPTER 11: *HANNAH* PUTS TO SEA

93   *Hannah's* first cruise: Broughton to Washington, NDAR 2, 36.

93   **thirty-nine men:** Beattie, *Washington's Fleet.*

93   **sailed on an unknown expedition:** Bowen, *Journal II,* 455.

93   **Colonel Glover has given the strongest proofs:** Moylan to Washington, NDAR 2, 368.

93   the frigate *Lively: Journal of Lively,* PRO/ADM 51/546.

93   **[A]bout 5 oClock:** Broughton to Washington, NDAR 2, 36.

94   **On August 28 Graves had ordered them to patrol:** Graves to Stephens, NDAR 2, 30.

94   **hove short at 1 A.M. weigh'd:** *Journal of Lively,* PRO/ADM 51/546.

94   **under my lee quarter:** Broughton to Washington, NDAR 2, 36.

94   **at ½ past 5 P.M.:** *Journal of Lively,* PRO/ADM 51/546.

94   **Light airs and fair Weather:** *Journal of Lively,* PRO/ADM 51/546.

94   **I perceived her** and following: Broughton to Washington, NDAR 2, 36.

95   **a sloop from St. Lucia:** *Journal of Lively,* PRO/ADM 51/546.

95   **Loaded with Horses:** Ibid.

95   **The Essex Cruiser:** Bowen, *Journal II,* 455.

Mutiny

96   **was such as I would rather have expected** and following: Broughton to Washington, NDAR 2, 56.

97   **Sailors worked more nearly as a collective unit:** For an excellent discussion of sailors as wage laborers, see Rediker, *Between the Devil and the Deep Blue Sea* and Lemish, *Jack Tar in the Streets.*

98   **The sailors . . . are the only people:** Gage to Ministers, quoted in Fischer, *Paul Revere's Ride,* 36.

98   **Mutiny, Riot and Disobedience** and following: Washington's General Orders, NDAR 1, 175.

99   **About 9 [A.M.] twelve Marblehead men:** Ingalls, *Journal,* 87.

99   **E're this you must have heard** and following: Washington to Langdon, NDAR 2169.

100   **as a Compliment:** Reed to Glover, NDAR 2, 490.

100   **Captain Broughton schooner:** Bowen, *Journal II,* 458.

100   **Broughton sailed again:** There is some question as to whether or not the schooner Broughton was commanding after the mutiny was *Hannah,* since her name does not appear in any other document relating to Broughton's activities. For a thorough discussion of this, see Smith and Knight, *Elusive Schooner* Hannah. In the absence of further proof, however, we will go on the assumption that the vessel was indeed *Hannah.*

100   **pursued a ship:** Bowen, *Journal II,* 459.

CHAPTER 12: *DOLPHIN* AND *INDUSTRY*

101   **expected to find a British man-of-war** and following: Journal of the Massachusetts House of Representatives, NDAR 2, 249.

101   **a number of our Marblehead men:** Bowen, *Journal II*, 457.

102   **one hundred and fifty turtles:** Journal of the Massachusetts House of Representatives, NDAR 2, 249.

102   **The Lovers of Turtle:** Tudor to Adams, NDAR 2, 248.

102   **Captains Somes & Smith** and following: Gloucester Committee to Washington, NDAR 2, 226.

102   **a present from the Tory merchants:** Warren to Adams, NDAR 2, 262.

103   *Prince George*: Portsmouth Committee to Washington, NDAR 2, 267.

Expanding the Fleet

103   Washington's letter to Congress: PGW/RWG 2, 24.

104   **Finding we were not likely:** Washington to Arnold, NDAR 2, 1283.

104   **Washington had decided on a course:** PGW/RWG 1, 450.

104   **his Excellency . . . has directed 3 vessels** and following: Reed to Warren, NDAR 2, 268.

105   **News from Headquarters:** Bowen, *Journal II*, 458.

105   **delivered to the Order of his Excellency:** Journal of the Massachusetts House of Representatives, NDAR 2, 278.

105   **Washington sent John Glover:** Reed to Committees of Salem and Gloucester, NDAR 2, 289.

105   **The Vote of the General Court:** Reed to Glover, NDAR 2, 289.

105   **let them [the ships] be prime Sailors:** Ibid.

"I have directed 3 Vessels to be equipped"

106   **a list of explicit instructions:** Instructions to Glover, PGW/RWS 2, 91.

106   Moylan: AA 4, 3:250; Clark, *Washington's Navy*, 16; PGW/RWS 1, 169n.

107   Church's treason: French, *First Year*; McCullough, *1776*; Washington to Hancock, PGW/RWS 2, 99.

108   Arnold's treason: Nelson, *Arnold's Navy*, 358.

108   **I shall now beg Leave** and following: Washington to Hancock, PGW/RWS 2, 99.

CHAPTER 13: BUILDING AND EQUIPPING AN AMERICAN FLEET

110   **the Continental Congress reconvened** and following: JCC 2, 239.

110   **accounts of the committee of Trenton** and following: JCC 3, 272–275.

Two North Country Brigs

111   **take into farther consideration the state of trade** and following: JCC 3, 276.

112   **most animated opposition:** Adams to Langdon, in JCC 3, 277.

112 **a very uncouth, and ungracefull Speaker:** Adams, *Diary and Autobiography, Vol. 2, 172.*

112 **He never appeared to me** and following: Adams, *Diary and Autobiography, Vol. 3,* 343.

113 **expressed much Zeal:** Adams, *Diary and Autobiography, Vol. 3,* 342.

113 **apply to the council of Massachusetts bay** and following: JCC *3,* 278.

Hannah's Last Stand

114 **Boats and Ships that are in the several Harbours:** Gage, *Correspondence,* 422.

114 **fired four shots:** Graves to Stephens, NDAR 2, 371.

115 **the best going Vessel:** Graves, *Narrative,* NDAR 2, 362.

115 **W^d. and Came to Sail:** Journal of *Nautilus,* PRO/ADM 51/629.

115 **I saw a ship off with her sails hauled up** and following: Bowen, *Journal II,* 459.

116 **saw standing into Salem a Schooner:** Collins to Graves, NDAR 2, 417.

116 ***Nautilus* tacked and stood in:** Journal of *Nautilus,* PRO/ADM 51/629.

116 **very near the beach:** Collins to Graves, NDAR 2, 417.

116 **The tide was ebbing:** Collins, *Hannah-Nautilus Affair.*

116 **the People speedily assembled:** *New England Chronicle,* NDAR 2, 416.

116 **six feet long and weighed:** Coggins, *Ships and Seamen,* 152.

116 **Came too of Beverly:** Journal of *Nautilus,* PRO/ADM 51/629.

116 **grapeshot range:** Collins to Graves, NDAR 2, 417.

116 **thought it best:** Ibid.

117 **two hundred or more:** Wetmore, *Almanacs,* EIHC.

117 **so well chosen:** Collins to Graves, NDAR 2, 417.

117 **got a nother Spring:** Journal of *Nautilus,* PRO/ADM 51/629.

118 **Cut the B.B:** Ibid.

118 **'tis very lucky:** Collins to Graves, NDAR 2, 418.

118 **hand blowed off:** White, *Almanacs,* EIHC.

118 **a bad Cold:** Glover to Washington, NDAR 2, 459.

118 **We fired very badly:** Wetmore, *Almanacs,* EIHC.

CHAPTER 14: MARBLEHEAD BOATS AT BEVERLY

119 **I hear Mr. Thomas Grant's schooner:** Bowen, *Journal II,* 458.

119 **appointed to inspect the schooners** and following: Appraisals of the *Speedwell* and *Eliza,* Prizes and Captures, LC.

119 **We were to sanguine in our expectation** and following: Moylan and Glover to Reed, NDAR 2, 368.

120 **seventy-four-ton schooner:** Appraisal of *Two Brothers,* Prizes and Captures, LC.

120 **the management of the Flour:** Reed to Moylan, Letterbook 1, image 62, GWP/LC.

A Second Front

121 Martindale and Washington's attitude toward: Clark, *Washington's Navy*, 18.

121 **a Captain in the Army:** Washington's Instructions to Martindale, NDAR 2, 354.

121 **Adams left Cambridge to begin the schooner's conversion:** *Instructions to Bowen*, Letterbook 1, image 65, GWP/LC.

121 **The Schooner *Harrison*:** Prizes and Captures, 69, LC.

122 **The officers of the Rhoade Island Forces:** *Orderly Book Kept at Cambridge*, NDAR 2, 387.

122 **inquire at Plymouth what Character** and following: *Instructions to Bowen*, Letterbook 1, image 65, GWP/LC.

123 **Bowen arrived at Plymouth** and following: Bowen, *Journal*, Image 443, GWP/LC.

123 **As he is somewhat of a Stranger:** Reed to Plymouth Committee, NDAR 2, 437.

123 **Bowen wrote to Washington:** Bowen to Washington, NDAR 2, 490.

123 **the several armed Vessels:** *Instructions to Watson*, Letterbook 1, image 75, GWP/LC.

124 **highly recommended** and following: Reed to Bowen, Letterbook 1, image 74, GWP/LC.

124 **I have no Friends** and following: Bowen to Reed, NDAR 2, 520.

CHAPTER 15: "NOT A MOMENT OF TIME BE LOST"

126 **It is Some Disappointment** and following: Reed to Moylan and Glover, Letterbook 1, Image 63, GWP/LC.

127 **on the Continental risque & pay:** Hancock to Cook, NDAR 2, 314.

127 Hancock wrote to the Massachusetts General Court: Hancock to Council of Massachusetts, NDAR 2, 312.

127 **two north Country built Brigs:** Hancock to Cooke, NDAR 2, 312.

127 **I think it my Duty:** Cooke to Washington, NDAR 2, 390.

127 **to sail with all possible dispatch:** Trumbull to Washington, PGW/RWS 2, 137.

128 **Before I was honoured with your favor** and following: Washington to Hancock, PGW/RWS 2, 147.

The Maddest Idea

129 Adams, Langdon, and Deane presented a report: JCC 3, 280.

129 **violent and boisterous** and Adams' descriptions of the other delegates: Adams, *Diary and Autobiography, Vol. 3*, 343; Adams, *Diary and Autobiography, Vol. 2*, 172.

129 **It is the maddest Idea in the World** and following: Adams, *Diary and Autobiography, Vol.* 2, 198.

131 **Washington's letter of October 5 was read to the Congress** and following: JCC *3*, 293, 294.

131 **Congress already had a certain ship in mind:** For a complete discussion of *Katy*'s history and her place in the American navy, see Rider, *Valour Fore & Aft.*

132 **We begin to feel a little of a Seafaring Inclination:** Adams to Warren, *Warren-Adams Letters, Vol. 1*, 140.

"What is the Admiral doing?"

132 **It may be asked in England:** quoted in French, *Siege of Boston*, 339–340.

133 **the utmost towards crushing the rebellion:** Sandwich to Graves, quoted in Yerxa, *Burning of Falmouth*, 122.

133 **seriously preparing for War** and following: Graves, *Narrative*, NDAR 1, 1252.

133 **punish the people** and following: Graves to Stephens, NDAR 2, 372.

133 **a small detachment** and following: Gage to Graves, NDAR 2, 7.

134 **if the Business had received:** Graves, *Narrative*, NDAR 2, 324.

134 **for suppressing . . . the Rebellion:** Lords Commissioners to Graves, NDAR 1, 1316.

134 Mowat's history: Yerxa, *Burning of Falmouth*, 125.

134 **burn destroy and lay waste:** Graves to Mowat, NDAR 2, 324.

135 **without Halfway Rock:** Bowen, *Journal II*, 459.

135 **The ships hove to for the night** and following: Mowat to Graves, NDAR 2, 513.

CHAPTER 16: THE EMPIRE STRIKES BACK

136 Description of Falmouth and pine board export: Yerxa, *Burning of Falmouth*, 127–128.

136 **a long and serious debate:** Minutes of the Committee of Inspection, NDAR 1, 120.

136 **the case was hard:** Deposition of Philip Crandell, AA 4, 2, 1169.

137 **a small bough of spruce** and following: Letter from Falmouth, Ibid, 552.

138 **hove taught the Spring:** Journal of *Canceaux*, NDAR 1, 297.

"My Design is to chastize . . . Falmouth"

139 **expressed his gratitude to the Town:** Letter from Falmouth, AA 4, 3, 553.

139 **great reason to be bound:** Account of the Destruction of Falmouth, AA 4, 3, 1169.

140 **the inhabitants generally were in a state of alarm:** Narrative of Daniel Tucker, NDAR 2, 488.

140 **amid a prodigious assembly:** Letter of Rev. Jacob Bailey, NDAR 2, 487.

140 **the People of Falmouth:** Mowat to the People of Falmouth, NDAR 2, 471.

140 **It is impossible to describe** and following: Letter of Rev. Jacob Bailey, NDAR 2, 487.

142 **by no means to deliver up the cannon:** Account of the Destruction of Falmouth, AA 4, 3, 1172.

143 **expressions of thankfulness** and following: Mowat to Graves, NDAR 2, 513.

"An horrible shower of balls"

143 **Mowat hoisted a red flag:** Narrative of Daniel Tucker, NDAR 2, 501.

143 **the flag was hoisted:** Letter of Rev. Jacob Bailey, NDAR 2, 500.

144 **an horrible shower of balls:** Account of the Destruction of Falmouth, AA 4, 3, 1172.

144 **absolutely necessary for some men:** Mowat to Graves, NDAR 2, 515.

144 **threw torches into the doors:** Narrative of Daniel Tucker, NDAR 2, 501.

144 **he chooses to fight for America:** Fogg to Washington, NDAR 2, 535.

144 **the body of the town:** Mowat to Graves, NDAR 2, 515.

145 **about three quarters of the town:** Letter of Rev. Jacob Bailey, NDAR 2, 500.

Fallout

145 **This is savage:** Warren to Adams, NDAR 2, 569.

145 **every manly exertion of power:** Gordon to Adams, NDAR 2, 603.

146 **From Portsmouth to Casco:** Callbeck to Shuldham, NDAR 3, 711.

146 **I can hardly believe this absurd:** Vergennes to De Guines, NDAR 3, 467.

147 **savage and brutal barbarity of our enemies:** *New England Chronicle*, quoted in Yerxa, *Burning of Falmouth*, 149.

147 **at present it seems to me:** Whipple to Langdon, NDAR 2, 997.

CHAPTER 17: *HANCOCK* AND *FRANKLIN*

148 **Lose no Time:** Reed to Glover, Letterbook 1, Image 65, GWP/LC.

148 **recruit your present Crew:** Reed to Broughton, Letterbook 1, Image 64, GWP/LC.

148 ***Hawk* of sixty-four tons:** Appraisal of *Hawk*, Prizes and Captures, No. 141.

148 **We are very anxious:** Reed to Moylan, Letterbook 1, Image 68, GWP/LC.

148 **This will acquaint you** and following: Glover to Reed, PGW/RWS 2, 169.

149 **The Price you mention:** Reed to Glover, Letterbook 1, Image 68, GWP/LC.

149 **two North Country Brigantines** and following: Washington to Glover, Letterbook 1, Image 70, GWP/LC.

149 **brig and a brigantine:** Falconer, *Marine Dictionary.*

150 **We learn with a good deal of Concern** and following: Reed to Glover, Letterbook 1, Image 77, GWP/LC.

151 **as we believe it will be difficult:** Glover and Moylan to Reed, NDAR 2, 517.

151 **fix upon some particular Colour:** Reed to Glover and Moylan, Reed to Glover, Letterbook 1, Image 84, GWP/LC.

151 **What do you think of a Flag:** Reed to Glover and Moylan, Reed to Glover, Letterbook 1, Image 84, GWP/LC.

152 **the *Appeal to Heaven*:** Letter from Cambridge, AA 4, 2:1687.

152 **The Schooners Commanded by Captains Broughton and Sillman:** Glover and Moylan to Reed, NDAR 2, 565.

152 **Not to be opened** and following: *Narrative of Captain John Selman,* NDAR 2, 565.

Harrison **and** *Washington*

152 **Your Conduct in fitting out the Vessels** and following: Reed to Bowen, Letterbook 1, image 82, GWP/LC.

153 Coit's background: PGW/RWS 2, 267n.; Woodward, *Captain Coit.*

153 **Pray forward both Vessels:** Reed to Bowen, Letterbook 1, image 82, GWP/LC.

155 **one top Gallant yard** and following: Prizes and Captures.

155 **a large Schooner Carrying 10 Carriage Guns:** Reed to Glover and Moylan, NDAR 2, 600.

155 **Set the Carpenters to Work:** Bowen, *Journal,* Image 443, GWP/LC.

CHAPTER 18: CONGRESS PAYS A VISIT

156 **to confer with General Washington:** JCC 3, 265.

156 **An Event which has given me:** PGW/RWS 2, 146.

157 **The discussions were wide-ranging** and following: *Minutes of the Conference,* PGW/RWS 2, 190–205.

157 **The Congress approve:** JCC 3, 401.

157 **Court for the Tryal & Condemnation:** *Minutes of the Conference,* PGW/RWS 2, 203.

"Mischievous Violators of the rights of Humanity"

158 **four 4-pounder carriage guns:** *Reed's Report of Washington's Armed Vessels,* NDAR 2, 637.

159 Weather and disposition of *Nautilus:* Journal of *Nautilus,* PRO/ADM 51/629.

159 **I shipped a sea:** Salman to Gerry, Waite, *Origin of the American Navy,* 26.

160 *Prince William* **and** *Mary:* Bartlett Papers, BHS.

160 **[B]y unfavorable Winds** and following: Broughton to Washington, NDAR 2, 850.

161 **Spanish River, now called Little River:** Clark, *Washington's Navy,* 48.

162 **a barrel of pork and one and a half barrels of "flower":** Bartlett Papers, BHS.

162 **The** *Phoebe* **was sent on to Beverly** and following: Order to Sargent Benjamin Doak, NDAR 2, 850.

162 **No Acct yet of the Armd Vessels:** Washington to Hancock, PGW/RWS, 2, 332.

162 **the** *Jacob* **and** *Elizabeth* **Brigs:** Graves to Parker, NDAR 2, 1249.

162 **10,000 stands of arms:** *London Chronicle,* December–January, 1775.

163 **in case he falls in at Sea with** *Elizabeth:* Dartmouth to the Lords Commissioners, NDAR 2, 722.

163 **would not suffer the stores to be landed:** *London Chronicle,* December–January, 1775.

163 **We attempted for some time after our last:** Broughton to Washington, NDAR 2, 899.

"It cannot be displeasing to the General"

164 **Bowen set out for Bristol:** Ibid.

164 **will much oblige the General:** Reed to Bristol Committee, NDAR 2, 538.

164 **Waited on the Committee** and following: Bowen, *Journal,* Image 443, GWP/LC.

165 **Most of which is already Swiveled** and following: Potter to Bowen, NDAR 2, 266.

165 **Made him One More offer:** Bowen, *Journal,* Image 443, GWP/LC.

166 **got the Guns off Rhode Island:** Bowen to Reed, NDAR 2, 639.

166 **Bowen paid the boatman five dollars** and following: Bowen, *Journal,* Image 443, 444, GWP/LC.

CHAPTER 19: "FOR GODS SAKE HURRY OFF THE VESSELS"

168 **For Gods Sake hurry off the Vessels:** Reed to Moylan, Letterbook 1, Image 80, GWP/LC.

168 **Capt Manley is to have one of the Vessels:** Reed to Glover, Letterbook 1, Image 78, GWP/LC.

168 Early life of Manley: Peabody, *Naval Career*; EIHC, 5; Greenwood, *Captain John Manley.*

168 **we give him credit:** Reed to Webb, NDAR 3, 820.

169 **Captain Glover will have the seventh Vessel:** Reed to Moylan and Glover, Letterbook 1, Image 69, GWP/LC.

169 **I wish with all my soul:** Moylan to Reed, NDAR 2, 589.

169 **to be introduced to Doctor Franklin** and following: Moylan to Reed, NDAR 2, 589.

169 **As Adams is well Acquainted with the Coast:** Reed to Moylan and Glover, Letterbook 1, Image 87, GWP/LC.

171 **Moylan and Glover alerted Reed** and following: Moylan and Glover to Reed, NDAR 2, 567.

171 **Winborn Adams and his crew were still in Cambridge:** Reed to Moylan and Glover, Letterbook 1, Image 87, GWP/LC.

171 **her guns provision &c on board** and following: Moylan to Reed, NDAR 2, 619.

171 *Franklin* **was in fact the smallest:** Prizes and Captures, No. 25.

172 **the appointment of agents in Marblehead:** Agents' Agreement, BHS, Reed to Moylan and Glover, Letterbook 1, Image 87, GWP/LC.

173 **moved upon so large a Scale** and following: Washington to Reed, PGW/RWS 2, 407.

"Yankeys & Punkings"

173 **rounding Cape North:** Selman to Gerry, Waite, *Origin of the American Navy,* 26.

173 **reaching Spanish River** and following: Broughton to Washington, NDAR 2, 899.

175 **Plaster Paris** and following: Selman to Gerry, Waite, *Origin of the American Navy,* 28.

176 **two merchantmen from the island of Jersey:** Selman to Gerry, Waite, *Origin of the American Navy,* 26, and Clark, *Washington's Navy,* 50.

CHAPTER 20: *LEE*'S AUTUMN CRUISE

177 **The skies were clear and blue:** *Log of* Nautilus, PRO/ADM 51/629.

177 **seventy-two-ton schooner:** Prizes and Captures, No. 267.

177 **Reports from Boston indicated:** Reed to Glover and Moylan, NDAR 2, 600.

177 **a glorious prize indeed:** Moylan to Reed, NDAR 2, 619.

178 **the wind had swung into the east:** *Log of* Nautilus, PRO/ADM 51/629.

178 **I hope *Lee* is out again** and following: Moylan to Watson, NDAR 2, 902.

179 **[A]t 8 standing in for Piscataqua:** Journal of *Cerberus*, NDAR 2, 890.

179 **The inhabitants and troops literally starving:** *Advices Received in England from America,* AA 4, 4:266.

179 history of *Ranger*: Pickering to Washington, PGW/RWG 517.

180 **dispose of the wood &c on board:** Moylan to Glover, Letterbook 1, Image 107, GWP/LC.

180 **in Such a Manner:** Memorandum of a Letter from Moylan to Glover, NDAR 2, 1154.

181 **four of whom are invalids:** Symons to Graves, NDAR 2, 1170.

181 *Hinchinbrook* **was cruising the waters of Cape Cod:** *Journal of* Hinchinbrook, NDAR 2, 893.

181 *Hinchinbrook* **. . . chaced a Pyrate:** Graves to Howe, NDAR 2, 1071.

182 *Lee* **resumed her hunt:** Movements of *Lee* from Bowen, *Journal II*, 462, 463.

182 **Two Resolute People** and following: Bartlett to Washington, NDAR 2, 879.

182 **As I am Willing and Desirus:** Bartlett to Washington, NDAR 2, 944.

182 **Beef, Tongues, Butter, Potatoes:** *Boston Gazette*, November 13, 1775.

183 **as to Capt. Manly Using any Voiolent measures:** Bartlett to Washington, PGR/RWS 2, 360.

The Prizes of *Hancock* and *Franklin*

183 **Captain Broughton and Selman:** Bowen, *Journal II*, 462.

183 Phoebe *arrived at Beverly:* Bartlett to Washington, NDAR 2, 928.

184 *Prince William* **and *Mary*** and following: Moylan to Glover, Letterbook 1, Image 107, GWP/LC.

184 **Should not a Court be established:** Washington to Hancock, PGW/RWS 2, 349.

184 **I should be very glad if Congress:** Washington to Lee, PGW/RWS 2, 333.

184 **it does not appear:** Moylan to Bartlett, NDAR 2, 1229.

184 **Friend to the Liberties:** Cooke to Washington, NDAR 2, 1204.

184 **to deliver the vessels to their owners:** Memorandum of a Letter to Glover, NDAR 3, 165.

185 **who, for some Reasons weare suspected:** Denison to Washington, NDAR 3, 679.

185 **he does not wish to have any Thing to do with her:** Harrison to Bartlett, Letterbook 1, Image 133, GWP/LC.

185 **over a hundred pounds to the *Speedwell*'s owners:** Account of Loss of Cargo and Damage, NDAR 3, 290.

Chapter 21: "The blundering Captn Coit"

186 **Captain William Coit and his crew:** Reed to Glover and Moylan, Letterbook 1, Image 87, GWP/LC.

186 **Her sides were painted black** and following description: *Intelligence Received from Sion Martindale*, NDAR 3, 64.

186 **old & weak:** Reed's Report of Washington's Vessels, NDAR 2, 637.

186 **Stupidity & Unskilfulness:** Reed to Bowen, Letterbook 1, Image 94, GWP/LC.

187 **we rather wish you should proceed in the *Harrison*:** Ibid, Image 93.

187 **provided Capts Martendal & Bowen:** Watson to Reed, NDAR 2, 644.

187 **Shall be Ready to sail:** Martindale to Reed, NDAR 2, 859.

188 **[T]he Intention of fitting out these Vessels** and following: Moylan to Watson, Letterbook 1, Image 102, 103, GWP/LC.

188 **the third time he ran the *Harrison* aground:** Bowen, *Journal,* Image 445, GWP/LC.

189 **Capt. Coit (a humorous genius):** Letter from Roxbury, NDAR 2, 967.

189 **I had just finished my Letter:** Washington to Reed, PGW/RWS 2, 335.

189 **Capt Coits mainmast Proves too rotten:** Bowen to Washington, NDAR 2, 903.

189 **To see me strutting about:** Coit to Webb, NDAR 2, 915.

190 **Drilling new touch hole:** Prizes and Captures 69, LC.

190 **he will Answer his Expectations:** Williams to Coit, NDAR 2, 945.

190 **On the 8 November we left Prospect Hill:** *Manvide's Journal,* NDAR 2, 932.

191 **shall we ever hear:** Moylan to Watson, Letterbook 1, Image 117, GWP/LC.

191 **I expected long before this:** Bowen to Reed, NDAR 2, 1043.

The Charlottetown Raid

191 **death to them would be inevitable:** Selman to Gerry, Waite, *Origin of the American Navy,* 26.

192 **commander in Chief of the Island St John:** *Petition from Phillip Callbeck and Thomas Wright to George Washington,* PGW/RWS 2, 504.

192 **the schooners carried one boat apiece:** Selman to Gerry, Waite, *Origin of the American Navy,* 27.

193 **two large Schooners:** John Budd to Lord Dartmouth, NDAR 2, 1125.

193 **Not having heard that the Rebellious Colony's had fitted out Privateers:** Callbeck to Lord Dartmouth, NDAR 3, 626.

193 **a very Civil reception** and following: *Petition from Callbeck and Wright to Washington,* PGW/RWS 2, 504.

194 **persecuted allmost to ruin:** Callbeck to Lord Dartmouth, NDAR 3, 626.

194 **were taken and sent on board:** Selman to Gerry, Waite, *Origin of the American Navy,* 27.

194 **[T]hey went onto Mr Callbeck's dwelling house** and following: *Petition from Callbeck and Wright to Washington,* PGW/RWS 2, 504.

195 **These unfeeling Monsters:** Callbeck to Lord Dartmouth, NDAR 3, 626.

195 **[T]o keep pace with their barbarity** and following: *Petition from Callbeck and Wright to Washington,* PGW/RWS 2, 505.

196   the amount of two thousand pounds: Ibid, 506.

197   left destitute of every support: Ibid.

197   should be blamed: Selman to Gerry, Waite, *Origin of the American Navy*, 27.

197   Broughton and Selman ordered the ships' masters: Arbuthnot to Graves, NDAR 2, 1216.

197   the New England schooners had taken twenty-two prizes: Minutes of the Royal Council of Nova Scotia, NDAR 2, 1198.

CHAPTER 22: CONVOYS AND CRUISERS

198   *Charming Nancy*'s landfall: Journal of *Charming Nancy*, NDAR 2, 927.

199   chased a large ship from Cape Ann: Bowen, *Journal II*, 463.

199   her captain, Hyde Parker, reported to Admiral Graves: Graves, *Narrative*, NDAR 2, 947.

200   above 40 Whale boats: Journal of *Charming Nancy*, NDAR 2, 952.

200   This morning passed three ships: Bowen, *Journal II*, 463.

200   There are many Transports from England: Harrison to Glover, Letterbook 1, Image 108, GWP/LC.

201   One of the Ships we saw Yesterday: Journal of *Charming Nancy*, NDAR 2, 952.

"Our Rascally privateers-men"

201   Our Rascally privateers-men: Washington to Reed, PGW/RWS 2, 409. The term "privateer," like many in the eighteenth century, was used more loosely than it is today. Strictly speaking, a privateer was a civilian who had received special permission from the government, in the form of a letter of marque and reprisal, to hunt for enemy shipping. The term also applied to a ship used in privateering. Washington's ships were in no way privateers; they were paid for and under the command of the army, "on the Continental risque and pay," as the Continental Congress phrased it. Nonetheless, Washington's ships and their men were often referred to as privateers.

202   Capt Coit has had much difficulty and following: Watson to Moylan, NDAR 2, 1107.

202   We have had a remarkably wet Autumn: Graves to Stephens, NDAR 2, 1083.

203   A fresh breeze was blowing: Journal of *Tartar*, PRO/ADM 51/972.

203   We had not gone 3 leagues and following: Manvide's Journal, NDAR 2, 1107.

204   The wind was light: Journal of *Raven*, PRO/ADM 51/771.

204   cut his jeers: Graves *Narrative*, NDAR 2, 1143.

204   At 1 saw a Schooner: Journal of *Raven*, PRO/ADM 51/771.

205 **He turned out and armed his boats' crews:** Journal of *Phoenix*, NDAR 2, 1118.

205 **Slipt both Cables** and following: Journal of *Raven*, PRO/ADM 51/771.

205 **they first dumped burning coals:** Letter from Boston, NDAR 2, 1169.

206 **the Ordnance Brig was safe:** Graves, *Narrative*, NDAR 2, 1117.

206 **A remarkable Instance:** Howe to Dartmouth, NDAR 2, 1155.

CHAPTER 23: "HARD GALES AND SQUALLY"

207 **so tempestuous that it was impossible:** Graves *Narrative*, NDAR 2, 1000.

207 **clear skies and fresh breezes:** Journal of *Lively*, PRO/ADM 51/546.

207 **Also in the area was the frigate *Cerberus*** and following: Journal of *Cerberus*, NDAR 2, 967.

207 **protect his Majesty's faithful Subjects:** Graves to Symons, NDAR 2, 462.

207 ***Cerberus* had been driven south:** Symons to Graves, NDAR 2, 1144.

209 **the Rebels Cruisers are ever watchful:** Howe to Dartmouth, NDAR 2, 1155.

209 **to put to Sea immediately:** Graves to Howe, NDAR 2, 1000.

209 **upon using every means to prevent her:** Graves, *Narrative*, NDAR 2, 1065.

209 **heartily wished she was in:** Graves, *Narrative*, NDAR 2, 1117.

209 **[S]poke the *Nancy* Brig,** and following: Journal of *Mercury*, PRO/ADM 51/600.

"This instance of Divine favour"

210 **Three ships for Boston** and following: Bowen *Journal II*, 464.

211 **Act for Authorizing Privateers:** Act for Authorizing Privateers, NDAR 2, 834.

211 **vessels are all manned by officers and soldiers:** Washington to Lee, PGW/RWS 2, 341.

211 **capturing the schooner *Rainbow*:** Wentworth to Moylan, NDAR 2, 1152.

212 **the officers in Boston:** Baldwin to Washington, PGW/RWS 2, 340.

212 **We have information upon which we can depend:** Moylan to Bartlett, *Bartlett Papers*, BHS.

212 **the sloop *Polly*:** Clark, *Washington's Navy*, 60.

212 **Raw cold:** Bowen *Journal II*, 464.

213 ***Nancy* was standing into shore** and capture of *Nancy*: *London Chronicle*, December–January, 1775.

213 **unluckily miss'd the greatest prize:** Washington to Reed, Reed, *Correspondence*, 132.

213 **Capt Manly would have taken her also:** *Edward Green to Joshua Green*, NDAR 2, 1247.

214 **What delighted me excessively:** quoted in Miller, *Sea of Glory*.

214 Inventory of *Nancy*: *Pennsylvania Evening Post*, December 12, 1775.

215 he would not had add'd one artic[l]e more: *Edward Green to Joshua Green*, NDAR 2, 1247.

215 we must be thankful: Washington to Reed, Reed, *Correspondence*, 132.

CHAPTER 24: "[U]NIVERSAL JOY RAN THROUGH THE WHOLE"

216 Your favor of the 27ᵗʰ: Moylan to Wentworth, Letterbook 1, Image 124, GWP/LC.

216 This day two years: Bowen, *Journal II*, 465.

217 [T]hat no part of it may slip through my fingers: Washington to Reed, Reed, *Correspondence*, 133.

217 All or part of fifteen militia companies and following: Prizes and Captures.

217 Part of the famos Prise: Wade and Lively, *Glorious Cause*, 36.

218 I wrote you last Thursday: Moylan to Reed, Reed, *Correspondence*, 133.

218 The loss must be very great: Tudor to Adams, NDAR 2, 1248.

218 the Agents have so much on their hands: Palfrey to Washington, PGW/RWS 2, 476.

218 a very open Harbour: Washington to Hancock, PGW/RWS 2, 462.

218 go into Cape Anne and Marblehead Harbours: Graves to Howe, NDAR 2, 1144.

219 [P]roceeds of the Sales: Bartlett Papers, BHS.

The British Loss

219 We have been these three weeks: Hutchinson to Haldiman, NDAR 2, 1267.

219 The Tempestuous Weather: Graves to Stephens, DAR XI, 202

220 most probably owning: Sandwich to Germain, NDAR 3, 460.

221 opened the eyes of the Ministry: *London Chronicle*, December–January, 1775.

The *Washington* at Sea

221 *Washington* stopped two vessels and following: Manvide's Journal, NDAR 2, 1130.

221 Strong gales, wᵗʰ Snow and Sleet and following: Journal of *Raven*, PRO/ADM 51/771.

222 the brigantine limped back to Plymouth and following: Manvide's Journal, NDAR 2, 1146.

222 She remained at anchor the next day and following: Ibid, 1158.

222 the same vessels of our mortal enemy: Ibid, 1171.

222 As we were about to get under way: Ibid, 1189.

222 have agreed to do no Duty and following: Watson to Washington, NDAR 2.

223 **determined to get *Washington* to sea** and following: Watson to Moylan, NDAR 2, 1268.

223 **the plague trouble & vexation I have had:** Washington to Hancock, PGW/RWG 2, 485.

224 **His majesty's frigate *Fowey*** and following: Journal of Fowey, PRO/ADM 51/375.

Chapter 25: "His people are contentd"

227 **so Old & Crazy as to be unfit** and following: Moylan to Watson, Letterbook 1, Image 126, GWP/LC.

228 **the *Thomas* out of Fayal:** Moylan to Watson, Letterbook 1, Image 137, GWP/LC.

228 **five Tory pilots:** *Commitment of George Price*, NDAR 3, 19.

228 **He had the schooner hauled on** and following: Watson to Moylan, NDAR 2, 1268.

228 **chimney of *Harrison*'s cookstove:** Prizes and Captures, 129.

Concord

230 **the *Concord*, from Greenock:** Glover to Washington, PGW/RWS 2, 475.

230 **350 chaldrons of coal:** *Boston Gazette*, NDAR 3, 48.

230 **loaded with woolen Goods:** Howe to Dartmouth, NDAR 3, 82.

230 **Captor and prize stood off the mouth of Marblehead** and following: Glover to Washington, PGW/RWS 2, 475.

231 **it is mention'd in the Letters:** Washington to Hancock, PGW/RWS 2, 483.

231 **in the Service of the ministerial Army:** *Instructions to Broughton* NDAR 1, 1287.

231 **His Excellency has no doubt:** Moylan to Glover and Bartlett, PGW/RWS 2, 476.

232 **I must beg of you my good Sir:** Washington to Lee, PGW/RWS 2, 611.

232 **a large Quantity of Potatoes:** Palfrey to Washington, PGW/RWS 2, 497.

232 **I am Credibly informed that James Anderson:** Washington to Hancock, PGW/RWS 2, 509.

233 **one BLL of Lemons:** Bartlett to Washington, PGW/RWS 2, 545.

233 **approves your taking such articles:** Hancock to Washington, PGW/RWS 2, 589.

233 **establishing proper Courts:** Washington to Hancock, PGW/RWS 2, 331.

233 **in a lawless manner:** JCC 3, 372.

234 **goods, wares or merchandizes:** Ibid, 437.

CHAPTER 26: "AND A PRIVATEERING WE WILL GO, MY BOYS"

235 Moylan to Reed: Reed, *Correspondence*, I, 137.

235 **You have no doubt heard:** *Letter from Beverly*, NDAR 3, 145.

235 *Manly: A Favorite New Song:* NDAR 3, 47.

236 **Five privateers were commissioned:** NDAR 3, 50n.

236 *Lee* **was cruising about fifteen miles offshore** and capture of *Jenny*: Wentworth to Graves, *Despatches of Shuldham*, 72.

236 **a crew of eighteen** and following description of *Jenny*: *Boston Gazette*, December 11, 1775.

237 **It was very unlucky:** Moylan to Bartlett, Letterbook 1, Image 139, GWP/LC.

237 **one Box of Pickles:** Bartlett to Washington, PGW/RWS 2, 545.

237 **you will please to pick up such things** and following: Moylan to Bartlett, Letterbook 1, Image 141, GWP/LC.

238 **[T]he General was Much Surprised:** Moylan to Bartlett, Letterbook 1, Image 147, GWP/LC.

238 **Captain Manly's good Fortune:** Moylan to Watson, Letterbook 1, Image 143, GWP/LC.

238 **Indian Corn, Potatoes & Oats** and following: Washington to Hancock, PGW/RWS 2, 573.

238 **This morning I find Captain Manley:** Bowen, *Journal II*, 467.

239 **Major Thomas Mifflin, the army's quartermaster general:** Bartlett to Mifflin, NDAR 3, 192.

239 **a very dirty condition:** Moylan to Bartlett, NDAR 3, 233.

The Final Cruise of Broughton and Selman

240 **made landfall first at the town of Winter Harbor** and following: Wentworth to Moylan, NDAR 2, 1244.

240 **by the Last Accounts from the Armed Schooners:** Washington to Hancock, PGW/RWS 2, 485.

241 **This morning arrived Captains Broughton and Selman:** Bowen, *Journal* II, 465.

241 **From the reception we met with at Head Quarters:** Wright to Dartmouth, NDAR 3, 290.

241 **my fears that Broughton & Sillman:** Washington to Hancock, PGW/RWS 2, 508.

241 **Capt Broughton with another Privateer:** Warren Diary, MHS.

242 **I beg you will be attentive to Mr Callbeck's goods:** Moylan to Glover, NDAR 3, 6.

242 **His Excellency cannot be a Competent judge:** Moylan to the Salem Committee of Safety, NDAR 2, 1284.

242 **determined by Judges:** Pickering to Moylan, NDAR 2, 1317.

242 **Manage the matter:** Moylan to Glover, NDAR 3, 6.

242 **My Reason for urging this Measure:** Legge to Dartmouth, NDAR 2, 1280.

CHAPTER 27: A NEW ARMY

244 **made us look over the Potatoes & Turnips:** Moylan to Wentworth, Letterbook 1, Image 125, GWP/LC.

245 **looked upon as friendly:** Lowrey to Hancock, NDAR 3, 979.

245 **Such a dearth of Publick Spirit:** Washington to Reed, PGW/RWS 2, 449.

246 **Our men inlist very slow:** Wade and Lively, *Glorious Cause*, 39.

246 **only 5917 Men:** Washington to Reed, PGW/RWS 2, 552.

246 **I returnd from Ticonderoga:** Knox to Washington, PGW/RWS 2, 563.

247 **I am Much affriad I Shall have a Like proposal:** Washington to Hancock, PGW/RWS 2, 546.

247 **has been thrown into Irons:** Washington to Howe, PGW/RWS 2, 576.

247 **has not forfeited his past pretensions:** Howe to Washington, PGW/RWS 2, 586.

247 **try persons Guilty of Acts of Rebellion:** Graves to Stephens, NDAR 3, 112.

247 **[T]his may account for General Howes Silence:** Washington to Hancock, PGW/RWS 2, 624.

248 **enter upon such a measure:** Howe to Dartmouth, DAR XI, 213.

248 **Howe also understood the psychological advantage** and following: Ibid, 112n.

Year's End

249 **Coit I look upon:** Moylan to Reed, Reed, *Correspondence*, I, 137.

249 **What is become of Coit?:** Reed to Webb, NDAR 3, 821.

249 **Sailed Captain Broughton:** Bowen, *Journal* II, 468.

249 **A list of** *Hancock* **and** *Franklin's* **expenses:** Prizes and Captures.

250 **[W]e let his Excellency understand** and following: Selman to Gerry, Waite, *Origin of the American Navy*, 27.

250 **indolent and inactive souls:** Moylan to Reed, Reed, *Correspondence*, 137.

250 **Our four cruisers:** Bowen, *Journal II*, 469.

250 **I am just informed:** Moylan to Reed, Reed, *Correspondence I*, 137.

"[E]very assistance the Fleet can afford shall be chearfully given."

251 **expressed his Apprehensions:** Graves, *Narrative*, NDAR 2, 1143.

251 **Your Excellency can make no request:** Graves to Howe, NDAR 2, 1144.

252 **Their Lordships well know the Situation:** Graves to Stephens, NDAR 2, 1266.

252 the White flag at the fore top Mast head: Hutcheson to Haldimand, NDAR 2, 1267.

252 originated with their wives: *Extract of a Letter from Boston*, NDAR 3, 85.

252 His plan—audacious for a man and following: Graves, *Conduct*, NDAR 3, 9n.

253 The whole of the Timbers: *Carpenters' Survey*, NDAR 3, 10.

253 Vessels of sufficient Force: Howe to Dartmouth, NDAR 3, 82.

254 If your Excellency thinks it advisable: Graves to Howe, NDAR 3, 82.

254 utmost prudence: *Letter from an Officer in Boston*, NDAR 3, 194.

254 *Fowey* made sail: Journal of *Fowey*, PRO/ADM 51/375.

254 keep in many of the Cruizers: Graves to Phillips, NDAR 3, 276.

254 Ashley Bowen noted *Fowey*'s arrival: Bowen, *Journal II*, 469.

255 first and only notice or intimation and following: Graves, *Narrative*, NDAR 3, 300.

CHAPTER 28: A NEW YEAR

256 Head Quarters, Cambridge: *General Orders*, PGW/RWS 4, 1.

256 the Old Troops went of: Baldwin, *Journal*, 20.

256 present situation of America: *King's Speech Opening the Session of Parliament*, NDAR 2, 777.

257 we gave great Joy to them: Washington to Reed, PGW/RWS 3, 24.

258 It is not in the pages of History: Washington to Hancock, PGW/RWS 3, 19.

258 a Surprize [attack] did not appear to me: Washington to Hancock, PGW/RWS 2, 28.

259 I have no doubt that you . . . are wondering: Washington to Tayloe, PGW/RWS 2, 537.

259 the town and the property in: JCC 3, 444–445.

259 the first moment I see a probability: Washington to Hancock, PGW/RWS 3, 19.

"The arch-rebels formed their scheme long ago"

260 the arch-rebels formed their scheme: Gage to Dartmouth, DAR XI, 58.

260 and the more it is considered: Ibid, 80.

261 Conditions in Boston: French, *Siege of Boston*, 397–402.

261 We are not in the least apprehension: Howe to Dartmouth, DAR XI, 191.

261 Neither is their army: Howe to Dartmouth, DAR XII, 46.

The Continental Navy

262 with all possible expedition and following: JCC 3, 311, 312.

262 immediately procured a Room: Adams, *Autobiography*, Vol. 3, 345.

262 to agree with such officers: JCC 3, 316.

263 **It is very odd:** Adams to Gerry, NDAR 2, 896.

263 **the founder of the greatest Navy** and following: Adams, *Autobiography*, Vol. 3, 350.

264 **How often have I exclaimed:** Moylan to Reed, NDAR 3, 572.

264 **Jones hoisted the new flag:** Thomas, *Jones*, Millar, *Early American Ships*.

265 **Rules for the Regulation of the Navy:** JCC 3, 378–384.

265 **Our instructions for an American fleet:** Quoted in Clark, *American Naval Policy*, 34.

266 **That a Committee be appointed:** JCC 3, 420.

266 **the pleasantest part of my Labours:** Adams, *Autobiography*, Vol. 3, 345.

CHAPTER 29: A NEW FLEET

268 **Two China Mugs:** Bartlett Papers, BHS.

268 **Captain and Commander:** *Washington's Commission*, NDAR 3, 553.

268 **take the Command of a Detachment of said Army:** *Instructions to Broughton*, NDAR 1, 1287.

269 **By virtue of the powers:** *Washington's Commission*, NDAR 3, 553.

269 **As the Harbour of Cape Anne:** *Sargent's Instructions*, Letterbook 1, Image 157, GWP/LC.

270 **[Y]ou mus[t] use all your diligence:** Washington to Glover, Bartlett and Watson, PGW/RWS 3, 15.

270 **Our men coming home** and following: Bowen *Journal II*, 472.

271 **Utterly Refused:** Bartlett to Moylan, NDAR 3, 631.

271 **he must give them to him:** Memorandum of Moylan's Letter to Bartlett, Letterbook 1, Image 164, GWP/LC.

271 **her hold stuffed with beef, potatoes, rice:** Account of Schooner *Hancock*, Prizes and Captures.

272 **a sufficient Number for these Small vessells:** Moylan to Bartlett, Letterbook 1, Image 166, GWP/LC.

272 **examine into the Condition:** Ibid, 161.

272 **strict enquiry** and following: Watson to Moylan, PGW/RWS 3, 100–101.

273 **His Excellency agreed to give Dyar command of *Harrison*:** Harrison to Watson, NDAR 3, 870.

The Armies Look South

273 **in the Command of His Majesty's Ships:** Lords Commissioners to Shuldham, *Despatches of Molyneux Shuldham*, 6.

273 **the ship unmoored and made sail:** Shuldham to Stephens, *Despatches*, 15.

274 **[T]he Voyage was almost a constant Succession of Storms:** Shuldham to Stephens, *Despatches*, 37.

274 **The sea continually washed over us:** Letter from a Captain of an English Transport, NDAR 3, 834.

274 **British officer was dispatched to the West Indies:** Howe to Dartmouth, DAR XII, 84.

275 **or whereever else you might hear:** Lords Commissioners to Shuldham, *Despatches*, 6.

276 **to receive Major General Clinton:** Graves to Graeme, NDAR 3, 659.

276 **a very Intelligent Gentleman:** Washington to Hancock, PGW/RWS 3, 19.

276 **but generally thought in Boston:** Ibid.

276 **there is great reason to believe:** Washington to Trumbull, PGW/RWS 3, 51.

"Sailed Manley in schooner"

277 **would not wish that great a Number:** Moylan to Bartlett, Letterbook 1, Image 177, GWP/LC.

278 **Montagu struck the topgallant masts and yards** and following: Journal of *Fowey*, PRO/ADM 51/375.

278 **at Noon Standing to wards** and following: Master's Log of *Halifax*, NDAR 3, 912.

279 **Sailed Manley in schooner . . . on a cruise:** Bowen, *Journal II*, 474.

CHAPTER 30: COMMODORE OF THE FLEET

280 **Robert Hanson Harrison, filling in for Moylan:** Harrison to Moylan, NDAR 3, 873.

280 **Broughton's instructions** and following: *Instructions to Broughton*, NDAR 1, 1287.

280 **The new instructions** and following: *Instructions to Dyar*, PGW/RWS 3, 149.

281 **On January 23, *Fowey* hove up her anchors:** Journal of *Fowey*, PRO/ADM 51/375.

281 **Captain Montagu hoped to find a supply of drinking water** and following: Graves, *Narrative*, NDAR 3, 1006.

282 **I have for his great vigilance:** Washington to Hancock, PGW/RWS 3, 217.

The *General Gage*

282 **halt to the practice of tearing down houses and wharves:** Frothingham, *Siege*, 293.

283 **within two miles of the *Renown*** and following: *Letter from Whitehaven*, NDAR 3, 996n.

284 **a schooner of eight carriage guns:** *Boston Gazette*, NDAR 3, 1133.

284 **receivd considerable assistance:** Watson to Washington, PGW/RWS 3, 212.

284 *Hancock* **had only six cartridges left:** *Letter from Whitehaven,* NDAR 3, 996n.
284 **sent the captured documents:** Watson to Washington, NDAR 3, 937.
284 **I congradulate your Excellency:** Watson to Washington, PGW/RWS 3, 192.
285 **had it not been for the cowardice:** Watson to Washington, PGW/RWS 3, 212.
285 **Let the General know:** Moylan to Watson, PGW/RWS 3, 213n.
285 **Conduct in engageing the eight Gun Schooner:** Washington to Manley, PGW/RWS 3, 206.
285 **This day smart cold:** Bowen, *Journal II,* 474.

Captains Ayres, Tucker, and Waters

286 **for assistance to bring up:** Brown's Orderly Book, 7.
286 **By January 28** and following: Prizes and Captures.
287 **fired 17 Nine Pdrs:** *Journal of* Fowey, PRO/ADM 51/375.
287 **deadeyes, scrub brooms:** Prizes and Captures.
287 **Tedious cold:** Bowen, *Journal II,* 475.
287 **45 Cords of wood about 10 Bushels of Potatoes:** *Report of Salem Committee,* NDAR 4, 3.
288 **claped a slip Bouy on the small Bower:** *Journal of* Fowey, PRO/ADM 51/375.
288 **Laden with wood:** Washington to Hancock, PGW/RWS 3, 277.
288 **fired 5 Guns & several swivells:** *Journal of* Fowey, PRO/ADM 51/375.
288 **Perkins, had produced his certificate from Newcastle:** *Report of Salem Committee,* NDAR 4, 4.

CHAPTER 31: "[A] STROKE WELL AIM'D"

290 **[W]e have not, at this time** and following: Washington to Reed, PGW/RWS 3, 89–90.
291 **laid before the Council** and following: *Council of War,* PGW/RWS 3, 103.
291 **Washington had rejected the idea:** Putnam to Washington, PGW/RWS 3, 298n.
292 **Washington suggested an assault on Boston** and following: *Council of War* PGW/RWS 3, 320–324.
292 **the Eyes of the whole Continent:** Washington to Hancock, NDAR 3, 1346.

Hancock **and** *Hope*

292 **Manly & the yankee Barnes:** Watson to Washington, PGW/RWS 3, 213.
293 **The** *Hope* **Brig is perhaps:** Graves to Stephens, NDAR 3, 992.
293 **said to be that same Manley:** Kemple Journal, NDAR 3, 1078.

293 **Cruize against the Rebels:** Graves to Stephens, NDAR 3, 992.

293 **Got up T-G-yds:** Log of *Hope*, PRO/ADM 52/1823.

294 **one of the Rebel armd Schooners:** Ibid.

294 **not less than 400 times:** *New England Chronicle*, NDAR 3, 1170.

294 **Manley ordered the *Hancock* scuttled:** Washington to Reed, PGW/RWS 3.

295 **being effectually disabled:** Grave, *Conduct*, NDAR 3, 1079.

296 **The *Harrison* Capt. Dyer:** Watson to Washington, PGW/RWS 3, 356.

296 **Saw two Sail:** Log of *Hope*, PRO/ADM 52/1823.

297 **every article belonging to the Continent:** Memorandum of Letter from Harrison to Watson, NDAR 4, 64.

The End of the Siege

297 **Bombardment and Cannonade caused a good deal of Surprize:** Washington to Hancock, PGW/RWS 3, 423.

298 **threw some shells:** Howe to Dartmouth, DAR XII, 82.

298 **full bright moon:** Thatcher, *Military Journal*, 38.

298 Fortification of Dorchester Heights: Frothingham, *History of the Sedge*, 298–300.

298 **in one hour's time:** Connecticut Officer, quoted in PGW/RWS 3, 427.

299 **so alarming and I presume unexpected:** Shuldham to Stephens, *Despatches of Shuldham*, 107.

299 **a warm desire:** Thatcher, *Military Journal*, 39.

300 **The weather continuing boisterous:** Howe to Dartmouth, DAR XII, 82.

CHAPTER 32: "IT IS WITH THE GREATEST PLEASURE I INFORM YOU"

301 **A thousand difficulties arose:** Howe to Dartmouth, DAR XII, 82.

301 **has no intention of destroying the town:** *Letter from the Boston Selectmen*, PGW/RWS 3, 434.

301 **was not obligatory upon General Howe:** Learned to Selectmen in Frothingham, *Siege of Boston*, 304.

302 **he had reason to believe:** Council of War, PGW/RWS 3, 460.

302 **I am justly sensible:** Howe to Dartmouth, DAR XII, 83–84.

302 **in the ordnance branch:** Howe to Dartmouth, DAR XII, 128.

302 **take into your possession:** Commission to Brush in Frothingham, *Siege of Boston*, 306.

303 **It is with the greatest pleasure:** Washington to Hancock, PGW/RWS 3, 489.

304 **direct Commodore Manly and his little Squadron:** Washington to Hancock, PGW/RWS 3, 425.

The Wolf Pack

304 Anchored here the *Hancock* cruiser: Bowen, *Journal II*, 476.

304 managed to take the brigantine *Nelly*: *Providence Gazette*, NDAR 4, 136.

305 at 1 [P.M.] Made Sail: Log of *Hope*, PRO/ADM 52/1823.

305 Night came on, they parted: Bowen, *Journal II*, 478.

306 4 Sail in Sight: Journal of *Lively*, PRO/ADM 51/546.

306 Coal, Porter & Krout: Washington to Hancock, PGW/RWS 3, 426.

306 [I]mmediatly the *Fowey* came to sail: Bowen, *Journal II*, 479.

307 Damaged his Vessel: Sargent to Washington, PGW/RWS 3, 455.

307 all the Sails & Most of the Rigen: Sargent to Washington, PGW/RWS 3, 469.

307 Saw a Vessel, on Shore: Log of *Hope*, PRO/ADM 52/1823.

The British Leave at Last

308 one of those unfortunate vessels: *Kemble's Journal*, NDAR 4, 435.

308 Our five cruisers sailed from Cape Ann: Bowen, *Journal II*, 480.

308 Slipp'd pr order: Journal of *Diligent*, NDAR 4, 435.

308 the brig's captain let his sails fly: Journal of Kemble, Ibid.

309 In the morning, to their great joy: *Sarah Sever to* ———, NDAR 4, 474.

310 Sailed 55 sail of shipping: Bowen, *Journal II*, 481.

310 in Company with HM Ships: Journal of *Chatham*, NDAR 4, 537.

310 made resistance: *Extract of a Letter from Cambridge*, NDAR 4, 694.

Epilogue: Washington Rides South

313 his health would not allow him and following: Washington to Reed, PGW/RWS 4, 10.

The New War at Sea

314 all the colonies . . . had established their own naval forces: Allen, *Naval History*, 138.

315 search out and attack: Congress to Hopkins, quoted in Ibid, 91.

316 Commander-in-Chief of the Fleet: AA 4, 4, 578.

316 an eighteen-gun brig, five thirty-six-gun frigates: Fowler, *Rebels Under Sail*, 71.

"Commodore Manley declines"

317 to intercept and send to this place: Shuldham, *Despatches*, 167.

318 the Men would not be induced: Ward to Washington, PGW/RWS 4, 54.

318 Defections from Washington's fleet: Clark, *George Washington's Navy*, 138–143.

318 Commodore Manley declines: Ward to Washington, PGW/RWS 4, 196.

318 John Manley and Isaac Cazneau: JCC IV, 290.

318 Subsequent career of Manley and other captains: Morgan, *Captains to the Northward*.

The Fleet Goes On

319 **cooper hooped, whole barrels** and inventory: *New England Chronicle*, NDAR 5, 216.

320 **Mann'd & Arm'd:** Journal of *Renown*, NDAR 5, 149.

320 **The intrepid Captain Mugford fell:** Ward to Washington, PGW/RWS 4, 347.

320 **This afternoon a grand funeral:** Bowen, *Journal II*, 487.

321 **Chaced by four Sail of Rebel Schooners:** Log of *Hope*, PRO/ADM 52/1794.

321 **to annoy the Enemies Ships:** Whitcomb to Ward, NDAR 5, 543.

"Removed at such a distance as his Excellency is"

322 **Not conceiving myself Authorized:** Washington to Hancock, quoted in Clark, *Washington's Navy*, 173.

322 **That the Marine Committee [of Congress] be directed:** JCC V, 631.

323 **Removed at such a distance:** Washington to Wentworth, quoted in Clark, *Washington's Navy*, 186.

323 **665 dozen Men's Shoes:** *Independent Chronicle*, NDAR 7, 232.

323 **the men seem loth to go out** and following: Bradford to Hancock, NDAR 7, 313

324 **wch were unfit:** Bradford to Hancock, NDAR 7, 1117.

324 **to support the dignity:** Bradford to Morris, NDAR 7, 1217.

325 **the *Lynch* pacquet:** Bradford to Adams, NDAR 7, 1293.

Power at Sea

327 **In any operation:** Washington to Rochambeau, quoted in Knox, *Naval Genius*, 64.

Bibliography

Manuscript Sources

Beverly Historical Society
  William Barlett Papers
  William Barlett Account Book
  Captain Moses Brown Orderly Book
Library of Congress
  Prizes and Captures, microfilm, Courtesy of the Naval Historical Center
Marblehead Historical Society
  John Manley Colony Ledger
Massachusetts Historical Society
  The Conduct of Vice Admiral Graves, Gay Transcript
  Thomas Hutchinson Diary
  Obadiah Brown Diary
  John Collins Warren Diary
  Phineas Ingalls Journal
Public Records Office, Admiralty Records
  Journal of *Lively*, PRO/ADM 51/546
  Journal of *Nautilus*, PRO/ADM 51/629
  Journal of *Raven*, PRO/ADM 51/771
  Journal of *Phoenix*, PRO/ADM 51/693
  Journal of *Fowey*, PRO/ADM 51/375
  Journal of *Mercury*, PRO/ADM 51/600
  Master's Log of *Hope*, PRO/ADM 52/1823

Printed Primary Sources

Abbot, W.W., ed., *The Papers of George Washington, Revolutionary War Series, Volumes 1, 2, 3*, Charlottesville, VA: The University Press of Virginia, 1985.

Adams, Charles Francis, ed., *Familiar Letters of John Adams and his Wife Abigail Adams, During the Revolution*, Boston: Houghton Mifflin Company, 1875.

Adams, John, *Diary and Autobiography of John Adams*, L.H. Butterfield, ed., vol. 2 & 3, Cambridge, MA: The Belknap Press, 1961.

Bartlett, John Russell, *A History of the Destruction of His Britannic Majesty's Schooner Gaspee in Narragansett Bay on the 10th June, 1772*, Providence, RI: A.C. Greene, 1861.

Barker, Lt. John, *The British in Boston*, Elizabeth Ellery Dana, ed., Cambridge, MA: Harvard University Press, 1924.

Belknap, Dr., *Journal of Dr. Belknap*, Boston: Massachusetts Historical Society Proceedings, Series 1, 4:79.

Bolton, Charles Knowles, ed., *Letters of Hugh Earl Percy from Boston and New York, 1775–1776*, Boston: Charles E. Goodspeed, 1902.

Bowditch, Nathaniel, *Chart of the Harbors of Salem, Marblehead, Beverly and Manchester, 1804, 5 & 6*, Beverly, MA: Reprint, Beverly Heritage Series #100, Cape An Syde Galleries.

Bowen, Ashley, *The Journal of Ashley Bowen (1728–1813) of Marblehead*, Philip Chadwick Foster Smith, ed., Boston: Publications of the Colonial Society of Massachusetts, Volume XLV, 1973.

Bowen, Ephraim, *Journal, George Washington Papers at the Library of Congress, 1741–1799: Series 4*, General Correspondence, Library of Congress, http://memory.loc.gov (accessed 28 August, 2007).

Carter, Clarence Edwin, *The Correspondence of General Thomas Gage with the Secretaries of State, 1763–1775*, New Haven, CT: Yale University Press, 1931.

Clark, William Bell, ed., *Naval Documents of the American Revolution*, Vol. 1–7, Washington: Naval Historical Center, 1968.

Clinton, Sir Henry, *The American Revolution: Sir Henry Clinton's Narrative of His Campaigns, 1775–1783*, William Willcox, ed., New Haven, CT: Yale University Press, 1954.

Dann, John C., ed., *The Revolution Remembered: Eyewitness Accounts of the War for Independence*, Chicago: The University of Chicago Press, 1980.

Davies, K. G., ed., *Documents of the American Revolution, 1770–1783*, Vol. IX, XI, XII, Dublin: Irish University Press, 1976.

Emerson, William, *Diaries and Letters of William Emerson, 1743–1776, Minister of the Church of Concord, Chaplin in the Revolutionary Army*, Amelia Forbes Emerson, ed., Boston: Privately Printed by Thomas Todd Company, 1973.

Falconer, William, *An Universal Dictionary of the Marine*, London: Latimer Trend & Company, 1970 reprint of 1780 edition.

Force, Peter, ed., *American Archives*, Fine Books Company, LeGrand J. Weller, Publisher, CD-ROM.

Holyoke, Dr. Edward A., *The Family Letters of Dr. Edward Holyoke*, Essex, CT: The Essex Institute Historical Collections, Vol. XIII, 1875.

Howe, William, *General Sir William Howe's Orderly Book: at Charlestown, Boston and Halifax*, London: B. F. Stevens, 1980.

Ingalls, Phineas, *Revolutionary War Journal Kept by Phineas Ingalls of Andover, Mass, April 19, 1775–December 8, 1776*, Essex, CT: The Essex Institute Historical Collections, Vol. LIII, 1917.

Jones, Stephen, *Autobiography of Stephen Jones, Sprague's Journal of Maine History*, Vol. III, No. 5, April, 1916.

————. *Historical Account of Machias, Maine Historical Society Quarterly*, Vol. 15, No. 2, Fall, 1975.

Journals of the Continental Congress, 1774–1789, Worthington Chauncey Ford, ed., Washington: Government Printing Office, 1905 (online version).

Mackenzie, Frederick, *Diary of Frederick Mackenzie*, Cambridge, MA: Harvard University Press, 1930.

Neeser, Robert Wilden, ed., *The Despatches of Molyneux Shuldham*, New York: Printed for the Naval History Society, 1913.

Reed, William B., ed., *The Life and Correspondence of Joseph Reed*, Philadelphia: Lindsay and Blakiston, 1847.

Rush, Benjamin, *The Autobiography of Benjamin Rush*, George W. Corner, ed., Princeton, NJ: Princeton University Press, 1948.

Taylor, Robert, ed., *Papers of John Adams*, Vol 2, 3, 4, Cambridge, MA: The Belknap Press, 1979.

Thatcher, James, M.D., *Eyewitness to the American Revolution: The Battles and Generals as Seen by an Army Surgeon*, Stamford, CT: Longmeadow Press, 1994, reprint of 1862 edition.

Waite, Henry E., *Extracts Relating to the Origin of the American Navy*, Boston: Published by the New England Historic Genealogical Society, 1890.

Warren, James, and John Adams, *Warren-Adams Letters, Volume 1, 1743–1777*, Boston: The Massachusetts Historical Society, 1917.

Washington, George, *George Washington Papers at the Library of Congress, 1741–1799: Series 3b Varick Transcript*, Library of Congress, http://memory.loc.gov (accessed 28 July, 2007).

Wetmore, William, *Interleaved Almanacs of William Wetmore, Salem*, Essex Institute Historical Collections, XLIII.

White, John, *Interleaved Almanacs of John White, Salem*, Essex Institute Historical Collections, XLIX.

Secondary Sources:

Ahlin, John Howard, *Maine Rubicon: Downeast Settlers During the American Revolution*, Calais, ME: Calais Advertiser Press, 1966.

Allen, Gardner, *A Naval History of the American Revolution*, Williamstown, MA: Corner House Publishers, 1970 (reprint of 1913 edition).

Arnold, Samuel Greene, *History of the State of Rhode Island and Providence Plantations*, Providence, RI: Preston & Rounds, 1899.

Batchelder, Samuel Francis, *Bits of Cambridge History*, Cambridge: Harvard University Press, 1930.

Beattie, Donald W., and J. Richard Collins, *Wasington's New England Fleet: Beverly's Role in its Origins, 1775–77*, Salem, MA: Newcomb & Gauss Co., 1969.

Billias, George Athan, *General John Glover and His Marblehead Mariners*, New York: Henry Holt and Company, 1960.

Bowler, Arthur R., *Logistics and the Failure of the British Army in America, 1775–1783*, Princeton, NJ: Princeton University Press, 1975.

Chapelle, Howard I., *The History of the American Sailing Navy*, New York: W. W. Norton & Co., 1949.

———. *The History of American Sailing Ships*, New York: W. W. Norton & Co., 1935.

Churchill, Edwin A., *The Historiography of the* Margaretta *Affair, Or, How Not to Let the Facts Interfere with a Good Story*, Maine Historical Society Quarterly, Vol. 15, No. 2, Fall, 1975.

Clark, William Bell, *George Washington's Navy: Being an Account of His Excellency's Fleet in New England Waters*, Baton Rouge, LA: Louisiana State University Press, 1960.

Drisko, George, *Narrative of the Town of Machias, The Old and the New, the Early and the Late*, Machias, ME: Press of the Republican, 1904.

Ellis, Joseph J., *His Excellency George Washington*, New York: Alfred A. Knopf, 2004.

Elting, John, ed., *Military Uniforms in America: The Era of the American Revolution, 1755–1795*, San Rafael, CA: Presidio Press, 1974.

Fischer, David Hackett, *Paul Revere's Ride*, Oxford: Oxford University Press, 1994.

———. *Washington's Crossing*, Oxford: Oxford University Press, 2004.

Flexner, James Thomas, *George Washington in the American Revolution, (1775–1783)*, Boston: Little, Brown and Company, 1967.

Fowler, William M., Jr., *Rebels Under Sail: The American Navy During the Revolution*, New York: Charles Scribner's Sons, 1976.

Freeman, Douglas Southall, *George Washington: A Biography*, New York: Charles Scribner's Sons, 1948.

French, Allen, *The First Year of the Revolution*, New York: Octagon Books, 1968.

Frothingham, Richard, *The History of the Siege of Boston and the Battles of Lexington and Concord, and Bunker Hill*, New York: Da Capo Press, 1970, reprint of 1903 edition.

Greenwood, Isaac J., *Captain John Manley, Second in Rank in the United States Navy, 1776–1783*, Boston: C. E. Greenwood & Co., 1915.

Hearn, Chester G., *George Washington's Schooners: The First American Navy*, Annapolis, MD: Naval Institute Press, 1995.

Higginbotham, Don, ed., *George Washington Reconsidered*, Charlottesville, VA: University of Virginia Press, 2001.

Humphreys, David, *The Life of General Washington*, Rosemarie Zagarri, ed. Athens, GA: University of Georgia Press, 1991.

Hurd, D. Hamilton, *History of Essex County Massachusetts with Biographical Sketches of Many of the Pioneers and Prominent Men*, Vol. 1, Philadelphia: W. Lewis & Co., 1888.

Isaacson, Walter, *Benjamin Franklin: An American Life*, New York: Simon & Schuster, 2003.

James, W. M., *The British Navy in Adversity: A Study of the War of American Independence*, London: Longmans, Green and Co. Ltd., 1926.

Knox, Dudley W., *The Naval Genius of George Washington*, Boston: Houghton Mifflin Company, 1932.

Leamon, James S., *Revolution Downeast: The War for American Independence in Maine*, Amherst: The University of Massachusetts Press, 1993.

Leckie, Robert, *George Washington's War*, New York: HarperPerrenial, 1993.

Mackesy, Piers, *The War for America, 1775–1783*, Lincoln, NE: The University of Nebraska Press, 1992.

Marshall, John, *The Life of George Washington, Vol. II*, Fredericksburg, VA: The Citizen's Guild of Washington's Boyhood Home, 1926.

McCullough, David, *1776*, New York: Simon & Schuster, 2005.

Middlekauff, Robert, *The Glorious Cause: The American Revolution, 1763–1789*, New York, Oxford: Oxford University Press, 1982.

Millar, John Fitzhugh, *Early American Ships*, Williamsburg, VA: Thirteen Colonies Press, 1986.

Miller, Nathan, *Sea of Glory*, Annapolis, MD: Naval Institute Press, 1974.

Morgan, William James, *Captains to the Northward: The New England Captains in the Continental Navy*, Barre, MA: Barre Gazette, 1959.

Morison, Samuel Eliot, *The Maritime History of Massachusetts, 1783–1860*, Boston: Houghton Mifflin Company, 1921.

Nelson, James L., *Benedict Arnold's Navy: The Rag Tag Fleet That Lost the Battle of Lake Champlain but Won the American Revolution*, New York: McGraw-Hill, 2006.

Phelps, Glenn A. *The Republican General* in *George Washington Reconsidered*, Don Higginbotham, ed. Charlottesville, VA: University Press of Virginia, 2001.

Randall, Willard Sterne, *George Washington, A Life*, New York: Henry Holt and Company, 1997.

Rediker, Marcus, *Between the Devil and the Deep Blue Sea: Merchant Seamen, Pirates, and the Anglo-American Maritime World, 1700–1750*, Cambridge, MA: Cambridge University Press, 1987.

Rider, Hope S., *Valour Fore & Aft*, Newport, RI: Seaport '76 Foundation, 1978.

Rossie, Jonathan Gregory, *The Politics of Command in the American Revolution*, Syracuse, NY: Syracuse University Press, 1975.

Sherman, Rev. Andrew M., *Life of Captain Jeremiah O'Brien, Machias, Maine*, Morristown, NJ: George W. Sherman, Publisher, 1902.

———. *The O'Briens of Machias, Me.*, Boston: Published for the American-Irish Historical Society, 1904.

Stephenson, Nathaniel Wright, and Waldo Hilary Dunn, *George Washington, Vol. 1*, New York: Oxford University Press, 1940.

Stone, Edwin, *History of Beverly Civil and Ecclesiastical From is Settlement in 1630 to 1842*, Boston: James Monroe and Company 1843, Facsimile reprint Friends of Beverly Public Library, 1975.

Sydney, James V., *Colonial Rhode Island: A History*, New York: Scribner, 1975.

Thomas, Evan, *John Paul Jones: Sailor, Hero, Father of the American Navy*, New York: Simon & Schuster, 2003.

Wade, Herbert T., and Robert A. Lively, *This Glorious Cause: The Adventures of Two Company Officers in Washington's Army*, Princeton, NJ: Princeton University Press, 1958.

Wiencek, Henry, *An Imperfect God: George Washington, His Slaves, and the Creation of America*, New York: Farrar, Straus and Giroux, 2003.

Wright, Robert K., Jr., *The Continental Army*, Washington, DC: Center of Military History, United States Army, 1983, online edition.

ARTICLES

Clark, William Bell, "American Naval Policy, 1775–1776," *American Neptune*, Vol. 1, No. 1, January 1941.

Collins, Dr. J. Richard, "The Hannah-Nautilus Affair," *Essex Institute Historical Collections*, Vol. CIII, No. 4, October 1967.

Dowdell, Vincent J., "The Birth of the American Navy," United States Navy *Proceedings*, Vol. 81, November 1955, 1250.

Lemisch, Jesse, "Jack Tar in the Streets: Merchant Seamen in the Politics of the American Revolution," *William and Mary Quarterly* 25, 1968, 377.

Massachusetts Historical Society *Proceedings:* 1st Series, 4:110.

Peabody, Robert E., "The Naval Career of Captain John Manley of Marblehead," Essex, CT: The Essex Institute Historical Collections, Vol. XIV, 1909.

Smith, Philip C.F., and Russell W. Knight, "In Troubled Waters: The Elusive Schooner *Hannah*," *American Neptune*, Vol. XXX, No. 2, April 1970.

Tutt, Richard, "Washington's Fleet and Marblehead's Part in its Creation," *Essex Institute Historical Collections*, Vol. LXXXI, No. 4, October 1945.

Woodard, Colin, "Why the Royal Navy Burned Portland in 1775," *Working Waterfront/Inter-Island News*, April 2007.

Woodward, P. H., "Captain William Coit," *Collections of the Connecticut Historical Society, Volume VII*, Hartford, CT: Published by the Society, 1899.

Yerxa, Donald A., "The Burning of Falmouth, 1775: A Case Study in British Imperial Pacification," *Maine Historical Society Quarterly*, Vol. 14. No. 3, Winter 1975.

INDEX

Montagu, George, 277, 281
Montgomery, Richard, 176, 201
Moore, James, 25, 28, 29–31, 32–34,
    34, 35
Mowat, Henry, 134, 135–45
Moylan, Stephen, 106–7, 119, 129, 148,
    151, 152, 168, 169–70, 172, 178,
    188, 202, 203–4, 212, 216, 231,
    232, 241, 244, 264, 268, 269, 280
Mugford, James, 319

Nancy (British ordnance storeship), 90,
    198, 206, 207, 208–10, 213
    British loss of, 219–21
Nautilus (British sloop-of-war), 115–18,
    128, 158, 206, 209, 304, 306
Navy, U.S.
    birth of, 327–28
    creation of, 261–67
    growth of, 314–16
    GW and, 316–17
    GW's recognition of importance of,
        53–54
    as "maddest idea," 129–32
    Second Continental Congress and,
        62
New York City, 260
Niger (British frigate), 306, 317
Noddles Island, 17
Norfolk (British transport ship), 283–84
North Briton (British sloop), 182–83

O'Brien, Jeremiah, 27–28, 32, 34, 35,
    77–78, 127, 327
Oliver Cromwell (Connecticut frigate),
    249, 314
Orne, Azor, 80, 81

Paine, Robert Treat, 130
Palfrey, William, 217, 218, 232
Parker, Hyde, 205
Patterson, Walter, 192
Peale, Charles Willson, 40
Perkins, Samuel, 287, 288
Phoebe (Canadian sloop), 161–62, 163,
    173, 184
Phoenix (British man-of-war), 90, 92,
    204, 205, 209, 227
Pickering, Thomas, 10
Pickering, Timothy, 180
Polly (British sloop), 26, 29, 32, 35,
    188–89, 212
Potter, Simeon, 164, 165, 166
Preston (British flagship), 5, 6, 17, 25
Prince George, 103, 108, 120
Prince William (Canadian
    merchantman), 160–61, 183, 184

Private property, capture of, 231–33
Prize courts, 184
Prize money, 128
Providence, 131, 263
Putnam, Israel, 20, 168, 189, 300
Putnam, Rufus, 291, 298

Quiberon Bay, Battle of (1759), 4

Rainbow (schooner), 244, 287–88, 324
Ramsay, William, 79, 217
Ranger (British sloop), 179
Raven (British sloop-of-war), 134, 204,
    205, 227
Reed, Joseph, viii, 53, 57, 79, 100, 104,
    105–6, 108–9, 122, 123, 124,
    148–49, 150–51, 152–53, 166, 168,
    173, 201, 215, 217, 257, 290
Renown (British man-of-war), 283, 317
Roche, John, 286
Rose (British frigate), 58–59, 73–74, 77,
    110
Roxbury Neck, 8
Rutledge, Edward, 112
Rutledge, John, 130

Sally (sloop), 244–45
Saltonstall, Dudley, 264
Saratoga, Battle of (1777), 326
Sargent, Winthrop, 269, 307
Savage (British sloop), 94
Schuyler, Philip, 42, 43, 86, 145
Second Continental Congress, 10,
    12–14
    creation of navy and, 62
    navy cabal of, 63–65
Selman, Arch, 119, 150, 152
Selman, John, 168, 191, 239–42,
    249–50
Sewall, Jonathan, 8–9
Shuldham, Molyneux, 255, 273–75,
    295, 299, 306, 317
Skimmer, John, 324
Somerset (British capital ship), 5, 18
Speedwell (American ship), 119, 185
Spencer, Joseph, 291
Spitfire (British sloop), 133–34
Stakesby (British transport), 307
Stanhope, John, 205
Stein, Leonard, 111
Stephens, Philip, 202, 273, 317
Stevens, James, 43
Sugar Act (1764), 65–66
Sullivan, John, 56
Symmetry (British transport ship),
    133–34
Symons, John, 179, 207–8